D1587998

THE
CORRESPONDENCE
OF WALTER BENJAMIN
AND GERSHOM SCHOLEM
1932—1940

Other Books by Walter Benjamin

Illuminations

Reflections

Other Books by Gershom Scholem

From Berlin to Jerusalem: Memories of My Youth

Major Trends in Jewish Mysticism

The Messianic Idea in Judaism: And Other Essays on Jewish Spirituality

On Jews and Judaism in Crisis: Selected Essays

On the Kabbalah and Its Symbolism

Walter Benjamin: The Story of a Friendship

Zohar—The Book of Splendor: Basic Readings from the Kabbalah (Ed.)

THE CORRESPONDENCE OF WALTER BENJAMIN AND GERSHOM SCHOLEM 1932–1940

EDITED BY
GERSHOM SCHOLEM

*Translated from the German by
Gary Smith and Andre Lefevere*

With an Introduction by Anson Rabinbach

SCHOCKEN BOOKS   NEW YORK

The translators were guided by Harry Zohn's excellent translations of portions of several letters that appear in Walter Benjamin's Illuminations *and Gershom Scholem's* Walter Benjamin: The Story of a Friendship.

First American Edition

English translation and introduction Copyright © 1989 by
Schocken Books Inc.

All rights reserved under International and Pan-American
Copyright Conventions. Published in the United States by
Schocken Books Inc., New York, and simultaneously in Canada
by Random House of Canada Limited, Toronto. Distributed by
Pantheon Books, a division of Random House, Inc., New York.
Originally published in West Germany as *Walter Benjamin/
Gershom Scholem Briefwechsel 1933–1940* by Suhrkamp Verlag.
Copyright © 1980 by Suhrkamp Verlag.

Library of Congress Cataloging-in-Publication Data

Benjamin, Walter, 1892–1940.
The correspondence of Walter Benjamin and
Gershom Scholem, 1932–1940.

Translation of: Briefwechsel 1933–1940.
Includes bibliographical references.
1. Benjamin, Walter, 1892–1940—
Correspondence.   2. Scholem, Gershom Gerhard,
1897–1982—Correspondence.   3. Authors, German—
20th Century—Correspondence.   4. Philosophers—
Germany—Correspondence.   I. Scholem, Gershom
Gerhard, 1897–1982.   II. Title.
PT2603.E455Z54813   1989   838'.91209   [B]   88-43132
ISBN 0-8052-4065-9

Manufactured in the United States of America

Schocken Books wishes to thank Inter Nationes of West
Germany for a grant subsidizing the translation of this book.

CONTENTS

INTRODUCTION

by Anson Rabinbach

In 1936 a collection of twenty-six letters appeared in a small Swiss edition under the name Detlef Holz, a pseudonym of Walter Benjamin. Its title, *Deutsche Menschen,* was chosen as a camouflage, to pass Nazi censorship, which it apparently did. Hardly what one might expect, these letters (including some by Hölderlin, Schlegel, Förster, and Nietzsche) convey rather ordinary moments in unadorned and sober prose. The Olympians of the German Romantic age reduced, as it were, to the earthly scale of their friendships, intimate relations, circumstances of exile, and sad occurrences—for example, the death of Hegel, reported by his student Schleiermacher. By this change of register, Benjamin hoped to achieve a reversal of perspective. The "meager, limited existence" and "true humanity" visible in this "secret Germany" was a modest assault on the Nazi pantheon, into which all spiritual "forebears" were posthumously initiated.[1]

Many years later Theodor Adorno remarked on the illusions and limitations of the book's subversive potential: "Benjamin shared with us other émigrés the error that spirit and cunning can possibly accomplish something against a force which no longer recognizes spirit as something autonomous, but only as a means to its own ends, and therefore no longer

---

[1] Typescript of "Deutsche Briefe I," Walter Benjamin, *Gesammelte Schriften,* (hereafter *GS*) vol. 4.2, ed. Tilman Rexroth (Frankfurt am Main: Suhrkamp Verlag, 1980), p. 945.

fears a confrontation with it."[2] There is nevertheless a close resemblance between the letters of *Deutsche Menschen* and Benjamin's correspondence with Gershom Scholem. What Benjamin valued in those older letters was, above all, "the light cast by substantive references, allusions, and details" in which the distinction "between the human being and the author, between the private and the objective" fades, and "we find ourselves surrounded by humanness."[3] In Scholem and Benjamin's correspondence too we find a wealth of detail, an austerity of style, and a depth of allusion, as well as a loyalty and intensity that recalls the legendary German-Jewish intellectual friendships of the post-Enlightenment generation. Those friendships, as Hannah Arendt recognized in her thoughts "On Humanity in Dark Times," were nurtured less by intimate confession than by a common intellectual discourse carried on in a society "without either Christians or Jews."[4]

Such intense friendships, which were not a flight from reality but a recognition of its terrors, allowed educated German Jews to create their own kind of tradition, one which took the best from German culture and ignored the rest. As George Mosse noted, the fierce attachment of German Jews to Goethe, Schiller, and the other titans of German philosophy and literature was not simply the chasing after noble illusions, but a bulwark against nationalism and anti-Semitism.[5] By the beginning of the twentieth century, however, dedication to the universal spirit of *Bildung*, or cultivation, was itself in crisis. This tradition reached its *denouement* in Scholem and Benjamin's generation, a century and a half after emancipation. Not the Enlightenment, but Marxism and Zionism were far more alluring for those intellectuals, like Scholem and Benjamin, who witnessed the collapse of what was later called the German-Jewish "symbiosis." By then exile was the only means of survival. And yet, the intensity of intellectual friendship seemed to increase with the growing irrationality of the world that surrounded it. The conflicts and shared passions that infuse their correspondence are not simply the surface topography of a tradition in dissolution; they are, as we shall see, an encounter with its deepest recesses. A passage from Benjamin's final letter to Scholem could serve as their epigraph: "Every line we succeed in publishing today—no matter how uncertain the future to which

[2] Theodor W. Adorno, "Nachwort," *Deutsche Menschen: Eine Folge von Briefen*, selected and introduced by Walter Benjamin (Frankfurt am Main: Suhrkamp Verlag, 1962), p. 121.

[3] Typescript of "Deutsche Briefe I," p. 944.

[4] Hannah Arendt, "On Humanity in Dark Times: Thoughts about Lessing," *Men in Dark Times* (New York: Harcourt, Brace and World, 1968), p. 24.

[5] George L. Mosse, *German Jews beyond Judaism* (Bloomington: University of Indiana Press, 1983), pp. 12–15.

we entrust it—is a victory wrenched from the powers of darkness" (127).[6]

Though many of Benjamin's letters were preserved and published earlier, Scholem's side of the exchange only emerged from the powers of darkness (they were confiscated by the Gestapo) through a series of accidents and circumstances which are described in his preface.[7] These letters begin a few months before Hitler's rise to power and end with the fall of France and Benjamin's death by suicide on the Spanish border on September 26, 1940. With the restoration of the full correspondence from 1933 to 1940, we have the record of an extraordinary intellectual relationship, and, at the same time, an extended discussion of the fate of the Jewish and German intellectual tradition on the eve of catastophe. It is fitting, therefore, that very few bear a German postmark. In these last years of their friendship, political circumstances and intellectual commitments placed Scholem and Benjamin at considerable geographic and spiritual distance from Germany and from each other. German and Jewish as these two men were in their learning and language, the backdrop of this correspondence is not the "unconsolingly clean" streets of Berlin, but "Jerusalem's battlements" and the "grayish blue façades of the boulevards" of Paris (91).

Together with Scholem's *Walter Benjamin: The Story of a Friendship*, this volume offers Anglo-American readers a more intimate and detailed insight into Benjamin's years of exile in Paris, and his relations with contemporaries (particularly members of the Frankfurt School). From Scholem's side, especially if we read his letters together with his autobiographical memoir *From Berlin to Jerusalem: Memories of My Youth*, we learn a great deal about his involvement with political events in Palestine, and of his reaction to the dire emergency of European Jewry. When these letters begin, Benjamin had already opted for Marxism, a decision he took shortly after Scholem's emigration to Palestine in 1923. Also in the past was his university career, which collapsed precisely when Scholem's began.

The tensions in their relationship—the result of Scholem's perception

[6] The numbers in parentheses refer to the standard numbering of the letters (not to page numbers) in both the German and the English editions.

[7] This edition, originally published as *Walter Benjamin/Gershom Scholem Briefwechsel 1933–1940* appeared in 1980. One letter, incomplete in that edition, has since been located and is published in full here. Twenty-nine of Benjamin's letters to Scholem during this period were originally published in the two-volume *Walter Benjamin–Briefe* edited by Scholem and Adorno and published in 1966, not all of them in full. Revised in 1978, the *Briefe* will be published in English by the University of Chicago Press. Subsequently, other Benjamin letters have come to light and to some extent have been included in the *Gesammelte Schriften*, as part of the apparatus to specific texts. An edition of Gershom Scholem's correspondence is currently in preparation in Jerusalem.

of Benjamin as a person "incapable of making a decision between meta-physics and materialism," and of Benjamin's frustrations with Scholem's insistence that he acknowledge the Jewish core of his work—were by now deeply sedimented. They are still very much in evidence, but no longer as personal discord or political disaffection. The most fascinating aspect of this phase of their correspondence is the emergence—through their ongoing discussion of Kafka—of the contours of their most serious philosophical dispute about the messianic core of Judaism and its rela-tion to exile and tradition. Thus, apart from any scholarly interest in the Scholem-Benjamin relationship, their correspondence assumes a place of importance on its own as a profound and moving commentary on the German-Jewish intellectual tradition in its final hour.

The letters published here thus chronicle a difficult period in a rela-tionship that had reached its "zenith" many years before. When they first met in 1915 Benjamin was twenty-three and Scholem seventeen. Scholem had heard of Benjamin several years earlier as a leading figure of a German youth movement influenced by the communitarian ideas of the experimental educationalist Gustav Wyneken. By then Scholem was already a Zionist, a direction he chose in 1911 when he was fourteen years old, and from which he never wavered. From the outset Scholem's Zionism was characterized by strong anarchistic and antibourgeois lean-ings which he later described as "post-assimilatory." [8] Both Scholem and Benjamin, like many others of their generation, were deeply affected by Martin Buber's powerful challenge to German-Jewish youth to repudiate their material comforts and find their spiritual identity in a decisive "transvaluation of values." In 1912 Benjamin too flirted with Zionism, but, unlike Scholem, rejected it for a different kind of Jewish self-definition. In a lengthy and crucial exchange with Ludwig Strauss, a young Zionist (and Buber's future son-in-law) who wanted to publish a journal of Jewish thought in Germany, Benjamin examined his attitude toward his "Jewishness" and found Zionism to be an inadequate re-sponse. "For me," he wrote, "Jewishness is not in any sense an end in itself but the noble bearer and representative of the intellect." [9]

In contrast to Scholem, whose father and grandfather were printers educated in the nineteenth-century traditions of German liberalism, and whose family belonged to the struggling middle class of Berlin's Jewish entrepreneurs, Benjamin grew up in a wealthy, bourgeois setting (his father was a successful art and antique dealer and collector). His bitter-

---

[8] "With Gershom Scholem: An Interview," *On Jews and Judaism in Crisis: Selected Essays,* ed. Werner Dannhauser (New York: Schocken Books, 1976), p. 1.

[9] Walter Benjamin to Ludwig Strauss, November 21, 1912, *GS* 2.3, ed. Rolf Tiedemann and Hermann Schweppenhäuser (Frankfurt am Main: Suhrkamp Verlag, 1977), p. 839.

sweet memoir, "A Berlin Chronicle," recalls a childhood spent in the villa on the Delbrückstrasse in the Grunewald section of Berlin where the physical presence of the Wilhelminian *fin de siècle* was preserved in the style and decor of the interiors.

And yet both reacted against the culture of middle-class, assimilated German Jewry. This was especially true of their reaction to World War I, which both abhorred and avoided. Scholem and Benjamin were united by a profound outrage at Buber, Wyneken, and other German and Jewish intellectual idols whose patriotism they saw as a "spiritual" betrayal. Their correspondence in those years gives an extraordinary portrait of the Swiss exile milieu in which they congregated with other "anti-Kaiser Germans" whose antipathy to rationalism was a badge of honor. Their associates in those years included the Jewish-Nietzschean expressionists Kurt Hiller and Salomo Friedländer, the Dadaist Hugo Ball, and their mutual friend Ernst Bloch, who was then a messianic anarchist *en route* to becoming a messianic Marxist.

Both Benjamin and Scholem combined a distaste for conventional academic scholasticism with a ravenous erudition (their private joke, the fictitious "University Muri" which parodied the pomposity of German University life stems from that period). They shared a chronic "bibliomania," a penchant for uncharted intellectual byways, obscure ideas (numerology, graphology), and a fascination with arcane spirits such as Franz von Baader, the early nineteenth-century philosopher who rediscovered sources of Medieval Catholic and Jewish mysticism (Benjamin's sale of a prized edition of von Baader's works to the Hebrew University Library is the subject of a lengthy transaction in these letters). Most importantly, they shared, as Scholem recalled, "a resoluteness in pursuing our intellectual goals, a rejection of our environment—which was basically the German-Jewish assimilated middle class—and a positive attitude toward metaphysics." [10]

In 1916 Benjamin completed his first major philosophical essay, "On Language as Such and the Languages of Man." [11] In it he describes human language as a condition of fall from its Adamic state where, as God's language, it was not yet plagued by confusion or ambiguity, or even distinct from the language of "immaterial" things and nature. God's language revealed a world "of all-sided and integral actuality," e.g., of complete immediacy and transparency; human language revealed only

---

[10] Gershom Scholem, *Walter Benjamin: The Story of a Friendship* (hereafter *W.B.*), trans. Harry Zohn (New York: Schocken Books, 1988), p. 21.

[11] Walter Benjamin, "On Language as Such and on the Language of Man," *Reflections: Essays, Aphorisms, Autobiographical Writings*, ed. Peter Demetz (New York: Schocken Books, 1986), pp. 314–32.

"decay" and "parody." Benjamin claims for language a status totally opposed to its denigration as a means to an end. His image of human language as identical with the "Fall" recalls the original state of language before its exile and decay into corrupt speech. For Benjamin, the affirmation of an identity between Jewishness and language sets out, in esoteric form, the attitude that he communicated to Strauss four years earlier. In a letter to Buber, in which he expressed his deep disappointment with the latter's partisanship for the war, Benjamin explained his idea of language as a human expression of the inexpressible as opposed to its "sullied" condition as a "means."[12] Since language can retain something of the "inexpressible" it contains a "residue of the creative word of God" and offers a glimpse of its original character. The esoteric language entrusted to "the elite in the party of the intellectuals (*die Geistigen*)," the Jews, is the absolute counterpoint to the disintegration of the word in the "abyss of prattle," an allusion to Buber's propagandistic efforts.[13] Benjamin's early philosophy of language thus contains the seminal idea of his life and career: human language, in its irreparable confusion, is the expression of a primal exile from God's word.

In the summer of 1918, which they spent together in Berne, Scholem and Benjamin read and discussed the great Jewish neo-Kantian philosopher Hermann Cohen's influential work *Kant's Theory of Experience* (1871). Cohen's philosophy, which assimilated the Jewish "religion of reason" to the Enlightenment, epitomized for Scholem and Benjamin the exorbitant price of the reconciliation of Jewishness to Germanness. Several months earlier Benjamin sent Scholem his paper "On the Program for the Philosophy of the Future," a set of reflections that subsequently played an important role in their conversations. Though he praised the systematic coherence of Kant's thought, he argued that by equating all human knowledge with the greatly reduced "minimum" of knowledge accessible to rational thought, the Enlightenment "worldview" sacrificed an entire realm of experience to its "historical and religious blindness."[14] At that time, Benjamin also remarked that Kant's (and, by implication, Cohen's) concept of experience was "inferior" because "a philosophy that does not include the possibility of soothsaying from coffee-grounds and cannot explicate it cannot be a true philosophy."[15]

[12] Walter Benjamin to Martin Buber, July 1916, *Briefe*, pp. 125–28.

[13] For a discussion of the political background of Benjamin's essay see Anson Rabinbach "Benjamin, Bloch, and Modern German Jewish Messianism," *New German Critique* 34 (Winter, 1985), pp. 78–124.

[14] Walter Benjamin, "Über das Programm der kommenden Philosophie," *GS* 2.1, p. 159. An English translation appeared in *The Philosophical Forum* 15:1–2 (Winter/Spring, 1983/84), pp. 41–55.

[15] Scholem, *W.B.*, pp. 58–60.

Though Scholem concurred with Benjamin's evaluation of Cohen's rationalism, which he considered to be a "major disappointment," and saw as illusory Cohen's conviction that there was "no discord between Germanism and Judaism," Scholem was drawn to an aspect of Cohen's work that apparently held little interest for Benjamin. As David Biale has shown, Scholem adopted Cohen's view of the true basis of the Jewish tradition as a revelation that does not guarantee truth, but only the possibility of its transmission through centuries of interpretation. Scholem's research into the Kabbalah spelled out the terms of that tradition as one in which God is alienated from the world, from Creation itself, and in which exile or *galut* is the most fundamental condition of existence. In contrast to Benjamin's purely linguistic messianism, Scholem's understanding of Jewish tradition is of a historical and exegetical enterprise: if "God is meaningless, but meaning-bestowing," then "not system but *commentary* is the legitimate form through which truth is approached." [16] For Scholem the problem was to redefine that tradition to include far more than rabbinic orthodoxy could ever admit. It had to come to terms with the inner nihilism of Judaism itself: "All that befalls the world is only an expression of this primal and fundamental *galut*. All existence, including God, subsists in *galut*. Such is the state of Creation after the breaking of vessels." [17] This philosophical distinction is enormously significant for Scholem's idiosyncratic view of Zionism, as it is for understanding his attachment to, and distance from, his most important philosophical partner, Benjamin.

Scholem was drawn to Zionism by a passion for Jewish learning and Jewish history, rather than by its contemporary political manifestations. For him, "return" was not only associated with an end to physical diaspora, but also with a restoration of the radical core of Judaism. Like many others of his generation Scholem was attracted by the lure of Eastern Europe as it appeared in the nouveau *Yiddishkeit* popularized among German-Jewish youth by Buber's famous literary renderings of hasidic legend (especially *The Tales of Rabbi Nachman*, 1906, and *The Legend of the Baal Shem*, 1908). "We did not come to Zionism because of politics," Scholem later recalled of his generation's desire for a renewal of Judaism as a cultural rather than as a strictly political revolt. An admirer of Ahad Ha'am, the Russian Zionist who emigrated to Palestine in 1891, Scholem shared Ahad Ha'am's vision of a spiritual regen-

[16] David Biale, *Gershom Scholem: Kabbalah and Counter-History* (Cambridge, Mass.: Harvard University Press, 1979), pp. 110–11; Gershom Scholem, "Revelation and Tradition as Religious Categories in Judaism," *The Messianic Idea in Judaism and Other Essays on Jewish Spirituality* (New York: Schocken Books, 1971), p. 289.

[17] Gershom Scholem, "The Star of David," *The Messianic Idea in Judaism*, pp. 45–46.

eration of Judaism in the land of Palestine as a beacon and a workshop for the emergence of a new Hebrew language and a new Jewish culture. Before his emigration to Palestine in 1923, Scholem was a sharp critic of the German Zionist *Blau-Weiss* youth movement, which he attacked as "German Romanticism in Zionist guise."[18] Yet Scholem's early Zionism, predicated as it was "on the power of a tradition thousands of years old," resisted conceptualization, because, he admitted, it "contains a secret life."[19] Beneath the tradition of normative Judaism, Scholem believed, there existed a deep vein of esoteric Judaism, embedded, above all, in the mystical and Kabbalistic writings, to which he devoted his career to unearthing and deciphering.

Scholem's lifetime project as a historian can thus be understood as an attempt to bring an authentically esoteric tradition to a modern Judaism incapacitated by a surfeit of rationalism and constrained by orthodoxy. For Scholem the message of modern Judaism was nihilistic: "the whole world was in exile." Though personally close to Buber, Scholem doubted that Buber's mystical and ecstatic vision of Judaism, drawn from the hasidic movement, was a sufficient basis to awaken contemporary Jewry to a new personal Judaism of deep feeling (*Erlebnis*). Buber and his closest followers in the Prague Jewish student association *Bar Kochba* (some of whom, like Samuel Hugo Bergmann, Robert Weltsch, and Max Brod became important writers and intellectuals) wanted to create a bridge between Western Jews and what Buber called the "Asian" Judaism of Eastern Europe, by updating a mystical Jewish tradition without too closely attending to its historical dimension, and by removing what Scholem called its "apocalyptic sting."[20] Nineteenth-century historicism, exemplified by the "Science of Judaism" of Heinrich Graetz and Leopold Zunz, was historical in its scholarly approach to the traditional texts, but estranged from the esoteric tradition in its anxiety over the irrational. Scholem tried to steer clear of the weaknesses of both by attempting to restore the esoteric tradition historically, with its "sting."[21] Rediscovering the ancient texts of Jewish mysticism and unlocking the anarchistic tradition of Kabbalah opened up a dimension of Judaism that he believed was of enormous significance for contemporary Jewish experience: "For the mountain, the corpus of facts, needs no key at all; only the misty wall of

[18] "With Gershom Scholem: An Interview," p. 13.

[19] Gershom Scholem, *From Berlin to Jerusalem: Memories of My Youth*, trans. Harry Zohn (New York: Schocken Books, 1980), p. 48.

[20] Gershom Scholem, "Martin Buber's Conception of Judaism," in *On Jews and Judaism in Crisis*, pp. 126–71.

[21] Gershom Scholem, "The Science of Judaism—Then and Now," *The Messianic Idea in Judaism*, pp. 304–13.

history, which hangs around it, must be penetrated. To penetrate it was the task I set for myself."[22]

Despite their philosophical differences, which persisted in appropriately esoteric form to the very end of their relationship, Scholem and Benjamin were always united by a deep religiosity of thought coexisting with an "anarchic suspension" of traditional and ritualistic forms of belief. Their religiosity took the form of a messianic sensibility or attitude, a spiritual radicalism that constituted a Jewishness without doctrinal Judaism. This messianic spirit, hostile to political gradualism in any form, skeptical of the Enlightenment, and thoroughly radical in its attitude toward philosophy and politics, became the thread connecting not only Scholem and Benjamin, but an entire generation of intellectuals who rejected the optimistic synthesis of rational Judaism and liberal politics that was the hallmark of the Wilhelminian German-Jewish world. Before World War I this new messianic attitude embraced an apocalyptic antipolitics, a spiritual redefinition of Jewishness, and, simultaneously, a Nietzschean vision of the transfiguration of European culture. As early as 1912 Ernst Bloch remarked that for his generation "the social manifestations of submissiveness and self-deprecation have disappeared." Instead "one sees an anticipation."[23] This messianic impulse appeared in many different Jewish-secular guises in the early decades of the century. It included the negative theology of Franz Kafka, the messianic Marxism of Georg Lukács and Ernst Bloch, the existential Judaism of Martin Buber and Franz Rosenzweig, the expressionist Nietzscheanism of Kurt Hiller and Salomo Friedländer, Gustav Landauer's mystical anarchism, and certainly Benjamin's linguistic messianism and Scholem's nihilistic and esoteric Zionism.[24]

If the prophetic tradition in Judaism expressed itself in public testimony, the messianic tradition invoked its opposite, an esoteric, or even secret, knowledge that defines redemption as a "restoration" of a lost truth. Since, as Scholem points out, messianism is always nourished by its dark vision of the absolute negativity of the existing order of things, it "is not directed to what history will bring forth, but to that which will arise in its ruin."[25] This accounts for its chronic tendency to oscillate between utter pessimism and contemplative withdrawal on the one hand, and

[22] Gershom Scholem, letter to Salman Schocken, October 29, 1937; cited in Biale, *Gershom Scholem*, p. 76.

[23] Ernst Bloch, *Durch die Wüste: Frühe kritische Aufsätze* (Frankfurt am Main: Suhrkamp Verlag, 1964), p. 122.

[24] On this movement, see Michel Löwy, "Jewish Messianism and Libertarian Utopia in Central Europe," *New German Critique* 20 (Spring/Summer, 1980), pp. 105–15.

[25] Gershom Scholem, "Towards an Understanding of the Messianic Idea in Judaism," *The Messianic Idea in Judaism*, p. 10.

impatient and inchoate bursts of radical activism on the other. The post–World War I garden of messianic Jewish radicalism, to which both Scholem and Benjamin belonged, grew according to this disorderly and apocalyptic design.

The Berne period (May 1918 to September 1919) was not only a time of great mutual intellectual influence for Scholem and Benjamin, but also brought out "a deep-seated bitterness and disillusionment over the images of one another that we had fashioned for ourselves."[26] As often proved to be the case in subsequent years, such mutual idealizations diminished with greater intimacy. After the war, their political and intellectual paths diverged still further. In the early 1920s Scholem was more "excited by Palestine than by the German revolution," while Benjamin was emphatic in his view that history as sphere of action was "incapable of fulfillment." Rejecting the promiscuous amalgamation of history and utopia which he found, for example, in Ernst Bloch's classic *Spirit of Utopia* (1918), he wrote that "the Kingdom of God is not the *telos* of the historical dynamic."[27] Benjamin's essays of the early 1920s took on an increasingly "anarcho-messianic" tone, distinguishing "pure violence" from the means-ends violence of the State and of the European revolutionary tradition. The political cataclysm of the postwar years was registered in terms of an inner conflict between language as the nonviolent sphere of redemption, and a Sorelian politics of revolutionary action.[28] Consistent with the inherent dilemma of messianism there is an unresolved tension between his antipathy to history and his embrace of revolutionary violence, between his total contempt for the German political landscape and his attraction to the "higher ethic" of the "deed." By the mid-1920s his apolitical stance had become a politics opposed to political goals.

The early 1920s were also personally difficult for Benjamin. In 1921 his relations with his parents completely broke down, his marriage to Dora Pollak (born Dora Kellner) collapsed (though they continued to live together intermittently until 1929), and a passionate liaison with Jula Cohn, sister of his school friend Alfred Cohn, ended with her marriage to another friend, Fritz Radt. Benjamin's study of Goethe's *Elective Affinities*, a novel of two couples whose loves tragically cross, is in part an evocation of his own circumstances at that time.[29] This period of personal disequilibrium coincided with Scholem's decision to emigrate to Jerusa-

---

[26] Scholem, *W.B.*, p. 68.

[27] Walter Benjamin, "Theologico-Political Fragment," *Reflections*, p. 312.

[28] See Rabinbach, "Modern German Jewish Messianism," p. 119.

[29] See the excellent brief biographical study by Bernd Witte, *Walter Benjamin* (Hamburg: Rowohlt, 1985), pp. 43–48.

lem in 1923, provoking Benjamin to consider a similar move. But, as Scholem observed, "Benjamin himself displayed an attitude of reserve toward Palestine precisely in the year in which the catastrophic development of inflation and the general breakdown of interpersonal relationships rendered the prospect of emigration acute for him."[30] In November Benjamin noted that "as regards Palestine, at this time there is neither a practical possibility nor a theoretical necessity for me to go there."[31] This reserve and ambivalence persisted, in varying degree, throughout the 1920s and well into the period after 1933.

Much less ambivalent were Benjamin's growing apprehensions about relations between Germans and Jews, which he elaborated in a letter to the critic Florens Christian Rang, whose "Christian-messianic" spirit was kindred to his own:

> Here, if anywhere, we are at the heart of the contemporary Jewish question: the Jew today, even if he *publicly* stands up for the best German cause, abandons it. Since every public German expression is necessarily purchased (in the deepest sense), it cannot be accompanied by any certificate of authenticity. Only in another way can the secret relations between Germans and Jews be legitimately maintained. For the rest, I believe that my sentence is valid: that everything in German-Jewish relations that today has a visible impact, works toward its destruction, and a healthy complementarity of the noble nature of both peoples today requires a silence about their ties to each other.[32]

Benjamin's insistence on a "secret" relationship to German traditions and a "healthy complementarity" is instructive. Scholem too believed in a "secret" core of tradition, but he did not think it could be found outside of Judaism itself.

In 1924 another difference began to divide the two friends. While on vacation in Capri Benjamin met and fell in love with Asja Lacis, "a Russian revolutionary from Riga," as he put it, who offered him "an intensive insight into the relevance of radical communism."[33] Through conversations with Lacis and with Bloch, who was also in Capri, Benjamin began his long encounter with Marxism. Among the first books he consulted at Bloch's recommendation was Georg Lukács's *History and Class Consciousness*. Lukács's messianic vision of the proletarian revo-

---

[30] Scholem, *W.B.*, pp. 116–17.

[31] Letter of Walter Benjamin to Florens Christian Rang, November 18, 1923, *Briefe*, p. 311.

[32] Ibid., p. 310.

[33] Witte, *Walter Benjamin*, p. 54; Scholem, *W.B.*, p. 122. Lacis describes their meeting in her *Revolutionär im Beruf: Berichte über Meyerhold, Brecht, Benjamin und Piscator*, ed. Hildegard Brenner (Munich: Rogner & Bernhard, 1971), pp. 41–51.

lution as the practical solution to all of the knotty epistemological problems posed by classical German philosophy naturally ignited a strong
attraction, though even before reading it Benjamin predicted that "my
essential nihilism" would assert itself against Lukács's hyper-Hegelian-
ism. If Benjamin's embrace of Marxism was enthusiastic, it was hardly
orthodox. Even at the outset it was colored by the political and ethical
ambiguities that his anarchist leanings—especially the ideas of Sorel—
already posed so acutely in the early 1920s.

Scholem did not conceal his "misgivings and apprehensions," noting
that he "knew more than he [Benjamin] did about the practices of the
Communists—not only through my brother, with whom I had had long
and rather heated discussions . . . but also on the basis of my own experience in Palestine."[34] Scholem's complex relationship with his older
(by two years) brother Werner and Werner's deep and longstanding communist involvement (he was a leading figure in the KPD's left wing until
he was finally expelled in 1926, and remained a Reichstag delegate for
some time afterward) contributed to Scholem's apprehensions. This association was not wholly lost on Benjamin, who commented ironically on
the "elective affinity between Walter Benjamin and Werner Scholem."
(Scholem's concern for and frustration with his brother, arrested by the
Gestapo in 1933, is also a theme of this correspondence.)[35]

For Scholem, Benjamin's Marxism was always an alien component in
his thought, though he conceded much later that "this interlocking of the
two elements that by nature are incapable of balance" accounts for the
"profound brilliance" of his Marxist writings.[36] To Scholem's charge that
he had "put himself behind some principles" which were once foreign to
him, Benjamin replied in 1926 that he could hardly "refrain from the
study, from the practice, in which things (and relations) and the masses
interact." Yet, from a Jewish point of view, he added that "a 'just' radical
politics, which does not claim to be anything more than politics, can
always be useful for Jewry and, what is infinitely more important, will
always find Jewry useful for its own purposes." The diminished status
accorded to "politics" is worth emphasizing. In any case, he admitted
that Scholem was, at least in concrete matters, "far more at home in
[his] current life and decisions than I am in mine."[37]

Scholem's version of Benjamin's divided self does not have to be taken
at face value. Even during his student days as a disciple of Wyneken,
Benjamin's ethical ideals were tied to a political program, just as his

[34] Scholem, *W.B.*, p. 122
[35] Walter Benjamin to Gershom Scholem, December 22, 1924, *Briefe*, p. 368.
[36] Scholem, *W.B.*, p. 124.
[37] Benjamin to Scholem, May 29, 1926, *Briefe*, p. 426.

linguistic messianism was tied to his antipathy to wartime politics. And it is no less true of Scholem himself that he conceived of his early Zionism in terms of the Kabbalah and its nihilistic conception of spiritual renewal. We can afford to be generous in retrospect. Scholem's assertion that the "split" between Benjamin's "metaphysical mode of thinking" and his "Marxist mode" left him "a theologian marooned in the realm of the profane" assumes, after all, that such a leap into praxis is somehow uncharacteristic for the messianic sensibility.[38]

Moreover, the attempt to disentangle these elements, whether from the Marxist or the theological side, yield little for a thinker like Benjamin, in whom, as in Freud's famous analogy of Rome, "all the earlier phases of development continue to exist alongside the latest one." The exhausting polemics between Benjaminians "of the left" and "of the right" during the 1970s attests to the poverty of the endeavor.[39] Benjamin gives no indication that he suppressed or abandoned earlier conceptions for later ones. In the same letter to Scholem, he emphasized that he was "not ashamed of my earlier anarchism" and that he "considered communist 'goals' to be nonsensical and nonexistent." This, he added, did not diminish the value of "communist action" at all, since it was a "corrective to its goals," and "because there is no such thing as meaningful *political* goals." If he were to join the Communist Party (needless to say, he didn't) he would "always proceed in a radical manner, but never consistently."[40] Messianic impatience demanded acts, not ends, which remained outside the realm of human affairs. As the letters in this volume indicate, even in 1932, during the first months of his exile on the island of Ibiza, Benjamin resumed the highly esoteric and messianic reflections on the correspondence theory of language which he had first set down in 1916 and discussed with Scholem in Berne in 1918.

Ironically, Scholem did not intend to become a scholar when he arrived in Jerusalem. But after serving briefly as librarian of the nascent university, he quickly advanced to a professorship in Jewish mysticism after the Hebrew University was established on Mt. Scopus in 1925. By contrast, Benjamin's academic career was far less auspicious. In 1925, after much "inner resistance" he completed his *Habilitation* on baroque drama, *Ursprung des deutschen Trauerspiels (The Origin of the German Tragic Drama)*. The first chapter, entitled "Epistemo-critical Prologue," surely one of the most impenetrable philosophical statements in the Ger-

[38] See Gershom Scholem, "Walter Benjamin," *On Jews and Judaism in Crisis*, pp. 187–88; Scholem, *W.B.*, pp. 123–25, and *passim*.
[39] For the prototypical Marxist defense see Terry Eagleton, *Walter Benjamin or Towards a Revolutionary Criticism* (London: Verso, 1981).
[40] Walter Benjamin to Gershom Scholem, May 29, 1926, *Briefe*, p. 426.

man language, was characterized by its author as a text of "boundless *chutzpah*." [41] Yet it presents Benjamin's most essential ideas in a highly compressed and abstract form. In this prologue we find an exposition of his crucial concept of "origin," through which the essence of phenomena, as they will one day be revealed in light of messianic fulfillment, can be glimpsed in their incomplete, ephemeral, and empirical existence. Here also is the "monadic" character of authentic knowledge "in which every idea contains the image of the world." Though it deals with seventeenth-century drama it is at the same time a commentary on aesthetic modernism which sets the microcosm, or fragment, in opposition to systems of thought or artworks whose totalizing or aestheticist pretenses offer more than they can deliver. [42] In this aesthetic, which condemns the work of art that lays claim to classical completeness, we can see both the Jewish proscription of idolatry and, at the same time, the modernist regard for allegorical representation. Indeed, Benjamin explicitly connects them by rejecting the notion that art could "be appointed a councillor of the conscience" or that it could "permit what is represented, rather than the actual representation, to be the object of attention." [43] The "anticlassical" attitude required a "melancholy immersion" in the detail or allegory as a possible site of truth; it opposed the illusory claims of art and metaphysics to "symbolically" represent reality—a central component of Benjamin's messianic modernism even in his later explicitly Marxist writings.

The hermetic *Trauerspiel*, published in 1928, was the rock on which Benjamin's academic career in Germany foundered. After he withdrew it from the University of Frankfurt (it was certain to be rejected), Benjamin assumed the role of literary critic and *feuilletonist* for a number of periodicals, including the prestigious *Frankfurter Zeitung*. Benjamin's position outside of the university made him dependent on his writing— he became a master of the review form, a largely unacknowledged accomplishment—but it also allowed him to pursue his "elliptical lifestyle Berlin–Paris." And it allowed him to indulge his "fanatical travel addiction" resulting in the masterful portraits of cities (Naples, Rome, Marseilles, and, significantly, Moscow) that he published in the 1920s. In December 1926 Benjamin visited the Soviet Union, homeland of the revolution, to renew his liaison with Lacis. Hardly the model revolutionary tourist of the 1920s, Benjamin's *Moscow Diary* reveals him adrift among

[41] Walter Benjamin to Gershom Scholem, February 19, 1925, *Briefe*, p. 372.
[42] For a thorough discussion see Richard Wolin, *Walter Benjamin: An Aesthetic of Redemption* (New York: Columbia University Press, 1982), pp. 90–106; also see Bernd Witte, *Walter Benjamin, Der Intellektuelle als Kritiker: Untersuchungen zu seinem Frühwerk* (Stuttgart: Metzler Verlag, 1976).
[43] Walter Benjamin, *The Origin of German Tragic Drama*, trans. John Osborne (London: New Left Books, 1977), p. 105.

uncomprehending apparatchiks (his essay on Goethe for the *Soviet Encyclopedia* was rejected) and distraught at Lacis's ambivalent reception. Politics play almost no role in his melancholic reflections. His random musings about whether to join the party or to remain an "outsider" whose "illegal incognito among bourgeois authors still might have some meaning" tell us more about his personal state than they do about that of the Bolshevik revolution.[44]

In April 1927 Scholem and Benjamin met for the first time since their parting four years earlier, this time in Paris. Scholem's perceptions of their changed relationship at that stage deserves full quotation:

> When I left Benjamin in 1923, I took with me the image of a man driven by a beeline impulse to fashion an intellectual world of his own, a man who unswervingly followed his genius and who knew where he was headed, no matter what the exterior entanglements of his life might be. I was heading for a world in which everything still seemed disorganized and confused, in which amid severe internal struggles I was seeking a stable position where my efforts to understand Judaism would more clearly fit together into an integral whole. When we saw each other again, I met a person caught up in an intensive process of ferment, whose harmonious view of the world was shattered and in disrepair and who was in transit—to new shores he was as yet unable to determine.[45]

During their reunion Benjamin told Scholem that he had been working on a new project, a cultural history of Paris in the Second Empire, focusing on the "Paris Arcades" which he had been researching since his enthusiastic discovery of the Surrealist Louis Aragon's cityscape *Le Paysan de Paris*. The Arcades Project was to be "a reconstruction of the 'primal history' of the nineteenth century," organized around a series of tropes (the "arcades," "panoramas," "fashion," "boredom," "prostitution," "gambling," "the *flaneur*"), all circumscribed by the changing city itself. This archaeology of modernity as urban experience was to be illuminated through the central category of the "phantasmagoria," which was for Benjamin the historical moment in which the commodity entered consciousness as a "hallucination," as novelty, as "the eternal recurrence of the new." And finally it was to be an exemplar of his theory of "dialectical images," the epistemological analogue of modernity's constant collisions, or shocks, in which the flow of thoughts is "arrested" in "a messianic cessation of happening."[46]

The Arcades Project, which he pursued with interruptions until 1934,

[44] Walter Benjamin, *Moscow Diary*, ed. Gary Smith, trans. Richard Sieburth (Cambridge, Mass.: Harvard University Press, 1986), p. 73.

[45] Scholem, *W.B.*, pp. 133–34.

[46] Walter Benjamin, "Theses on the Philosophy of History," *Illuminations*, ed. Hannah Arendt, trans. Harry Zohn (New York: Schocken Books, 1969), p. 263.

and steadily thereafter, became the most ambitious undertaking of his life, his *raison d'être* during the years in exile. It became a labyrinthine work, "in truth the theater of all my struggles and all my ideas."[47] And yet, as he himself recognized in his notes to the project, "the labyrinth is the home of the hesitant," the path of "someone who does not want to reach a goal."[48] Benjamin was not simply "in transit"; he had found a place, the arcades, in which his restlessness could be at home and where exile could be thematized as the labyrinth of modernity itself.

In Paris, Benjamin also declared that he would soon begin learning Hebrew, an announcement of more than ordinary interest to Scholem, whose investigations of Kabbalah, Jewish mysticism, and of the seventeenth-century Sabbatian movement were beginning to bear fruit, and who had not yet abandoned hope for Benjamin's eventual emigration to Palestine. Scholem arranged a meeting with Judah Leon Magnes, chancellor of the Hebrew University, whom Benjamin impressed with his plan to become a "critic of Hebrew texts" and to emigrate to Palestine where, as Scholem suggested, he might be given a position in German and French literature. But by 1929, as plans for Benjamin's departure took shape (Scholem had secured *via* Magnes a stipend for him to study Hebrew) the Hebrew studies faltered and Benjamin confessed to Magnes that he was "encountering a pathological vacillation which, I am sorry to say, I have already noticed in myself from time to time."[49]

The collapse of what Scholem, with more than wishful thinking, called "the Palestine project" took its toll on their friendship. In February 1930 Scholem asked for an accounting, "if it turns out that in this life you can no longer reckon with, and do not reckon with, a real encounter with Judaism except in the medium of our friendship. . . . To me it is far more important to know where you really are than where you hope to go someday, for the way your life is constituted it is certain that you, more than anyone else, will always wind up some other place than where you wanted to get."[50] Benjamin's response called attention, perhaps exaggeratedly, to his sense of Scholem as the link to the Jewish side of his intellectual preoccupations, but also to the limits of that alternative: "Living judaism I have certainly encountered in no other form than in you."

In the early 1930s Benjamin's "vacillation" intensified with his stormy divorce from Dora, and with Lacis's arrival in Berlin.[51] Another new

[47] Benjamin to Scholem, January 20, 1930, *Briefe*, p. 506.
[48] Walter Benjamin, "Central Park," trans. Lloyd Spencer (with Mark Harrington), *New German Critique* 34 (Winter, 1985), p. 40.
[49] Scholem, *W.B.*, p. 156.
[50] Ibid., p. 161.
[51] Lacis took full credit for Benjamin's decision not to pursue that option: "The path of a normal thinking progressive person led to Moscow, but not to Palestine. I can safely say,

element in his life was his admiration for and friendship with Bertolt Brecht, whom Benjamin met through Lacis in 1929. Brecht fulfilled Benjamin's need for a "secret relation between Germans and Jews," a role once played by Rang (who died in 1924), and even earlier by the poet C. F. Heinle, who committed suicide in 1914.[52] By the beginning of 1931 Benjamin's relationship with Scholem was strained almost to the breaking point. Scholem's frustration and disappointment with Benjamin's Marxism, and his antipathy toward Brecht, his antipode, is evident from the tone of his missives, above all the one launched from Jerusalem on March 30th. Adopting the self-assumed role of an "old theologian," Scholem accused Benjamin of confusing religion and politics and of "engaging in a singularly intensive kind of self-deception." Benjamin's essay on Karl Kraus, the Viennese moralist, he said, exhibited "an astonishing incompatibility and unconnectedness between your real and your pretended modes of thought" and in general "stamps your output in this period as the work of an adventurer, a purveyor of ambiguities, and a cardsharper." The Communist Party, with no uncertainty, would "unmask you as a typical counterrevolutionary and a bourgeois." "The only question is," Scholem concluded, "how long the morality of your insights, one of your most precious possessions, can remain sound in such a dubious relationship."[53]

That Benjamin evaded Scholem's thrust is predictable. But a previously overlooked source shows to what extent he was wounded by the crisis in their relationship. At that time Benjamin wrote a brief commentary on a 1799 letter from the romantic philosopher Friedrich Schlegel to the "old theologian" Schleiermacher at the point of a similar crisis in their friendship. Published only a few weeks later in the *Frankfurter Zeitung* of May 1931 (and significantly *not* included in the original edition of *Deutsche Menschen*) it contains Schlegel's reaction to the severe "judgments" on his ideas which Schleiermacher offered, and, perhaps, Benjamin's unspoken answer to Scholem:

> As if I could demand that you should understand the ideas . . . or, as if I should be unhappy that you did not understand them. Nothing is more despicable to me than this entire business of understanding or misunderstanding something. I am truly pleased if someone I love or hate grasps to some degree what I want or sees what I am. You can readily imagine whether I am often in a situation where I can expect this sort of pleasure. . . . But if my writings only provide you with the occasion to thrash about in the empty spirit (*hohlen Gespenst*) of understanding

that if Walter Benjamin did not go to Palestine, that was my achievement." Lacis, *Revolutionär im Beruf*, p. 45.

[52] Cf. Witte, *Walter Benjamin*, pp. 90–91.

[53] Scholem to Benjamin, March 30, 1931, in *W.B.*, p. 229.

or not understanding, put them aside. . . . Or do you really believe that torn flowers can be made to grow again through dialectic?[54]

The crisis was acknowledged in Jerusalem as well. Despite the collapse of the Jerusalem project, Benjamin remained for Scholem the "living link" to his own past in the German-Jewish messianic resurgence of the postwar years, and to his reevaluation of its legacy. At that same moment, 1931, Scholem expressed doubts about ever realizing his conception of Zionism as a "religious-mystical quest for a regeneration of Judaism." Scholem's sense that this regeneration had little to do with political matters is evident: "Now, Zionism as a movement certainly always has been far more than the empirical form of its organization, but surely in all these years there was the chance for people like me to pursue our cause—which, God knows, originally had nothing to do with Englishmen or Arabs."[55]

Here we get a rare glimpse of the depth of Scholem's political involvements in Palestine, especially with Brit Shalom, an organization founded in the mid-1920s by Arthur Ruppin and a group of university intellectuals (in which Magnes, Hugo Bergmann, and Martin Buber were also active). Brit Shalom called for a binational state with equal rights for Arabs and Jews, and in contrast to the "political Zionists" of left and right (Ben-Gurion and Jabotinsky, respectively), it prophetically foresaw that a perpetual conflict between Arabs and Jews would threaten Zionism itself. But after the 1929 Arab riots significantly strengthened the hand of the revisionists, Brit Shalom increasingly came under attack from critics of its "unrealistic" posture, and for reflecting a diaspora mentality. Zionism, Scholem believed, endangered itself by becoming prophetic or messianic in the secular realm, before it could achieve inner cultural renewal "in the invisible realm, . . . in the regeneration of language."[56]

In a remarkable article written in the heat of debate over the 1929 Arab riots Scholem explained: "I absolutely deny that Zionism is a messianic movement and that it has the right to employ religious terminology for political goals. The redemption of the Jewish people, which as a Zionist I desire, is in no way identical with the religious redemption I hope for in the future."[57] At the historical moment that political Zionism

[54] *Deutsche Menschen*, *GS* 4.1, p. 232. Scholem wrote: "That Benjamin himself did not particularly welcome such clarification I could easily grasp, but it took me some time to understand that at bottom that clarification was not possible for him. His later work proved that he was incapable of making a decision between metaphysics and materialism (as he conceived of the latter)." *W.B.*, pp. 168–69.

[55] Scholem to Benjamin, August 1, 1931, in Scholem, *W.B.*, p. 171.

[56] Ibid., p. 172.

[57] Gershom Scholem, "Three Sins of Brit Shalom," *Davar*, December 12, 1929. Cited in Biale, p. 177.

"has triumphed itself to death" in its thisworldly expectations, Scholem placed even greater weight on the otherworldly dimension of messianism that his historical studies illuminated. His withdrawal from politics in 1931 was the ironic counterpoint to Benjamin's engagement.

In 1931 Benjamin justified his communism by likening himself to "a castaway who drifts on a wreck by climbing to the top of an already crumbling mast. But, from here he has a chance to give a signal for his rescue." The descent of their correspondence into "controversy" at that time also required a rescue, provided by the figure of Franz Kafka. That Benjamin at the nadir of their relationship asked for Scholem's opinions on Kafka, the writer most admired by both of them, was an act of "diplomacy," as Adorno once described Benjamin's posture as a correspondent. This diplomacy restored the Jewish substance to their communication, and was unmistakably a gesture of reconciliation (coinciding, incidentally, with a brief reconciliation with Dora). At this juncture of a crisis narrowly overcome, the phase of their correspondence published here begins.

The Mediterranean sun was not much balm for Benjamin, as we see from the dour photographs of him in rumpled white shirt and tie on the veranda of Jean Selz's beach house on Ibiza, where he spent three months in the summer of 1932.[58] Benjamin's letters from Ibiza, and from Nice, which serve as a kind of prelude, give only surface signs of serious depression over his work, his marriage, and his uncertain future. Two suicidal episodes, in May 1931 ("battle fatigue on the economic front") and in June 1932 in Nice, testify to his diminished state even before the trials of a life in emigration commenced. In March 1933 Benjamin left Germany for France. His political antennae were so poorly attuned, he later recalled, that if it had not been for the insistence of Gretel Adorno and other friends, he might not have sensed the danger of remaining. Yet, he writes, "I did not act on panic: the German atmosphere in which you first look at people's lapels [for the Nazi party insignia AR] and after that usually do not want to look them in the face anymore, is unbearable"(14). Benjamin occupied a somewhat different place in the Parisian émigré milieu than other German exiles. He stayed aloof from "the great mass of refugees in France [who] lived cut off from French contacts" and "read their emigré papers, frequented their emigré clubs and cafés, lived immersed in their emigré universe."[59] "I have hardly ever been as lonely as I am here. If I were seeking opportu-

[58] Benjamin to Scholem, April 17, 1931, in *W.B.*, p. 233.
[59] Arthur Koestler, *The Invisible Writing* (New York: Macmillan, 1969), p. 303. Koestler was director of the Institut pour l'Etude du Fascisme, a communist front organization in

nities to sit in a café with emigrés, they would be easy to find. But I avoid them" (43).

Though he too lived in cheap and dreary hotels, was supported by the Alliance Israélite Universelle and experienced day-to-day economic insecurity, Benjamin was also more at home in Paris, having considered a move there as early as 1926. He was highly regarded as the German translator of Baudelaire and Proust, he had reported on French literary developments for the *Frankfurter Zeitung* and *Die Literarische Welt*, and his contacts in the world of French literature included some of the most influential figures in French letters, including Adrienne Monnier and André Gide. At the outset, he could still publish in Germany under pseudonyms, and his association with the Frankfurt Institute for Social Research (then in Geneva) provided a small but adequate financial basis. Nevertheless, Benjamin's experience of exile was harsh: "Life among the emigrés is unbearable, life alone is no more bearable, and a life among the French cannot be brought about" (42). Georg Förster, whose letter from Paris exile almost 150 years earlier Benjamin included in *Deutsche Menschen*, mirrored his own exile: "I have no homeland, no fatherland, no friends anymore, everything which once clung to me has abandoned me to assume new bonds and when I think about the past and what of it I am still bound to, it is merely a matter of my own choice and my imagination." [60]

Even earlier, Benjamin's difficult material circumstances exacted a heavy toll. In July 1932, after contemplating suicide, he wrote to Scholem that "the literary forms of expression that my thought has forged for itself over the last decade have been utterly conditioned by the preventive measures and antidotes with which I had to counter the disintegration constantly threatening my thought as a result of such contingencies. And though many—or a sizable number—of my works have been small-scale victories, they are offset by large-scale defeats" (4). In May 1933 Benjamin wrote of his first few months as an emigré: "My constitution is frail. The absolute impossibility of having anything at all to draw on threatens a person's inner equilibrium in the long run, even one as unassuming and as used to living in precarious circumstances as I am" (23). This entirely pessimistic evaluation would be repeated many times over the next few years, especially in his last year of exile.

In Paris, Benjamin saw his situation as exemplary for the "decline of the 'free floating intelligentsia' " in the era of fascist ascendancy. He

Paris where Benjamin delivered his "Author as Producer" in April 1934. He does not mention the lecture or Benjamin in his memoirs.

[60] Walter Benjamin, *Deutsche Menschen, GS* 4.1, p. 160.

became his own best case for a theory of the precipitous descent of intellectuals from the social rank and moral latitude they enjoyed in an earlier, less catastrophic era. Goethe, he once remarked, was permitted far greater room for "compromise" than the intellectual allied with the proletarian movement. "On the Social Situation of the French Writer," written in 1933 for the Institute's *Zeitschrift für Sozialforschung*, to which Scholem vehemently objected because of its theme of class betrayal as the duty of intellectuals, is striking for the parallel it implicitly draws between his own impoverished condition as a writer in exile, and his diagnosis of the social and political eclipse of those great authors—like Zola, or Gide—who maintained a moral and social position above the class conflict: "the intellectual mimics proletarian existence, without in the least being connected with the working class."[61] When Scholem asked unsympathetically if this article "is intended to be a Communist credo," Benjamin characteristically pointed to his own situation: "That, among all the possible forms and means of expression, a credo is the last thing my communism resorts to; that—even at the cost of its orthodoxy —my communism is absolutely nothing other than the expression of certain experiences I have undergone in my thinking and in my life; that it is a drastic, not infertile expression of the fact that the present intellectual industry finds it impossible to make room for my thinking . . ." (50).

This vision of intellectual debasement at once reinforced Benjamin's bleak outlook and, paradoxically, provided a source of hope, albeit limited. Until the late 1930s, consistent with his earlier reflections on the debasement of art, Benjamin did not completely equate social decline with political defeat. He still saw in the descending social position of intellectuals and in the disappearance of the artwork's "auratic" halo, a hidden potential for releasing those "divine sparks" which, according to the messianic ideal, are buried in the debris of history. Benjamin's attraction to Surrealism was largely to its "poetry of decline," the creation of a new type of intellectual whose liberation from social constraints permitted "the profane illumination."[62] He was drawn to Brecht as much as a consequence of the dramatist's asceticism and his refusal of the mantle of genius—the "artist" as "producer"—as to his Marxism. At his most optimistic, even his own journalistic activity took on similar meaning: "the place where the word is most debased—that is to say, the newspaper—becomes the very place where the rescue operation can be mounted."[63]

---

[61] Walter Benjamin, "Zum gesellschaftlichen Standort des französischen Schriftstellers," *GS* 2.2, p. 789.

[62] Walter Benjamin, "Surrealism," *Reflections*, pp. 177–92.

[63] See Walter Benjamin, "Author as Producer," in Walter Benjamin, *Understanding*

Benjamin's 1934 observation that the man of today is "a reduced man, therefore, a man kept on ice in a cold world," recalls his description a decade earlier of "the realm of dead objects, the supposed infinity of a world without hope" in the *Trauerspiel* book.[64] "For it is precisely the vision of the frenzy of destruction, in which all earthly things collapse into a heap of ruins," which permits a glimpse of redemption.[65] As Irving Wohlfarth has pointed out, Benjamin's ubiquitous figure of the "rag-picker" *(chiffonier)* in the Arcades Project is a self-image, "the 'salvation' or 'salvaging' of the phenomenal world is thus synonymous with its 'dissolution' or 'dispersal.'"[66] Above all, the Arcades Project, "the attempt to retain the image of history in the most inconspicuous corners of existence—the detritus of history," offered solace, "the actual, if not the only reason, not to abandon courage in the struggle for existence."[67]

After 1931, "Marxism" and "Palestine" remained the headings under which the most fundamental strains in their friendship can be assembled. They are at once emblems of a personal difference, and, at the same time, the polarities of European Jewry during the first quarter of the twentieth century. In 1933, when Benjamin again considered emigrating to Palestine, Scholem replied, "My life here is only possible . . . because I feel devoted to this cause, even if in the face of despair and ruination" (29). Scholem's uniformly pessimistic assessment, however realistic, of Benjamin's employment prospects in Palestine, and Benjamin's own guilt over the earlier fiasco, did not augur well for Benjamin to put his Jewish convictions to the "test of experience." As Hannah Arendt, who knew him in Paris, noted, "what strikes one as indecision in [Benjamin's] letters, as though he were vacillating between Zionism and Marxism, in truth was probably due to the bitter insight that all solutions were not only objectively false and inappropriate to reality, but would lead him personally to a false salvation, no matter whether that salvation was labeled Moscow or Jerusalem."[68] Scholem's letters show that after 1933, as far as Benjamin's often-planned and just as often postponed visit to Palestine is concerned, the vacillations and hesitations were mutual.

In 1934, Scholem reopened the file on Benjamin's Marxism: "I have

---

Brecht (London: New Left Books, 1973), p. 90. This translation differs slightly from the one in *Reflections*, pp. 220–38.

[64] Walter Benjamin, "Author as Producer," p. 100.

[65] Walter Benjamin, *The Origin of German Tragic Drama*, trans. John Osborne (London: New Left Books, 1977), p. 232.

[66] Irving Wohlfarth, "Et Cetera? The Historian as *Chiffonnier*," *New German Critique* 39 (Fall, 1986), p. 161.

[67] Benjamin to Theodor Adorno, May 31, 1935, *Briefe*, p. 664.

[68] Hannah Arendt, "Walter Benjamin: 1892–1940," introduction to *Illuminations*, p. 36.

been waiting for years for an exposition on such implicit questions as I asked you for then and which you must have long *forgotten*"(53). Characteristically, Benjamin responded (as he had in 1931) in terms that called attention to their respective experiences, rather than their ideological commitments. "A memory that has to digest impressions imparted by unforeseeably changing living conditions will rarely be as reliable as one sustained by continuity"(55). "A correspondence," he emphasized, "such as we maintain is, as you know, something very precious, but also something calling for circumspection"(49).

With crisis again on the horizon, Kafka was once more called upon to assist.[69] In the same letter (May 6, 1934) in which he replied to Scholem's question about his "Communist credo," Benjamin asked for some "pointers" on Kafka's position within Judaism. At this juncture Kafka's significance became not so much their mutual attraction to his greater unifying vision, as a less delicate atmosphere in which their most urgent intellectual and personal differences could be aired. Kafka offered a common language in which they could avoid violating circumspection or risking destruction. As if to underline the point, Benjamin called his Kafka essay and their exchange "the crossroads of the different paths my thought has taken"(65).

For both Benjamin and Scholem, Kafka belonged to the messianic sensibility. Their dispute concerns his precise relation to it. Significantly, the identity of the "great rabbi" who anticipates Kafka when he "once said that he did not wish to change the world by force, but would only make a slight adjustment in it" is divulged as Scholem himself.[70] Already in 1931 Scholem put the crucial distinction in parentheses: "I have already had 'individual thoughts' about Kafka, although these do not concern Kafka's position in the continuum of German literature (in which he has no position of any sort, something that he himself did not have the least doubt about; as you probably know, he was a Zionist)."[71] For Benjamin, however, Kafka belonged not only to a Jewish but to a German tradition, a point which Adorno rightly called "decisive."[72]

---

[69] The immediate occasion was provided by Scholem's efforts to convince Robert Weltsch, a childhood friend of Kafka and the editor of the *Jüdische Rundschau*, which was still published in Germany, to commission an article by Benjamin on the tenth anniversary of Kafka's death. The essay was published, though greatly reduced, on December 12, 1934. See the extensive notes in *GS* 2.3, pp. 1190–1270 and the English language translation, "Franz Kafka: On the Tenth Anniversary of His Death," *Illuminations*, pp. 111–40.

[70] "Franz Kafka," *Illuminations*, p. 134.

[71] Scholem to Benjamin, August 1, 1931, in Scholem, *W.B.*, p. 170.

[72] Adorno to Benjamin, December 17, 1934, *GS* 2.3, p. 1177. Cited in Hans Mayer, "Walter Benjamin and Franz Kafka," *On Walter Benjamin*, p. 204. Adorno noted: "If Kafka is not a founder of a religion—and how right you are! How little he is that!—he is certainly not in any sense a poet of Jewish *Heimat*. Here I find most decisive your sentences on the

Scholem's Kafka was the most modern of Jewish gnostic commentators on the Law: his moral vision is what "a halakhist who attempted a *linguistic* paraphrase of divine judgment would have to be like."[73] Kafka descends from a Jewish tradition of commentary, and yet is not at home in it. It is Kafka's sense of the commentary as a broken vessel that Scholem alludes to when he admonishes Benjamin, "You had the *moral world of Halakhah* right before your eyes, complete with its abysses and its dialectics" (58). Kafka was thus able to express the "fine line between religion and nihilism" in Scholem's own thought, as he wrote to Salman Schocken in 1937: "I later [found in Kafka] the most perfect and unsurpassed expression of this fine line, an expression, which, as a secular statement of the Kabbalistic world-feeling in a modern spirit, seemed to me to wrap Kafka's writings in the halo of the canonical."[74] If revelation has lost its binding character, for him "the central Jewish nerve" in Kafka, is not the loss of tradition but the "unenforceability" of revelation and Law.

Scholem's vision of Kafka is best expressed in the poem he sent Benjamin in July 1934, which is published here (with letter 57). In it, God appears as an agent of nihilism—the nothingness of experience is the concrete form of the "last judgment"—that does not preclude the possibility of redemption, only of human intercession on its behalf. "Kafka's world is the world of revelation, but of revelation seen of course from that perspective in which it is returned to its own nothingness" (58).

This is both close to, and yet, remote from Benjamin, who calls Kafka's world "prehistoric," a world where "laws and definite norms remain unwritten" and where "transgression in the sense of the Law is not accidental but fated." It is not divine judgment as "martial law," but the mythical condition of exile that is paramount in Benjamin's reading of Kafka: "Exile—his exile—has gained control of him." This exile is not simply an individual fate, but a collective exile from the sources of knowledge and truth, from the doctrine or teaching, which is of course synonymous with the tradition itself. The question Benjamin asks—"But do we have the doctrine which Kafka's parables interpret and which K.'s postures and the gestures of his animals clarify?"—is answered negatively.[75]

To understand this brilliant and freighted controversy—the most ex-

intertwining of the German and the Jewish elements." It is clear from the letters published here that Mayer's view of Scholem as rejecting "a Kafka whose laws and teachings were mere appearance" is wide of the mark.

[73] Scholem to Benjamin, August 1, 1931, in *W.B.*, p. 171.
[74] Biale, *Gershom Scholem*, p. 75.
[75] "Franz Kafka," *Illuminations*, pp. 122, 126.

traordinary in this collection—is finally to come to terms with their respective conceptions of the interpreter and the text, the tradition and the Law, the German and the Jew. Extending from their wartime discussions of language as a condition of fall or exile from God's word, Scholem and Benjamin shared a conception of truth as embedded in commentary, but often hidden or dispersed in the prosaic stream of language. Truth emerges as "divine sparks" or emanations, often where least expected. Both were fond of quoting the proverb that "each word in the Torah had seventy—according to some, 600,000—possible levels of meaning," but each interpreted the proverb differently. For Scholem, tradition is not rooted in unambiguously revealed truth or doctrinal orthodoxy, but in the esoteric tradition of commentary which both restores and transforms its meaning: "Authentic tradition remains hidden; only the decaying [verfallende] tradition chances upon [verfällt auf] a subject and only in decay does its greatness become visible."[76] The closest Scholem comes to his own credo is this passage in the letter to Salman Schocken:

> Certainly, history may seem to be fundamentally an illusion, but an illusion without which in temporal reality no insight into the essence of things is possible. For today's man that mystical totality of "truth" [des Systems], whose existence disappears particularly when it is projected into historical time, can only become visible in the purest way in the legitimate discipline of commentary and in the singular mirror of philological criticism.[77]

Although both equated system with myth, already in the *Traverspiel* Benjamin identified both criticism and commentary as estranged from "a primordial form of perception in which words possess their own nobility as names, unimpaired by cognitive meaning." The Adamic state in which there is "as yet no need to struggle with the communicative significance of words" can only be glimpsed in the "most singular and eccentric of phenomena"—through a "gestural" or "physiognomic" mode of knowledge in which the "bits and pieces" of historical experiences offer more in their dissipation than does the most coherent philosophical system in its completeness. For this reason, the "meaning" of tradition cannot simply be sought in historical or philological interpretation, but is itself irrevocably lost.

Thus, Benjamin claims that Kafka's "assistants are sextons who have lost their house of prayer, his students are pupils who have mislaid the Holy Writ"; Scholem replies that they "cannot decipher it." The "main

---

[76] Gershom Scholem, "Zehn Unhistorische Sätze über Kabbala," *Judaica* III (Frankfurt am Main: Suhrkamp Verlag, 1973), p. 264. Quoted in Biale, *Gershom Scholem*, p. 101.

[77] Biale, *Gershom Scholem*, p. 76.

point" as Scholem put it, is that Benjamin regards the Law "only from its most *profane* side," whereas Scholem also regards it from its religious side. "Its problem," he admonishes, "is not, dear Walter, its *absence* in a pre-animistic world, but the fact that it cannot *be fulfilled*" (58). Benjamin's reply to Scholem indicates that he considered "Kafka's constant insistence on the Law to be the point where his work comes to a standstill . . . (63). For Benjamin, the tradition is "lost" or "mislaid," replaced only by a condition of exile in which the commentators "have nothing to support them on their 'untrammeled happy journey.' " [78]

For Scholem, then, the fate of the Jews is bound up with the inherent nihilism of their own tradition: the cosmic exile of the Jews is also an exile from the meaning of the Law, but not from the Law itself. This was the error of the Sabbatian apostates whose heresy proclaimed that the coming of the Messiah and the restored world had already occurred. For Benjamin, however, it is bound up with an irreparable condition of exile which is the (German-Jewish) tradition of modernity. In Benjamin's Kafka the Law is *absent*, "the work of the Torah—if we abide by Kafka's account—has been thwarted" (63). And most significantly: "It is in this context that the problem of the Scripture [*Schrift*] poses itself. Whether the pupils have lost it or whether they are unable to decipher it comes down to the same thing, because, without the key that belongs to it the Scripture is not Scripture, but life" (63). And, adds Benjamin, Kafka identifies "life" with "life as it is lived in the village"—his image of exile. Benjamin later calls this condition "the sickness of tradition."

In all its esoteric splendor and subtlety, the Kafka discussion is an inner-messianic dispute about the "tradition" of Judaism and the meaning of commentary in exile and in catastrophe. Expressed through their Prague connection, it is a debate between a Zionist whose nihilistic impulse and admiration for the heretics and mystics did not fully abandon the tradition of the commentators, and an exiled "student" whose messianic commentary had lost its original text, its Holy Writ. [79]

[78] "Franz Kafka," *Illuminations*, p. 139.

[79] It is interesting to note that in an earlier essay on Benjamin, written prior to the emergence of this correspondence, Scholem reconciled his friend's interpretation of Kafka with his own: "Benjamin perceived the negative inversion to which the Jewish categories are subjected in Kafka's world; there the teaching no longer conveys a positive message, but offers only an absolutely Utopian—and therefore as yet undefinable—promise of a postcontemporary world. We are left nothing but the procedures of a 'Law' that can no longer be deciphered. These procedures became the central feature of Kafka's vision. Benjamin knew that in Kafka we possess the *theologia negativa* of a Judaism not a whit less intense for having lost the Revelation as a positive message." Scholem, "Walter Benjamin," *On Jews and Judaism in Crisis*, p. 196. Scholem, as Henry Pachter recognized, is ambivalent about the messianic tradition: he "wants to condemn heresy while lovingly proclaiming the heretics saints." Henry Pachter, "Masters of Cultural History: Gershom Scholem—The Myth of the Mythmaker," *Salmagundi* 40 (Winter, 1978), p. 33.

These letters do not dwell on the political details of the "magnificent global catastrophe." Their sobriety alone is enough to invoke its presence. There are, of course, pressing personal worries: Scholem's despair over his brother Werner's long imprisonment (Werner Scholem died in Buchenwald, in 1940); Benjamin's similar fears for his brother (Georg Benjamin died in Mauthausen, in 1942), and his concern for his son Stefan and for Dora. Scholem comments at length on the Arab riots in Jerusalem in 1936, and on the various schemes for partition that followed the British Royal Commission report the following year. That Brit Shalom could not translate its moral vision into a viable politics was already evident to Scholem in the early 1930s when he wrote Benjamin, "I do not believe that there is such a thing as a "solution to the Jewish Question' in the sense of a normalization of the Jews, and I certainly do not think that this question can be solved in Palestine in such a sense." [80] Yet, when the British plan for partition was made public Scholem reluctantly accepted it—against many of his former colleagues in Brit Shalom who remained skeptical of a Jewish state.

Benjamin's laconic comments in October 1936 about the "political world that is more closely touching if not already engulfing me" (86) refers to his complex attitude toward the French and émigré left, an aspect of his life which, for obvious reasons, he chose not to elaborate to Scholem. In a letter to Max Horkheimer, written only a few days earlier, he castigated the "local French intellectuals" for their illusions "arising from the cult of the Great Revolution." [81] Those illusions, revived by the Popular Front and canonized at the 1935 Paris Congress for the Defense of Culture were, like the overstuffed rhetorical furniture of an obsolete historial style, embodied in the political vocabulary of "progress," "the people," and "the nation." [82] Yet, despite his professions of isolation in Paris, there were also productive contacts among the small group of intellectuals still caught up in the vapor trail left by Surrealism after its descent to the Popular Front. Benjamin was in close contact with Georges Bataille, Pierre Klossowski, Pierre Missac, and attended meetings of their "closed and secret group," the Acéphale ("acephalic," or "headless"). The association with Bataille—to whom Benjamin en-

[80] Scholem to Benjamin, August 1, 1931 Scholem, Story, p. 172.

[81] Benjamin to Horkheimer, October 13, 1936, Walter Benjamin—Briefe, p. 724.

[82] On Benjamin's relation to the Popular Front, see Philippe Ivernel, "Paris, Capital of the Popular Front, or the Posthumous LIfe of the 19th Century," New German Critique 39 (Fall, 1986), 61–86; Chryssoula Kambas, "Politische Aktualität: Walter Benjamin's Concept of History and the Failure of the French Popular Front," New German Critique 39 (Fall, 1986), 87–98; and her Walter Benjamin im Exil: Zum Verhältnis von Literaturpolitik und Ästhetik (Tübingen, 1983).

trusted his papers—deserves greater attention because of the natural affinity between these two early explorers of the then uncharted waters of fascist irrationality.[83]

Scholem's "dark broodings" about Benjamin's Marxism did not allow him to read all the signs of his friend's growing disenchantment. In the "Expressionism controversy" of 1935, a debate on the mythologies of communist Popular Front politics, Benjamin defended a revolutionary avant-garde already eclipsed (and in some cases about to be liquidated) by the Stalinist norms of "bourgeois realism" and "literary heritage" officially prescribed in 1934. Benjamin commented that among the "most interesting" reactions to his famous essay "The Work of Art in the Age of Mechanical Reproduction" was the effort of "the party members among the writers to suppress the debate, if not the lecture" when he delivered it to an organization of German emigré writers in June 1936.[84] The Gide Affair of November 1936, a scandal on the left unleashed when André Gide, that holiest of "bourgeois writers" in the antifascist firmament, who sanctified the 1935 Paris Congress by his presence on the podium, published a (very mild) critical report of his travels in Russia, produced his ironic remark that "the outrage of the party-people knows no boundaries."[85] Though never explicitly mentioned in these letters, the confusion and anxiety that the Gide Affair and the Moscow trials elicited in Benjamin are evident from his confession to Horkheimer: "For the current events in the Union I have no key."[86] In the summer of 1937 he wrote to a friend, Fritz Lieb, that "The destructive effect of the Russian events will necessarily extend itself ever further. And, in this regard, the worst is not the premature disarming of the stalwart fighters for 'freedom of thought'; much sadder and much more necessary appears to me the muting of thinkers, who precisely as thinkers, can hardly be considered to be in the know. This is my case."[87]

Scholem and Benjamin did not meet again until 1938 when Scholem passed through Paris on his way to New York, where he spent the spring semester of that year. This final meeting, which is a missing piece to the story told in these letters, is described by Scholem in detail in *Walter Benjamin: The Story of a Friendship*. "The focus of our discussions," he notes, was, of course, Benjamin's Marxist orientation.

[83] See Pierre Klossowski, "Lettre sur Walter Benjamin," *Mercure de France* 315 (1952), pp. 456–57.

[84] Benjamin to Alfred Cohn, June 1936, *Briefe*, pp. 715–16.

[85] Cited in Albrecht Betz, *Exil und Engagement: Deutsche Schriftsteller im Frankreich der Dreissiger Jahre* (Munich: Text und Kritik, 1986), p. 130.

[86] Benjamin to Horkheimer, January 31, 1937, *Briefe*, p. 728.

[87] Benjamin to Fritz Lieb, July 9, 1937, *Briefe*, p. 733.

Years laden with a heavy cargo of political events had intervened, and both of us could not help contemplating our reunion with some tension. If Benjamin wrote to Kitty Steinschneider after my departure that "our overdue philosophical discussion came off in good fashion," that was a friend's extenuation, for the discussion had taken place in an emotionally rather charged atmosphere, and even had included two or three downright dramatic moments relating to Benjamin's own feelings, his relationship to the Institut für Sozialforschung and to Brecht, as well as to the trials in Russia, which greatly excited the entire world at the time.[88]

That Benjamin remained noncommittal about Stalinism, despite what Scholem describes as the "passionate stance" of close friends like Hannah Arendt and Heinrich Blücher, only partly reflects his fidelity to Brecht's apologetics and equivocation. He was unwilling to acknowledge what his diaries of conversations with Brecht later that summer record explicitly: "Brecht yesterday evening: 'There is no longer any doubt— the struggle against ideology has become a new ideology.'"[89] In any case, the testimony of another Parisian exile, Manès Sperber, that he repressed his natural political skepticism because as a good antifascist emigré he had become "hope-addicted," is hardly applicable to Benjamin, for whom it would be more apt to say that his own skepticism was suspect because of his natural addiction to pessimism. Scholem, however, has put together sufficient testimony to understand that Benjamin's remark about "the *Zeitgeist*, which has set up markers in the desert landscape of the present that cannot be overlooked by old Bedouins like us,"(127) was referring to the Hitler-Stalin pact.[90] When in early 1940 he spoke of "prostrate" politicians who "confirmed their defeat by betraying their own cause," his deep reaction to the events in the political arena are evident.[91] This explains why his last letter to Scholem anticipates— of course with the necessary distance and circumspection—their eventual, though never consummated, rapprochement: "Even though it is a sad thing that we cannot converse with one another, I still have the feeling that the circumstances in no way deprive me of such heated debates as we used to indulge in now and then. There is no longer any need for those today. And it may well be fitting to have a small ocean between us when the moment comes to fall into each other's arms *spiritualiter*"(127).

Benjamin's last reflections on Kafka, written to Scholem in 1938, are

[88] Scholem, *W. B.*, p. 206.
[89] Walter Benjamin, "Conversations with Brecht," *Reflections*, p. 217.
[90] Scholem, *W. B.*, p. 221.
[91] Benjamin, "Theses on the Philosophy of History," *Illuminations*, p. 258.

entirely apocalyptic, which makes them no less prophetic: "Kafka's world, frequently so serene and so dense with angels, is the exact complement of his epoch, an epoch that is preparing itself to annihilate the inhabitants of this planet on a massive scale. The experience that corresponds to that of Kafka as a private individual will probably first become accessible to the masses at such time as they are about to be annihilated" (109). These thoughts complement Scholem's own sense of the coming catastrophe, when he writes from Jerusalem, after *Kristallnacht*, of "unmitigated despondency and paralysis, which have gripped me for months in the face of the state of things here. It is indeed impossible *not* to reflect on our situation, and by 'our' I am not merely referring to us Palestinians. The horrifying catastrophe that Jewry has gone through these last six months, and whose dimensions nobody is really able to grasp, this utter hopelessness in a situation in which hopes are invented only to mock us . . ." (123). For Scholem, whose comments on the destiny of the European Jews are normally reserved, this passage articulates the absolute negativism that informs his postwar essays on Germans and Jews. The lesson he drew from Hannah Arendt's biography of the most important German-Jewish woman of the Enlightenment, Rahel Varnhagen, was that "a relationship built on fraud, such as the German Jews' relationship to 'Germanness,' could not end without misfortune" (123). And yet, in accord with his view of history as a catastrophic experience, he does not offer prophecies, unless we take his beginning work on Sabbatai Zvi to be a warning against false prophets in a cataclysmic era.

During 1939 Benjamin suffered a series of reversals. His relations with the Institute in New York worsened, beginning with Adorno's long letter rejecting the chapters of a planned book on Baudelaire which Benjamin had submitted to the *Zeitschrift*. Benjamin's "astonishing representation of facticity," Adorno wrote, of his "absolute concreteness" and interpretive asceticism, did not distinguish between the empirical world and its critical illumination, a charge that certainly went to the core of his hermetic and esoteric procedure. The impact registered: "The isolation I live in, and especially work in here, creates an abnormal dependence on the reception my production encounters." In March he received a letter from Horkheimer warning of a possible reduction of support: "this new barge is setting out to sea freighted far beyond the load line with much heavier cargo—my heavy heart" (120). With the outbreak of war in early September, Benjamin, along with 20,000 other German and Austrian exiles, was interned by the Daladier government as a threat to national security. Sent first to the notorious collection point Stade Colombe, and, after two weeks of deprivation, to a primitive camp at Nevers, his health, which was already poor, worsened, and he suffered a collapse *en route*.

In the camp, despite his weak condition and helplessness "in all things practical," he managed to give lectures in exchange for cigarettes, and even tried to found a small journal, "naturally of the highest niveau."[92] But shortly after his release at the intercession of a number of leading French writers, he wrote to Horkheimer that he was "extremely fatigued" and often had to stop on the street to catch his breath. The German invasion of France was the final ordeal. Like many emigrés, he fled south, first to Lourdes, then to Marseilles, and, by foot across the Pyrenees to the border, a journey which has now been described in detail by the woman who led Benjamin's party, Lisa Fittko. At Port Bou, where he was detained by Spanish border authorities, he ended his life.[93]

Scholem, who knew him best, offered the judgment that even before his physical exile, Benjamin was a person whose "harmonious view of the world was shattered" and who "was in transit." Whether by choice, by circumstance, or by "pathological vacillation," Benjamin's own fate was bound up with a tradition—the German-Jewish tradition—which had lost its most important Writ, and was irrevocably and permanently in exile. Spengler's caricature of the "civilized, nomad intellectual" must have struck home, since he noted it down. And our suspicion that the village of Kafka is the city of exile of Benjamin, is confirmed by yet another clue found in the notes to the Arcades Project: "emigration as a key to the metropolis."[94]

Even in the catastrophic 1930s and '40s, Scholem never abandoned his lifelong conviction that all Judaism somehow "fit together into an integral whole." Perhaps this also accounts for what Benjamin once called his "ostentatious self-assurance." Scholem's Zionism, for all its nihilistic and anarchist tendencies, remained tied to Jewish history as an "invisible stream" of commentary, in which Benjamin held important place, the latest in a long line of "ancient sages," commentators, heretics, and apostates. In New York, shortly after their final visit, Scholem ended his lectures on Jewish mysticism (dedicated to Benjamin's memory) with this comment: "The story [of Jewish mysticism] is not ended, it has not yet become history, and the secret life it holds can break out tomorrow in you or in me."[95] This explains why he did not, or pretended

[92] Benjamin to Adrienne Monnier, September 21, 1939, *Walter Benjamin—Briefe*, p. 827. Also see Hans Sahl, "Walter Benjamin in the Internment Camp," *On Walter Benjamin*, pp. 346–52.

[93] Lisa Fittko, "Der alte Benjamin—Flucht über die Pyrenäen," *Merkur* 403, 36:1 (January 1982), 35–49. English version, "The Last Days of Walter Benjamin," *Orim* 1:2 (Spring 1986), 48–59.

[94] Benjamin, "Central Park," p. 42.

[95] Gershom Scholem, *Major Trends in Jewish Mysticism* (New York: Schocken Books, 1961), p. 350.

not to, understand Benjamin's conviction that Kafka had "failed." After all, he tried to reassure him, "he *really* did comment," even if it was commentary on the futility of commentary, "the nothingness of truth"(115). And yet, as if to confirm that his friend's view of Kafka revealed the essential about Benjamin, Scholem recalled many years later that "there was an element of purity and absoluteness" about Benjamin, "a devotion to the spiritual like that of a scribe cast out into another world, who has set off in search of his 'scripture.'" [96]

[96] Scholem, *W.B.*, p. 53.

THE
CORRESPONDENCE
OF WALTER BENJAMIN
AND GERSHOM SCHOLEM
1932–1940

PREFACE

The present book owes its existence to an unexpected event which for many years I no longer believed would ever come about. It fills a gap I was fully aware of when I wrote *Walter Benjamin: The Story of a Friendship*[1] in 1975, but one I did not see a way to close during my lifetime. I had in my possession the complete collection of all of Benjamin's letters to me, but not the ones I had written to him. We used typewriters only in the rarest of cases, which meant that neither of us automatically had copies of our letters, although on occasion I preserved separate sections for special reasons. As a result, I had complete drafts or transcriptions of very few items. After 1945, I realized that I could not count on my letters ever resurfacing. It had become obvious early on that most documents that had fallen into the hands of the Gestapo had been destroyed.

What I did not know then, of course, was that I was dealing with two separate courses of events. The one is linked to the confiscation of all the papers Benjamin had left behind in his Berlin apartment, including all letters addressed to him prior to March 1933. The other had led to the confiscation of the papers left behind in his Paris apartment (10 rue Dombasle) shortly after the entry of the German army into the city. That these two sets of correspondence were never combined is certain.

---

[1] [Trans. Harry Zohn (New York: Schocken Books, 1988).—TRANS.]

Whether such a combination would have come about at all under the system used by the Gestapo is something I cannot judge. But I learned firsthand from the deputy director of the Central Archives of the German Democratic Republic in Potsdam, where I was received with considerable graciousness in October 1966, that Benjamin's papers—owing to a technical slipup made while being packed—had been incorporated into the archive of the *Pariser Tageszeitung*. Although virtually all papers and documents in Gestapo archives had been destroyed following a February 1945 directive, issued once the Gestapo realized that the war was lost (hence my letters to Benjamin up to March 1933 were destroyed in that process), the *Pariser Tageszeitung* archive escaped destruction when the directive was sabotaged by the staff member in charge. Benjamin's Paris papers then traveled to Russia as a part of this archive, which remained intact for about fifteen years. It was only as a result of a highly political decision made around 1960, according to which museums, libraries, and archives began to be returned to the G.D.R., that the collection reached the Central Archives in Potsdam.

When the collection was being inventoried, it became obvious that it contained two filing boxes without any material connection to the *Pariser Tageszeitung* and that these boxes contained Benjamin's confiscated Paris papers. Benjamin's own writings accounted for only the smallest part of these papers; for the most part, they contained correspondence addressed to him. It was Benjamin's practice—most likely a feature of his personality—to keep letters and postcards written to him. As a result, we have at our disposal a storehouse of documentation on Benjamin's life for the years 1933 to 1940 in the form of these letters, even if almost all of them represent only one side of the correspondence.

Following their return to the Potsdam Central Archives, these holdings were sorted, although generally not in a very detailed manner. Particularly striking collections, such as my letters, those written by his former wife, Dora, and those from his son, Stefan, were kept in separate files. It took several years for rumors of the existence of these letters to reach the publishing house of Suhrkamp, partly through colleagues working in the Brecht archive, which at that time was also kept separately in East Berlin, but also partly through stories told by a former associate at the Institute for Social Research, the political economist Alfred Sohn-Rethel (Birmingham, England), who had seen these papers during a visit to Potsdam. In this way I received word that my letters from those days were also in Potsdam, a fact that Dr. Gerhard Seidel (who at the time worked at the Brecht archive) immediately confirmed upon my inquiry. I was advised to apply to the Ministry of the Interior, which held jurisdiction over the papers, for permission to study these holdings. I did so, but received no response. This situation did not change until the end of September 1966, after—at an academic gathering in Bucharest—I was able to describe my situation and interest in the matter to two leading members of the German Academy of Sciences. Only days later, I received an invitation to come to Berlin and Potsdam as a guest of the German Academy of Sciences, where I would be allowed to study the holdings of Benjamin's papers and obtain photocopies of them. Hence I was able to work there for several days in October 1966 and to satisfy myself that indeed practically every letter I had written to Benjamin during those years was there. I was assured that photocopies of this correspondence, as well as some others of value to my work, would be sent to me. But nothing was sent in 1967, apparently on instructions from higher authorities. In the meantime, Benjamin's papers had been transferred from the Central Archives in Potsdam to the Literary Archives of the Academy of Arts of the German Democratic Republic in East Berlin.

In *Walter Benjamin: The Story of a Friendship* (p. 195), I wrote about this exceptional primary source that I would not be able to make use of for another decade: "If this material became accessible, I could provide a complete book-length documentation of our relationship in those years." This volume now presents that documentation. It unexpectedly came into being thanks to the help and initiative of the writer Stephan Hermlin and the G.D.R.'s Minister of Culture, Johannes Hoffmann, to whom I again would like to express my gratitude. The photocopies I received in November 1977 were the most precious and welcome present I could have received on my eightieth birthday.

I have devoted no small share of my working hours in 1978 and 1979 to preparing this publication. It turned out that virtually all of my letters had survived intact. Two letters are only halfway intact—in one case, the first page and, in the other, the second page have not yet been located. This is especially regrettable in the case of a letter in which I wrote at length about Kafka.[2] In addition, it has not been possible to locate the original of my last letter (128), of which I kept only a partial transcription of a passage of importance. Two postcards, which merely addressed the technical details regarding arrangements for our Paris meeting in February 1938, are also missing. Perhaps these items will also surface once Benjamin's papers are reexamined more thoroughly.

The letters from both correspondents are presented in their entirety. I have repositioned words only in a very few passages, and in four places

---

[2] [The missing portion of letter 57 was subsequently discovered and published in a posthumous collection of Scholem's essays on Benjamin, *Walter Benjamin und sein Engel*, ed. R. Tiedemann (Frankfurt am Main: Suhrkamp Verlag, 1983), pp. 193–94. The complete letter has been included in this edition.—TRANS.]

I omitted observations of a very personal nature, some of which refer to people still living and which might be considered defamatory. I accept full responsibility for these elisions. I wish to emphasize that these observations concern neither the Institute for Social Research nor anyone actively engaged there at that time.

In order to underscore the utter precariousness of Walter Benjamin's predicament in the months preceding Hitler's seizure of power, I have incorporated the eleven letters and cards he sent me between June 25, 1932, and February 28, 1933, in their entirety. I regard them as essential to any understanding of Benjamin's situation as it was already developing at the beginning of the von Papen government. Of these letters, in which the terrible despair of his predicament appears but summarily, in retrospect and innuendo, only two were included in the 1966 collection.[3] Thus, the present volume now contains 128 letters. Eleven serve as an introduction, followed in strict chronological order by our correspondence, which includes 61 letters and cards from Benjamin, 55 from me, and a letter to me from his former wife, Dora. In the 1966 selection, I could include only 29 of the letters Benjamin wrote to me, and some of them only in abridged form. Just as the letters written in the summer and fall of 1932 serve to orchestrate our correspondence in a way, I have added a passage on Benjamin's death to the somewhat abrupt end, or rather suspension, of our correspondence after February 1940. (A reply to my last letter never reached me, even though at the time Hannah Arendt confirmed its existence.)

The present publication will shed considerable light on Walter Benjamin as well as on our relationship. It will furthermore rectify a number of details I noted from memory in my book on W.B., although most of the claims in that book are corroborated by the letters presented here. There is also precise information about our shared deliberations on a visit, or rather an extended (permanent?) stay by Benjamin in the land of Israel. The secondary literature on Benjamin published to date bristles with false information and assertions on this subject, among others, which are due primarily to unfamiliarity with the documents, but also to a fundamental misunderstanding of my position.

Time and again I have been (and still am) accused of having wanted to "induce" Benjamin to come to Palestine/Israel. Nothing could have been further removed from my real position. In the long years of our friendship, as well as in the letters written before 1933, there could obviously never be any doubt about my chosen destiny or life's decision.

---

[3] [The two-volume selection of Benjamin's letters published as *Briefe*, ed. Theodor W. Adorno and Gershom Scholem (Frankfurt am Main: Suhrkamp Verlag, 1966).—Trans.]

Nonetheless, I have never even attempted to talk another person, let alone one as complex as Benjamin, into making such a decision; indeed, I would not be capable of doing so, as it would go against my very grain. To claim that I did so is nonsense, and the letters presented here show just how differently these discussions proceeded. The coarse simplifications made by many who have commented on this have missed the mark. Moreover, Benjamin knew very well how to distinguish between coming to terms with the phenomenon of Jewishness, on the one hand, and a possible decision to go to Palestine, on the other. His letters to Florens Christian Rang—not to mention my own testimony—offer eloquent proof of that.

I think this is also the place to say a few words about Ernst Bloch, who, ever since 1920, played a somewhat problematic role in Benjamin's letters to me, including the letters printed here. I had to ask myself whether or not I should substantially abridge my letter of August 25, 1935, in which I expressed myself in very pointed terms about Bloch's relationship to Benjamin. My present regard for Bloch, after so many years and much more extensive attention to the entirety of his production, does not correspond to what I impetuously put to paper in the twenties and thirties. I have expressed my considered, mature view of Bloch and his work in an essay that appeared in the magazine *Der Spiegel* on July 7, 1975, on the occasion of his ninetieth birthday. The relationship between Bloch and Benjamin was subject to powerful tensions and fluctuations, and for many years I was probably the main recipient of Benjamin's reactions to this state of affairs. The fact that a—one is tempted to say, delicate—equilibrium was maintained, despite all tensions, and that a break never occurred proves how strong the ties were that existed between these two exceptional men. No one can say how their relationship might have developed had Benjamin survived. I thus decided against omitting the relevant testimony pertaining to this, even though I may now view it critically or have second thoughts about it. The special situation of these two men, as close and at once as different as they were—who in conversation both inspired each other and opened fire on one another—cannot, in my opinion, be comprehended by any of us today.

One other question will be raised by the reader of these letters: Why didn't I draw any direct conclusions from Benjamin's often catastrophic and distressing portrayals of his financial situation, which comes to light in this book? This is a question I could answer, but choose not to.

Needless to say, this edition corrects some of the errors that slipped into the transcription of the previous, incomplete publication. It also improves upon the annotation, which is much more extensive here. Mistakes in the spelling of people's names have been rectified silently wherever I was able to spot them. Benjamin's memory for orthography was poor. On the other hand, his original punctuation has been preserved as often as possible, since it helps portray the characteristics of our style of writing in those years. The dates of the letters have been uniformly set in the upper right-hand corner, to make chronological orientation easier for the reader. In Benjamin's original letters, the date always appears at the end of the letter, in the lower left-hand corner.

Gershom Scholem
Jerusalem
July 1979

1

BENJAMIN TO SCHOLEM

SAN ANTONIO, IBIZA
JUNE 25, 1932

Dear Gerhard,

Your letter was a profound disappointment as concerns the possibility of our arranging a meeting, since the dates you mention have meanwhile flown by. Hence the comfort I could draw from your postcard was slight. There is a good chance, however, that we will see one another in Berlin, no matter how great my inclination to keep my distance from there, in any way I can. But our chances of being together would have been so much greater here, and there is much we won't be able to speak about. To say nothing of the fact that in Menton my "Catholica" would have been safe from you.[1]

The University of Muri[2] must now consider how it is going to extricate itself from the matter.[3] To be perfectly honest, I hope that it will prove to be somewhat less ready to give way than the gazettes and my friends, who won't have any difficulty granting my wish not to make a fuss about this day. I plan to spend the day in Nice, where I am acquainted with a

---

[1] I had written him of my intention to establish a section on Catholic theology in my library.

[2] We named our fictitious university—a satirical counterpart to the University of Berne where we studied from 1918 to 1919—after the village of Muri (near Berne, now a suburb), where we lived in 1918.

[3] Walter Benjamin's fortieth birthday on July 15, 1932. Here, as in other notes, I refer to my *Walter Benjamin: The Story of a Friendship* [hereafter cited as Scholem, *W.B.*]; cf. p. 58.

rather eccentric fellow[4] whose path has often crossed mine in the course of my various travels. I might invite him for a glass of white wine, if I decide not to be alone. At any rate, my departure from here has apparently drawn nearer, since the Noeggeraths[5] are expecting other *paying guests* (I'm probably spelling this wrong, for fear of writing *goasts*), and I would be hard pressed to recreate the incomparable seclusion of these quarters in San Antonio. All else depends on the ongoing state of my finances. I have worked hard these last few weeks, and all of this would be bearable had I not also to contribute to the upkeep of my apartment in Berlin, because of the fraud I told you about.[6]

As to your villa in Jerusalem[7]—speaking as Goethe might—lay garland after garland upon its threshold.[8] A propos Goethe, did I write you that last year Insel Verlag came close to commissioning a book on Goethe from me if . . .[9] I fear I have lost my précis, but I would be able to relate enough about it to bewilder the Muri faculty, especially its professors of Kabbalah Studies and Medieval Jewish Philosophy. And you are no doubt fully aware that his (the professor's) career on this Earth represents but a faithful reflection—speaking as Marx might—of that in Muri.

[4] The "eccentric fellow'" was Death, as we can infer from papers now well known. W.B. seriously considered taking his life on that day; cf. Scholem, *W.B.*, pp. 178f., 185–89.

[5] Felix Noeggerath (1880–1961), with whom W.B. had frequent contact from the time of their Munich student days until later in Berlin. W.B. lived as Noeggerath's guest on Ibiza. Cf. Scholem, *W.B.*, p. 181ff. In a letter from 1915, W.B. documents Noeggerath as being twelve years his senior. [Cf. also "Walter Benjamin und Felix Noeggerath" in Scholem, *Walter Benjamin und sein Engel*, pp. 78–127.—Trans.]

[6] Both W.B. and Noeggerath had rented their apartments to a swindler who was being sought by the police and who fled.

[7] The house my first wife, Escha, and I were building in Jerusalem and which was completed while I was abroad.

[8] Specialists have confirmed that there is no such line in Goethe's works. But I am grateful to Frau Exleben of East Berlin for the following reference (in a letter to Werner Kraft): Verse 460 of *Iphigenia in Taurus* (second version) has the lines

> Rejoicing, as for one new-born, might loop
> Her fragrant garlands high upon the pillars!

Benjamin's allusion might have been an unconscious rewriting from memory, since he definitely knew Goethe's *Iphigenia*. I have Siegfried Unseld to thank for a second suggestion. In the Artemis edition, the following poem is listed as no. 57 under the heading "Inschriften: Denk- und Sende-Blätter":

> When wreath upon wreath encircles the day,
> Then may that day be turned to her,
> And when she finds a known face here
> She may have recognized herself.

Benjamin might have meant this poem, although he might not have had a specific quotation of Goethe's in mind and just wanted to "speak as Goethe," that is, in Goethe's style and manner.

[9] The word "if . . . " [*wenn . . .*] occurs in the letter exactly as printed here. I am unable to explain what is meant by the ellipsis.

—Incidentally, are you, as a Kabbalah scholar, familiar with the novel *Cabala* by the American Thornton Wilder?[10] I recently read it for the second time and must say that it deserves to be read by you, if only for its last 6 pages (it has 280).

I also hope to be able to work while on the Riviera, where I may visit Dora and Stefan for a day or two, since they plan to travel to Pardigou. While I'm still here, I shall endeavor to pay homage to the *genius loci* in the form of some reflections on Gracian.[11] I must admit that up to now only a dubious herald of these thoughts has arrived, in the form of my longstanding admiration of the *Handorakel*. Perhaps the next envoy, Borinski's monograph on *Gracian und die Hofliteratur in Deutschland*, will bring more precise findings. Anyway, it was recently borne out that "Baroque" was the right horse after all (I was simply the wrong jockey), since the best of the Baroque specialists, the Berlin *Privatdozent* [an unpaid assistant professor] Richard Alewyn, has been named to Gundolf's chair in Heidelberg. Perhaps now that he's become a full professor, he will find the time to write the review of *The Origin of German Tragic Drama*, which the editors of the *Deutsche Literaturzeitung* commissioned four years ago.[12]

I am really looking forward to your offprint from the encyclopedia.[13] Make sure I get it soon. Above all, write as soon as you can. Sometimes I believe you find this a little difficult, now that you can no longer start off letters by resorting to your traditional laments concerning my epistolary indolence. You should feel free to use this address through the 1st or 2nd of July. After that: Poste restante, Nice. You should then abbreviate my first name, so that the letter does not end up in the W box. All the best, most cordially,

Yours, Walter

[10] Thornton Wilder's *Cabala* appeared in 1926. W.B. must have read the 1929 German translation. I had already glanced through it in 1927, on the mistaken assumption that it bore some relation to my field of study.

[11] As far as I know, W.B. never wrote this essay, even though he also mentions it in other letters.

[12] Richard Alewyn (1902–1979), at that time Extraordinary Professor of Modern German Literature. After World War II he became a professor at the Free University of Berlin. He never published a review of *Ursprung des deutschen Trauerspiels* (Berlin: Rowohlt, 1928) [*The Origin of German Tragic Drama*, trans. John Osborne (London: New Left Books, 1977)].

[13] W.B. is alluding to my article "Kabbalah" in the *Encyclopaedia Judaica* (Berlin: Eschkol, 1932). I was able to send him the offprint only later; cf. letter 11.

2

BENJAMIN TO SCHOLEM

SAN ANTONIO, IBIZA
JULY 5, 1932

Dear Gerhard,

Just a brief greeting today, to inform you that I am still on the island and will be staying here at least until July 10th. I hope to be able to leave then, but that still depends on financial arrangements. So I don't even know myself where I can be reached on the 15th, whether here or in Nice. At least by now you will, I imagine, have received my series of notes from Ibiza—which are expanding slowly and quietly.[1] I started reading Proust again today for the first time in five or six years. I am curious to observe the likely contrast between its effects on me then and now, and thus to learn something about myself and the time I have behind me. Not that I believe this contrast will be all that striking or far-reaching. Should you come to Germany in the near future, you will certainly be in for an eye-opener.[2] I presume that the Italian newspapers aren't keeping you as up to date as my German correspondents are.[3] You have sufficient experience, though, to piece together the appropriate images, which you then need only arrange as a montage. Let me hear from you soon. Most cordially,

Yours, Walter

3

BENJAMIN TO SCHOLEM

POSTE RESTANTE
NICE (A.M.)
[BARCELONA, JULY 12, 1932]

Dear Gerhard,

My plans have taken a new turn which makes your change of dates distressing. At the request of Speyer,[1] who has meanwhile arrived in

---

[1] "Ibizenkische Folge," *Gesammelte Schriften* 4: 402–9. Henceforth Benjamin's collected works will be cited as *GS*.

[2] I went to Munich at the end of July 1932.

[3] All those letters are presumably lost.

[1] The author Wilhelm Speyer (1887–1952), with whom W.B. had a close literary relationship during these years and in whose car he often traveled. Speyer was well known for his novels and plays, but above all for his juvenile literature: books such as *Der Kampf der Tertia* [*Galahads and Pussy-cats*, trans. Margaret Juers (New York: J. Cape and H. Smith, 1929)], *Die goldne Horde*, etc. Alfred Döblin wrote an obituary on him.

Poveromo (near Pisa) and made intriguing proposals for a joint project, I will probably arrive in Italy around the 28th of July. Should your itinerary change again—and even if it doesn't—please inform me in Nice, Poste restante. It looks as if I'll arrive there on the 22nd, or the 23rd at the latest. On Sunday the 10th I travel from here to Palma, and from there to Marseilles by boat.

I had two clippings[2] mailed to you as "printed matter," and I hardly need to say that I send you certain such scholia solely in the interest of the relative comprehensiveness of the *editio hierosolemitana* of my *opera*.

Most cordial regards, and let me hear from you soon.

Yours, Walter

4

BENJAMIN TO SCHOLEM

Dear Gerhard,

NICE
JULY 26, 1932

While you were in Milan, writing the lovely letter that reached me here, I was still on Ibiza. My stay there ended up lasting a week longer than planned. Indeed, a somewhat impromptu celebration even materialized, which owed its élan not so much to those characters in the repertoire, with whom you are acquainted, but to two French people who have recently arrived on the scene: a married couple[1] I found quite delightful. Since this affinity was reciprocal, we stayed together—with only slight interruptions—until my departure. Their company was so captivating— right up to midnight of July 17th, when my ship was to sail for Mallorca —that when we finally arrived at the quay, the gangplank had been removed and the ship had already begun to move. I had stowed my baggage on board in advance, of course. After calmly shaking hands with my companions, I began to scale the hull of the moving vessel and, aided by curious Ibizans, managed to clamber over the railing successfully.

Thus, at this very moment I am on my way to Speyer. There, in

---

[2] "Pestalozzi in Yverdon" (*GS* 3:346–49) and "Goethebücher, aber willkommene" (*GS* 3:352–54).

[1] Jean Selz and his wife. Selz published his recollections of their time together on Ibiza in *Le dire et le faire* (Paris: Mercure de France, 1964), pp. 52–72. [Cf. Selz, "Walter Benjamin in Ibiza," in G. Smith, ed., *Walter Benjamin: Critical Essays and Recollections* (Cambridge, Mass.: MIT Press, 1988), pp. 354–66.—TRANS.]

Poveromo, I will learn whether I must return to Germany in August or whether there is any way for me to extend my stay abroad. Even taking into account the circumstances you are familiar with, you still cannot begin to imagine just how averse I am to returning. To do so, you would need not only to have before you the letter in which the building-safety authorities demand I give up my apartment—because its condition fails to meet certain regulations—you would also need more than just a clear idea of how the reactionary movement you allude to has affected my work for radio.[2] Above all, you would have to grasp the profound fatigue that has overcome me as a result of these very circumstances. That brings me to the important insights contained in your birthday letter.[3] They require no commentary—other than on the concept of the "counterrevolutionary." I hope you will find occasion to enlighten me as to its precise meaning as a characterization of my deeper insights.[4] I can indeed imagine what this concept might mean; all the same, I find it ambiguous. I preface my remarks with this qualification only in order to accord full weight to the expression of my complete agreement with your remaining observations. Your remark that the chances of what you wish for me actually coming to pass are the smallest imaginable thus gains in significance. We would both be well advised to face up to these facts—in view of which the failure of your Palestinian "intervention" was indeed fateful.[5] And if I do so with a grimness verging on hopelessness, it is surely not for want of confidence in my resourcefulness in finding alternatives and subsidies. Rather, it is the developing of this resourcefulness, and the productivity that corresponds to it, that most seriously endangers every worthwhile project. The literary forms of expression that my thought has forged for itself over the last decade have been utterly conditioned by the preventive measures and antidotes with which I had to counter the disintegration constantly threatening my thought as a result of such contingencies. And though many—or a sizable number —of my works have been small-scale victories, they are offset by large-scale defeats. I do not want to speak of the projects that had to remain unfinished, or even untouched, but rather to name here the four books that mark off the real site of ruin or catastrophe, whose furthest boundary

2 Franz von Papen's so-called "gentlemen's club," which deposed the Prussian (Social Democratic–led) government in a sort of coup d'état only days before this letter was composed, had formed its reactionary cabinet on June 2, 1932.

3 My letter had been written for W.B.'s fortieth birthday on July 15, 1932.

4 Strangely enough, W.B. had already forgotten our exchange of letters between March 30 and April 17, 1931 (Briefe, pp. 257, 531), in which he had termed my characterization of his writings as "counterrevolutionary'" from the Communist Party's perspective as "quite correct."

5 Cf. the chapter "The Failed Project" in Scholem, W.B., pp. 143–56.

I am still unable to survey when I let my eyes wander over the next years of my life. They include the "Pariser Passagen," the "Gesammelte Essays zur Literatur," the "Briefe,"[6] and a truly exceptional book about hashish.[7] Nobody knows about this last topic, and for the time being it should remain between us.

So much about me. This hasn't told you anything new. Perhaps by seeing the relative equanimity with which I can, on occasion, lucidly describe my situation, it might appear to you in a new light and give you something to think about.

You will be pleased to learn that I briefly met the cousin you mentioned[8] at the State Library and gently but firmly gave him the cold shoulder, recalling how frowningly you wrote of him. I now find it very amusing to discover him in the gallery of Goethe mavens circling the Earth this year./ Even more momentous is the establishment of the photography section of your Kabbalah archive, for which I send my most sincere congratulations. I include here Ernst Schoen's address to whom you should of course convey my kindest regards: Südwestdeutscher Rundfunk, Eschersheimer Landstrasse 33. You will also come across many other remarkable people in Frankfurt, perhaps even Theodor Wiesengrund, the *Privatdozent* who conducted a seminar on my *Traverspiel* book last semester.[9]

Write as soon as you can, c/o Wilhelm Speyer, Casa Mesquita, Poveromo (Marina di Massa).

I will be prompt in claiming my present. All the best,

Yours, Walter

[6] W.B. has in mind the collection of German letters (with brief introductions) that subsequently appeared in 1936 under the title *Deutsche Menschen* [Lucerne: Vita Nova Verlag]. The letters were first published in the *Frankfurter Zeitung* during 1931 and 1932.

[7] The materials Benjamin collected for this book appeared in 1972 under the title *Über Haschisch: Novellistisches, Berichte, Materialien* (Frankfurt am Main: Suhrkamp). [Cf. *GS* 6:558–618.—TRANS.]

[8] My parent's cousin Heinz Pflaum (1900–1962), who had been teaching Romance languages at the Hebrew University in Jerusalem since 1928.

[9] Ernst Schoen (1894–1960) was program director of Frankfurt Radio. I visited him and his wife often during August 1932, but did not yet meet Theodor Wiesengrund(-Adorno), who had received his *Habilitation* [postdoctorate degree] in Philosophy the year before.

5

BENJAMIN TO SCHOLEM

Mon très cher

I expected some news from you by now. Or did I neglect to send you my Italian address from Nice? The following few lines are only meant to accompany the enclosed clipping, which you may find of interest, my address being the main point. Anyway, this will be all the briefer because my stock of good news is low. The building-safety authorities intend to throw me out of my Berlin apartment and are thus in complete harmony with both my economic difficulties and my disinclination to take up the hopeless struggle in the press and radio to create some *Lebensraum* for myself on Berlin soil. But how things could develop far away from Berlin is also hard to tell. For the time being, I keep myself going with cigarette money that Speyer has advanced me, and otherwise live on credit. At least the time here is not lost, because the work I am doing with Speyer is some of the most financially rewarding available to me; it is just that the term of payment is quite protracted. In the meantime, we admire the northern Etruscan Alps from afar, or even from close up when we take the car. If Speyer's rather fluctuating finances allow, we are going to refresh my memories of San Gimignano, Volterra, Siena, and Lucca. Poveromo lives up to its name: it's a seaside resort for poor people, or at least for families, from Holland, Switzerland, France, and Italy, with limited funds but lots of children. I live away from all the bustle, in a simple but quite satisfactory room, and I am rather content, insofar as conditions and prospects allow me to be. But I must ask you not to read into this any intention on my part to mitigate the detailed view of my situation I gave in my last letter. So now I hope to hear from you as soon as possible, and to learn the dates of your October visit to Berlin. Sincerely,

Yours, Walter

6

BENJAMIN TO SCHOLEM

Dear Gerhard, [AUGUST 24, 1932]

I am troubled to hear that you are unable to write and work effectively. But I was glad to hear of your whereabouts,[1] even though your letter's brevity enabled me to increase the surprising lead I have gained on you as a correspondent in recent months. This would not have deterred me from increasing my lead even further, had not factors that have for some time been threatening become totally oppressive. Unfortunately, it is beginning to look as if your present trip to Europe is going to make you a witness to the most severe crisis I have ever faced. If you could only be an eyewitness! But I sit here with dark thoughts indeed as I watch all my attempts even to scratch together the bare minimum—at the very least to settle my bill—go awry, because events at Berlin Radio have completely robbed me of the income I could always rely on. I don't know how I am supposed to get to Berlin. Once I'd been there for a while, I might hit on something. But in the meantime?—At least keep me informed of your travels and let your thoughts dwell on my situation once more. It is of the essence. All the best. Affectionately,

Yours, Walter

7

BENJAMIN TO SCHOLEM

Dear Gerhard,

FORTE DEI MARMI
SEPTEMBER 1932

Your letter of August 27th got here quickly. My sincerest congratulations on the expansion of your academic activities![1] May I take this occasion to remind you of your promise to forward me a copy of your letter to Herr

---

[1] I had arrived in London in the course of a six-month research tour of Italy and England, mainly devoted to studying kabbalistic manuscripts. After stopping in Cambridge, I traveled to Berlin in mid-September.

[1] There was a plan to expand my professorship of Jewish Mysticism by awarding me a professorship of either History of Religion or Jewish Philosophy.

Schoeps (on the subject of the philosophy of religion)?[2] Nothing has arrived as yet.—Yes, it would be most desirable to see one another in Berlin. But how do I know if that will come about? I haven't a penny to my name these days and am altogether dependent on the maneuvers that Speyer (who is here with me) makes with his car. The real miracle is that I can still summon up the concentration to work. But I can: I have begun a small series of vignettes, half of which are now finished, called "Berliner Kindheit um 1900"—a portrayal of my earliest memories.[3] That's all for today. The *Frankfurter Zeitung*—which suddenly doesn't seem to be printing anything of mine anymore—did bring out a review, "Erleuchtung durch Dunkelmänner," which I will mail to you in Berlin.[4]

Fondly,

Yours, Walter

8

BENJAMIN TO SCHOLEM

VILLA IRENE
POVEROMO (MARINA DI MASSA)
SEPTEMBER 26, 1932

Dear Gerhard,

You can imagine how depressing I find the prospect of not seeing you at all. Unfortunately, we must take this possibility into account. The situation is quite simple: I cannot finance the trip from my own resources, but must depend upon Speyer, who will take me along in his car when he drives back himself. I can't make any plans beyond this, and what might await me in Berlin remains unclear. This much seems to be clear: Speyer is hardly likely to leave Italy before the end of October. This has to do with a play we are working on together here,[1] as well as the generally high hopes entertained here with regard to October. As for myself, such trains of thought are all beyond the present horizon of my thinking. I have but a single cause for joy: my *pension* has given me a rather long

[2] My "Open Letter" to the author of the monograph *Jüdischer Glaube in dieser Zeit*, which I had given to Ludwig Feuchtwanger in Munich, appeared only after my departure (in the *Bayerische israelitische Gemeindezeitung* 8:241–44), and I hadn't even received it by then. It was a polemic against Hans-Joachim Schoeps (born 1909, professor in Erlangen after World War II). Cf. also letter 12.

[3] First published in book form in 1950, it can now be found in *GS* 4:235–304. [See also letter 10, note 2.—TRANS.]

[4] *GS* 3:356–60. A sharp polemic against an anthroposophical book, *Die Geheimwissenschaften im Lichte unserer Zeit*, by Hans Liebstoeckl (Zurich: Amalthea, 1932).

[1] It was a detective play that I am not sure was ever published.

18

credit line, so in any case [I] am relieved of day-to-day bother or even unpleasantries. I am making use of this still-advantageous situation—relatively speaking and all misery notwithstanding—to permit myself the great luxury of concentrating on a single project, for the first time since who knows when. The work for Speyer I just mentioned only requires my services as a consultant, and, as such, it merely provides a fascinating respite from my own work. It is, by the way, my sole diversion, since I write all day and sometimes well into the night. But it would be a mistake for you to imagine a voluminous manuscript. It is not only slim, but written in small sections: a form I am repeatedly led to adopt, first, by the materially threatened, precarious nature of my work and, second, by considerations as to its commercial prospects. Moreover, the subject matter seems absolutely to demand this form. In short, I am working on a series of sketches I will entitle "Berliner Kindheit um 1900." For you, I shall even divulge its motto: "O Victory Column baked brown / With winter sugar from the childhood days." Someday I hope to be able to tell you the origin of these lines.[2] The text is now largely finished, and it might have influenced my material situation very favorably in the near future if only my relationship to the *Frankfurter Zeitung* had not abruptly ended a few months ago as a result of a totally inexplicable constellation of events, which I haven't yet been able to investigate. Things have reached the point where I no longer even receive a reply, be it to manuscripts or to letters. But I hope, by the way, that these childhood memories (you will have guessed that they are not narratives in the form of a chronicle, but rather portray individual expeditions into the depths of memory) can be published in book form, perhaps by Rowohlt. Since he has, incidentally, been pressuring me about the essay volume,[3] it is not inconceivable that—should everything proceed smoothly—two books of mine might come out simultaneously in the not-too-distant future and stand in a similarly cockeyed relation to each other as the Baroque book and *One-Way Street*.[4]—I am experiencing every imaginable difficulty with this new stationery, which I wanted to inaugurate in your honor, but writing on it turns out to be possible only in pencil. Nonetheless, I still

[2] I explain that this motto originated from a kind of surrealist poem W.B. wrote down in the final stages of a hashish experience, in my afterword to W.B.'s *Berliner Chronik* (Frankfurt am Main: Suhrkamp, 1970), pp. 130–32, ["A Berlin Chronicle," in Walter Benjamin, *Reflections: Essays, Aphorisms, Political Writings*, trans. Edmund Jephcott, ed. Peter Demetz (1978; New York: Schocken Books, 1986)].

[3] A collection of Benjamin's literary essays—a book never published.

[4] [The English translation, a selection from the original *Einbahnstrasse* (Berlin: Rowohlt, 1928), was first published in *Reflections*, pp. 61–94. The identical translation appeared in England as *One-Way Street and Other Writings* (London: New Left Books, 1980), pp. 45–104.—TRANS.]

hope to succeed in inscribing it with the urgent request that you let me hear from you as soon as possible. Above all, let me know the precise date of your departure from Berlin.[5] Write me what you thought of Stefan. Let me conclude by again requesting that the details of this letter remain between us. For the time being, I especially don't want anyone in Berlin to learn of the new book. More on better paper next time, and I hope also with better news than what I unfortunately had to begin with this time.

Most cordially,

Yours, Walter

9

BENJAMIN TO SCHOLEM

VILLA IRENE
POVEROMO (MARINA DI MASSA)
OCTOBER 25, 1932

Dear Gerhard,

Let me first of all confirm that your letter from Port Said has reached me safely. I am pleased that you can look back on your months in Europe with such great satisfaction. I assume that you will be resuming your scholarly production on a markedly expanded basis—expanded not merely by the wealth of new material, but also by the greater compass of your new teaching assignment. Under such auspices, I trust that your life in your own house will get off to a happy start.[1]

Your encounters in family circles in Berlin seem to have been somewhat oppressive. Let's hope that your brothers, who to my knowledge have never made much of an effort in your direction, will survive the economic crisis relatively unscathed.[2] As for myself, I am engulfed in it like a fish in water, but I am hardly as well off as the fish. Although I am still in Poveromo, there is nothing voluntary about this stay, notwithstanding certain agreeable aspects it offers despite the autumn storms. I have to return to Germany, no matter what evil awaits me there. But I can't at the moment. I simply don't have the funds to travel.

I would like to have received you in my Berlin apartment—which has endured so much adversity recently, in the form of a larcenous tenant,

[5] I left Berlin around October 18, 1932.

[1] These wishes were unfortunately not fulfilled, and I left the house to my first wife, Elsa (Escha) Burchhardt-Bergmann (1896–1978), when we divorced in 1936.

[2] The printing shop founded by my father and taken over by two of my older brothers was already being liquidated as early as 1932.

threats from the building-safety authorities, and demands to return furniture put at my disposal—because it would have told you something of my life. But why speak of all that when so much more of consequence has been denied us. I had hoped to read a few words by you about Stefan: what you thought of him and how you got on together.[3] I had a most charming letter from him today.

Other than the work with Speyer, which unfortunately brings in no rewards at the moment and only promises something for next year, I have continued my "Berliner Kindheit um 1900." I don't know whether or not it will be possible to publish parts of it soon, let alone what the chances are of it ever appearing as a book. The only information I could get from here indicates that my works are the object of a boycott in Germany which could not be better organized if I were a small Jewish clothes dealer in Neu-stettin.[4] The *Frankfurter Zeitung*, for example, has left all my letters and manuscripts unacknowledged and unpublished for four months now, and I shall leave the letter that the editor of the *Literarische Welt* wrote—to inform me of their disinterest in my contributions at present—to the manuscript department of the Jerusalem library. And if the German fatherland has its way, it might land there quite soon.[5]

Just to keep you up-to-date, I note that the Cologne-based Romance philologist [Leo] Spitzer reserved an appendix for references to my Baroque book in his latest short monograph, *Die Literarisierung des Lebens in Lopes "Dorothea,"*[6] a work dedicated to Vossler. The essay is quite sound, by the way, but insignificant. Somewhat more novel was the personal encounter with an academic I had here a few days ago. [Alfred] Kühn, professor of Zoology in Göttingen, turned up at the *pension*. This cheerful and clever gentleman is among the very few who know the details of the famous theft of the Hawaiian feather dress that came to Göttingen in the 1880s, together with other acquisitions from Cook's expedition, and was pilfered from the local museum a few months back, as you may know from the papers.[7] Before his departure today—which

---

[3] Stefan Benjamin (1918–1972) was then fifteen years old and very much under the sway of Communism. He conspicuously avoided me at the time, and I didn't see him again until 1946, in London.

[4] Neustettin in Pomerania (not far from Bismarck's estate of Vartzin) was known in Jewish families as the scene of the first Prussian pogrom, which took place in 1881 and lived on as a shock in the memories of my parents' generation, even in assimilated families.

[5] This is an allusion to W.B.'s will, which he had written in Nice only three months earlier. The relevant passage is printed in Scholem, *W.B.*, p. 187. I wasn't aware of the existence of the will and didn't then interpret the passage as literally as it was intended.

[6] Leo Spitzer (1887–1960), *Die Literarisierung des Lebens in Lopes "Dorotea"* (Cologne, Bonn: L. Röhrscheid, 1932), pp. 61f. (The work treats Lope de Vega's prose drama *Dorotea*).

[7] The Hawaiian royal cloak and helmet were stolen from the ethnographic collection in Göttingen during the night of March 7–8, 1932, under circumstances that remain unclarified, and they were then presumably taken to Berlin. The cloak seems to have been kept

leaves me here as the last guest—he initiated me into the circumstances of the affair, unveiling one of the most astonishing criminal stories of the century.

Finally, I want to bring two books to your attention, and offer my apology if I have already happened to mention the first one. It is Rosenberg's *Geschichte des Bolschewismus*, published by Rowohlt, to which I am indebted for much revealing information.[8] The second book is a small study in the philosophy of language, which, despite its utter lack of theoretical foundation, provides an uncommon amount of thought-provoking material. Its author is Rudolf Leonhard, until now a relatively inconsequential man of letters, and the book's title is *Das Wort*, published by Ida Graetz Verlag, Berlin-Charlottenburg.[9] It is an onomatopoetic theory of the word set forth by means of examples.

If my memory serves me correctly, you should be celebrating your birthday about now. Tell me the exact day sometime. But above all, accept my most heartfelt congratulations intertwined with the following regards, and let us hope that very soon we will be able to present each other with the gifts we can exchange this year only in thought.

Fondly,

Yours, Walter

---

there (in the old castle?), where it vanished or was destroyed at the end of World War II. The helmet was recovered there at the end of 1945 and returned. The Berlin press played up the case on March 8 and over the next few days (when W.B. was still in Berlin). The value of the unique, stolen objects was estimated to be more than two million German reichsmarks. Professor Kühn's version, which pointed to political circumstances, seems not to have become widely known; in fact, this seems to be the sole mention of it. (Cf. *Göttinger Monatsblätter*, March 1975, pp. 6f., as well as information kindly provided by Dr. Ernst Pfeiffer and Prof. Albrecht Schöne, Göttingen.)

[8] Arthur Rosenberg (1889–1943) was a close friend and colleague of my brother Werner in the Reichstag. They remained friends even after they broke with the German Communist Party, which is how I came to meet him at the beginning of October 1932. Shortly before my departure, he presented me with the book W.B. mentions, which was published in 1932 [Berlin: Rowohlt], and made a great impression at the time, inscribing it "From Luria [the kabbalist he read about in my work] to Lenin!" [*A History of Bolshevism: From Marx to the First Five Years' Plan*, trans. Ian F. D. Morrow (1933; New York: Doubleday, 1967).]

[9] Rudolf Leonhard (1889–1953) belonged to the circle around Kurt Hiller and kept intermittently in touch with W.B. in Berlin and Paris. The book appeared, undated, in 1931. W.B. also mentions the book in his notes on the philosophy of language.

10

BENJAMIN TO SCHOLEM

PRINZREGENTENSTR. 66
BERLIN-WILMERSDORF
DECEMBER 10, 1932

Dear Gerhard,

Even though you may have little or no understanding of how I am furthering our mutual cause by wresting a message, however brief, from the present moment, it shall be done. And yet you could have trained your eye to spot certain difficulties in correspondence (which you too encountered) during your travels in Europe, in that for me it is often as difficult to find the next source of funds as to reach the moon. But it shall be done, all the more so since I want to flank your birthday with congratulations from both sides, having missed the target this December 5th. Above all, though, this is to inform you that there are no more obstacles to your sending your "Kabbalah" here. It pleases me to fill, in such a dignified manner, one of the gaps that appeared in my library as a consequence of my tenant's zeal. The fellow was arrested at about the time of my return, and he is now in prison pending trial somewhere in the Rhineland.

As an illustration of my situation, I would have liked to enclose a letter [Willy] Haas wrote to me in Poveromo, but I do not have it at hand.[1] In order to know how someone fares who deals with such "intellectuals," in the form of editors or newspaper owners, you need only remember that the "intellectuals" among our "coreligionists" are the first to offer the oppressors hecatombs from their own circles, so as to remain spared themselves. True, I have been able to stem the boycott led against me simply by showing up. But whether the energy I invested over these first few weeks will avert the worst cannot yet be judged. It certainly could not be accomplished merely by switching my activities to French. Despite all my familiarity with the stuff of life there, the position from which I approach things is still much too much in the vanguard to fall within the view of the reading public. I mulled over this problem while in Italy, and not for the first time. The result was always the same.

I ask you to consider this letter more or less as a note accompanying a manuscript which will be posted off to you in a day or so. I send it to you only because I find it important to show you as nearly as possible the sunniest side, relatively speaking, of my present state of being, since we haven't seen each other for such a long time and won't be doing so for

[1] W.B. mentioned this letter, which has not been preserved, in the preceding letter. [Haas was editor of the *Literarische Welt.*—TRANS.]

quite a while. I hope that this side can be found in the pages of the "Berliner Kindheit um 1900," even though the epithet "sunny" can't really be applied to its contents in any strict sense. The manuscript you will receive is provisional in two ways: first, in the matter of its staying with you, since I can only send it to you with the binding stipulation that you return it a week after its arrival at the very latest; second, the number of its sections is provisional: the definitive manuscript will have thirty,[2] but the twenty-four you are getting are *ne varietur* in their versions, which is the seventh or eighth for many of them. I don't believe it necessary to accompany the manuscript with very many words. If I entertain any hopes for its fate in the world, it is because, of everything I have written, this work may be most liable to be misunderstood. But that is something I don't have to consider where you are concerned.

I will try to send you, in the near future, everything you requested from the series of letters.—I am displeased to hear such dismal news about Hüne Caro,[3] but am glad to hear you take an interest in Leo Strauss,[4] who always made an excellent impression on me, too.—And who is "Tom Freud's niece"?[5]

So much, or so little. I close now in the hope that I will soon receive a few words concerning my work, as well as the work itself, but not before mentioning that I can think of much that is fitting about your rejection of the planned professorship and your proposal for another.[6]

All the best to you and Escha,

Yours, Walter

[2] Concerning this book's various stages, see the remarks of its editor, Tillman Rexroth (who didn't know this letter), in *GS* 4:964–69. That edition contains forty-one sections. [Benjamin's recently discovered final version, which in fact did have thirty sections, will be published in *GS* 7.—TRANS.]

[3] Siegfried Caro, 1898–1979 (whom everybody called Hüne because he was so small; he later lived in Jerusalem), had known W.B. for many years; cf. *Briefe*, pp. 208, 222, 252. I myself had known him since 1919.

[4] Leo Strauss (1899–1973), an important philosopher who was then working at the Academy for Jewish Studies in Berlin and who was extremely influential as a political philosopher, especially in the U.S., where he taught in New York and Chicago. We first met in 1927, and became increasingly close.

[5] I wrote about Tom Freud, a niece of Sigmund Freud, who lodged in the same house as I in Munich from 1919 to 1921, in Scholem, *From Berlin to Jerusalem* [trans. Harry Zohn (New York: Schocken Books, 1980)], p. 124. Her "niece," in fact a somewhat distant relative belonging to the Galician branch of the Freud family, was Fania Freud, then a student in Jerusalem and later my second wife. W.B. knew Tom Freud (and respected her as a writer and illustrator of children's books), having met her during his visit to Munich in 1921.

[6] I had initially been offered an expansion of my professorship in the direction of history of religion; I proposed instead an expansion in the direction of Jewish philosophy.

11

BENJAMIN TO SCHOLEM

Dear Gerhard, [JANUARY 15, 1933]

I gladly confirm that your last letter contains much that is worth knowing. Yet it leaves much to protest against: that I learn much too late what I should have known long ago, such as your news of Seidmann-Freud, which you brazenly kept to yourself while I unsuspectingly sent you my reviews of her books;[1] that so much worth knowing breaks off before my hunger for it is quite appeased, as with your innuendos about Magnes, of whose adversaries—who they are, what they want, and where they live[2] —I would like to be able to form a clearer picture.

What—despite such grave faults—graced your letter in my eyes are the truly edifying and apposite sentences you write on my "Berliner Kindheit." "Apposite," of course, is not meant to refer to the praise you award it, but rather to the place you reserve for this series within my work, and also to the very special thoughts you devote to the piece on "Sexual Awakening."[3] Your thoughts have convinced me and I shall proceed accordingly. Moreover, you could hardly have said anything more encouraging than that in fact now and again certain passages seemed to bear on your own childhood. Your letter, then, is not among the least of the reasons why I have taken up the work again, in order to add several pieces. Yet here, where I lack the tranquility of a vast beach and a secluded place to stay, [I] must proceed with twice the care.

There is some chance that the *Frankfurter Zeitung* will soon start printing the complete series.[4] Incidentally, changes are in the offing there, whose course I cannot predict. I have therefore recently tried to establish new contacts, and have in the process hit upon the *Vossische Zeitung* on the one hand and the Frankfurt *Zeitschrift für Sozialforschung*

[1] Tom Freud took her life after the death of her husband, Jakob Seidmann. W.B.'s very positive reviews of three of her books are printed in *GS* 3:267–74 and 311–14.

[2] Albert Einstein was the most important opponent facing Dr. Judah L. Magnes, the chancellor of the Hebrew University. Einstein was close to him in views and Zionist politics, but challenged his ability to administer a university.

[3] I urgently advised him to delete this section because it was the only one in the whole book in which Jewish matters were explicitly mentioned, thus creating the worst possible associations. There would have been no point in leaving out this section if his Jewish experiences had been voiced in other sections as well, but it would have been wrong to have kept it in this isolated position. Adorno, who did not know about this correspondence, printed the section in the first book edition of the "Berliner Kindheit" anyway, and that is why it is now contained in all editions to date.

[4] Publication began on February 2, 1933.

on the other. The latter has given me a few assignments and promised me others. I will soon receive a large volume to review on the social relations and the ideology of the Baroque, written by a certain Borkenau, who is rumored to have done some very remarkable work.[5] Furthermore, several restrained remarks I heard you make about Wiesengrund won't deter me from drawing your attention to his newly published *Kierkegaard*.[6] I only know the book in excerpts thus far, but have already found much in it of merit. What's more, the author's case is so complex as to defy treatment in a letter. When I disclose that he is continuing to use my *Traverspiel* book in his seminar for the second semester running, without indicating this in the course catalogue, then you have a small cameo that should serve for the moment. But you should definitely take notice of his book, all the same.

For my part, I am very eager to receive your open letter on *Jewish Faith in Our Time*.[7] At the same time I wish to thank you very much for sending me the "Kabbalah." Though no judgment can arise out of the abyss of my ignorance in this area, you should still know that the rays of your article did force their way even down there. Otherwise, however, I have to content myself with cobweb-thin esoteric knowledge; at the moment—for the purpose of a radio play about spiritism.[8] I am about to cast a glance over the relevant literature, not, to be sure, without having constructed, slyly and for my private pleasure, a theory on these matters which I intend to put before you on a distant evening, over a bottle of burgundy. You should regard some of my more recent products, like "Das Taschentuch" or the—pruned—"Kaktushecke" [Cactus Hedge][9] as originating from the same evident motives as the spirit revue. I only send them to you to honor your archive, if even at my own expense.

By no means consider this letter short. Besides, it's been written very quickly. Tell me all that transpires in the struggle for your professorship and accept—not for it[10]—my kindest regards.

Yours, Walter

[5] Franz [von] Borkenau, *Der Übergang vom feudalen zum bürgerlichen Weltbild*, Publications of the Institute for Social Research, vol. 4 (Paris: Librairie Félix Alcan, 1934). Cf. my letter 67 of September 20, 1934.

[6] Theodor Wiesengrund [-Adorno], *Kierkegaard: Konstruktion des Aesthetischen* (Tübingen: J. C. B. Mohr, 1933), the first German book written under W.B.'s decisive influence. It was Adorno's *Habilitationsschrift* [postdoctoral thesis]. [*Kierkegaard: A Construction of the Aesthetic*, trans. Robert Hullot-Kentor (Minneapolis: University of Minnesota Press, 1989).—TRANS.]

[7] Cf. letter 7, note 2.

[8] As far as I know, none of W.B.'s notes on this subject have been preserved.

[9] *GS* 4:741–45, 748–54.

[10] Perhaps this should read: "not *solely* for it."

12

BENJAMIN TO SCHOLEM

Dear Gerhard,

BERLIN
FEBRUARY 28, 1933

I'm using a quiet hour of deep depression to send you a page once again. The immediate occasion is receipt of your utterly remarkable article in the [Bavarian] *Israelitischen Gemeindeblatt,* which I received only this morning—from Fräulein [Kitty] Marx from Königsberg, along with your letter of introduction and the announcement of her arrival.[1] The rest of the day was taken up with work and the dictation of a radio play, "Lichtenberg,"[2] which I must now send in, in accordance with a contract the better part of which has long been fulfilled and which facilitated my flight to the Baleares.

The little composure that people in my circles were able to muster in the face of the new regime was rapidly spent, and one realizes that the air is hardly fit to breathe anymore—a condition which of course loses significance as one is being strangled anyway. This above all economically: the opportunities the radio offered from time to time and which were my only serious prospects will probably vanish so completely that even "Lichtenberg," though commissioned, is not sure to be produced. The disintegration of the *Frankfurter Zeitung* marches on. The editor of its feuilleton page[3] has been relieved of his duties, even though he had demonstrated at least some commercial aptitude by his acquisition of my "Berliner Kindheit" at a ridiculously low price. Heinrich Simon[4] now seems to be in charge there. Publication of my work has now been stopped for more than a fortnight.

Prospects of seeing the work published as a book are minimal. Everyone realizes it is so superb that it will be called to immortality, even in manuscript form. Books are being printed that are more urgently in need of it. By the way, as of last week I can consider the text finished, if I wish: with the composition of the last piece—serially the first,[5] for as such it has become a pendant to the last, the "Buckligen Männlein"—

---

[1] Kitty Marx-Steinschneider (born 1905), a niece of my friend Moses Marx and his sister Esther, the wife of the writer and Nobel Prize winner S. Y. Agnon. On Moses Marx, see *From Berlin to Jerusalem,* pp. 143f.

[2] *GS* 4:696–720. The radio play was not broadcast.

[3] Werner Diebold.

[4] Part owner of the *Frankfurter Zeitung.*

[5] The "Tiergarten" piece was published in the *Frankfurter Zeitung* on February 2, 1933.

the number of thirty has been reached, not including the one deleted on your advice.

When not captivated by the fascinating world of Lichtenberg's thought, I am absorbed by the problems posed by the next months. I don't know how I will be able to make it through them, whether inside or outside Germany. There are places where I could earn a minimal income, and places where I could live on a minimal income, but not a single place where these two conditions coincide. If I report that, despite such circumstances, a new theory of language[6]—encompassing four small, handwritten pages—has resulted, you will not deny me due homage. I have no intention of having those pages published and am even uncertain whether they are fit for a typescript. I will only point out that they were formulated while I was doing research for the first piece of the "Berliner Kindheit."[7]

Even without being familiar with Schoeps's work, I think I can discern the horizon of your observations, and I am in complete agreement that nothing is more necessary than to finish off those hideous pacesetters of Protestant theologoumena within Judaism. But that is a minor matter compared with the definitions of Revelation given in your text and held by me in high esteem: "The absolutely concrete can never be fulfilled at all."[8] These words (putting aside the theological perspective) say more about Kafka, of course, than that man Schoeps will ever be capable of understanding. Max Brod is just as incapable of understanding this, and I think I have discovered here a dictum possibly embedded in the earliest and deepest layers of your thought.

It would be quite nice to hear from you soon. I am sending this short letter with the reassuring certainty that it will be complemented anecdotally by the stories Fräulein Marx will relate.

With all the best,

Yours, Walter

---

[6] "Über das mimetische Vermögen," *GS* 2:210–13 ["On the Mimetic Faculty," *Reflections*, pp. 333–36], a text that will be mentioned frequently in these letters. The reference might also be to the longer alternate version, "Lehre vom Ähnlichen," *GS* 2:204–10 ["Doctrine of the Similar," *New German Critique* 17 (Spring, 1979), pp. 65–69,], but I consider this unlikely, since this version probably wasn't written before the spring of 1933, on Ibiza. The first manuscript version, which is still extant, indeed consists of no more than four and a half small handwritten pages, though he sent me only the first text.

[7] This sentence has remained a riddle to me. If it means that W.B. was writing down notes that led to the formulation of this philosophy of language before he wrote down the "Tiergarten" piece, the relation is not clear. To establish a connection between philosophy of language and the "Weihnachtsengel" piece would be just as difficult.

[8] Thirty years later I incorporated these remarks—with small modifications—into an Eranos lecture. They can be found in the volume *Über einige Grundbegriffe des Judentums* (Frankfurt am Main: Suhrkamp Verlag, 1970), p. 110. ["Revelation and Tradition as Religious Categories in Judaism," in *Judaism* 15, no. 1 (1966), pp. 23–39.—Trans.]

Glancing through your last letter, I see that I must oblige with a small postscript. I am doing it on that noblest of papers, which I bought fifteen years ago in a small shop I discovered in Sarnen—on a walking tour—and which was sold to me by a Herr Narziss von Ach, whose memory is much dearer to me than that of a psychologist of the same name.[9] As this paper is usually reserved for my deepest meditations, please consider it a mark of esteem.[10]

My essay on Kafka is still unwritten, for two reasons. First, I really wanted—and still want—to read the essay announced by Schoeps before I start working on mine. I expect Schoeps's essay to be a codification of all misguided opinions that can be distilled from a specifically Prague-bound interpretation of Kafka, and, as you know, such books have always inspired me. But the publication of this book is not unimportant to me for a second reason as well: it is obvious that I could only undertake the work such an essay would involve if it were commissioned. And where should such a commission come from, out of the blue, unless you obtained one for me in Palestine.[11] The best way to get such a thing done in Germany would be to write it in the form of a review of Schoeps's work, but then again, I don't know whether the book will be published or not.[12]

As to your other requests for your archive, i.e., my works for the radio: Even I haven't been successful in collecting them all. I am speaking of the radio plays, not the series of countless talks, which [will] now come to an end, unfortunately, and are of no interest except in economic terms, but that is now a thing of the past.[13] Moreover, most of these radio plays were written together with others. Notable from a technical point of view perhaps is a piece for children, which was broadcast last year in Frankfurt and Cologne; I may be able to secure you a copy at some point. It's called "Radau um Kasperl."[14] If you don't receive the *Kierkegaard*

[9] Sarnen, on the way from the Brünig Pass to Lucerne. Narziss Ach was, at the time, Professor of Psychology in Göttingen.

[10] It is a page in duodecimo, which belonged to a tear-sheet notebook I often saw on W.B.'s desk. Many more pages, closely covered with writing, are still among his papers. The paper is indeed of excellent quality.

[11] I was instrumental in helping W.B. secure such a commission from the *Jüdische Rundschau* in Berlin, which was the official publication of the German Zionists. Its editor-in-chief, Robert Weltsch (Prague, 1891–Jerusalem, 1985), was a friend of Max Brod's.

[12] The book did not appear.

[13] This denigratory assessment of W.B.'s radio work, which has only been partially published and is for the most part housed in the G.D.R. literary archives, must be interpreted in the context of his negative attitude toward much of the work he did for money. Yet most of these texts also contain sediments of his decidedly original way of seeing. His Berlin lectures were mostly for the children's radio, where he had a quarter of an hour at his disposal. [The several dozen radio texts in East Berlin are now being published in *GS7*. —Trans.]

[14] This radio play was published in *GS* 4:674–95. It was first broadcast in Frankfurt at the beginning of March 1932.

from Wiesengrund within a reasonable time, I'll be honored to dedicate to you a copy of the page proofs which is in my possession.[15]

[Beginning of the Two-Way Correspondence]

13

SCHOLEM TO BENJAMIN[1]

JERUSALEM
Dear Walter,   [CA. MARCH 20, 1933]

The day before yesterday, returning from a Purim visit with friends near Tiberias, I found your letter waiting for me. I had hoped for a detailed message, especially under these new conditions, but, having learned to be content with little, I am happy that you are still among the living and I hasten to assure you that the same holds true for me. Perhaps you will now write more often. The turmoil caused by my brother's arrest—which you certainly heard about[2]—has temporarily subsided following his release several days later, and given that he expects nothing else to happen. Otherwise, we hear little positive news—and, insofar as we receive any news at all, you can imagine that it is not very generously meted out. The agitation here about what has happened is widespread and persistent, all naive souls being amazed and confused by the inglorious end to which the old order has come. In light of recent disclosures, I allow myself to await eagerly the companion piece to your theses in the "Reise durch die deutsche Inflation,"[3] even though you are perhaps not even aware that you are going to author such a piece. But I expect you will agree that you must instruct your muse (should you have one), or in any

[15] I did indeed receive the book in this form only.

[1] This is the first of my existing letters from 1933. I had sent it to Berlin, and it was forwarded to Paris.

[2] My brother Werner (1895–1940) was arrested the night of the Reichstag fire. He was arrested again at the end of April 1933 and never released.

[3] Prior to my departure from Germany at the beginning of September 1923, W.B. presented me with these notes in the form of a scroll (cf. *GS* 4:928–35). They were printed in a slightly different version—under the title "Imperial Panorama"—in *One-Way Street* [*Reflections*, pp. 70–76].

case orient your friendship toward providing me with the pages of the new theory of language you announced, even at the cost of transcribing them yourself. Apart from that, I expect to learn something of how you are in two or three weeks' time, since I was gratified to gather from Kitty Marx's letter from Germany that she visited you twice, that she has much to relate, and even that she regrets not having been able to bring you along with her. I would be pleased to hear that her visit did not meet with your disapproval, since she belongs to those who benefited, so to speak, from your absence in Berlin during my last visit. Instead of you —given that your projected trips to Palestine have all been ill fated— Gustav Steinschneider[4] has turned up here for a (longish?) stay. I regard this with great misgivings, as agreeable as I (and Escha) find him. The clear impossibility of your making a living here won't exactly guide your steps this way in case of a move, although circumstances here are basically favorable, even if only for a more or less limited time.

Neither I nor the library have received the book by Wiesengrund that you mentioned. I would therefore be very grateful if you would act on your suggestion to send me a copy of the page proofs. I am definitely interested in such reading matter. As far as Kafka is concerned, in my estimation you *cannot* count on seeing the book you are awaiting from Herr Schoeps. The young man—I must have written you that I also made his acquaintance in Berlin and have little interest in its continuation, since he is *bursting* with vanity and the desire to be on everybody's lips —is so busy trying to connect up with German fascism in every way, *sans phrase* [without further ado], that he will not have time for any other activities in the foreseeable future.[5] He has now published a book that defies the imagination—it is rather decent reading matter—namely, correspondence between said Schoeps and good old [Hans] Blüher,[6] in which Schoeps, playing the Prussian conservator of Jewish faith, tries to prevail against the ideology of "cultivated" anti-Jewishness. The spectacle is despicable, and—once you accept the immanent level of discussion—it is then just and edifying that in this discussion, with all its trumpery, the superior logic and more dignified posture are still on the side of the anti-Semite. I confess that one did not expect such a spectacle

[4] My friend, whom W.B. also knew quite well, arrived with his brother Karl and his future wife, K.M. Concerning Gustav Steinschneider, see Scholem, *From Berlin to Jerusalem*, pp. 122–24.

[5] Schoeps later republished his relevant publications under the title *Bereit für Deutschland . . . 1930–1939* (Berlin: Haude & Spencer, 1970).

[6] Blüher (1888–1955) published his "refined" anti-Semiticum *Secessio Judaica* in 1922 [Berlin: Der Weisse Ritter Verlag] and later voiced this attitude in more detail in *Die Erhebung Israels gegen die christlichen Güter* (Hamburg, Berlin: Hanseatische Verlagsanstalt, 1931).

from the editor of Kafka's papers,[7] even if he is but a lad of 23, who was by no means selected by the deceased. The tome is entitled *Streit um Israel*.

Definitely send me the radio play "Lichtenberg"! How could it possibly be missing from my archive? This coming year I must drastically limit my own work in order to concentrate on [medieval] Jewish philosophy, since I will probably have to begin lecturing on it in October, if my appointment as professor of Jewish Philosophy and Kabbalah Studies indeed comes through this summer. At long last the university has formally made the proposal, after a long struggle. I would have preferred other alternatives, but this is the one likely to materialize, if nothing unanticipated comes up. This means I will have much more to do, since my workload will swell, albeit without bringing a financial improvement in its wake, owing to the university's precarious situation. Even though the general economic and financial situation in Palestine at the moment is superb—a fact that seems to have given this land a kind of mythical renown in far-flung circles—the plight of public scholarly institutions like the university, whose funds essentially come from America, remains perilous. Otherwise I wouldn't have had to assume this responsibility, since they would have made a separate appointment expressly for that subject. Even now I have undertaken the philosophy part only as a provisional obligation, so that [I] can disengage myself from it should circumstances improve enough to permit the appointment of an assistant, associate, or full professor. But that is not foreseeable over the next few years.[8] By the way, please treat this information about my professorship as strictly confidential, since it would not be good to make much ado about it before final negotiations are concluded.—It is also quite possible that they may allow unpaid lecturers here (given intense pressure from outside and otherwise), even though they have always rejected this as a matter of principle. I dare not envisage the scene here should Jews—including professors who have already made a name for themselves—be expelled from university careers in Germany (which I regard as a real possibility). People are generally unsure, both here and in Germany, whether or not to expect a strong wave of emigration from Germany. To some extent this can already be seen very clearly in Tel Aviv, and the government here would certainly not be displeased if ten or fifteen thou-

---

[7] Schoeps edited the volume *Beim Bau der Chinesischen Mauer* (Berlin: Gustav Kiepenheuer Verlag, 1931) together with Max Brod. [*The Great Wall of China*, trans. Willa and Edwin Muir (New York: Schocken Books, 1946, 1970).—Trans.]

[8] In fact, this came about much faster than expected, and Julius Guttmann (1880–1950), who had taught these subjects at the Academy for Jewish Studies in Berlin, was offered the professorship that very year.

sand German Jews—rather than Polish or Rumanian Jews—were to obtain the hotly contested "certificates" (i.e., permission to immigrate for impecunious Jews, which the government issues as blank forms twice a year, depending on the labor market, to the Zionist organization, which handles their distribution). But as much space as there is in Palestine now for workers, there is precious little room for the academics who arrive with every ship in greater numbers, particularly from Germany. One recent ship alone had fourteen architects and engineers on board, and before long we will be receiving doctors from municipal hospitals, professors, and lawyers. The only profession likely to do well under these circumstances will be that of the Hebrew teacher!

Please write me in as much detail as you can. Especially given the present state of affairs, in which no letter's arrival is sure, it would be doubly fitting to reintroduce the good old custom of the immediate reply, which we practiced when I was in Jena. Should you change your address, please inform me separately.

Accept my most sincere regards and wishes,

Yours, Gerhard

14

BENJAMIN TO SCHOLEM

HOTEL ISTRIA
RUE CAMPAGNE PREMIÈRE
PARIS
MARCH 20, 1933

Dear Gerhard,

So here we are again, about to inaugurate a new chapter in our correspondence, one that will definitely not proceed uniformly on my part, as far as postmarks and addresses are concerned. What you hear about me these days from Kitty Marx will certainly provide you with an accurate image of my internal and external circumstances before they were assailed by events that once again entirely transformed them. But before I tell you more about this, I mustn't neglect to point out how lamentable it was that a farewell visit—if I may call it that—should constitute the beginning of an acquaintance whose potential I considered very attractive. Since this letter will follow close on the footsteps of her arrival in Jerusalem, I wish to place a modest welcoming bouquet for her atop the heavy freight of news the letter itself holds.

33

I doubt whether you have already spoken with people who left Germany after, say, the 15th of March. Only especially reckless people would have sent you news by mail. It can be very risky to write from there without a carefully contrived disguise. Since I have my freedom, I can express myself clearly and all the more succinctly. A sense of the situation there is better conveyed by the totality of the cultural state of affairs than by the particulars of individual acts of terror. It is difficult to obtain absolutely reliable information about the latter. Without any doubt there are countless cases of people being dragged from their bed in the middle of the night, and tortured or murdered. The fate of the prisoners may be of even greater significance, but harder to probe into. Horrifying rumors are circulating about this, and one can only say that some of them have turned out to be untrue. Otherwise, matters stand as always in times like these: for the few cases that were subject to exaggeration, there may be many you never hear about.

In my case it was not these conditions—more or less foreseeable for some time—that prompted me barely one week ago to transform what were ill-defined wishes to leave Germany into a hard and fast decision. Rather, it was the almost mathematical simultaneity with which every conceivable office returned manuscripts, broke off negotiations either in progress or in the final stages, and left inquiries unanswered. Every attitude or manner of expression that does not fully conform to the official one is terrorized—a reign of terror that has reached virtually unsurpassable heights. Under such conditions, the utmost political reserve, such as I have long and with good reason practiced, may protect the person in question from systematic persecution, but not from starvation. In the midst of all this, I had the good fortune to rent my place for a year to a reliable man. Only through elaborate arrangements did I succeed in raising the few hundred marks that will enable me to live on Ibiza—where I plan to go next—for a few months. What will come after that, however, may one day be as completely closed to me as it is now open. I can at least be certain that I did not act on impulse, out of panic: the German atmosphere in which you look first at people's lapels and after that usually do not want to look them in the face anymore, is unbearable. Rather, it was pure reason, which bid all possible haste. Nobody among those who are close to me judges matters differently.

However, not that many of them were still in Germany at the time of my departure: Brecht, Kracauer, and Ernst Bloch left at the right time —Brecht one day before he was to be arrested. Ernst Schoen was arrested but then released. They presumably took his passport away, as in most such cases. Mine unfortunately expires in August of this year, and one can obviously not count on its being renewed under present circumstances.

These lines are intended to inform you with broad strokes about my situation and the measures I have taken. The details can wait until later. I must ask you to address your reply to me in Paris, even though I won't be here long—if need be, mail will be forwarded. Please give Fräulein Marx my kindest regards, and tell her that the books she has from me should remain with her in Jerusalem, for the time being. Later on, I'll give her an address where she can send the proofs of [Brecht's] *Mother* —only after you've subjected them to detailed study, I hope.

Did I tell you that I wrote a small and perhaps peculiar text about language—eminently suitable to adorn your archive?

Answer as swiftly as possible and share my most cordial regards with Escha,

Yours, Walter

P.S.: I found a reference to Hubert Grimme's *Althebräische Inschriften am Sinai* among my Berlin notes, which [I] came across here. I am sending you this title—I don't even know whether it's the title of a book or an article—because I read a truly noteworthy iconographic decipherment of the *Sistine Madonna* by this author some years ago.[1]

15

SCHOLEM TO BENJAMIN

Dear Walter, MARCH 23, 1933

I am disturbed not to have heard from you for so long. I hope you received my last letter. Fräulein Marx arrived here on Monday, but she will only be making her way to us in Jerusalem next Sunday, so I have to tame my curiosity about you until then. Please write!

Kindest regards,

Yours, Gerhard

[1] Hubert Grimme (1864–1942) was professor of Semitic Studies in Münster. The work in question, which unleashed considerable controversy, appeared in 1923. Benjamin confuses Grimme with the art historian Hermann Grimm.

16

BENJAMIN TO SCHOLEM

Dear Gerhard,   [PARIS, APRIL 4, 1933]

Both the letter and the card you sent to Berlin arrived today. In the meantime you have most likely received my missive from Paris. Tomorrow evening I leave for Ibiza, in the company of a Parisian couple I'm friendly with.[1] I can sustain myself there for two months. There is hardly anyone among those touched by the events who can look further into the future.

All of this, which belongs to the realm of the most highly private matters, would be bearable, if only Stefan weren't where he still is. In my first letter from here, I urged Dora to send him to Palestine, where her brother[2] owns a plantation.

I don't wish to go into details today. You will certainly have spoken with Kitty Marx and had a chance to convey intact my especially kind regards to her. I must ask her to send Brecht's *Mother* to me in Ibiza. I can certainly assume that she will enclose a letter with it.

I was quite delighted to read what you had to say about Schoeps. Whenever I hear things like that, I am as happy as when a thick novel, bought at the last moment, fits into my suitcase after all. The upshot: There is order in the world. And the Schoepses are looked after—if not by God, then by Satan.

The most important things at this moment are my address in Ibiza and the undelayed dispatch of two letters to it—one from you and one from Kitty Marx:

       Fonda Miramar, San Antonio, Ibiza (Baleares)

All the best,

                                   Yours, Walter

[1] Jean Selz and his wife.
[2] Viktor Kellner, one of the founders of the village of Benyamina.

17

SCHOLEM TO BENJAMIN

Dear Walter, MONDAY, APRIL 3, 1933

I received your letter on Friday, after Kitty Marx and I had talked about you late into the night on Thursday!—and I hasten to write you at once. First this: Just days before you left for Paris, I sent quite a detailed letter to you in Berlin. Please confirm whether you received it, i.e., that it hasn't fallen victim to censorship by dint of the double border crossing, first into Berlin and then out again to Paris. It's important that I know this. I also wrote to Ernst Schoen, who wrote me before he was arrested, and I fear he will never have received my letter if he is treated as a suspect and subject to censorship. From examples of letters we have received here from Germany, we can indirectly perceive the terrible burden and intimidation being brought to bear upon the writers. I hardly have to elaborate on how pleased I am that you have left after all: in the near future, there will be no room in Germany proper for writing such as yours. But what now? Do you plan to switch over to writing in French, at least in part? Or will you be able to take up "strictly scholarly" work in Ibiza? With things as they are, it would be foolish to presume that you could or would even want to return to Germany soon. We are all of the opinion that things will become even more awful and that for Jews the situation will be utterly beyond repair. In view of these alarming times, I would like to ask you to send news of yourself more frequently—we can ill afford to interpose such long intervals in our correspondence. I told you about myself in the letter to Berlin mentioned earlier.

At the moment, large numbers of people are continually arriving here from Germany, both in transit and permanently, and one hears more than one would really like to.

And on top of it all, frightened Jewish families still send telegrams (!!) to people outside (obviously under gentle pressure), in which they implore them to stop the "fabricated horror propaganda" abroad!! At least the postal service, if nobody else, profits from this. But if the economy continues its downslide there, what happens next will be unpredictable. And yet socialism has suffered a setback of such mammoth proportions in all this that it is hard to see how it will ever recover, except by means of a war—which, suddenly, many people are hoping for. Just as a curiosity, I note that your *LW*–Willi Haas,[1] who no longer feels at ease now that he's fallen prey to the *Völkischer Beobachter*, made inquiries here as to whether there might be a position for him in Palestine. I saw his letter and had to think about your fairly unenthusiastic allusions to the way he behaved toward you.

Kitty Marx, who already started a job today and will stay in Jerusalem for the time being, was very taken with you, and I also truly regret that you did not meet her before. She gave me the Wiesengrund proofs, which I have not been able to get to yet, but for which I am most grateful. I have yet to receive Brecht's *Mother*. She confessed she had initially forgotten many of the things she wanted to tell me about you, as well as what you had told her to tell me. I expect to elicit this bit by bit over the next few weeks. I will relay your regards to her tomorrow evening.

I mentioned in the letter to Berlin that I hope and want *very much* to receive a transcription of your new jottings on language. If you no longer have a typewriter, then please make use of a few idle half-hours to perform this service of friendship. I would very much appreciate it. Write *as soon as possible!*

All the best, and most sincere wishes to you from Escha and myself.

Yours, Gerhard

Unfortunately I haven't been able to convey news about you as well as I had hoped, but anyway.—Thank you very much for your greetings; did you receive those I sent from Cyprus? How far is it from the Baleares to Palestine?!

Kind regards,

Yours, Kitty Marx

18

SCHOLEM TO BENJAMIN

Dear Walter,   APRIL 13, 1933

We just received your card from Ibiza, i.e., the one you wrote en route, and Kitty happens to be here with us, so I am making use of today's mail to give you the best possible impression of the livelier pace of our correspondence, which should—at least attempt to—accurately convey the

[1] Willy Haas of the *Literarische Welt*.

incredible nature of what is happening. I am happy that you received the letter I had sent to Berlin, as I had more or less given it up for lost, and by now you should also have the letter I sent to you in Paris. I hope that you will finally have the peace and quiet you desire during the next few weeks or months, so that you will have some idea of where to go from there. Here in Palestine there is tremendous commotion, as you can imagine: every ship brings hundreds of people from Germany, conveying a harrowing picture of the medieval events. Ever since the mass exodus of many thousands of people on March 30 and April 1, telegrams from all possible relatives and friends (not my family, as it happens, but almost *all* others) have been raining down like hail, left and right, and you can see from them how almost everybody took off headlong and especially how, apparently, anybody who is remotely able to do so is taking his children out of this new hell. No matter whom you run into, everybody is thinking about how he can get his family, or at least part of it, out of there. A major emigration of the bourgeois class of German Jewry is doubtless in the offing, and a sizable part of it will most likely end up here—but will things remain as they are, or will they give way to even bloodier conditions? The horrible thing about it, though, if one dares to say so, is that the human cause of the Jews in Germany only stands to benefit if a real pogrom were to take place, instead of the "cold" pogrom that they will be trying to restrict themselves to. It represents almost the only chance of bringing about something positive from such an eruption. For, although the extent of the catastrophe is of historic proportions, and it can teach us something about 1492,[1] the stuff of which resistance is made has been reduced in German Jewry to a very small fraction of what existed in those days. The magnitude of the collapse of the communist and socialist movements is frightfully obvious, but that of German Jewry certainly does not pale by comparison.

We had a visit from our friend Käthe Becher (Johannes R. Becher's divorced wife),[2] who will probably come over here like so very many others and establish herself here (as a doctor). She told us a lot about things in Berlin. It is as if we were experiencing everything ourselves. Please write us whatever you know about the details of Dora's and Stefan's plans. You are aware of Escha's and my concern for them. So much for today.
Sincerest regards from Escha and myself,

Yours, Gerhard

---

[1] The year of the expulsion of the Jews from Spain, one of the gravest events of Jewish history in the Middle Ages.

[2] On Käthe Becher, née Ollendorf, a niece of Alfred Kerr's, cf. Scholem, *From Berlin to Jerusalem*, p. 146.

Dear Herr Benjamin,

As enchanted as I was and am to receive your regards, I am just as pleased about the certitude with which you expect a letter from me. My words on this subject in Berlin should have taught you differently. But I would reply to a letter of yours with the utmost delight.

With many regards,

Yours, Kitty Marx

19

BENJAMIN TO SCHOLEM

FONDA MIRAMAR
SAN ANTONIO IBIZA (BALEARES)
APRIL 19, 1933

Dear Gerhard,

If I'm not mistaken, you must have already received confirmation from Paris that your letter to Berlin reached me there. A few days ago I received the first letter you addressed to Ibiza. To dwell for a moment on the first one, I wish to turn your news about Steinschneider's stay with you into the object of a small inquiry. As you will have read, among the grains of sand that the awakening Germany rubbed from its eyes was —besides Herr Rotter[1] and his wife—Hanussen, the clairvoyant. According to a press report, his real name was supposedly Steinschneider. Please, by all means, let me know if he, too, should turn out to be a member of Gustav's already remarkable family.[2] If Gustav were to share the talent of that putative member of his family, then I foresee a significant boom in your kabbalistic studies, since it would presumably eliminate the costly business of photographing manuscripts.

Your news about Schoeps and Blüher was extremely valuable to me, as I may already have told you. Under the circumstances, I am now doubly impatient to receive his book on Kafka. For what would be more in character for the angel who looks after the destroyed part of Kafka's works than to hide the key to it under a dungheap? Whether comparable enlightenment can be expected from the latest essay on Kafka, I cannot say. It can be found in the April issue of the *Nouvelle Revue Française* and is by Bernhard Groethuysen. Once I have seen it, you may have it, in exchange for something else to read.

---

[1] The director of a Berlin theater.
[2] See my affirmative reply in the next letter.

Even though a modest house library of thirty or forty volumes has been assembled here, partly from Noeggerath stock and partly from what I left behind here last spring, it is still only a meager base. As irony will have it, this is precisely the moment I am supposed to write an essay on the sociology of contemporary French literature, commissioned by the *Zeitschrift für Sozialforschung,* which managed to escape with its funds and equipment to Geneva. And I have to write the essay, since I can at least count on being paid by them. The essay, which in any case is sheer fakery, acquires a more or less magical mien by virtue of the fact that I have to write it here, with next to no source material of any kind. It will boldly exhibit that visage in Geneva, but keep it hidden in your presence. I don't know anything more about this yet. On the other hand, I now especially praise the impulse that made me give Brecht's book (and, if I'm not mistaken, several other books on loan[3]) to Kitty to take with her, since by doing so I hope they will return into my possession before too long. It will amuse you to know, by the way, that at the last moment I was suddenly seized by the idea of packing an enormously provocative and well-written work of Brecht's into my suitcase, after I had meticulously sifted through my archive, which means that I have only a fraction of it at my disposal here, and only totally innocuous pieces politically. The Brecht text is unpublished and exists only in galleys. It is entitled "The Three Soldiers"[4] and will also have found—or soon find—its way to Palestine.

By the time your prognoses regarding the fate of German Jewry arrived here, they had been fulfilled. Needless to say, they concur with mine. It was three weeks ago that I asked Dora to send Stefan, if at all possible, to her brother in Palestine. For the moment, however, she does not seem to be contemplating this course of action. I dwell upon my own situation only reluctantly. After having implemented the last option I had —that is, by moving here, to reduce my living expenses to the European minimum of about 60 or 70 Reichsmarks a month—I feel incapable of indulging in too much activity for the moment. Not every literary association with Germany has been dissolved as yet: an essay or a review might still sneak through every now and then. However, the foundation of a "writers' union" that excludes Jews from its ranks and from the press, has to be imminent. I am extremely skeptical about the prospects of securing a livelihood for myself in France, unless emigré organizations were to provide me with a framework within which I could work. With

[3] Robert Musil's *Der Mann ohne Eigenschaften,* 2 vols. (Berlin: Rowohlt, 1930, 1932). [*The Man Without Qualities,* trans. Eithne Wilkins and Ernst Kaiser (1953; New York: Perigee, 1980).—TRANS.]

[4] First published in volume 6 of the *Versuche* (as no. 14).

41

this in mind, I am making use of every opportunity during my stay in Paris, introducing myself in various places. A return to Paris, however, even if it should seem to be the right course to take, poses not only a financial but legal problem, since my passport won't be valid after this summer. And it is highly unlikely that it will be extended. Needless to say, I will not return to Germany under any circumstances. I only wish that Stefan were already out, as well.

Kitty Marx sends me a congenial postscript, which has not so bewitched my eyes, however, that they would lose the image of the letter she promised, especially since her Cyprian greetings did not reach me at all. Give her my kindest regards, and convey such to Steinschneider as well. I return Escha's greetings and yours most wholeheartedly.—I'll copy the text on language for you. Even though it turned out to be very short, I am sure manifold thoughts and objections will stay my hand and hold it back as I write, and that you will not come into possession of the two or three pages for many weeks.

Yours, Walter

P.S. Your letter of the 13th arrived at this very moment. I can only confirm that I received it, and K.M.'s postscript as well. I have also tried to reflect on the implications of events in Germany for the future history of the Jews. With very little success. In any event, the emancipation of the Jews stands in a new light. Nothing new from Dora. But she lost her job.

20

SCHOLEM TO BENJAMIN

Dear Walter,   MAY 4, 1933

I am replying by return mail to your letter of April 19—which only arrived yesterday, by the way, and therefore must have caught the least propitious steamer—because I want to live up to my recently announced resolution, even if it should lead me into the hell in which cultural bolshevists stew. We would like to have a better idea of how you have organized your life on the European subsistence level in Ibiza and what is happening there with you now. Further, whether you won't attempt to take the first opportunity to save your books—Kitty told us so much about the ingenious way you have arranged them—from the auto-da-fé of all that is un-German in the Third Reich. We have already received oral reports from an acquaintance of ours from Frankfurt about the flight of the Institute for Social Research to Geneva, and hope that this will at least help you somewhat—I really don't seem able to discover another reason for its existence. Reports from Frankfurt reaching us at the same time as your letter tell us that things are otherwise also quite fierce in the city of your academic past. The name of that poor wretch who inherited your *Privatdozentur*, Herr [Martin] Sommerfeld, is listed beside more illustrious names on the lengthy list of Jews who have just been dismissed and which includes everybody and anybody, so to speak, even Max Wertheimer[1] and Weil[2]—the sole exception being Buber perhaps,[3] but this is probably also only a matter of time—and anyway, not a single one of those who "remain" will ever be able to lecture again (and, anyway, to whom would they lecture?). The implications that these mass expulsions of the Jewish intelligentsia—except those who have been ostentatiously baptized—might have for the University of Jerusalem[4] are the object of a vehement debate here, which should come to fruition in the course of the summer months. Our position would be quite comfortable, if we only had some money. In any case, there will obviously be a number of scholars among the expected abundance of German immigrants.

We are personally very alarmed by the second and, we fear, irrevocable arrest of my brother Werner and his wife (who was immediately taken away with him this time), the day before they planned to go to Switzerland. I truly cannot fathom my brother's behavior—as imprecisely as I can reconstruct it from my family's veiled messages—specifically, why he didn't put the border behind him the minute they released him from custody the first time. He was to have gone to our uncle, the mathematician,[5] in Zurich. My mother has collapsed under the pressure of all these events and the extravagance with which the German soul has exhibited itself this time: she has aged considerably. We still do not know if the further course of events will necessitate bringing her here—a move

[1] Max Wertheimer (1880–1943), one of the founders of Gestalt psychology.

[2] Gotthold Weil (1882–1960), professor of Semitic Languages, who was reinstated for a short time, since he did not fall under the provisions of the "Law to Reestablish the Cadre of Professional Civil Servants."

[3] At this time, Martin Buber had only forgone lecturing in the summer semester, after receiving a strongly "suggestive" letter from the dean. He was not formally expelled until the beginning of October 1933. (Information to the contrary in biographies of Buber is incorrect.)

[4] [Scholem is referring to the Hebrew University of Jerusalem, founded 1925.—Trans.]

[5] Arthur Hirsch (1860–1946), a cousin of my mother's, a professor of Mathematics at the Eidgenössische Technische Hochschule in Zurich.

we would only want to risk, as you will easily understand, if she is no longer able to live with the family over there. It is more likely that there will be an addition to the family from the younger generation.[6] I must say that I cannot at all understand why Stefan is still in Germany when it's possible for him to be elsewhere. I doubt that things can remain that way, and, of course, Dora herself—I haven't heard from her since October [1932]—will soon find the air in Germany unbearable, since the prospects for Jewish translators and journalists will soon become nonexistent.[7] Many of our acquaintances are already sending their children here, even though they must naturally count on a major change in their career prospects and a corresponding change in their schooling.

Regarding your inquiry about the clairvoyant, Hanussen, I can unfortunately only reply that he is in fact, without a doubt, a distant relation of the Steinschneider family, whose origins go back to Prossnitz in Moravia, and which has endured this peculiar career. Gustav told me that this had always been denied by the family, since no one could pinpoint the exact connection until a Viennese family member finally revealed it. Incidentally, the whole family indignantly rejects this additional branch, even if it is a dead one. The Steinschneider family has proven itself to be remarkable rather more through the incorporation of a living member, likely to be of much greater interest to you and me; it has succeeded, in the person of Gustav's brother Karl,[8] in persuading Kitty Marx to join it, which is a great occasion in every respect, and not merely because we are dealing with the undisputed world record holder for rejected marriage proposals. I acted as a witness at the wedding, which was held in extreme privacy the day before Passover. I even assumed "direction" of the ceremonial part of the act myself, with all the more unrestrained emotion since Karl St. is one of the people in Palestine closest to my heart, and he could assure himself of my immeasurable affection for him when we met again after nearly six years of his working in California. Since she will probably be joining her husband in two weeks (he works at the agricultural experimental station in Rehovot, a large Jewish colony an hour from Tel Aviv), we will be losing her from Jerusalem—even though this means that there will be another place I can travel to in Palestine without sighing. Do you think that Rowohlt still dares to sell books such as your *One-Way Street*? I wanted to include it among my

[6] Two of my cousins came to the country.

[7] Dora worked primarily as a translator from English, in which she was fluent. Her father, Leon Kellner, was a professor of English Literature at the University of Czernowitz.

[8] Karl Steinschneider (1900–1979), whom I had known since 1916, came to Palestine in 1922. He met W.B. in 1935 in Paris.

various wedding presents to them. But, from this distance, the fate of all those publishing houses and books is entirely impenetrable. Anyway, I urgently advised Kitty to send you an announcement of her destiny, in her own hand, but nevertheless I did not want to delay mailing this letter. You should soon receive Brecht's *Mother*,[9] but I confess that I would also like to read the Musil books myself, if I can find the time. Do you mind?

I am also sending you an issue of the *Jüdische Rundschau*, whose firm and honorable stance is especially remarkable under the prevailing conditions in Berlin.[10] Among the riddles of the times is that the *Rundschau* was not banned—especially following a stormy "interview" the author held with Herr Goering, the most important man in the current government—but has managed to maintain its convictions all these weeks. No literature by Herr Schoeps has gotten through to me, thank God. You will not be deprived of it—for your gruesome enjoyment—should it still arrive.—Incidentally, Kraft[11] has now also been relieved of his post in Hanover.

The library here carries the *Nouvelle Revue Française*, so I will endeavor to look at Herr Groethuysen's essay. More about literature another time.

Regarding your passport, I wanted to tell you that if you are able to procure a *permanent* residence permit for Spain, it should be entirely possible for you then to have yourself entered in the *register* of the nearest German consulate (as you can in Jerusalem, for example), which would give you (at least until now) the right to obtain a new passport there at any time. Generally speaking, German consulates abroad have an interest in registering as many people as possible, for obvious reasons having to do with sphere of influence, and to show a liberal face abroad. You should at least make inquiries of people who are in the know over there. In the meantime, the flight from German "citizenship" has reached considerable dimensions[12] here in Palestine. I suspect that, if need be, you could be naturalized in France or Spain.

I await the copy of your text on language with gratitude and eagerness.

---

[9] The first version of this letter, which I still possess, reads: "Brecht's *Mother*, which left me cold," etc.

[10] It was the April 4 issue, which created a stir with the superb article by Robert Weltsch, the editor-in-chief, entitled "Tragt ihn mit Stolz, den gelben Fleck" [Wear It with Pride, the Yellow Stain].

[11] Werner Kraft was a librarian at the Hanover State Library.

[12] I had already renounced German citizenship in 1926, when British Mandate authorities promulgated a law making Palestinian citizenship available after two years of permanent residence.

So much for today. Please write soon, and at length. Should you be in touch with Ernst Schoen, could you ask him if he received my letter? Kindest regards from Escha and myself,

Yours, Gerhard

21

BENJAMIN TO SCHOLEM

FONDA MIRAMAR
SAN ANTONIO, IBIZA
MAY 7, 1933

Dear Gerhard,

Just a few lines, even without having heard any news from you.

I have learned, from a serious but not necessarily infallible source, that my brother Georg, who practices medicine in Berlin N[orth] Brunnenstrasse, fell into the hands of the SA, was severely brutalized, and lost an eye. He is presumed to be in the state hospital, either as a prisoner or in preventive detention, and is most likely cut off from the outside world.[1]

This story was told in Zurich by Reni Begun, a Jewish doctor, who is said to have left Berlin ten days ago. She is now in Paris; I am trying to establish direct contact with her, but this will take some time.

The last news I received from my sister[2] was before Easter, from Switzerland. At the time, everything was still all right.

My brother's predicament has given us reason to fear the worst. The matter is too serious—and the prospects of my being able to help too futile—for me to turn to Berlin[3] for information, since such an inquiry could endanger either the recipient or the person giving the information. Perhaps you can extract some information about my brother from the

---

[1] The information was not correct in this form. Georg Benjamin was taken into "preventive detention" on April 12. At the time this letter was being written, he was already in the "relatively legal" remand prison of Plötzensee, where my brother Werner was also being held. More precise details about these events can be found in Hilde Benjamin's biography of her husband, *Georg Benjamin: Eine Biographie* (Leipzig: S. Hirzel, 1977), pp. 210–13.

[2] Dora Benjamin (1901–46), a political economist and the youngest of Benjamin's three siblings, worked in the fields of social welfare and psychology. At the time, she was still in Germany, but she had an apartment in Paris from 1934 to 1935. She managed to escape to Switzerland during the war and died in Zurich, after many years of a severe illness. I visited her there at Paracelsus Hospital three days before her death.

[3] He probably means his ex-wife, Dora, and his sister-in-law, Hilde Benjamin, his brother's wife (and biographer), who at the time was still a lawyer in Berlin; she later served for many years as Minister of Justice in the G.D.R.

people who have just arrived. Please try this and inform me at once. My sister is meanwhile back in Berlin.

Such news was scarcely required to heighten my desire to know that Stefan is safely outside of Germany; reading the papers is enough. I encouraged Dora along these lines while I was still in Paris. Judging from her reply, she seemed then to want to wait and see how things developed. In the meantime, the regulations about the *numerus clausus* for Jews in high schools and middle schools have been published. I do not yet know if Stefan is affected by them. But much more germane is the fact that he is squarely on the Left and probably does not possess the constant prudence that a Jew has to have in Germany today if he wants to have a chance of saving his skin.[4]

I cannot write Dora about these things without putting her in danger. I relate them to you both under the seal of secrecy and yet in the hope that you might have some way of passing on news of this letter by word of mouth. I realize that this is quite unlikely, since you would need *a person you could trust absolutely* to deliver the message. There are spies everywhere.

I am pessimistic about the business of my passport, especially since just today I heard a long-standing suspicion of mine confirmed, namely, that officials at the consulate may demand, under some pretext, that people hand over their passports, in order to keep them. I am going to pretend that mine has been lost. But of course I don't believe that I will get another one. I will then think about staying in Spain, more or less illegally, or returning to France before my passport expires. I have been assured of receiving a *carte d'identité* there. But how I am to get there is another matter, not to mention what I will live on.

The writer "Detlef Holz"[5] requests, through me, that you keep his writings in your archive of my works. The first one just appeared in the *Frankfurter Zeitung.* I don't yet have a specimen copy. Should you catch sight of the article—in the issue of April 30, 1933[6]—without my efforts at mediation, he wants you to know that you must always keep editorial meddling in mind where Holz's articles are concerned. This first article is no exception. Perhaps I can make it accessible to you sometime in its unadulterated form. The young author hopes to create a stir with his second essay, which has just been sent to the paper. It is entitled "Am

[4] W.B's correspondence with his son is only partially extant; it is now in the Literary Archives of the Academy of Arts of the G.D.R.

[5] W.B.'s frequently employed pseudonym for his publications in Germany from 1933 to 1935. He also used it for his *Deutsche Menschen* in 1936, so that the book might have a chance of being sold in Germany.

[6] This refers to a very positive review of the poet Max Dauthendey (*GS* 3:383–86), in which Paul Scheerbart also receives praise.

Kamin"[7] and includes a theory of the novel that bears no resemblance to Lukács's theory.[8]

Many regards to Kitty Marx. I would like to know if I lent her a book for her trip to Palestine and, if so, which one?

All the best to you and Escha,

Yours, Walter

22

SCHOLEM TO BENJAMIN

Dear Walter, MAY 23, 1933

Your letter only arrived here the day before yesterday, which means that every now and then the mail takes a rather long time, and I strive to make up for this by replying at once. You will have received my crossing letter in the meantime. I was very alarmed by what you write about your brother, but it is unfortunately necessary to take that kind of information very seriously and to try to establish the truth. I will do what I can. I venture to say that you have certain misconceptions about the things that can be written without endangering anyone. My very considerable experience has shown me that it is possible to write much more than you might think, and, if sensitive inquiries are disguised in innocuous poetic dress, you can write very nearly anything. For my part, I will be writing to two people in Berlin to ask them to look into the matter as far as possible, but of course I do not know whether they will be able to give a positive reply or whether they, too, have already left Berlin by now. And I will also write to Dora again myself, in suitably veiled terms. It is very, very unfortunate that a young man left here only the day before your letter arrived. He was the only one I could have entrusted to take things

---

[7] "Am Kamin" treated Arnold Bennett's novel *Konstanze und Sophie*, published in German in 1932. [Translation by Daisy Brody of *The Old Wives' Tale* for R. Piper & Co., Munich.] The review was printed in the *Frankfurter Zeitung* on May 23, 1933 (*GS* 3:388–92), and provides a model of how W.B. would conceal sweeping theoretical considerations of his own in reviews. He spoke unequivocally of his profound affinity to Bennett in a letter to Jula Radt (*Briefe*, 587).

[8] Georg Lukács, *Die Theorie des Romans* (Berlin: Paul Cassirer, 1920) [*The Theory of the Novel: A Historico-Philosophical Essay on the Forms of Great Epic Literature*, trans. Anna Bostock (Cambridge, Mass.: MIT Press, 1971)]. (This was Lukács's last pre-Marxist publication in German.)

directly to Berlin, and there was nothing more I could do to reach him. Otherwise, I know of nobody traveling to Berlin, but I will certainly look around. The people we trust most are as a rule not inclined to take the road back there these days.

My brother and sister-in-law are also still under arrest, and nothing has been heard from them yet. You may have read that Gutkind's brother-in-law [1] "took his own life" in the Moabit prison, to quote the official version. They arrested one of my cousins, a 16-year-old high schooler in Hamburg, for suspected communist activities, because he belonged to a Jewish-socialist (Zionist) youth organization, and kept him in jail for more than two weeks.

After what you wrote about Stefan, it seems worth raising the question whether it makes sense to send him to Palestine if, as I understand from you, he has communist leanings. In that case, he will not get the feeling of satisfaction he might need, certainly not in the *strictly reactionary* environment (which is known as such all over Palestine) that Dora's brother happens to be living in. The attitude of Jews here is *very* hostile toward communism;[2] the question is whether it makes sense to expose a 15-year-old boy to the certain conflicts connected with this. Lacking a strong, positive attitude toward Judaism, he will find life here difficult to bear. But I may be wrong, and Stefan is, after all, at an age when new ideas can still make an impression on the mind. These things must be considered carefully from all sides. If he were to go to school here (which is no longer possible in Benyamina, because of his age), then he would first have to learn Hebrew in a very different way, and he would not be able to get any higher education in this country if he did not.

As to your worries about your passport: I understand that you could run into difficulties if you wanted to come to Palestine, but France's position is well known, so I cannot really understand why an expired passport would be an obstacle to crossing the French border at a time when hundreds of people from Germany are constantly doing it without any passport—and without being deported. I think you should look at these matters with more optimism. Another thought: Aren't many regions in Italy as cheap as your present place of asylum? Or am I underestimating things there? If the writer Detlef Holz, whose birth I have noted with great pleasure, were to establish himself—here I am fairly skeptical—perhaps it would be advisable to consider a closer part of

---

[1] Erich Baron, Lucie Gutkind's brother, had been very active in the Organization of Friends of the Soviet Union.

[2] Due to the Comintern's strictly anti-Zionist policy in general and the practice of its Palestinian branch (consisting almost exclusively of Jews until 1930), which led to many a split within the Palestine Communist Party.

Europe. (Not having seen Holz's work thus far, I am very eager to do so. By the way, I am also still missing many of your own recent products, which you withheld, such as a critique of Wiesengrund's *Kierkegaard* I came across in the *Vossische Zeitung*[3] purely by chance.) You would need about eight to ten pounds to live in Palestine. How much of that might you have at your disposal? The problem whether you (a) could (b) should live here has often been discussed in the circle of your male and female admirers. Kitty says she wanted to give you her ticket straight off.[4] Would you perhaps like to participate in our discussion by giving us your opinion? I often think about this. I hope I will soon have the opportunity to write you again. Magnes recently wrote and asked about you. So I wrote him a reply. I passed your regards on to Kitty and I admonish her with silent looks to reply to your letter, which was quite a success.

Many kind regards from all of us,

Yours, Gerhard

P.S. If I thank you for your letter here, then I won't have a beginning for my own anymore. But you shall receive it very soon.

Until then, kind regards,

K.M.

23

BENJAMIN TO SCHOLEM

FONDA MIRAMAR
SAN ANTONIO, IBIZA (BALEARES)
MAY 23, 1933

Dear Gerhard,

Your letter of May 4th has arrived. I have all the more time to answer it, because exchanges with German correspondents turn out to be increasingly sparse. Understandably, the people there are not anxious to put themselves in danger for the sake of an exchange of views. On May 4 you had not yet seen my last inquiry, but did have the somber news about your brother. You write that you are unable to imagine why he behaved as he did. I feel the same way about my brother. I spoke with him on the telephone before I left. At that time rumors of his death had already

---

[3] This review in the *Vossische Zeitung* of April 2, 1933 (*GS* 3:380–83) was still signed with his initials.

[4] Meaning that she was still prepared to pay for W.B.'s passage to Palestine.

50

surfaced twice in Wedding, where he lives. Meanwhile, the rumors I asked you to help me check have turned out to be basically true. He fell into the hands of the SA five weeks ago and since that time has been held prisoner in the state hospital. I don't know anything about the nature of his injuries . . .[1]

Tell me if you are able to find out anything else—which I doubt. Today I exchanged a few words with someone newly arrived from Germany. On the whole, all one knows and suspects is confirmed. A week ago I urged Dora once again—insofar as this is possible in a letter—to send Stefan out of Germany. As long as he is still inside, I must proceed with the greatest caution imaginable in what I allow to be printed.

My constitution is frail. The absolute impossibility of having anything at all to draw on threatens a person's inner equilibrium in the long run, even one as unassuming and as used to living in precarious circumstances as I am. Since you wouldn't necessarily notice this if you were to see me, its most proper place is perhaps in a letter. The intolerability of my situation has less to do with my passport difficulties than with my total lack of funds. At times I think I would be better off if I were less isolated. Nonetheless, the choice of this place was naturally a clever one. The odd letter gives me hope now and then that acquaintances might put in an appearance, although experience of course teaches me not to set great store in their plans. Even last year, nobody actually showed up. When I let more than a week pass—as I have now—without seeing my Parisian friends in Ibiza, it puts me in a dismal state. By the way, the husband is absorbed in his ambition to translate small sections of the "Berliner Kindheit." He doesn't know any German but is capable of following my paraphrases with excellent comprehension.[2]

Since I must assume that the new press law being drafted in Germany will deprive me of the last remnants of my journalistic opportunities there, Paris would offer me the only remaining base for my work. And isn't this formulation utterly optimistic! But since the most I could earn in Paris would just suffice to cover my living expenses *here*, a dilemma presents itself for which I see no solution.

So much in answer to your kind inquiry.

In the meantime, I apply myself to my ongoing projects as best I can, isolated from all means of production. Both these tasks and my living conditions, which differ somewhat from last year's, have conspired to keep me away until now from what matters most to me: continuing the "Berliner Kindheit." Did I manage to send you "The Little Hunchback,"

[1] See above, note 1 to letter 21.

[2] These translations, which went through many stages, are printed as an appendix in *GS* 4:979–86. Tillman Rexroth, the volume's editor, reports on their origin on pp. 969–70.

51

the concluding piece, or did that first come into being after I had sent you the rest? Once I am done agonizing over my extended study on the state of contemporary French letters, which I'll soon have ready, I will devote myself again to the subject of the novel, which I recently explored in an essay that regrettably hasn't yet been printed.[3]

At about the same time I will probably exchange my present quarters for quarters in a lonely mill—without windows: they will probably make a hole in the door. There things will either become bearable[4] (and then I might remain indefinitely) or (and this is at least as likely) become unbearable, in which case I may leave San Antonio for Ibiza, or leave the island altogether.

I am very much looking forward to the *Mother*. If you want to read the Musil you may keep it, though only for the time being. I have lost my taste for it and have taken leave of the author, having come to the conclusion that he is far too clever for his own good.

And now for something that will line your brow with furrows. But it must be said. After further misgivings about the plan of sending you my recent jottings on language, I realized that this project, hazardous as it is, would only be viable if I could first conduct a comparison of these notes with my early "On Language as Such and on the Language of Man."[5] The latter, however, is of course out of reach, since it is among my papers in Berlin. But I know you possess a copy. I therefore urgently request you to send it as soon as possible by registered mail to my present address—which remains valid even if I move to the mill. Don't lose any time: you will receive my new notes all the sooner. Incidentally, I am waiting for just a few more mailings of printed matter from Berlin before I send you another package to supplement your archive of my writings. I must really congratulate myself now on the conscientiousness with which I have attended to this archive. I hope to hear soon, however, that the largest and most current part of my own archive is secure in a Paris safe; somebody wants to take charge of having it transported there.[6]

Kitty Marx received a long letter from me, sent from here. I honor and welcome an occasion that must have eclipsed this shining event in her eyes, but I can only tell her that once she has paid even slight tribute to it. Be quick about ordering her the *One-Way Street*, before the German booksellers have read it.

What kind of position did Kraft have in Hanover? And is he still among

[3] See note 7 to letter 21.
[4] W.B. did not want to stay at the Noeggeraths' any longer.
[5] [See *Reflections*, pp. 314–32.—TRANS.]
[6] Although this person's identity is not known to me, it could most likely be ascertained from the letters to W.B. that are in East Berlin.

your correspondents? And what has happened to him?[7] What will become of him?

Write without delay! Adorn your letter once more with enclosures like the *Jüdische Rundschau,* for which I am indebted. Kindest regards to you and Escha,

Yours, Walter

24

BENJAMIN TO SCHOLEM

IBIZA
MAY 31, 1933

Dear Gerhard,

There can be no doubt at the moment as to which side has been more diligent in keeping up our correspondence. I also realize that I do not improve matters by writing more often, since it is precisely the vision of the admonitions and remonstrances with which you can start your letter that so often quickens your hand. It almost seems as if the Jews who are strewn about the world—not to mention your most able pupil in Palestine—have picked up your laxness in correspondence with me. For silence, in this case, is to be preferred to the expression of just wrath.

But now the moment has come when you must allow me to shake a few meager fruits from the tree of conscientiousness which has its roots in my heart and its leaves in your archive. A technical mishap so heavily damaged three pages from my newspaper folder that important sections of the text are missing. This includes *Literarische Welt* 5:25, with the article "Bücher, die übersetzt werden sollten" (June 21, 1929), *Literarische Welt* 6:21 with the third section of the "Pariser Tagebuch" (May 23, 1930), and above all the heavily damaged article in the Frankfurt *Illustriertes Blatt* of April 1, 1929, with the article "Dienstmädchenromane des vorigen Jahrhunderts."[1] I would like to ask you especially to leave me the last one, in any case. I would welcome the other two on a loan basis, if need be; I could then use your copy to reconstruct the missing text. I am simultaneously trying to secure replacements from Germany. But it is very questionable indeed whether they are still to be had.

---

[7] He came to Palestine in 1934, and is still living in Jerusalem.
[1] The articles are reprinted in *GS* 3:174–76, 4:567–87, and 4:620–22.

Nothing would make me happier than for you to enclose the essay "On Language as Such and on the Language of Man" with these pages. And the sooner I receive it, the better.[2] I now have the time to devote my attention to the comparison of both texts on language. And since I will have a secretary for the next few weeks, you have every prospect of gaining possession of the second text on language quickly. But I absolutely must have access to the first beforehand.

Bear in mind that I must do everything alone here, under the most difficult of circumstances, while you have a house—and within it a hundred hands—at your service.[3] I do not count Escha's hands here in connection with such humble tasks.

If you still need either encouragement or a bonus after all this, I would be inclined to offer you one in the form of the manuscript (on loan) of the essay on "The Present Social Position of the French Writer,"[4] which I finished yesterday. The article was produced for that Institute for Social Research which moved to Geneva, or rather for its journal, and has been wrenched from the most difficult of circumstances. It wasn't possible to produce something definitive. Nonetheless, I believe that the reader will gain insight into connections that until now have not been brought out so clearly.

Did I write you that I have meanwhile received grim confirmation of the news about my brother? Yet I am still in the dark concerning the nature of his injuries.

I spent eight days with friends in Ibiza and managed to relax a little over the last three days, despite seven hours of dictation. I am returning to San Antonio today.

Affectionate regards, if only under the condition that you grant my requests immediately.

Yours, Walter

---

[2] I had given this essay to Kitty to copy, in order not to endanger the important original through the mail.

[3] This was sheer exaggeration. I didn't even have a secretary; otherwise, many of the texts I sent W.B. over the years and which are now missing would be preserved today.

[4] "Die gegenwärtige gesellschaftliche Stellung des französischen Schriftstellers," *GS* 2:776–803.

25

SCHOLEM TO BENJAMIN

Dear Walter,   JUNE 15, 1933

Both your letter of the 23rd and the note of May 31 required quite some time for their voyages; it seems that no letter from Ibiza makes it here in under two weeks, which is why I ask you not to be impatient if everything can't be taken care of as rapidly and promptly as when we were writing to and from Germany. At the same time, I am sending you, under separate cover, registered and as printed matter, a copy of the first text on language, which you may keep. When your first letter arrived, Kitty immediately offered to make a transcription for you, but we have been severely set back by illnesses and family matters. Don't think poorly of her that she hasn't written you yet, she has really been a harried creature, and I have misgivings about communicating your displeasure to her. She is leaving her job in Jerusalem any day now, and will then certainly have more leisure to show her true colors. At any rate, I wasn't able to muster up a copy until now, and I enclose the requested essays, whereas I *strongly* request that you return at least the third part of the "Pariser Tagebuch." In the rush, I didn't find time to copy the few lines on penny novels—might I expect this back as thanks for having fulfilled each of your wishes? It won't have escaped you that I'm looking forward to the second text on language with the unfeigned interest of the Black Magician who expects a theory to shore up his formulae. Only a week has passed since your first entreaty reached me, so I confess that I don't really feel stung by the remark about laxness in matters of correspondence. Hopefully, your secretary didn't disappear in the mills at the "maw of the great abyss" spoken of in the Zohar[1] before our transaction could take place (*almost* by return mail).

I wasn't able to infer from your letter whether or not you received the one I wrote immediately after receiving your news about Georg. But I hope so. By the way, I wrote to Dora twice in the last two months, without the slightest sign of life from her (since my visit to Berlin).

Escha left for Rome yesterday after receiving a telegram from her sister; the family is meeting at my cousin [Loni]'s to negotiate its future. Escha will remain there only very briefly, until about July 1, or at most a week longer, if someone from my family is able to come down. Because

---

[1] The place where the demons retreat to on the Sabbath, according to the kabbalistic book Zohar (1:48a).

they are supposedly preparing proceedings against my brother Werner[2] on a charge of high treason (as the district attorney threatened my mother, who incidentally writes most uninhibitedly and in detail about these conditions and her experiences with the new German "mentality"!),[3] my wife—since she bears the same name—is certainly not about to cross the German border. We urged my mother to come to Rome. It's a great pity you aren't in Italy now. We don't expect my mother to come live with us as long as Werner and his wife are in jail, as it would go against her maternal feelings. The prevailing sentiment in Escha's family, on the other hand, seems to be for leaving Germany. My German acquaintances are meanwhile streaming in here in growing numbers, to say nothing of many more people I do not know. This has consequences that are not negligible in terms of the demands both groups make on our time. One hears German spoken on the streets to such an extent here, and even more conspicuously in Tel Aviv (where I observed this last Saturday), that it makes people like me feel even more like withdrawing into Hebrew. I have unfortunately already been guilty of an encounter that ended in my female partner's fit of tears, simply because I engaged in an uncharitable analysis of the dream world German Jews have been living in.[4] I never would have dreamed—given my opinions about present-day matters—that I could acquire a reputation for extreme chauvinism, but this is probably the just revenge of the *genius loci*. Our old thesis, that Zionism shows superior insight in the diagnosis of the Jewish condition but has tragic weaknesses as a therapy, will probably be uncannily reconfirmed, in view of the unfolding events. Well, this will hardly be the last letter you receive about these matters.

I enclosed several issues of the *Jüd[ische] Rundschau* in the package of printed matter. The journal seems to have been banned late last week, because of an article—which I will send you as well, if possible—of the highest moral courage and import, and with the quite topical title of "Herr, mache unsere Rücken gerade" [Lord, Straighten Our Backs].[5] If this is the end, it would be the most honorable one. If not, so much the better.

Kraft, to answer this question as well, is by no means one of my correspondents, although I am well acquainted with his sister-in-law,

---

[2] It did in fact come to a court case against my brother, on a charge of undermining military strength. He was acquitted, but then immediately arrested by the Gestapo as he left the courtroom and taken to Torgau concentration camp.

[3] [An edition of these letters is forthcoming, to be published by C. H. Beck Verlag in cooperation with the Leo Baeck Institute, Jerusalem.—TRANS.]

[4] My conversation of June 8 with a wealthy lady, a certain Dr. Weil, got me so worked up that I made a note of it.

[5] Robert Weltsch's long article appeared May 30, 1933. The most amazing thing about it was that the *Jüdische Rundschau* was *not* banned thereafter.

Toni Halle,[6] who works in Tel Aviv as a teacher. He was librarian at the Hanover State Library for four years, or even longer, and he now faces the void, like all of German-Jewish intelligentsia. He just sent his son to Palestine to continue his education, but I don't see a potential livelihood here for the man himself. We already have an almost incalculable supply of librarians, and no money to begin to do anything with them. For all that, it is conceivable, by the way, that the university might be able to use a part of the emergency funds, which people are now endeavoring to raise with great élan, for the resettlement of German Jews in Palestine. In that case, we would be gaining a few new colleagues.

The semester ends in two weeks, and then I will have to get started on rather strenuous work: to prepare for next year and to finish off a few large projects. A large book of mine, an analysis of the turn of mind of an especially difficult thirteenth-century kabbalistic specialist, has been appearing in installments of 20 to 40 pages for some time and should gradually be nearing its conclusion.[7] Only then will I receive copies of the book; if you were able to read Hebrew by then, you would find it of interest.

Write me the bare facts of your life on Ibiza. Do you live alone, in a boarding house, with farmers, or with Europeans? Do you speak the local dialect? I have been told by others that one sees the name Ibiza rather often in the papers these days; does that imply immigration and more expensive living conditions?

With kindest regards and the wish to hear from you soon,

Yours, Gerhard

26

BENJAMIN TO SCHOLEM

Dear Gerhard,   JUNE 16, 1933

A few days have passed since your letter of the 23rd arrived—it, too, took a long time to get here. When it finally did come, I happened to be

---

[6] Toni Halle (1890–1964) had been a friend of mine since the Heidelberg and Jena days. Late in her life she married Gustav Steinschneider. She was one of the best-known teachers and the director of a progressive secondary school in Tel Aviv for many years.

[7] A monograph on the kabbalist Isaak ben Jakob Kohen of Soria and his school, published from 1932 to 1934 [cf. Fania Scholem et al., *Bibliography of the Writings of Gershom G. Scholem* (Jerusalem: Magnes Press, Hebrew University, 1977), entries 107, 112, 127, 140.—TRANS.]

away for a few days, as I take every opportunity to turn my back on San Antonio. If you take a hard look at things, then you realize that there are no peaceful spots left—let alone peaceful moments—in its vicinity, which has been smitten with all the horrors accompanying the activities of settlers and speculators. Even the cheapest place becomes too expensive if the price is the sheer possibility of getting any work done, and my relocation to the city is only a matter of days, as difficult as it is to find a place both affordable and bearable on Ibiza.

Meanwhile, I am using this situation as an impetus for extended exploratory hikes into the heart of the island. I undertook one recently in the very pleasant company of a grandson of Paul Gauguin, who bears his grandfather's name. We had a lobster fisherman drop us off at a deserted spot on the coast—not before watching him at work—and marched from there into the mountains. Yesterday I was away with my French friends for fourteen hours. As soon as one is out of earshot of the blastings and hammer blows, the gossip and debates that constitute the atmosphere of San Antonio, one feels the ground again beneath one's feet. My long-held mistrust of the whole business of developers which I first experienced in Grünau as a guest in the Gutkinds' house,[1] has been all too drastically confirmed here in the Noeggeraths' house. Add to this the very unpleasant nature of the villagers. In short, I already yearn for those saturated shadows with which the wings of bankruptcy will bury this whole glorious paradise of narrow-minded shopkeepers and vacationers within a few short years.

Ibiza also has its drawbacks, although such an atmosphere is not among them. Keep writing to me here, anyway, before you find out my address over there. All my mail will be forwarded.

.I want to backtrack to my last letter once again and tell you how very definitely I hope to get my hands on your copy of my manuscript on language, so that I can go through it and then transcribe my new essay and have it sent off to you. Besides this imminent expansion of your holdings, a lesser acquisition will have reached you by now—at least I sent you an envelope of new material a week ago, containing the first pieces written by Detlef Holz. But even his obligingness has its limits. I must forgo his assistance on an essay I am working on at the moment, because it would immediately compromise his name, the way his [predecessor's] name has been compromised.[2] Two review copies are forcing me into the disagreeable position of having to speak about Stefan George,

[1] 1920–21. See W.B.'s letter in *Briefe*, p. 239.
[2] This explains why he chose a new pseudonym ("K. A. Stempflinger") for the review he subsequently refers to, which was of two books on Stefan George. [Cf. *GS* 3:392–99.— TRANS.]

58

now, before a German audience. I believe I have understood this much: If ever God has smitten a prophet by fulfilling his prophecies, then this is the case with George.

I most likely wrote you that I finished an extended study on "The Present Social Position of French Writers," and to my credit have found a place for it in that very Frankfurt archive which escaped to Geneva. They have presented me with yet another commission, which will perhaps be more demanding and certainly less pleasurable.[3] Most peculiar, though, are the requests for my contributions that keep arriving from Germany, from offices that showed little interest in me in the past. The *Europäische Revue*, for example, asked me for suggestions about possible contributions.

But I am jotting down these brief bits of information for you mostly to give you some idea of the condition of my budget, or rather to demonstrate the utter impracticability of drawing up a budget at all. Since leaving Berlin, I have averaged a monthly income of about 100 Reichsmarks,[4] and this under the most unfavorable conditions. I don't wish to imply that I might not manage to earn even less than this tiny sum. But presumably not in the long run. On the contrary: I assume my earnings would increase in the long run, that is, if I am not completely severed from every means of production, as I am here. I could say more—but only tentatively—if I knew more about the impending German press laws.

And with that I have contributed to the discussion I learned of through your letter. I won't deny that I have more to say about it. To begin with, I should state that such a discussion does not leave me indifferent, by any means. It is of tremendous importance to me. But I would not be forty if I did not approach with extreme caution the idea of the mere possibility of change it contains. I tell myself that I might appear at this new shore in an ambiguous light. Thousands of intellectuals have made their way to you. One thing distinguishes them from me—and this seems to work in my favor at first glance. But thereafter—as you well know—the advantage becomes theirs. Precisely this: They represent blank pages. Nothing would have more fateful consequences than an attitude on my part that could be construed as though I were attempting to cover up a private calamity with a public one. This is something that has to be considered, since I have nothing and am attached to little. In such circumstances, one must shy away from every doubtful situation, since they

[3] This may well refer to the essay on Eduard Fuchs, which Benjamin was not keen on writing from the outset.

[4] About seven English pounds in those days, in the valid currency of the British Mandate of Palestine. Compare my reply of July 26, 1933 (letter 29).

can bear disproportionate consequences. I would be glad and fully prepared to come to Palestine, if you, or others concerned, assume that I could do so without provoking such a situation. And as far as I can tell, the same proviso can be couched in the question: Is there more room for me—for what I know and what I can do—there than in Europe? If there is not more, then there is less. This sentence needs no explanation. And neither does this final one: If I could improve upon my knowledge and my abilities there without abandoning what I have already accomplished, then I would not be the least bit indecisive in taking that step.

My brother is in a concentration camp.[5] God only knows what he has to endure there. But the rumors about his wounds were exaggerated in at least one respect. He did not lose an eye. I recently found this out from my sister. I only learned of Erich Baron's death from you.

I allowed K.M.'s greetings to take effect on me. The story of her first letter to me seems to be unfolding in the purest *Tristram Shandy* style.[6] With this observation we also best do justice to the utter uncertainty as to whether the letter will ever come into being.

All the best for today,

Yours, Walter

27

BENJAMIN TO SCHOLEM

FONDA MIRAMAR
SAN ANTONIO, IBIZA (BALEARES)
JUNE 29, 1933

Dear Gerhard,

This letter allows you to share a rare moment of bliss with me. What's more, your share has been earned, whereas I only come upon mine through one of those moods that enable Schluck or Jau[1] to wake up in a palace. Indeed, I have a whole house—if not a palace—all to myself for an entire day. And I started off the day early this morning with a bath. But as for your claim to the share I am transferring to you with this letter, I see it as accruing from the registered parcel and letter of the 15th, which both arrived here a few days ago.

---

[5] Georg Benjamin was in Sonnenburg concentration camp; see Hilde Benjamin, *Georg Benjamin*, p. 214. The discrepancy between the date in this letter and the date in Hilde Benjamin's book requires explanation, since H.B. fixes the transfer from prison to the concentration camp as not taking place until September. Could it be that his sister, Dora, who is referred to as a source for at least some of the particulars, was imprecise?

[6] An allusion to the way imbroglios are portrayed in Laurence Sterne's novel.

[1] In Gerhart Hauptmann's play of the same title.

The words "Fonda Miramar" are an empty phrase, which I request, however, that you continue to include in the address. Actually, I have been living with the Noeggeraths, as I must have written. I finally ended this situation, carrying out a plan I have harbored for some time. Although last year I found their house pleasant and the atmosphere bearable, both were just as unbearable, and, what's worse, became more and more so, when I sought them out this year. They had exchanged the house for a building on the opposite, much less pleasant, side of the bay, and the building is most aptly compared to a sounding board. The atmosphere has been poisoned by the extremely sad decline of the man's external, and above all his internal, quality of life, to say nothing of other events which I vastly prefer not to go into. I haven't really been following his fate; but the two excerpts I am familiar with—the one from Munich and the one from San Antonio—represent the most bitter contrast.[2]

As a first step, I managed to regain the old shore. True, I won't completely recover the solitude I found there last year. To avoid any economic burden, I will be living in a room—which happens to be already finished—in a new building still under construction. I hardly expect to find more furniture in it than a bed. The whole affair won't be without its difficulties, but it will allow me to spend the whole day in the immediate vicinity of water and woods. And I will be able to wrest opportunities to work from the latter. Before I try out this new arrangement, I have to go to Mallorca for a few days, to try to straighten out my passport problems. I will be very careful not to surrender my old passport. If anything, I'll tell them I lost it. I will then travel from Palma to Cala Ratjada for one or two days, where there is a colony of German writers around [Franz] Blei, and see what my colleagues are up to.

Since I am leaving tomorrow, I have to defer making the promised copy of the notes on the philosophy of language until my return. But the anticipation with which you are waiting for them fills me with some apprehension. For one thing, it's only a matter of a gloss of two or three typewritten pages. Moreover, you should think of them only as an addendum to the larger essay and—I add this in passing—by no means as commentary. If hints serve any purpose here, the text deals with a new turn in our old tendency to show the ways in which magic has been vanquished. But I want neither to overburden you with sharing the responsibility for this turn nor to raise your expectations, which could easily end in utter disappointment. Until now, I have done nothing more with the copy than to note the place where this kind of thinking might fit in the context of the first, earlier work.

[2] W.B. held a very high opinion of Felix Noeggerath in Munich in 1916, as is documented in his letters.

Did I write you that I have willy-nilly—or to say it in German, *nolens volens*—brought myself to do a small piece on Stefan George, whose topical nature was confirmed only days later by an essay of Eduard Korrodi's[3] on the same author. I need hardly add that he assures readers of the *Neue Zürcher Zeitung* of the very opposite of what I wish to convey to readers of the *Frankfurter*. It likewise goes without saying that those persons left in the decimated editorial office of the latter newspaper are of good Zurich persuasion on this point. This makes publication of my review, which I unfortunately had to send in handwritten, most doubtful.[4]

It occurs to me on this occasion that the University of Muri has seen fit to publish the first question for its competition. The name of its recipient will be publicly announced at the Ibiza Cercle Nautique. The contest theme is: Who was the first and who is the last cultural bolshevist? Entries are requested before July 15th, if possible. I believe that Kitty Marx should officially be requested by the dean's office to participate.

She wrote me a very nice letter, which includes laudatory mention of our correspondence, and I feel obliged to pass this on to you. You should convey my best wishes for her new life in Rehovot, wrapped in the tissue paper of the promise of an early reply.

In the meantime, you will have received a letter that deals with Palestine and me. I will probably find your reply, which means a great deal to me, only after I return from Mallorca. Meanwhile, as I already mentioned, the texts I requested from your archive have arrived. You will get the "Dienstmädchenromane" back, of course. But I am not sending it just yet, because I've taken steps to secure you a replacement copy, if at all possible. The same goes for the other pieces. You will be getting back the "Pariser Tagebuch" in any case. The first part of a new parcel is lying next to it, ready for mailing.

My brother is in prison. But the news of an eye injury did not prove to be true, thank God. Fascism is making great strides, outside Germany as well. I can see how things stand in Switzerland not merely by reading Korrodi, unfortunately, but also from certain editorial emendations the *Zeitschrift für Sozialforschung* proposes for my essay "Die gegenwärtige gesellschaftliche Lage des französischen Schriftstellers." The published form will probably contain so many deletions and distortions that I have reserved an original for your archive.[5]

My last parcel to you included an essay on Arnold Bennett. I cannot

---

[3] The editor of the literature section of the *Neue Zürcher Zeitung*.

[4] It appeared on July 12, 1933 (*GS* 3:392–99).

[5] I did not receive any such copy. In the editorial apparatus in *GS* 2:1515, only the publication in the *Zeitschrift für Sozialforschung* is mentioned, without reference to an unedited version.

deny great empathy for this author, even though he may not figure among the greatest novelists. I usually glide past modern popular fiction, with the exception of detective novels. But I am now reading Bennett's second two-volume novel, *The Clayhanger*, which is even longer than his first, and I am getting a lot out of it.—Have you heard of Leo Weisgerber? I was sent his "Die Stellung der Sprache im Aufbau der Gesamtkultur," an offprint from the truly noteworthy journal *Wörter und Sachen*, for review.[6]

Write back soon. Send my greetings to Rome, where I myself would like to be, and carry more greetings to Rehovot, so that you will be able to keep those due you with a clear conscience.

Yours, Walter

28

SCHOLEM TO BENJAMIN

Dear Walter,   JULY 6, 1933

This letter might have a chance to land in your hands on your birthday, and so I enclose my best wishes to you. You won't be able to say that you don't need them this year. The unfolding of events has led you so far away from the lifestyle you deserve that one immediately wants to think about the beginnings of a swing back in the other direction. I dare not think about the extent to which the events of this past year have assailed the very foundations of your inner existence, and it means little that you must easily have been able to conceive of them beforehand *in abstracto*. The event itself is always a different thing altogether, and in this respect you are very reticent, which is not to say that I do not find your attitude completely understandable, nor that I am not prepared to show deference to it.

Your letter postmarked June 16 also arrived only last week. In the interim, you should have in hand a second letter of mine, as well as the transcription of the essay on language and the other articles you wanted. I am mulling over what you wrote in connection with Palestine and your predicament, and would have liked to have been able to talk it over with

---

[6] Leo Weisgerber (born 1899), linguistic scholar. [*Die Stellung der Sprache im Aufbau der Gesamtkultur*, 2 vols. (Heidelberg: C. Winter, 1933).—TRANS.]

Escha. But she has been away for three weeks now; she has gone to Rome, where she met her sister from Hamburg to talk about her possibly settling in Palestine,[1] and she will only be back in Jerusalem next Sunday. I would therefore like to postpone my remarks about this for now. Suffice it to say that you are wrong if you think that intellectuals have been arriving here by the thousands. Nothing of the kind! The new arrivals belong to totally different social strata. Many are young, many are merchants, and many are Orthodox. Intellectuals—apart from doctors, teachers, and lawyers—are mainly represented only by the somewhat difficult figure of Gustav Steinschneider, and I can't imagine that his stay in this country is likely to last much longer.[2]

Your brother in a concentration camp, mine charged with "high treason," awaiting trial in Moabit's remand prison. And my mother writes letters that make me fearful every time that they could well land her before a special court, accused of "atrocity propaganda."

The semester has been over for a week and I am working at home. I have to write a few pages in German for the *Almanach des Verlages Schocken*,[3] the publishing house likely to bring out my major books, and once again I find this a difficult task. Summer happens to be very beautiful here just now, and since I am only half a married couple, I am making use of the opportunity to fulfill my various visiting obligations and the like in a successfully summery way. In between, I am learning Maimonides.

I take it that in the meantime you have received the letter you coveted from Kitty. She herself has moved to Rehovot and can undoubtedly look forward to a meaningful career there.

So much for today.

Accept my kindest regards,

Yours, Gerhard

---

[1] Therese (Tescha) Neufeld, a doctor's wife, came to the country in 1934 and has lived in Tel Aviv ever since.

[2] I was wrong about this, and G.S. still lives here today.

[3] "Nach der Vertreibung von Spanien" in the (first) *Almanach des Schocken Verlags auf das Jahr 5694* (1933–34), pp. 55–70.

29

SCHOLEM TO BENJAMIN

Dear Walter, JULY 26, 1933

Escha is back from Europe, and we are awaiting with little suspense the mechanical unfolding of the several family catastrophes that are now starting to occur with great speed. Various members of both our families will probably resettle here by winter, but God only knows to what extent the living space in this country can still be stretched and how all this will continue. To date, about five or six thousand immigrants have turned up from Germany, not counting those who have left again, and in such a small country one notices this very keenly. It is pretty much impossible to predict what changes ten times that number may cause. Many will undoubtedly be ready enough to come here; but it is more likely that the British government won't be prepared to allow such large groups into the country if the German government has robbed them of everything but the shirts on their backs.[1] As long as a fairly large group succeeds in getting its money out of Germany, things will still be possible, but the latest Berlin laws are of course designed to usher in the final campaign of plundering. Have you actually taken any steps to rescue at least your library from confiscation as property of an "enemy of the German people"? Have you been able in the meantime to have all your papers sent abroad?[2] It is still possible to do so at present, without undue difficulty. We are appalled to hear that valuable libraries have been sold off for absurdly trifling sums, in the rush to emigrate—because what cannot be taken along has simply lost all value. But one should at least keep as much as possible from the clutches of the *boches*.

As to your prospects here: It seems to us that it would be impossible for you to live here on 100 reichsmarks. Not that this is impossible prima facie—100 Reichsmarks are now £7 here, sufficient for a minimal existence—but we believe such a minimum would not be the end of it. There are also immense psychological difficulties: we see no possibility of your finding work or an occupation here that would be even halfway suitable. And it isn't good to live without work in this country, since to do so would put you in a psychologically unbearable position. You would no longer be able to get your ideas across to people. And the most important question

---

[1] Overall, about 60,000 German Jews stayed in Palestine/Israel.

[2] A thematically organized inventory of the papers W.B. kept in Berlin around 1930–31 exists in his handwriting. The larger part of these papers has been lost.

is whether you would have to live in the same isolation as on some Ibiza, or whether you would find a means of participating in such a wholly different way of life. There is no reason as such why you could not do your literary work here as well: Jerusalem has an advantage over Ibiza in this respect, first, because a few people like us are around, and second, because there are books. All of this would be quite fine if it were conceivable that you could pursue the present course of your work—so conspicuously European in orientation—without any difficulty. But we find it questionable whether a person could possibly feel well in this country without directly participating in life here, whether (*exempla docent*)[3] this would not rapidly bring about a morally unbearable state of estrangement in which life cannot be sustained. Perhaps all of this can only be decided by putting it to the test, but, on the other hand, the most elementary considerations tell us you would not be faced by moral and psychological tribulations of this sort in Paris. In our experience, in the long run only those people are able to live here who, despite all the problems and depressions, feel completely at one with this land and the cause of Judaism, and things are not always so easy for the new arrival, particularly for someone who occupies an intellectually progressive position. Indeed, such persons are the first to encounter difficulties, and they meet them the most easily; and such difficulties can only be overcome by means of a steady and resolute attitude. The questions you raise—whether there is more room for you here than there, and whether you could augment your knowledge and abilities here without relinquishing what you have already achieved—are not one and the same. To answer the first question would mean to assess the degree of your commitment to Judaism, a judgment that can be decided only here and not over there—and neither of us is in the position to judge this, after so many years. The second question can certainly be answered in the affirmative—only it is not the decisive question. What is decisive for your life here is whether you would also be able to put your knowledge and capabilities to use. My life here is only possible, as I think I have written you on various occasions, because I feel devoted to this cause, even if in the face of despair and ruination. Otherwise, the suspect nature of a renewal that tends to manifest itself mostly as hubris and linguistic decay would have torn me apart long ago. It is impossible, particularly for a person of your experience and insight, to be spared having to make such a decision here. That is how things stand, if I am correct in my perceptions.

I hope to receive samples from your most recent work soon, especially

---

[3] I was thinking of persons such as Arnold Zweig, and the many stories that circulated about his behavior. See also the end of letter 48.

the George essay. My productivity is slowly reawakening, and thus I have just written a few pages on the consequences of the expulsion of the Jews from Spain—you will also receive these promptly once they are in print.

Ernst David[4] died suddenly two weeks ago today, and I did not want to fail to inform you of this. He was one of the most pleasant people I have ever met; his purity and decisiveness of purpose, combined with the utmost humility and tact, made the many years of his acquaintance a joy. In the end he lived a mere minute away from us, but of course worked a lot in Cairo, where he simply, without any warning, dropped dead. I spoke at his funeral on behalf of his friends, and I feel a real loss. Would you like to send your condolences to his wife? He was, incidentally, a very pious man and lived here strictly according to Jewish Law. He kept steadfastly silent about his connections—and break—with the Goldberg circle,[5] even though he energetically solicited my opinion on the matter. I inherited a few very interesting books from what he left behind.

The day after tomorrow my favorite relative, Loni Ortenstein,[6] arrives from Rome for a two-week visit, which we are already looking forward to. And beyond that there is no shortage of new arrivals, such as our friend Käthe Ollendorf, Johannes R. Becher's divorced wife, who combines a rare faith in God, Judaism, and Zionism with an ever rarer goyish constitution in a remarkably attractive way, and who intends to set up as a doctor in Jerusalem. By contrast, the Steinschneider family, including its newest member, has, since the beginning of July, totally disappeared into the darkness of the plantation regions. In parting, I presented Karl and Kitty with *One-Way Street*, supplemented by a critical poem of my own. Your work will accordingly be well represented in Rehovot.

So much for today, because it is time for the mail. Please write soon, often, and at length; you can be assured of the most ardent interest at this end.

Kindest regards,

Yours, Gerhard

[4] W.B. had known Ernst and Lotte David from the war years until 1925. He held Ernst in high esteem; his wife less so.

[5] Regarding Oskar Goldberg and his circle, see Scholem, *From Berlin to Jerusalem*, pp. 146–48, as well as Scholem, *W.B.*, pp. 95–98. Ernst David financed the printing of Goldberg's main work, *Die Wirklichkeit der Hebräer* (Berlin: David, 1925).

[6] On Leonie (Loni) Ortenstein (1896–1944), see *From Berlin to Jerusalem*, pp. 109–12.

30

BENJAMIN TO SCHOLEM

FONDA MIRAMAR
SAN ANTONIO, IBIZA (BALEARES)
JULY 31, 1933

Dear Gerhard,

The mere sight of this stationery should suffice to make you, as the unchallenged authority on my letter writing, realize that something is amiss.[1] And that fact exonerates me for at least part of the three weeks I let go by without thanking you for the beautiful letter you sent me for my birthday. In particular, it covers me for the continued nonappearance of the notes on language you are entitled to.

You see, I have been ill for about a fortnight now. And because the outbreak of the illness—not very serious in itself—coincided with the first fits of July heat (perhaps no coincidence), I had my hands full to keep myself somewhat going under such difficult circumstances. I did so, on the one hand, by drawing upon all available reserves of detective novels, and, on the other, by intensively resuming my work on the "Berliner Kindheit um 1900." A new section, which I fitted into the existing ones, had me sequestered from all other work for a while. A few pages have come into being under the title "Loggien," and I can only say very good things about them and add that they contain the most precise portrait I shall ever be able to give of myself. I hope you will see the piece in print in the near future.[2]

With it, of course, the Detlevian Holz[3]—which I have thrown upon the flame of my life—will flare up for more or less the last time. The new press laws are already taking shape, and after they go into force, my appearances in the German press will require a far more impenetrable disguise than heretofore.

And of course, probably more seldom. This would have left the future completely overcast had not a somewhat more hopeful perspective become visible over the last few days. It was imparted in a letter promising me free living quarters in a house that Baroness Goldschmidt-Rothschild has reserved in Paris for refugee Jewish intellectuals. Speyer made use of his connections with the world of Jewish finance,[4] apparently with success, in that a dispatch arrived here yesterday making the invitation

---

[1] The letter was written on irregularly sized, grayish blue paper, of a kind he never used.

[2] "Loggien" first appeared in the *Vossische Zeitung* on August 1, 1933 (*GS* 4:294–96).

[3] [The German means "wood."—TRANS.]

[4] Wilhelm Speyer, who himself had been baptized, came from a Jewish banking family in Frankfurt, which in its time was as well known as the Goldschmidts.

official. But even this—a free place to live—is an extremely unstable foundation in an expensive city like Paris. However, I do not want to rule out the possibility that the same route that has led me this far may take me somewhat farther still, for this invitation undoubtedly also implies a more or less far-reaching introduction. Furthermore, the steps I took in the matter of my passport have been rewarded with success because of a fortunate constellation for which I may also claim some of the credit. I am now the owner of a new passport, even before my old—supposedly lost—one has expired.

I can of course only regard the Paris invitation as a happy intermezzo; in no way do I see that it opens up any long-term prospects. And precisely because the matter our last letters warily touched upon—the Palestinian options—deals only with the long term, whatever we are able to discuss in this regard must definitely take precedence over short-term European combinations. Yet you have a sufficient picture of my situation in your mind's eye to know how reassuring even a mere breathing spell must be for me. At any rate, I would have faced a winter on Ibiza only with unmitigated horror.

With regard to my poor health, I have a very unpleasant inflammation of a wound on my lower right thigh. Luckily it started up just when I happened to be in the town of Ibiza for a few hours. In San Antonio, my situation would have become grotesque. I live here in a hotel room at one peseta a day—the price indicates what the room looks like—and I drag myself through the town for unavoidable errands. If the situation doesn't improve in the next two or three days, I will be forced to keep myself completely immobile. A German doctor whom I have unearthed here delights in painting daily pictures of my chances of dying, should a complication arise.

I am separated from all books and papers, since they are in San Antonio. If I had the necessary books, I could at least start work on a commission from the *Frankfurter Zeitung* to write something for the 200th anniversary of the death of Wieland,[5] whom I hardly know at all. But I have been supplied only with pitiful occasional pieces. The French translation of the "Berliner Kindheit" is, by contrast, making progress. We work on it every day. The translator doesn't know a word of German. As you can imagine, the technique we use is not to be trifled with. But the results are nearly always outstanding.

As I told you, the truly hot spell has begun here. The Spaniards, who are familiar with its effects, speak of "August madness" as a very com-

[5] *GS* 2:395–404. It appeared in the national edition of the *Frankfurter Zeitung* of September 5, 1933.

69

mon occurrence.[6] I find it quite amusing to observe its manifestations in foreigners. Their numbers are growing, and, as you might easily imagine, there are some quite remarkable specimens among their ranks.[7]

I was interrupted here by the doctor, who told me that they will probably have to make an incision. That means an imminent return to San Antonio is out of the question. Nonetheless, send mail only to that address.

Even though you will now have to wait a while longer for the theory of language, I hope to receive a copy of your Schocken manuscript very soon, all the more as I have been exemplary in replacing with substitutes all those items you were kind enough to let me have from your archive of my material. Moreover, my essay on Stefan George should also be in your hands by now. If I can believe what I am told, there must have been a few bright lights who knew what to think of "Stempflinger." I would like very much to know what you think of the article.

So much for today. With kindest regards,

Yours, Walter

31

BENJAMIN TO SCHOLEM

FONDA MIRAMAR
SAN ANTONIO, IBIZA (BALEARES)
SEPTEMBER 1, 1933

Dear Gerhard,

Nearly a month has gone by since I received your last letter. But this time I don't have to search for reasons for my long silence, even though I would gladly trade actual reasons for such embarrassment. First, I have hardly emerged at all from poor health over the last two months. It is nothing serious.[1] But periods of exhaustion and complications in the external circumstances of my life are meshing so perfectly into a chain

[6] Days later (August 12 and 13), Benjamin was to write the autobiographical note "Agesilaus Santander," which I published in the volume *Zur Aktualität Walter Benjamins*, ed. S. Unseld (Frankfurt am Main: Suhrkamp Verlag, 1972), pp. 94–102. [See letter 31, note 3; English translation by Werner Dannhauser in Scholem, *On Jews and Judaism in Crisis* (New York: Schocken Books, 1976), pp. 204 –8.—TRANS.]

[7] Since W.B. kept all, or nearly all, of the cards and letters sent him during that time, it might be possible—if one had access to his papers in the East Berlin Academy of Arts—to identify the people he had in mind here. The woman mentioned in the next letter was certainly among them.

[1] He was thus not yet ill with malaria, as has sometimes been supposed. See my essay cited in note 6 to the preceding letter.

of mishaps, that I am held in check for days or weeks. Add to that an urgent, agonizing article that had to be finished by a certain deadline, and which it was virtually impossible to prepare because of the dearth of documentation. The *Frankfurter Zeitung* commissioned an article for Wieland's 200th birthday, and I had never read a line of his. I hope they get it in time and that the drudgery of the last ten days won't have been in vain.

But these weeks of silence have not been lost in terms of what is the most important object of our correspondence at the moment. I reread your last letter—with more distance—and noticed that a misunderstanding threatens to arise. When, many, many weeks ago, you first considered the prospect of my coming to Palestine, I did not imagine this for a moment to mean that Palestine would, in such a case, represent just another—more or less expedient—place for me to reside. But since it is precisely this conception that you attribute to me, and which you seem to be arguing kindly but firmly against in your last letter, I cannot let the opportunity pass to reject it. No, I never for a moment conceived that my stay could take a shape such that the present direction of my work would be left entirely intact; I never viewed this as belonging to the realm of possible solutions. And, in raising, as you did, the question of my coming to Palestine, I thought I perceived a bold, and in no way frivolous, readiness on your part to put the question of my solidarity with the cause of Judaism to the vote of experience. What's more, I wholeheartedly agree with you that we can know nothing about this question "after so many years," as your last letter put it. But I never had the merest shadow of a doubt that the decision on this question—and thus on the most essential matters we touched on with each other—has to be made before a Hebrew forum, as difficult as circumstances make it for me to express this in words that must seem more or less like a shabby excuse. But I insist on doing so, not least in order to distinguish clearly between this forum and others one might consider. For it is obvious that neither of us is prepared to investigate my "solidarity with the cause of Zionism"; the issue is just as unsure as my presumable empathy with the Orthodox way of life of an Ernst David or the faith in God of a Käthe Ollendorf is. The result of the investigation could only turn out to be completely negative. I do not disavow connections. But it seems important to me, after your last letter, to tell you that I did not for a moment see the perspective of your previous letter as being defined by anything other than the base line drawn by the Hebrew.

To return to Ernst David: After receiving your news, I was amazed to find a precise impression of his appearance and physiognomy in my memory. It is hardly possible for me to write to his wife, but you would

71

definitely be acting in accord with my feelings if you would tell her this in a few words.

Regarding my condition, I am once again lying sick in bed, suffering from a very painful inflammation in the leg. Doctors, or even medicine, are nowhere to be found here, since I am living totally in the country, thirty minutes away even from the village of San Antonio. Under such primitive conditions, the facts that you can hardly stand on your feet, hardly speak the native tongue, and in addition even have to work, tend to bring you up against the margins of what is bearable. As soon as I have regained my health, I will return to Paris. But I do not know how long [it] will take. In any case, you should keep writing to this address, since I have my mail forwarded. I will send you word as soon as I arrive in Paris.

Meanwhile, the rest of my archives—above all, the part that contains my political work on literature—is now out of Germany and has arrived in Paris. The transfer took place with such discretion that even I do not know who brought it about. A man I have known for many years, who left Berlin at about the same time as I did, had offered to take care of the matter. But the fears for my library persist. The problem is primarily a financial one. Even if I could find a trustworthy person in Paris, within whose four walls I could set up the library again, I still wouldn't know how to finance the packing and the transport.[2]

It hardly needs to be stated that I am facing my stay in Paris with the utmost reserve. The Parisians are saying: "*Les émigrés sont pires que les boches*" ["The emigrés are worse than the Krauts"], and that should give you an accurate idea of the kind of society that awaits one there. I shall try to thwart its interest in me the same way I have done in the past.

I am somewhat depressed at not having yet sent you the promised meditations on the philosophy of language. It is as hard for me to relinquish them in this unrevised form as it is to revise them. As soon as my health improves, I shall presumably be capable of cutting through this Gordian knot. *En attendant*, I must ask you to be patient just a bit longer.

If these excuses have mollified you, then the way should be clear for a few requests. To begin with, you know I cannot possibly be uninterested in a critical dedicatory poem to *One-Way Street*. On the contrary, I would like you to send me a certified copy of it *very, very* soon [!]—complete with all insinuations and sarcastic comments. And since I am on the topic of this branch of your production, I really must renew my request for a copy of your poem on the Angelus Novus. I have met a

[2] A large portion of these books later reached Svendborg and Paris, where I saw them in 1938.

72

woman here who is his female counterpart,[3] and I do not want to withhold from her the beautiful greeting you addressed to her brother. I am furthermore awaiting with utmost eagerness your gloss on the expulsion of the Jews from Spain. You should long ago have received the printed matter you had sent me and the other pieces I returned from your archive of my stuff. Work on the piece commemorating Wieland kept me away from things closer to my heart for some time. I just completed a new section of the "Berliner Kindheit um 1900" entitled "Der Mond."[4]

Please write me if you have read Wiesengrund's *Kierkegaard* in the meantime.

A fond farewell, and let me hear from you soon,

Yours, Walter

32

SCHOLEM TO BENJAMIN

Dear Walter,   SEPTEMBER 4, 1933

Your letter of July 31 took more than two weeks to reach me, after which I left it unopened for another two weeks, because I was completely caught up in my work following my cousin Loni's departure—and this is

---

[3] This formulation, which had slipped my mind, is remarkably similar to the one he used on August 13 in the sketch "Agesilaus Santander." There he writes that the angel of whom he is speaking "sent his female form after the masculine one reproduced in the picture [*Angelus Novus* by Paul Klee] by way of the longest, most fateful detour, even though both happened to be—although they did not know each other—intimately connected with each other." In my commentary on this text, I related this and other sentences dealing with the woman in question to Jula Cohn, who for years was the object of his love (see pp. 115–19 of my essay in *Walter Benjamin zu ehren* [the commemorative volume published privately on the ninetieth anniversary of Benjamin's birth and reprinted, in revised form, as *Zur Aktualität Walter Benjamins*; cf. "Walter Benjamin and His Angel," pp. 219–22.— TRANS.]). Thus, I also remarked that it was possible that the sentences which follow later might refer to a number of women who fascinated him. The present letter now raises the possibility that the text does not (or not only) deal with Jula Cohn, but also with a previously unidentified woman (perhaps Hélène Léger?), whom he first met "here," i.e., on Ibiza. He also speaks of her at the end of his next letter (no. 33). Both versions of the final sentence of "Agesilaus Santander" could also very well refer to her. Of course, my earlier interpretation of this final sentence ("Walter Benjamin and His Angel," pp. 227–28) as referring to his experience with Jula Cohn remains plausible, since he had written a letter shortly before (on July 2, 1933) that attests to his enduring bond to her (*Briefe*, no. 224). In any case, renewed thought needs to be given to the whole mysterious problem of these sentences.

[4] In an undated letter to Gretel Adorno (*Briefe*, p. 591), apparently written during the second half of August 1933, he states that he still has to finish this section (*GS* 4:300–302).

the result. In the meantime, you will have received another letter of mine, which mainly deals with the Palestine Question and which must have crossed with your letter. First and foremost, I truly hope your health has improved. I read a long feuilleton about Ibiza in the *Prager Tagblatt*, written by a female colleague of yours who appears to live just around the corner from you. Although I didn't glean any news from it about you, I did learn about the increasing worldliness of your paradise. After your last letter, however, I believe I am justified in conjecturing that, once you have fully recuperated, your stay there won't last much longer anyway. I gather from your happier news about the invitation to Paris, as well as the successful extension of your passport, that you are likely to be in France during the winter. Just today I read the list of the first 35 fortunate ones to be relieved of the burden of German citizenship, and of their assets at the same time. I take this occasion to reiterate my very urgent advice to attend to the transfer of all your papers abroad, and to do so in time, for very soon it could be too late. If you do not have a secure location, I am always prepared to keep as many of your things for you as possible. Perhaps you can make use of this offer. Your library— for whose housing I admittedly have no advice or proposal to make— should also be exposed for as short a time as possible to the chance of being auctioned off one day for some sin or other committed in your family's past, present, and future.

Is there any hope of bringing out the "Berliner Kindheit" in French as a book? And what else are you working on? With regard to your George article, suffice it to say that I would welcome your trying to express your opinion, which is very relevant to current events, even if it is not generally accepted, in a neutral place, unequivocally, and without any watering down or diplomacy. For, in the final instance, it is here and nowhere else that the seeds of the Third Reich lie buried, and the perspectives that a thoughtful observer like you can discern in George's work in the light of the Reich's sad victory should not be obscured or diluted by a concern for the censors.

August has been very beautiful and rather cool here, in contrast to the weather in Spain. The three weeks my cousin spent here—she is now back in Rome—were pleasant and enjoyable in every respect. We also traveled around the country, and she was completely enthralled and left as an enthusiastic Zionist, as far as such a thing can be imagined (and it is, of course) in the case of a "Nardeg" ("Nicht-arierin im Sinne des Gesetzes") [Non-Aryan under the Law], the most popular expression in the new jargon that has accommodated itself to the times), meaning in this case a woman who is half Jewish. The day after her departure from Jaffa, I was in Rehovot at the Steinschneiders', where I conveyed your greetings and news to Kitty Marx and otherwise talked a great deal about you. There—as everywhere in Palestine—people are extremely preoccupied with moving their families out of Germany. But the affairs of my own family are utterly unclear at present. My mother spent a short holiday convalescing in France, from where she wrote extensively about the (hopeless) situation my brother [Werner] is in; my sister-in-law's situation is even worse and seems to be threatening the whole family as well. They seem to have acted with a carelessness totally incomprehensible to anyone else and without the slightest feeling for the situation created by Hitler's seizure of power—operating instead on the assumption that things under fascism would be much as they had been under Brüning and that nothing could happen to them anyway. It is impossible to predict what will happen to them, one has to expect the worst. My mother doesn't want to leave yet. My brother Erich, however, is reportedly already diligently learning Hebrew.

I am working, and feel quite good doing so. As soon as the article on Spain is published, I'll send it to you. Otherwise, I am writing in Hebrew, as is appropriate under the circumstances. The German catastrophe has made my work at the university easier insofar as I probably won't have to take on giving the lectures, etc., on Jewish philosophy, since Julius Guttmann will most likely be invited here from Berlin. Should this occur, which I would find very congenial, I would be provided with a professorship solely for Kabbalah studies, once all the negotiating has been completed. This is likely to happen at the next trustees' meeting, which has been postponed from August to December on account of the elaborate negotiations regarding the university's expansion and the creation of new positions. This will afford me the opportunity to once again turn my full attention to my real work, and in any case I have already canceled the announcement of my lectures on Jewish philosophy—with a huge sigh of relief. I have bigger projects in mind, exploiting last year's travel souvenirs. I will write to you about this as soon as affairs here are clearer. Incidentally, the study of medieval Arabic-Jewish philosophers, which took up the greater part of last year, was by no means unproductive for my real interests, and my library especially profited [from] this section.

I hope to hear from you soon.

Best regards and wishes for your health and the New Year in general, which begins, here at least, two weeks from now,

Yours, Gerhard

33

BENJAMIN TO SCHOLEM

Dear Gerhard,   [CA. SEPTEMBER 10–12, 1933]

I am taking advantage of a dismal situation, in which I am only capable of writing letters and dictating—and barely of the former, since I have lost my fountain pen and have to make do as best I can—to prepare the parcel I long ago promised you. The somewhat lessened sense of responsibility, a symptom accompanying the ever-present pain and the dearth of soothing perspectives, turns out to be a relief in this case. Who knows when I would have decided to send the enclosed—or what will follow it —had circumstances been different.

It should by no means be assumed that the unauthoritative methodological thoughts I am presenting to you (and no one else) will ever result in the humblest stabs at an exemplification. So please stow them away in the least accessible chambers of your archive.[1]

I do not know when I will be capable of making the trip to Paris. I am bedridden here in the countryside, virtually without help, with no doctor, and unable to take a few steps without the greatest pain. A sorry state of affairs. The case itself is not that serious: many sores, small ones, that have become infected, and—whether from the heat or my problematic diet of recent months—an obvious shortage of recuperative powers.

There is hardly anything new to report since my last letter, and I don't even know if I wrote that one in a fundamentally different situation. As for this one, bear in mind that every single word has been born from within a swarm of flies.

You will understand that in this condition I am reading a hodgepodge of things. Even theology,[2] for want of acceptable detective novels.[3] Thanks to a—quite decent—French book on Luther,[4] I have now grasped for the fifth or sixth time in my life what is meant by justification through faith. But I have the same trouble here as I have with infinitesi-

---

[1] The short text on the mimetic faculty.

[2] He read Albert Mirgeler, *Geschichte und Dogma* [Hellerau: Hegner, 1928], which he had been wanting to review since 1928, and Detlev Nielsen, *Der geschichtliche Jesus* [1924; Munich: Meyer & Jessen, 1928].

[3] As always in those years, he preferred to read anything by Georges Simenon he could lay his hands on—which in Ibiza numbered six volumes.

[4] The reference is to Lucien Febvre, *Un Destin: Martin Luther* (Paris: Rieder, 1928) [*Martin Luther: A Destiny*, trans. Roberts Tapley (New York: E. P. Dutton, 1929)].

mal calculus: as soon as I have mastered it for a few hours, it vanishes again for just as many years.

Do you know under what sign the literary emigrés are beginning to gather within the framework of an Amsterdam-based periodical? Well, precisely under the sign they deserve most, namely, with Klaus Mann as editor-in-chief. His uncle opens the first issue with a polemic against the regime,[5] so feeble that it is provocative. I can even see the day approaching when I will attempt to have myself published in these surroundings.[6]

The activity of German publishers last winter was limited, as concerns me, to robbing me of all my copies of "Berliner Kindheit," and I will now have to replace them in Paris at great expense. It now contains 34 sections. I have already sent you the "Loggien" and would have liked to hear what you think about it. I consider it my self-portrait. A new section, recently completed, is called "Der Mond."

Up to this point, the only thing these lines have left out is an explicit addendum characterizing my condition. This now makes its way into this letter on the back of this page,[7] on the occasion of an attempt to change my bandages. The incredible difficulties endured in obtaining any water make me bemoan its improper use much more than my breach of etiquette.

My last letter included several requests, which I hereby repeat in brief, especially the appeals for the two poems: the one on *One-Way Street* and the one on *Angelus Novus*. The latter will be welcomed here with full honors, since I plan to bring it to the attention of the only person I intend to introduce as a neophyte to this narrow sector of angelology, which happens to be the only one I have been familiar with since acquiring the *Angelus*.[8]

If you knew how bad the worst mattress in the world is (I am lying on it), you would call the state of affairs described by this letter relatively euphoric.

All the best. Write soon. Fondly,

Yours, Walter

[5] Heinrich Mann introduced the first issue of *Die Sammlung*.

[6] See *Briefe*, p. 657. Benjamin's participation failed to come about owing to his demand for higher remuneration for his (already typeset) review of Brecht's *Dreigroschenroman* (Amsterdam: A. de Lange, 1934) [*Threepenny Novel*, trans. Desmond Vesey, verses trans. Christopher Isherwood (1937; New York: Grove Press, 1956)].

[7] A streak caused by water runs through the letter's first page and discolors the paper to look bluish because of its effect on the ink.

[8] See letter 31, note 3. This very obvious reiteration of his intimation in that letter suggests that the letters to W. B. housed in East Berlin could yield more precise information about this "great unknown."

34

Scholem to Benjamin

Dear Walter,

JERUSALEM
SEPTEMBER 19, 1933

Last Friday I received your letter of September 1, which I read with the greatest concern after such a relatively long interval. Early Sunday morning I drove to Tel Aviv to deliver to the printer an essay on the Provençal origins of the Kabbalah—an essay I wrote in recent weeks with great satisfaction—and when I returned I found a letter from Kitty together with one from you to her. The remarks in it directed at me reached their addressee after the letter written ten days later. In the meantime, I have already written you once and hope that the promptness of my reply will spur you on to similar feats.

It would depress me greatly if my statements on the possibility of your living here kindled any discord. True, the issue of your residence in Palestine should be judged as you indicate: the question of your solidarity with the cause of Judaism must indeed be put to the vote of experience, but I cannot lose sight of the external difficulties. Since you are inclined to throw yourself into your work with such intensity, one of two eventualities is likely to occur: either the work on Hebrew won't leave you time for any other—and for now I see no other work than the kind that feeds you at present, however inadequately—or else work and the necessities of material existence will push the other aside. This is a very important consideration, particularly given your special temperament and situation. I am afraid that there is no possibility of guaranteeing your livelihood here; there is nothing left to hope for from the university, so how could we find a way that would not embitter life for you here from the very beginning? I have racked my brains on this and other ways of making a living. Beyond all this, even if it were possible, the duration of your stay here would, as I must have written, depend on still other powers—call them what we like, they always boil down to the same thing.

Your persistent illness makes me fear that something more serious might be behind it. Have you seen a doctor in the meantime? We wish you a truly complete recovery and the best of health!

I have no idea of how the emigrés live in Paris—we hear that, apart from a minority, they must be in dire poverty. Perhaps you could fill me in, once you have gained some insight into the situation there. I will send you the essay on Spain in the Schocken *Almanach* as soon as I receive it

78

myself. The book should be coming out any day now. I am still stubbornly awaiting the notes on language with undaunted courage because I am convinced that the final review will turn out to be all the more remarkable.—*My* philological inclinations were unleashed again in full force in an essay[1] in which I undertook to interpret a 30-line letter from the earliest period of the Kabbalah and managed to conclude the essay in as many pages, without feeling any guilt about this excess. Nothing quite compares with the attraction of working out an incisive interpretation of a text. The consequences of such pursuits are as follows: I was appointed in August (but I was only told now) Professor of Jewish Mysticism and perhaps also of History of Jewish Religion, and you can therefore congratulate me. This does not mean more money, of course; things remain unchanged in that respect, but otherwise it is very pleasant: a full professorship of my own, since the other one for Jewish Philosophy has been given (with my happy and relieved consent) to Julius Guttmann of the Academy for Jewish Studies in Berlin (who is twenty years older than I). I am more than pleased with this solution, which leaves me free to concentrate on my real work and also keeps the broader field completely covered. So much for today. You will receive this letter on Yom Kippur, the day that marks my first ten years in Palestine.—The poems are included. What might an Angela Nova look like?[2] More next time.

Yours, Gerhard

Since I happen to be here & undertaking research (& = and) at the behest of Prof. Dr. Scholem (read Gerhard), I must tell you that my information about "Gerhard and the *Mother*" was incorrect & I refer to the disclosures of said Gerhard himself, who claims to have told you that [Brecht's] *Mother* leaves him cold. Since I already began to mention the Jewish holidays in my letter to you, allow me to note, as the correspondent above has done, that this will probably reach you on Yom Kippur, which will no doubt evoke the greatest interest in you.

Your dear Frau Steinschneider

Greetings from Angelus

I hang nobly on the wall
Looking at nobody at all.
I have been from heaven sent,
A man of angelic descent.

---

[1] The essay (already mentioned at the beginning of the letter) appeared in 1934 in the (Hebrew) *Festschrift* for the poet C. N. Bialik's sixtieth birthday.

[2] This very personal question remained unanswered.

The human within me is good
And does not interest me.
I stand in the care of the highest
And do not need a face.

From where I come, that world
Is measured, deep, and clear.
What keeps me together in one piece
Is a wonder, it would appear.

In my heart stands the town
Whence God has sent me.
The Angel who bears this seal
Does not fall under its spell.

My wing is ready to beat,
I am all for turning back.
For, even staying in timeless time
Would not grant me much fortune.

My eye is darkest black and full,
My gaze is never blank.
I know what I am to announce
And many other things.

I am an unsymbolic thing.
My meaning is what I am.
You turn the magic ring in vain.
I have no sense.

[*Gruss vom Angelus*

*Ich hänge edel an der Wand / und schaue keinen an / Ich bin vom
Himmel her gesandt / Ich bin ein Engelsmann. / Der Mensch in
meinem Raum ist gut / und interessiert mich nicht / Ich stehe in des
Höchsten Hut / und brauche kein Gesicht. / Der ich entstamme, jene
Welt / ist massvoll, tief und klar. / Was mich im Grund
zusammenhält / erscheint hier wunderbar. / In meinem Herzen steht
die Stadt / in die mich Gott geschickt. / Der Engel der dies Sigel
hat / wird nicht von ihr berückt. / Mein Flügel ist zum Schwung
bereit / ich kehrte gern zurück / denn blieb ich auch lebendige Zeit /
ich hätte wenig Glück.[1] / Mein Auge ist ganz schwarz und voll /*

---

[1] [Benjamin used the fifth stanza as the epigram to the ninth of his "Theses on the Concept of History," *Illuminations*, p. 257.—Trans.]

Mein Blick wird niemals leer / Ich weiss was ich verkünden soll /
und weiss noch vieles mehr. / Ich bin ein unsymbolisch Ding /
bedeute was ich bin / Du drehst umsonst den Zauberring / Ich habe
keinen Sinn.]

To Karl and Kitty
With a Copy of "One-Way Street"

Is this the picture of the one-way street's landscape,
Which you want to walk through?
I almost doubt it. But know
Where you should go.
And many streets have return alleys
Which you don't see.
And it is untrue that nothing happens to you
When you're unsure which direction to take.
No negotiating here when collisions occur;
Lightning strikes.
And if you find yourself suddenly completely transformed:
It is not just seeming.
In the old days all roads led
To God and his name, somehow.
We are not pious.
We remain in the Profane,
And where God once stood now stands: Melancholy.

[An Karl und Kitty
Mit einem Exemplar der "Einbahnstrasse"

Ob dies das Landschaftsbild der Einbahnstrasse ist, / die Ihr
durchlaufen wollt? / Ich darf es fast bezweifeln. Aber wisst, / wohin
Ihr sollt. / So viele Strassen haben Rückfahrtwege, / die man nicht
sieht. / Und kommt man mit der Richtung ins Gehege: / Es ist nicht
wahr, dass einem nichts geschieht. / Bei Kollisionen wird hier nicht
verhandelt; / der Blitz schlägt ein. / Und findest Du Dich plötzlich
ganz verwandelt: / Es ist kein Schein. / In alten Zeiten führten alle
Bahnen / zu Gott und seinem Namen, irgendwie. / Wir sind nicht
fromm. Wir bleiben im Profanen / und wo einst Gott stand, steht:
Melancholie.]

35

BENJAMIN TO SCHOLEM

HÔTEL REGINA DE PASSY
6 RUE DE LA TOUR
PARIS XVI
OCTOBER 16, 1933

Dear Gerhard,

Even if these wishes arrive far too late for Rosh Hashanah,[1] they will at least reach you in time for the long-sought and now official establishment of your academic duties, not to mention the title of Professor.

Before I touch on this or anything else from our last exchange, let me just sketch out my situation. I arrived in Paris seriously ill. By this I mean that I had not recovered at all while on Ibiza, and the day I was finally able to leave coincided with the first in a series of very severe attacks of fever. I made the journey under unimaginable conditions, and, immediately after my arrival here, malaria was diagnosed. Since then, a rigorous course of quinine has cleared my head, even though my strength has yet to be fully restored. It was considerably weakened by the numerous hardships of my stay on Ibiza—not the least of which was the wretched diet.

You won't be surprised to learn that I am faced here with as many question marks as there are street corners in Paris. Only one thing is certain, that I have no intention of making a futile attempt to earn my living by writing for French journals. If I could place something in a representative journal (*Commerce, NRF*) once in a while—although even this seems unlikely—I would welcome it because of the attendant prestige. But to try to make a French literary career my means of subsistence, so shortly after a series of still lingering setbacks, would soon rob me of what's left of my no-longer-unlimited power of initiative. I would prefer any occupation, even a menial one, to whiling my time away in the editorial antechambers of the street tabloids. Probably the best I can hope for right now is a chance to earn something doing part-time bibliographical or library work.

I have hardly been out of my bed, and hence have been unable to activate my local contacts. I would welcome any assistance toward broadening them in a fruitful way. Is Robert Eisler by any chance in Paris?[2]

Friends have transported the major part of my archives[3] to Paris, at

[1] Rosh Hashanah, the Jewish New Year.

[2] On Robert Eisler (1882–1949), see Scholem, *W.B.*, pp. 131–32, and *From Berlin to Jerusalem*, pp. 127–32. At that point he had already been back in Austria for some time.

[3] By "my archives" W.B. evidently meant something other than the totality of his papers and correspondence, most of which, as already mentioned, was lost.

least the manuscript section. The Heinle papers are the only manuscript material of any importance still missing. The problem of securing my library is mainly a question of money, and that by itself presents a formidable enough task. Add to this that I have rented my Berlin apartment out furnished and cannot simply remove the library, which is an essential part of the inventory. On the other hand, the person renting it only pays what the landlord demands.

I am still waiting with a certain sense of uneasiness for acknowledgment that you've received the notes on language I sent you in typescript from Ibiza. You should have gotten them shortly after the 19th of September, the date of your last letter. I myself am looking forward to your contribution to the Schocken *Almanach*. I read your poem on the *Angelus Novus* again with undiminished admiration. I would place it among the best that I know.—I reread the dedication in *One-Way Street* with sympathy[4] enlivened by recent written news from K.M.-S. Please convey to her my kindest regards the next chance you have and assure her that a letter will soon notify her when I have regained my strength somewhat.

Haas is editing a journal in Prague called *Die Welt im Wort*. I would much rather send you the first issue—which has just reached me—if you wish, than comment about it at great length. Please consider even these three lines confidential.

Whether or not I will be able to move into the quarters Frau von Goldschmidt-Rothschild promised me has become rather problematic because of a series of oversights and delays far too complex to recount here.[5] It is also gradually becoming clear that the apartment is by no means free of charge.

Take it to heart that this is the first long letter I have written since my illness, and let me hear good news from you soon and at length.

Yours, Walter

36

SCHOLEM TO BENJAMIN

JERUSALEM
OCTOBER 24, 1933

Dear Walter,

It troubles me that I haven't heard anything from you for a long while. My fear is that your health, which I was certain you would have regained

---

[4] The reserve in Benjamin's formulation is unmistakable.
[5] It didn't work out in the end.

by now, is still far from the best, even to the point of leaving you weary of writing. I therefore also have to assume that you are still on Ibiza. I am amazed that no Jewish doctor from Germany, plentiful as they are in Spain, has yet made it to Ibiza to take charge of your treatment. The ones I know have already pressed on as far as Palma. Please report to me soon on your condition and your situation in general. Has the new German press law we have observed (from our vantage point) here already had repercussions for you, or are you, as a mere contributor, not yet caught up in the whole mendacious muzzling of people? It has been a long time since I received anything published of yours—with the exception of one section from "Berliner Kindheit." I suspect that you will have to decide whether you want to give up working for journals inside Germany—if this hasn't already become impossible—in order to contribute to German journals published abroad.

I have thus far read about two-thirds of the book on Kierkegaard by Wiesengrund—whose name I just read next to 50 others on the official list of people dismissed from [the University of] Frankfurt—and to my mind the book combines a sublime plagiarism of your thought with an uncommon chutzpah, and it will ultimately not mean much for a future, objective appraisal of Kierkegaard, in marked contrast to your analysis of the *Trauerspiel*. I regret that our opinions probably differ in this matter. If you yourself had taken the trouble to write this book as a kind of "applied one-way street into melancholy,"[1] the result would have been infinitely more real and somewhat less "schnokes." My immediate thought at many a passage was: *utinam Walter ipse scripsisset!*[2] I am convinced that you would not have indulged in the pleasure of certain "unmaskings," which seem especially to fascinate the author in question. Much of it is of course quite good; other passages I purely and simply didn't understand.

Much is happening here. I have already written to you about myself, my professorship, etc. I have also been given the chance to lecture on Jewish religious history and I plan to make use of this opportunity later, at the right time. The semester begins next week, and I will go to work with great pleasure. Baumgardt[3] (who has not been dismissed) was among the latest visitors who were able to fill me in about the situation in German universities. He will stay here throughout the winter, if not

[1] An allusion to the poem on *One-Way Street*, enclosed with letter 34.

[2] "Oh, if only Walter had written that himself!" (i.e., less affectedly).

[3] David Baumgardt (1890–1963), who lectured on philosophy at the University of Berlin from 1924 to 1935, had been an acquaintance of W.B. since the days of the "Neopatheticians" (1912–14). I got to know him in 1918. His book referred to here was entitled *Der Kampf um den Lebenssinn unter den Vorläufern der modernen Ethik.*

forever. I had not seen him for 16 years, but I will have ample opportunity to form an opinion. He just published a ponderous new tome, which is not exactly included in my reading plans.

I am very much occupied with my Kabbalah, and I am at the moment negotiating with Schocken about some of my publications. I still have not received the Schocken *Almanach* which I promised to send you; parcels take a long time getting here. You will be sent a copy at once.

How is your brother? I recently received a long letter from mine, who has been imprisoned in Moabit for half a year now, waiting to learn whether or not he will be tried on a charge of high treason.[4]

A fortnight ago I was in Rehovot, where everyone wants to know about you. The Steinschneider family will be my guests this Sabbath and, as the main event, I shall declaim Herr Heidegger's rectorial address from beginning to end (in appropriate style).[5]

I sent you all my "poetry" you requested. I would like to make the acquaintance of the Angela Nova as a reader of the "Angelus Novus."[6]

Kindest regards from us all,

Yours, Gerhard

37

BENJAMIN TO SCHOLEM

PALACE HOTEL
1 RUE DU FOUR, PARIS VI
OCTOBER 31, 1933

Dear Gerhard,

I was pleased to receive your lines from Rehovot. Yet you still have not confirmed receipt of my note "On the Mimetic Faculty."

Today I am putting aside the indecisiveness being fed by deep and well-founded depressions to formulate a short query. It is based on information I received from Dora. She writes: "A Frau Shoshanah Persitz, a Russian Jew of British nationality, is undertaking to expand the existing Palestine Publishing Co. in Jerusalem. In agreement with English and German publishers, this should result in the publication of works that cannot at present be published in Germany. She intends to publish them in English and German, but first, provisionally, in Hebrew (translation)."

---

[4] I still have this letter, the last one I ever received from my brother.

[5] Heidegger's rectorial address of May 27, 1933, entitled "Die Selbstbehauptung der deutschen Universität."

[6] This restated question was again left unanswered.

This supposedly has to do with scholarly writings. Do you think it possible to arrange to have an article commissioned for me there? A history of contemporary German or French literature? Or something along that line. Would it be wholly unrealistic to entertain the thought of having my collected essays published in Hebrew? Please write me whether you see any prospects here.

I have moved in the meantime. My health has been making real progress. I have also written a new section for "Berliner Kindheit." But I still have not at all successfully established a firm foothold here, and I have everything to fear.

So much for today. Send me news as soon as you can.

Cordially,

Yours, Walter

38

Scholem to Benjamin

Dear Walter,   NOVEMBER 10 [1933]

I had just sent a detailed letter to you on Ibiza—you have undoubtedly received it by now—when your first letter from Paris arrived. I have received your second letter, and the references in it to your steady recovery put my mind at ease, at least on this important point. I am hastening to reply by return mail, which means I have to rush to meet the last collection.

I received your notes in good order and with the utmost gratitude. I hope that you have the Schocken *Almanach* by now, which I sent you immediately on arrival. If I have yet to comment on the notes, it is only because I am still making a serious effort to understand them—a task that doesn't seem to be all that easy. Please grant me a moratorium until such a time.

You don't need to send me *Welt im Wort*, since the library here subscribes to it. I must admit that I honestly do not understand either your secrecy in reporting the fact of its publication or your wish not to state your views about it, for I really do not know what one could possibly have to say about such an indifferent object. I do not understand what your desire for discretion refers to, since you were not telling me anything other than a notorious fact. I consider this Haas a fraud.

As to Frau Persitz,[1] she is a lady who makes a grand entrance, promising left and right whatever suits her at a given moment. Indeed, it is by no means certain whether (a) her publishing venture, which has been launched with such great hullabaloo, will turn out to be more than a bluff and whether (b), even assuming it got off the ground and they began to print in Tel Aviv, you would ever see any remuneration, and that is, after all, the heart of the matter. I do not hold the lady in particularly high esteem, even though we are acquainted, and I can only counsel caution. She is primarily looking for "big names," people with polished images, and deep down I have the quiet suspicion (this is just between the two of us) that it might all turn out to be a fraud.[2] Yet the lady is *very* diligent and energetic, and she knows very well how to put herself in the limelight, not to mention how to turn things to her advantage. If you want to make contact with her enterprise, you should not pin any hopes on my personal intervention but had better contact her directly: Mrs. Schoschana Persitz, Tel Aviv. Your letter will reach her, since her name is on everybody's lips and half of Tel Aviv considers her the real soul of the Jewish nation. A translation of your essays would probably prove to be difficult. They will not interest the circle of readers in question, since they occupy a position far too advanced, in terms of educational background alone. If you should want at some point to write for such readers, then you would have to express yourself in a completely different way, which could be very productive if you do indeed intend to deal with contemporary German literature. Moreover, Hebrew as a language is simply not yet able to keep pace with your manner of expression.[3]

Whether there is another way for me to help you in a concrete manner, as I would like, will become apparent when I have the chance to speak with [Salman] Schocken, who is coming to Palestine at the end of the year to pay his family a short visit; they are in the process of settling here. If he does in fact come, I will no doubt be seeing him, and I shall steer the conversation toward you and determine whether anything can be effected. His son [Gustav] did not seem to be a great fan of your writing, but I am doing my best to bring about a change of opinion here.

So much for now, in haste. The semester has started, and I have loads of new students and work.

Write soon and at length. Kindest regards,

Yours, Gerhard

[1] Frau Persitz (1893–1969) was very active as a publisher and politician.
[2] This suspicion proved to be unfounded, even though nothing came of the whole undertaking.
[3] The literary Hebrew of 1930 didn't yet have the flexibility it displays fifty years later.

39

DORA SOPHIE BENJAMIN TO SCHOLEM

Dear Gerhard, [BERLIN] NOVEMBER 29, 1933

This time around I am only sending you my very best wishes for your birthday, as well as cordial greetings to you and Escha, since I don't know what is on your list of desiderata. I don't know which of us is the more indolent letter writer, but I am prepared to assume the guilt gladly and to promise to better myself if that helps me receive a letter from you. You must be inundated with fellow countrymen by now, but when I look at those who leave here, I see that such an increase does not always necessarily mean a gain. On the other hand, my sister, along with her husband, left Vienna last week to settle in Haifa—a most respectable feat for a couple their age—she is 48, he is 66![1]

I wrote to Frau Persitz, who either opened or built up a publishing company in Tel Aviv, and she plans to help me get an editorial position. I seem to have had a few good ideas. If it works out, I would come over. Otherwise, there would be little sense in such a move. Stefan is doing very well in school, he is at the top of his class and doesn't have to struggle. I still have the house,[2] which I keep improving so that one day it will bring me a little extra—this small profit would, of course, become illusory if I left. It would also be very difficult to sell, if I wanted to leave for good. Nevertheless, I would like to leave, but only if I can make a living. I am sure you agree with me there. For the time being, I am diligently learning Italian together with Stefan, since Italy is likely to be our next stop. After only four weeks of lessons, we can already chatter away like magpies (*le gazze*). You will of course say that it would be better to learn Hebrew, but I will begin with that only if and when I need to. At present it would also be too hard on Stefan, who has, as it is, to cope with Latin and Greek, English and Italian.

How are things with you both? Are you pleased with the house? I often hear about you indirectly, through Erna Mayer's sister.[3] But I would prefer direct communication. I think I must have a complete collection

---

[1] Dora's sister, Paula Arnold (1885–1968), wrote English quite well and was a respected contributor to the English-speaking Zionist press for many years. She and Dora did not get along well.

[2] Delbrückstrasse 23, where she remained after her separation from W.B.

[3] Erna Mayer was the wife of Dr. Max Mayer, from whom W.B. had begun to learn Hebrew in 1929. He settled in Palestine in 1932 and remained in close contact with me in Jerusalem.

of Scheerbarts by now. Even the *Mondrevolution* you kidnapped seems to have now found its way back to me.

You must have heard that Walter had malaria and that he is now living in Paris under very reduced circumstances. We are writing each other once again on a regular basis. The stories at the time about Georg were untrue, of course, as I wrote Walter at once. I am now trying hard to do something for him. Even the editors are already referring to him as "the best living writer in the German language"—but only those editors who happen to be Jewish.

Once again, all the best, and write soon,

Yours, Dora

40

BENJAMIN TO SCHOLEM

Dear Gerhard,

1 RUE DU FOUR, PARIS VI
DECEMBER 7, 1933

The 15th of December is drawing near, and after this date the grapes of the press will be hanging even farther out of reach for an old fox like me, and what little fruit still beckons from over the shard-strewn walls of the Third Reich has to be snatched away with the nimblest of bites indeed. I had to select this shabby stationery in order to keep the narrow temporal frame set for my letter in front of me in spatial terms. And I could say a great deal more. If I could present things to you as they truly are, I would most certainly not need to ask you to pardon my longish silence: you would understand. But, as matters stand, I can only allude to things and say that someone who was a close acquaintance of both Brecht and myself in Berlin has fallen into the hands of the Staatspolizei.[1] He was freed after someone from the same circle of friends intervened, and he subsequently turned up here and filled us in about the dangers threatening the few who are still close to us. All this is complicated in the most fateful way by the fact that we may one day have to face the possibility that the denunciations originated from a man in Paris we all know. The problem has by no means been resolved; and we cannot at all gauge the possible repercussions. But since the last few days have passed some-

---

[1] [The reference is to the Geheime Staatspolizei (secret state police), or Gestapo.—TRANS.]

what more tranquilly, I have been able to find time for these short sentences.[2]

I want to treat other matters just as cursorily and inform you first of all about the attempt to rescue my library. It remains to be seen whether the support friends can muster for this project will suffice, and whether other problems arise. If it proves to be feasible, I would have the library dispatched to Denmark, where I am thinking of going at the end of the winter.[3] Brecht is there, as well as several others; life should not be much more expensive in the small town in question than it was on Ibiza, and the cost of transporting the books there would be relatively moderate.

For the first time in months, I once again have a library at my disposal, and I was amazed how quickly I found my way back into the complicated catalogue system of the Bibliothèque Nationale. I will first begin work on two major commissioned articles: one is a review of new publications on the philosophy of language; the other is an analysis of the work of Eduard Fuchs, the well-known author of books on the history of customs and the history of art. Fuchs is here at the moment; his collections are in the hands of the police. He is a remarkable person, who inspires reverence and allows you to imagine what the men who were Social Democrats at the time of the Anti-Socialist Law must have been like.

It remains for me to thank you for your information about Frau Persitz. It kept me from contacting her, which I would not have done willingly anyway. Such hasty contacts hardly ever lead to anything. In the meantime, her project may already have taken on firmer contours, and you could sketch them for me someday.

Has Schocken already arrived? Thank you very much for sending me his *Almanach*. I was pleased with your Kabbalah essay and with the extracts from the Jewish reader as well. I will write to you soon at greater length. But send me some news as soon as you can.

With the kindest regards,

Yours, Walter

P.S. Have you heard anything about Erich Gutkind? I dreamed very vividly about him last night.[4]

---

[2] The circumstances to which this communication refers are unknown to me, even though one might assume that they could be illuminated on the basis of papers or reminiscences by people belonging to Brecht's circle. Perhaps other letters from or to W.B. may also contain information about persons not mentioned here.

[3] He undertook the trip to Brecht much later, in the summer of 1934.

[4] Erich Gutkind (1877–1965) was an old acquaintance of W.B.—since 1916—and is often mentioned in the *Briefe*. In 1920 the Benjamins spent a number of months at the Gutkinds', in the Falkenberg settlement near Grünau.

41

SCHOLEM TO BENJAMIN

Dear Walter,   DECEMBER 24, 1933

I waited for news from you for a long time, and I couldn't find an explanation for your silence. But I finally received your short letter-card last week, which at least gave me half a hint. Though of course I did not understand a single thing. I don't know what you are all so terribly afraid of that even you won't entrust a pragmatic report on concrete experiences to the stationery of the French postal service. I find all of this quite unfathomable, and I hope you will find an evening sometime soon to explain to me—at least for my domestic consumption, so to speak— what was really troubling you and why it cannot be set to paper. Until such time, I must be satisfied with your hints, *nolens volens*. I am most of all delighted that you seem to be rid of your Spanish malaria, or whatever it was. That the German laws have brought your journalistic work for the German papers to a definite end does not come as a surprise. And what now? Where will you publish your major work? It must be some time, in fact all of 4 months now, since I received a contribution to my archive. Have the various pseudonyms all died so suddenly? I don't see why you don't make contact with the *Prager Tagblatt*, which right now must be among the German newspapers with the widest readership. The feuilleton section is edited by Max Brod, and regardless of what you think of him, he nevertheless has the greatest respect for your work (I know that from him directly), is very receptive to it, and in my judgment could do something for you there. That seems a great deal more real to me than Frau Persitz.

I was very pleased to hear that you may be able to get your library to Denmark. Let me hear how this operation develops—I hope for the best possible outcome. It might then again be possible, on some occasion (i.e., when we have the funds here), to raise the question about which we corresponded a number of years ago, namely, that of the library acquiring your complete Baader. Together with this letter I am sending you a thin volume of Agnon's stories, two-thirds of which I translated myself.[1] Perhaps you'll get something out of it.

I am working hard and enjoying it. Among the most recent discoveries

---

[1] *In der Gemeinschaft der Frommen* (Berlin: Schocken, 1933), six stories, three of which I had translated and published in earlier versions in the monthly *Der Jude* at the beginning of the 1920s.

to enrich my knowledge is proof of the existence of the "proto-Bahir," fragments of which I found in a handwritten Roman MS last week and whose discovery has provided one of my most beloved hypotheses about the origins of the Kabbalah with a totally unexpected basis in fact.[2] Starting this week, I will be holding a two-hour introductory lecture on the Kabbalah in Tel Aviv every fortnight, for which I am at present putting together a kind of manuscript. I am otherwise devoting myself, with good cause, to the study of Manichaean religion. You may not know this, but one of the biggest sensations in the history of religion for a long time is experiencing a tragic collapse. The discovery of undoubtedly authentic writings by Mani and his first disciples is filling many a heart with highly justified expectations.[3] The writings have been found in Coptic papyri, which have been unearthed in terrible condition. The only person who can save the papyrus in the 1½ years before it disintegrates into dust is the Berlin bookbinder of genius [Hermann] Ibscher, who is fatally ill, and the only person who can read it is a Russian Jew[4] who is soon to be thrown out by a Prussian government loyal to the best traditions of the old Germanic tribes of the migratory period. Which is to say that the parts of the papyrus that are not in English hands, and which contain an irrecoverable treasure (Mani's authentic letters and his *Book of Psalms and Prayers*) will soon dissolve into the dust from which they originated before the eyes of the Berlin Academy of Sciences, which owns them. The report connected with this, which has been published in the 1933 Academy proceedings, is one of the most highly recommended detective stories of recent times—along with all the other things it is besides. You should read it in the Bibliothèque Nationale one of these days!

Many people have been visiting here. (A propos, 40,000 Jews have entered the country this year, a quarter of them from Germany.) I met Baumgardt, whom I had not seen since 1918, a prime example of a high-school philosophy teacher, who incidentally has not been dismissed. You asked about Gutkind: He emigrated to America months ago, as I hear from many people who have more detailed information about him.[5]

---

[2] On the discovery referred to here, see my book *Ursprünge und Anfänge der Kabbala* (Berlin: de Gruyter, 1962), pp. 94–109 [*Origins of the Kabbalah*, ed. R. J. Zwi Werblowsky, trans. Allan Arkush (Princeton: Princeton University Press, 1987), pp. 105–23]. The book of Bahir, the oldest extant kabbalist text, was the topic of the dissertation I wrote in Munich from 1920 to 1921 and was printed in 1923 [as *Das Buch Bahir: ein Schriftdenkmal aus der Frühzeit der Kabbala, auf Grund der kritischen Neuausgabe von Gerhard Scholem* (Leipzig: W. Drugulin, 1923)].

[3] The 1933 Academy publication on this scientific sensation referred to at the end of this letter, was entitled "Ein Manifund in Ägypten," by Carl Schmidt and H. J. Polotsky.

[4] Hans Jakob Polotsky (born 1905), who was appointed to the university in Jerusalem in 1934 and became one of the most important authorities on Egyptian and Coptic linguistics.

[5] Gutkind was a close friend of the well-known American writer Upton Sinclair, who

Schocken has yet to arrive, and he most likely won't do so before February.

Please write soon. Most sincere regards,

Yours, Gerhard

42

BENJAMIN TO SCHOLEM

1 RUE DU FOUR, PARIS
Dear Gerhard,   [DECEMBER 31, 1933]

Even though you haven't written for quite some time, I want to return the cordial wishes you so regularly send me for Rosh Hashanah on the threshold of the European New Year. But you will have to take into account my profound weariness with the moment. For some time now, these moments have turned into days and the days into weeks. It's not surprising that the pressure to put three new irons in the fire daily should lead to severe fatigue. I am not achieving much in my dejected state because I am convinced that I cannot ask very much more of myself. The top priority among the little I am still capable of would probably be a change of scenery. Paris is much too expensive, and the contrast with my previous stay here is much too harsh. I see nothing encouraging when I survey my surroundings, and the only person I find of interest finds me less so.[1] Otherwise, the town seems dead to me, now that Brecht is gone.[2] He would like me to follow him to Denmark. Life is supposed to be cheap there. But I am horrified by the winter, the travel costs, and the idea of being dependent on him and him alone.[3] Nevertheless, the next decision I can bring myself to make will take me there. Life among the emigrés is unbearable, life alone is no more bearable, and a life among the French cannot be brought about. So only work remains, but nothing endangers

helped him and his wife to emigrate quickly to New York, where they lived in wretched conditions until their deaths.

[1] The reference may well be to the woman he met on Ibiza and described as the "female counterpart" to the Angelus Novus (letter 31). On the other hand, he could be referring to Margarete Steffin, Brecht's friend, who was then staying in Paris for an extended period. W.B. was very fond of her. But Steffin was on very friendly terms with W.B., so I am more inclined to the first interpretation.

[2] Brecht had spent several weeks in Paris (see Klaus Völker, *Brecht: A Biography*, trans. John Newell [New York: Seabury Press, 1978], pp. 206–12) and tried to talk W.B. into emigrating to Denmark. He gave him to understand that he would be able to live there on 60 reichsmarks a month.

[3] He wrote a similar letter to Gretel Adorno a day earlier (*Briefe*, pp. 596–97).

it more than the recognition that it is so obviously the final inner mental resource (it is no longer an external one). I have accepted a commission from *Le Monde* for an article on Haussmann, the prefect of the Seine.[4] The *Zeitschrift für Sozialforschung* is waiting for a review on recent philosophy of language,[5] as well as the long essay on Eduard Fuchs.[6] But preparations are only at a stage where things creep along. And I cannot permit myself to work on the only project I am often attracted to—the continuation of the "Berliner Kindheit um 1900."

I chose this smallish sheet of paper very conscious of the fact that I would not be able to fill a larger one. And plenty of room still remains for the signature. I hope to hear better news from you than I am capable of communicating,

Most cordially,

Yours, Walter

43

BENJAMIN TO SCHOLEM

PALACE HOTEL
1 RUE DU FOUR, PARIS VI
JANUARY 18, 1934

Dear Gerhard,

This obstreperous format is giving me the courage to prepare a longer letter. First of all, thank you for your letter of December 24th and for the book. You know the exceptional interest with which I read all of Agnon's writings that are accessible to me. I have just finished this volume, and I will often refer back to it. For now, I bring it into the conversation whenever possible. I have yet to find anything more beautiful in his works than "The Great Synagogue," which I regard as a tremendous masterpiece. And then the story about the guardian of books seems to me to be of great significance. Agnon displays mastery in every piece, and if I had become "a teacher in Israel"[1]—but I could have just as easily become an ant lion—I would not have been able to refrain from a lecture on Agnon and Kafka.[2] (By the way, should I ever regain possession of my

[4] The essay was never written (see *Briefe*, p. 602), but he did treat Haussmann in "Paris, Capital of the Nineteenth Century" [in *Reflections*, pp. 146–62].

[5] Published in 1935 as "Probleme der Sprachsoziologie" (*GS* 3:452–81).

[6] He spent (or rather, tarried) more than three years on the essay, as the following letters document.

[1] A Jewish expression (taken from Hebrew) of highest honor.

[2] That was a very broad hint to me. I had once written that a revision of Kafka's *Trial*

library, Kafka's *Trial* will be missing from it. It was stolen a long time ago. If you could come up with a copy, then the worst devastations the con man subjected my place to in his day would be repaired. I managed to wrest the other irreplaceable piece—the first edition of Brecht's *Hauspostille*, of which there are only 25 extant copies—from the author in the course of difficult negotiations.) I cannot predict, by the way, what will become of my library. It would require 16 pages to set out the facts. But there is hope that I may get it back. I may be able to say more (or less) about it in the near future.[3]

Mentioning Kafka causes me to tell you that I have struck up an—albeit reserved—relationship with Werner Kraft.[4] He spotted me in the Bibliothèque Nationale and approached me afterward, in writing. I was surprised to read several texts of his from which I can withhold neither agreement nor respect. Two of them are attempts at a commentary on short pieces of Kafka's, subdued and definitely not without insight.[5] He has undoubtedly grasped much more of the matter than Max Brod. Among the maxims and reflections that have been discovered among Goethe's papers after his death (and one can guess why he never published the most important ones), one reads the following interesting sentence: "A child once burned is twice shy; an old man many times singed is afraid to warm himself."[6] I allude to it to convey in a few words the kinds of moods with which I have to struggle—often for weeks on end—to bring myself to take some initiative aimed at getting my writings printed somewhere. Overcoming these moods has, in the recent past, hardly ever resulted in anything other than having my inhibitions confirmed. They turned out to be justified in an especially uncomfortable way in the case of Max Brod, to whom I sent an essay at your urging, even referring to you by name. Not only did he reject it, but he was brazen enough to pass it on to Willy Haas without first getting my permission. Since the latter fellow has not sent me any remuneration at all

---

takes place in Agnon's writings. [In "Das hebräische Buch: eine Rundfrage," *Jüdische Rundschau* 33 (1928), p. 202.—TRANS.]

[3] He did in fact get "the more important half" (even if the smaller half) of his library, as he wrote to Brecht (*Briefe*, p. 602).

[4] Benjamin and Kraft had not been in contact between 1921 and 1933.

[5] The reference is to Kraft's essays "Über Franz Kafkas 'Elf Söhne' " and "Der Neue Advokat," both of which W.B. read in manuscript. (They were reprinted in Kraft's *Franz Kafka: Durchdringung und Geheimnis* [Frankfurt am Main: Suhrkamp Verlag, 1968], pp. 13–16, 49–62.) See the bibliography in *GS* 2:1247.

[6] Maxim 931, in vol. 9, p. 620 of the Artemis edition. Also in Max Hecker's edition of the 1907 *Maximen und Reflektionen*, republished as an Insel pocketbook, p. 168. The maxim can be found in both editions under "Aus dem Nachlass: Über Literatur und Leben" and is called "Ein gebranntes Kind . . ." [*The Maxims and Reflections of Goethe*, trans. Bailey Saunders (New York: Macmillan, 1893).]

up to now, for two contributions—one of which must be in your possession by now—I will consider myself fortunate if I ever get back the
manuscript.[7] I think you will permit me to refrain from listing similar
attempts that came to a similar end. It seemed more interesting—even
if hardly more promising—to send the "Berliner Kindheit um 1900" to
Hermann Hesse, which I did just recently.[8]

Did I write you that my brother was freed from Sonnenburg concentration camp around Christmas? But for all I know, proceedings on
charges of high treason are still pending. If it comes to the worst, he and
his one-year-old son[9] can be supported by his in-laws. Anyway, I consider it practically certain that he will resume illegal work in one way or
another.[10] This in strictest confidence, of course. You may also infer
from this passage that it is by no means fear of censorship—what censorship?—that makes me occasionally speak of my own affairs in a laconic manner. Rather, the fault lies with the decidedly depressing
conditions—and I am not speaking only about the external ones. I have
hardly ever been as lonely as I am here. If I were seeking opportunities
to sit in a café with emigrés, they would be easy to find. But I avoid
them. Just call to mind how exceptionally important—and at the same
time exceptionally small—the circle was that shaped my existence during my last years in Berlin. None of those who were at the center of
it are here now, ever since Hauptmann, Brecht's secretary, went to
America. And only two people who belonged to its periphery are
around.[11]

I am postponing the trip to Denmark, and not only because of the time
of year. As close as I am to Brecht, I do have my reservations about
having to rely solely on him once I am there. Moreover, it is good to be
able to seek the anonymity that a large city has to offer when you are
completely destitute. Moreover, steps have been taken on my behalf at
the Israélite Alliance Universelle, and they may provide me with some

[7] The two contributions, "Erfahrung und Armut" (GS 2:213–19) and remarks on J. P.
Hebel's Schatzkästlein (GS 2:628), were in fact published in Haas's journal Die Welt im
Wort. Because the journal failed, it defaulted on the payments, and the two pieces W.B.
sent to Brod did in fact get published in the Prager Tagblatt (GS 4:757–61), as originally
intended.

[8] W.B.'s letter of January 13 and Hesse's very positive reply have been printed in a
Suhrkamp publication on Hesse (1975), pp. 83–84. Hesse was among the very few writers
who tried to do something for W.B. He tried to interest two publishers, S. Fischer and
Albert Langen, in Benjamin's work, and he later brought Benjamin to the attention of an
emigré publishing company in Holland.

[9] Michael Benjamin, born December 27, 1932.

[10] See Hilde Benjamin's biography of her husband, pp. 233–39.

[11] I don't know whom Benjamin might have had in mind. In Klaus Völker's aforementioned book on Brecht, the reader can find out who the people at the center of Brecht's
Berlin circle were.

support for a short period, even though my information suggests that it cannot come to very much. I may have written you that I made contact with the magazine *Le Monde*. I am going to write a long article for them, a critical exposé of Haussmann's actions in Paris, about which I have already collected interesting materials over the years.

Your news about the Mani manuscript has made me curious. I will try to get the relevant Academy report. Besides the work just mentioned, I am currently working on the philosophy of language. I had the *Zeitschrift für Sozialforschung* assign me an extensive survey of that field—and this gives me the opportunity to write about it. Are you familiar with Heinz Werner's *Sprachphysiognomik*,[12] which Barth published in 1932? I am studying it at the moment.

If you are in Rehovot again, pass on my fondest regards. And to Escha as well. Write soon.

Yours, Walter

44
SCHOLEM TO BENJAMIN

Dear Walter,   [EARLY FEBRUARY 1934]

Your latest news was all very discouraging and I understand that, the longer things continue this way, the deeper you get caught in a mood of despair which doesn't especially encourage you to express yourself. I cannot imagine the kind of life you are forced to lead in Paris these days, and I only see from what you write that, even avoiding German emigré circles, your present Paris existence has fundamentally changed (and not for the better) from the way it was during your stay a few years ago. Have your French doors closed as well? Has the mass influx brought out a special reserve on their part, which didn't inhibit relations to the same extent before? All this seems to have become an agonizing burden for you, judging from the tenor of your sparing remarks about Paris. I am desperately racking my brain as to which direction the kind of literary work you have been doing up to now could continue with some meaning and in the expectation of a certain effectiveness. What you intimate about your experience with Brod is a severe disappointment to me, and

---

[12] [*Grundfragen der Sprachphysiognomik* (Leipzig: J. A. Barth, 1932).—TRANS.]

I won't neglect to make my feelings known to Brod in a very emphatic way. But really, where could your work be placed? And even more: *where* will the work flow from if your present situation continues? You know of my intention to bring your case to the attention of [Salman] Schocken and to ascertain if there is any chance of achieving something in this direction. The man is now here for a short visit, and he will settle here for good in the fall. If I succeed in putting my contact with him on a firmer footing, then I will come out with my suggestions. Even if that isn't yet possible, or if it doesn't lead to any tangible results, I should still be able to find out if there is any hope at all of getting him interested in your work. Your *Elective Affinities* essay should be the point of departure for this kind of enterprise. In any case, rest assured that I do not for a single moment lose sight of the possibility of undertaking something there.

Things are going very well with me, except for Escha's illness, which hardly contributes to my well-being. She has spent six weeks in bed with a severe attack of sciatica and is in great pain. There seems to be precious little one can do about it. This is also the worst climatic season for it. Otherwise, I am working a great deal and am very busy with kabbalistic analyses. The winter semester will be over 14 days from now, and I will then travel in the country for a few days.—You write that you are seeing Kraft; I, on the other hand, am seeing his little son, who has developed from a Hannoverian into a very nice Hebrew in only half a year. He speaks Hebrew with amazing ease and comprehension. Even I cannot help laughing when not only do I speak Hebrew with the son of a follower of Rudolf Borchardt, but I am actually compelled to speak it, since the child expresses a very strong aversion to speaking German! That should only happen to Kraft!

If you get your hands on your library again, which would be grounds for the most heartfelt congratulations, then please reconsider selling your Baader to our library. I already wrote you some time ago that this oeuvre is missing here and that the library would very much like to purchase it at a reasonable price.

Kitty Steinschneider was here the day before yesterday, and I passed on your greetings. It looks as if they will be leaving Rehovot.

I heard with joy that your brother is free again. Unfortunately, I cannot say the same about mine. There are also no signs of any development in his case up to now. He has been in detention pending trial for ten months —and he has been taken before an examining magistrate only once thus far.

Please write in as much detail as you can. Sincerest regards,

Yours, Gerhard

45

BENJAMIN TO SCHOLEM

PALACE HOTEL
1 RUE DU FOUR
PARIS VI
MARCH 3, 1934

Dear Gerhard,

I am making use of a late hour to reply to your last letter.

I gather from it that your image of my life is accurate, even if the news you base that image on is sparse. My existence is about as precarious as it could be and depends each day anew on the good Lord himself—to say the same thing in a more prudent way. And by that I do not mean just the help I get from time to time, but also my own initiative, which is more or less aimed at a miracle.

It would almost take a miracle to find an appropriate use here for my abilities. I have undertaken my latest experiment in this direction by announcing a series of lectures on the "Avant-garde alle-mande,"[1] for which I have been promised a small room in the form of an art salon as well as a few French subscribers. All of this is planned on the smallest of scales and is still on the drawing board. Such a series of lectures in French would at least provide good practice in the language.

To return to the "help": The only small crutch I can lean on at the moment is support in the form of 700 French francs a month, which I will receive until April from the Israélite Alliance Universelle, to whose president, Sylvain Lévi, I was personally recommended. The extension of the subsidy is vitally important to me. But as things stand, I could only expect it if a new factor entered the game. Would you know of some way to bring this about?

You may be familiar with Sylvain Lévi by name: he is an Indologist.[2] I will go to see him in the near future, to speak with him about the planned lecture series and to present him with my work on contemporary French literature, which you will also receive in the near future. But I won't dare broach the subject of having the subsidy extended. If you were able to effect something—directly or indirectly—the situation might change.

[1] He intended to speak on Kafka, Ernst Bloch, and Brecht, among others. The lecture series never took place.

[2] In his letter to Brecht W.B. strangely anoints the famous Indologist Sylvain Lévi (1863–1935) chief rabbi of France without mentioning Lévi's name. Cf. *Zur Aktualität Walter Benjamins*, p. 33. He didn't mention the then–chief rabbi of France, Israel Lévi, to whom I could have recommended him.

I might mention that Jean-Richard Bloch[3] is a nephew of Sylvain Lévi's. I believe I read in one of your letters that you once met Bloch when he was traveling in Palestine.

The "Arcades" project is the *tertius gaudens* these days between fate and me. I have not only been able to do much more research recently, but also—for the first time in a long while—to imagine ways in which that research might be put to use. That this image diverges greatly from the first, original one is quite understandable.

In my situation, one can only give oneself up to the feeling of hope with great dietary precautions. This should give you an idea of what a successful intervention with Schocken would mean to me.

That Haas's Prague journal has gone under is gratifying. Brod—what a peculiar man—had his publisher send me his latest novel (which I certainly won't read). More enjoyable was a letter from Hermann Hesse, to whom I had sent the "Berliner Kindheit um 1900." Not only did he comment on the book with great insight, he also offered to intervene with S. Fischer. Unfortunately, though, the situation there is such as to render his intervention fruitless,[4] and he seems to sense that himself. Anyway, the impulse that made me turn to him did not deceive me.

In these times, when my imagination is preoccupied with the most unworthy problems between sunrise and sunset, I experience at night, more and more often, its emancipation in dreams, which nearly always have a political subject. I would really like to be in a position to tell you about them someday. They represent a pictorial atlas of the secret history of National Socialism.

I know that my library—or rather, the most important part of it—is on its way to Scandinavia, but I do not know if it has crossed the border yet and arrived safely. It is going to Brecht, who will house it; I could neither set the books up here nor come up with the storage fees. On the other hand, I have hopes of soon regaining my large *Geschichte des deutschen Buchhandels*, about which I want to write an essay for *Die Sammlung*.[5]

---

[3] Jean-Richard Bloch (1884–1947), a well-known French author who retained a lively interest in Jewish issues even after joining the Communist Party. I met him twice when he was in Jerusalem in 1925.

[4] During the last months of his life, Samuel Fischer—who died on October 15, 1934—could play only a reduced role in his publishing company. In his recollections of Fischer, Thomas Mann wrote of a meeting in May 1934: "The seventy-four-year-old had been suffering for a long time; his mental powers were waning." The position of the two leading figures in S. Fischer Verlag, G. Bermann-Fischer and Peter Suhrkamp, must have still been unclear.

[5] This review was never written. W.B.'s reference is most likely to Kapp-Goldfriedrich, *Geschichte des deutschen Buchhandels: Im Auftrage des Börsenvereins der deutschen Buchhändler, herausgegeben von der Historischen Kommission desselben*, vol. 1 by Friedrich

So much—and it is by no means little—for today. I don't want to close without best wishes for Escha's recovery. I know sciatica is terribly painful—from the days I had to simulate it.[6]

Kindest regards,

Yours, Walter

P.S. I received [Nahum] Glatzer's *Geschichtslehre der Tannaiten* by mistake.[7] Even though the book is very brief in its explanations, it seems just as significant for the problems it raises. Write me what you think about it.

46

BENJAMIN TO SCHOLEM

25 RUE JASMIN
PARIS XVI
APRIL 8, 1934

Dear Gerhard,

I hope the causes of your long silence are not to be found in your health. At this moment I really miss having news from you, which would also have included an answer to my last letter concerning Sylvain Lévi.

You will find my address [above] which changed several weeks ago. I couldn't keep the hotel any longer; some of my things are still there and have to be redeemed. I found a very temporary place to live, at my sister's. This is also not something that could have been anticipated.[1] Anyway, I will soon be leaving here, because the room I am in has been rented.

I devoted my stay in Paris over the last few weeks exclusively to preparing a lecture, which was to familiarize guests invited to a very respected private house with the starting point for a series of observations on contemporary German literature.[2] The plan was to follow this lecture with seminars the participants would have had to pay for, unlike the lecture. Well, shortly before the agreed date I learned that the orga-

---

Kapp, vols. 2–4 and Index volume by Johann Goldfriedrich (Leipzig: Börsenverein, 1886–1923).

[6] In May and June 1917. The doubts expressed in Werner Fuld, *Walter Benjamin: Zwischen den Stühlen* (Munich: Hanser, 1979), p. 81, are totally unfounded.

[7] *Untersuchungen zum Geschichtsbild der Tannaiten* (Berlin: Schocken, 1932).

[1] His sister Dora moved to Paris in 1934, where W.B.'s relationship with her—which in the past had been strained and conflict-ridden—became closer.

[2] This plan had taken the place of the project mentioned in the previous letter.

nizer, a very well known gynecologist, had fallen ill with pneumonia. Everything had to be canceled. And printed invitations had already been sent.[3]

That's why I cannot foresee at all what the coming weeks will bring. If the lecture takes place later, the problem of whether more lectures could follow would be still more uncertain than before. The season will probably have advanced too far by then. But before I come nearer to the thought of leaving, I must try out every opportunity to take at least this first step before a Parisian audience.

I sent you my essay on the current social situation of the French writer a few days ago, together with an article on Kommerell's Jean Paul book.[4] The planned lecture was to have been the companion piece to the essay "Courants politiques dans la littérature allemande actuelle."

I finished off a long review essay, "Probleme der Sprachsoziologie" for the *Zeitschrift für Sozialforschung*. By the way, its editorial staff tried to procure me a *service de presse* with a number of large Paris publishers. I am currently supplementing their endeavors with *démarches* of my own, and so I hope again to have a small French library here shortly. My original one reached Denmark a few days ago, together with a sizable part of the rest of my library. For various reasons I had to leave half of it in Berlin—the less valuable half.

I hope soon to be received by Sylvain Lévi. I gather from your silence that you would be unable to achieve anything where he is concerned. It remains to be seen what I myself can bring about this time.

But there might be another step within the realm of what you can do. Wiesengrund writes me from Berlin that Erich Reiss has expressed a lively interest in the "Berliner Kindheit um 1900." But the publishing house seems to be following a more Zionist course of late. Wiesengrund sees certain difficulties in that, and he is probably right. There might be some hope of overcoming them if you could point out certain Jewish aspects of my book, in a kind of expert's report.[5]

You won't think for a moment that I write without realizing that such a report would amount to a tour de force. But the mere fact of your statement would already represent the better half of an argument. And your wisdom, if not your archive of my work, might give you some support for the other half.

Whether you want to send such a letter—if you decide to write one— directly to Erich Reiss (I don't know his address) or via me is a question of lesser importance.

[3] I don't know if a copy of this invitation still exists.

[4] "Der eingetunkte Zauberstab" (*GS* 3:409–17) appeared under the pseudonym K. A. Stempflinger in the *Frankfurter Zeitung* of March 29, 1934.

[5] See letter 48.

It would probably not be right to dismiss the—for the time being admittedly vague—project out of hand simply because the chances of publication of the "Berliner Kindheit" are minimal. But I don't think the same holds true for its chances of success.

Among the books that are safe with Brecht in Denmark are the Kafka volumes. And this makes the loss of *The Trial* I suffered through robbery a few years ago relevant once again. Do you see any opportunity—perhaps even through Kitty Steinschneider's mediation, whom I told about the loss while in Berlin—to schnorr a copy somewhere for me?!

That's all for today, besides the request for a prompt reply.

Yours, Walter

P.S. The doctor's condition has deteriorated. There is no chance of the lectures for the moment.

47

SCHOLEM TO BENJAMIN

Dear Walter,   APRIL 11, 1934

The weeks have passed without my replying to your letter of March 3. But in the meantime your situation has preoccupied me more than such a prolonged silence might betray. I did not find any reasonable way to intervene with Sylvain Lévi, who is completely unknown to me. The one or two occasions I met his nephew—I don't know how many years ago— are not a bridge that could carry me. On the other hand, I have invested a lot of energy in recommending your work, viz. yourself, to Herr [Salman] Schocken. But great illusions about this might well turn out to be exaggerated, unfortunately. He doesn't seem to want to come near. In the meantime, he temporarily left again, and very suddenly, while I was with Escha in Tiberias, so I didn't have a final interview with him, but I believe that he doesn't want to get into it. I had several extended conversations with him about you, in the course of which he spoke about what he had read of yours with a mixture of respect, admiration, and resolute rejection: he repeatedly declared his incomprehension of most of what you have written. That is unfortunately how things stand. But how your situation will really develop is becoming increasingly uncertain to me. I hope to hear from you what became of the various projects you touched on in your last letter: the lectures, S. Fischer, the work on the "Arcades"

103

project. My most heartfelt congratulations on your library's transfer, which must have meanwhile taken place. At least this way you will not be entirely deprived of it.

The news from this end is that Escha is still bedridden with her (lingering) sciatica, which is more and more earning the name of "eschiatica." She was in Tiberias for six weeks to take the waters, but to no avail so far, and she suffers greatly. Only the warmth of summer, which should be starting about now, will really be of some use. I am working and reading a great deal, and the latter activity especially makes demands on my energy. Even though I generally read kabbalistic and mystical literature—I started reading Jakob Boehme's writings, rather curious reading matter—two volumes of Rilke's letters also found their way into my hands *en passant,* and they have moved me profoundly. They include some astonishing pieces. Rumor also has it that Julien Green has published a new book. Do you know anything about it?

I am familiar with the book by Glatzer you ask about. It does quite nicely when it comes to posing the problem, but is feeble in addressing it, and also completely wrong in parts. On top of that, it manages to camouflage rather a lot of factual shortcomings. In my opinion he gives an utterly erroneous interpretation of the "historicization" of unhistorical biblical passages in the talmudic way of thinking, and that is a capital matter.

It will soon be a whole year that my brother has been in jail. Did I write to you that his wife fled? She had been "provisionally" released.[1] That makes his plight even worse, of course.

Things here remain lively and brisk, with no change. Else Lasker-Schüler—who would fit in better in any other country in the world than in the real Orient[2]—is here for the time being, and, as far as I can tell, is right on the brink of madness. All the same, she continues to be a really bewildering figure. She had a thirty-minute conference with King David, about which she now demands kabbalistic edification from me. And I am unfortunately not even convinced that she really saw him.[3] I am careful and methodical in avoiding other literary coryphaei.

Kindest regards,

Yours, Gerhard

[1] My sister-in-law Emmy Scholem (1896–1968) crossed the border a few days after being released, going first to Prague and later to London. She tried to organize support for my brother from abroad.

[2] She arrived in Jerusalem about March 10, 1934.

[3] I was much in her disfavor following this conversation, and she referred to me as "Herr Dispute." I regarded her visions as fiction.

48

SCHOLEM TO BENJAMIN

Dear Walter, APRIL 19, 1934

I wrote to you a week ago, if I'm not mistaken, and still to your old address, of course. I told you the story—at least allusively—of my endeavors with Schocken on your behalf. I received the last dispatch of printed matter from you three days ago and your letter today (dated the 8th—thus a conspicuously long time on its way!). I am hastening to reply and to inform you of the various steps I have taken.

First, I forcefully brought you to the attention of Dr. Robert Weltsch, the *Jüdische Rundschau*'s editor-in-chief, who was in Jerusalem these past weeks and who is a man relatively close to me ideologically. I advised him most urgently to have you collaborate on the critical evaluation of recent literary publications, etc. The *JR*, which has a very large circulation (40,000), would be in a position to pay royalties. The only *concrete* suggestion I could give him with regard to you was: to solicit, from you and nobody else, a commemorative article on the *tenth* anniversary of Franz Kafka's death, which is coming up in June or July, and which is reason for the *JR* to feature Kafka prominently. He (W.) assured me that he would write to you following his return to Berlin. As to his question of whether you were not on the blacklist of authors he is a priori forbidden to print, I could only give him an imprecise answer, as I had just received your pseudonymous article in the *FZ*. He said he would print your work unless he was directly forbidden to do so; because of your esoteric style, however, he doesn't believe this will happen, as long as you haven't been expressly labeled as a contributor to political emigré journals and newspapers. I believed myself safe in denying the latter. Otherwise, Weltsch said he could obviously only print your work periodically, since "not a soul" among his readers would understand you, meaning your writings could be something for a small (but obviously extant) circle of the intellectually and linguistically ambitious.[1] I didn't want to contest this, things being what they are. Much more difficult, if things become more concrete, will be the

---

[1] In 1946, when I had to examine what was left of Jewish libraries (both of public and private origin) in Germany to prepare for their custody by Jewish institutions, I found clear evidence that such a readership existed for Benjamin's work. I came across carefully filed clippings from the *Jüdische Rundschau* containing W.B.'s Kafka essay. I managed to put a copy aside for myself as a memento, and I own it to this day.

question of what you should write about, since the *Rundschau* is restricted [by the censor] to Jewish themes. I am inclined to believe that a really fine essay on Kafka in this publication could be very useful for you. But you won't be able to avoid making explicitly formulated references to Jewishness.

Second: I asked the editor of the Schocken Library,[2] those small Jewish pocket volumes, Dr. M[oritz] Spitzer, Hunsrückstrasse 22, Bensheim, if he couldn't recruit you for one or more small books. He would *very much* like to do so, if he only had some *proposals:* for what. The Library has a relatively popular profile and he—he asks me in his last letter to induce you to send him proposals if you can think of any that would fit in with the Library's approach. I proposed to let you make a selection of Molitor's work.[3] But that is too exclusive for his taste, not popular enough. If you have an idea, I urge you to establish contact with him: he has a high opinion of you.

Now to your letter: I detest Herr Reiss, a fat Berlin-W[est] Jew, half jobber, half snob, and I am not very charmed by the prospect you raise of my intervening with him. On the other hand, it is also unclear to me whether he has read your book or whether the whole thing is just Herr Wiesengrund's idea. That Reiss is vigorously riding the Zionist wave is well known, but that wave is not so much mine as that of Herr Joachim Prinz, Herr Kastein,[4] or similar contemporaries. It is utterly unclear to me how you imagine I—acting as the "expert"—could possibly discover *Zionist* elements in your book, and you will have to lend me a real hand with a list of hints. The only "Jewish" passage in your manuscript was the one I urgently asked you to leave out at the time,[5] and I don't know how you imagine what the procedure will be if you are unable to add sections that are directly relevant in *content*, not just inspired by some

---

[2] The *Schocken Bücherei* [Library] was one of the most important phenomena in the intellectual life of German Jews from 1933 to 1938 (until Schocken Verlag was closed down, a few months after *Kristallnacht*). It published 93 volumes of uneven but often remarkable value and distinction. Its editor, the Indologist Moritz Spitzer (born 1900), lives in Jerusalem.

[3] Franz Joseph Molitor's *Philosophie der Geschichte, oder Über die Tradition*, 4 vols. (Münster: Theissing, 1827–57), the most remarkable German book on the Kabbalah, written by a Christian theosophist and follower of Franz von Baader. Volume 1 appeared in 1827, but it was republished in 1857 in a second edition that almost doubled the size of the first.

[4] The rabbi Joachim Prinz (born 1902) and the writer Joseph Kastein (1890–1946) were at the time very influential lecturers and authors. In 1931 Prinz published a popular *Jüdische Geschichte* (Berlin: Verlag für Kulturpolitik). Kastein (a pseudonym for Katzenstein) published *Eine Geschichte der Juden* (Berlin: Rowohlt, 1931) [*History and Destiny of the Jews*, trans. Huntley Paterson (New York: Viking, 1933)]. Both advocated a strict Zionist line with great bravura and found many readers, especially after 1933. Kastein emigrated to Palestine in 1933.

[5] See note 3 to letter 11.

106

metaphysical *posture* which will certainly leave Herr Reiss utterly indifferent. You unfortunately also considerably overestimate my wisdom when you assume I could make your book's "Jewish aspect," which is very obscure to me, clear to a publisher. By the way, I don't know Herr Reiss personally. It goes without saying that, were the publishing house to turn to me *of its own initiative,* I would make every possible effort on your behalf—of that I can assure you—but I must, with a certain skepticism, leave it up to you whether you think it advisable to propose me as a prospective "authority."

How about doing something really daring in Paris and going to see Leo Shestov?[6] That shouldn't present such immense difficulties.

I have not yet understood your essay in the *Zeitschrift für Sozialforschung.* Is it intended to be a Communist credo? And if not, then what actually is it? I have to admit that I don't know at all where you stand this year. Despite all the attempts, which you will recall, I have never succeeded—even in the past— in gaining a clarification from you as to your position. And now, following the dawn of the new eternity, when you seem even less predisposed to it because of your horrible external circumstances, I will manage to do so even less. And that is really lamentable. But you know all that much better than I do. You seem to have filed all my intensive questions, which have never been answered by any Brecht-style *Versuche,*[7] away in your inner registry.[8]

Many have been trying to get hold of *The Trial* for you—without success so far. Incidentally, Schocken wants, as he told me, to buy up all publisher's rights to Kafka's books and to reprint everything.

I am afraid that Escha is in very poor health. She is very worn down. If her condition doesn't improve, she will have to go to the hospital. She sends her cordial regards and many thanks.

I hope that your Parisian *démarches* have led to some success or other. Write me immediately if possible.

Our latest guest in Palestine these days—as I may have written

[6] Lev Shestov (Schwarzmann, 1866–1938), a Russian-Jewish philosopher of religion and author, whose books, which were usually translated into German (e.g., *Auf Hiobs Wage,* 1929), had impressed me. [*In Job's Balances: On the Sources of the Eternal Truths,* trans. Camilla Coventry and C. A. Macartney (1932; Athens, Ohio: Ohio University Press, 1975).] He moved to Paris in 1922.

[7] [A play on the title of Brecht's *Versuche,* the journal-format vehicle for many of his publications between 1930 and 1955. Literally translated as "attempts" or "experimental writings."—TRANS.]

[8] This assumption, confirmed two letters later, turned out to be completely incorrect, which came as no small surprise to me. He kept my letter of March 30, 1931, the original of which he had removed from the sheaf of my letters and saved separately, with his Paris papers, which years later came to Frankfurt. But he had forgotten about it (or ascribed it to Max Rychner) and therefore also about the two letters that followed it. All pertinent documents are to be found in *Briefe,* pp. 522–33, and in the appendix to my *W.B.,* pp. 227–34.

you—is Else Lasker-Schüler. A ruin, more haunted than inhabited by madness.

All the best for today,

Yours, Gerhard

49

BENJAMIN TO SCHOLEM

[UNMAILED DRAFT OF THE BEGINNING
OF THE LETTER OF MAY 6, 1934][1]
HÔTEL FLORIDOR
28 PLACE DENFERT-ROCHEREAU
PARIS XIV
APRIL 28, 1934

Dear Gerhard,

I am writing to you with unaccustomed promptness and in an unaccustomed form. I do not want to fail to make use of the rare constellation of events that puts a typewriter at my disposal, the more so since your letter of the 19th of this month has already intensely preoccupied me.

Intensely and sorrowfully. Is our understanding really threatened? Has it become impossible for such an expert on my development as you are, an expert on almost all the forces and conditions influencing this development, to keep up to date? Do you and I stand in danger of your interest one day taking on the color of pity?

A correspondence such as we maintain is, as you know, something very precious, but also something calling for circumspection. This circumspection by no means precludes touching on difficult questions. But these can only be treated as very private ones. To the extent that this has happened, the letters in question have definitely been filed—you can be sure of that—in my "inner registry." On the other hand, I sometimes get the impression that you don't raise those questions as very private ones, which they are and remain, but more as the stages of a controversy.

This is the only way in which I can explain to myself that you respond to the latest essay I sent you with the question: "Is it intended to be a Communist credo?" You know very well that I have always written according to my convictions—save perhaps a few minor exceptions—but that I have never made the attempt to express the contradictory and

[1] This typewritten draft is among W.B.'s papers in East Berlin and was sent to me together with the copies of my own letters.

108

mobile whole that my convictions represent in their multiplicity, except in very extraordinary cases and then never other than orally.

And some shabby literature survey is supposed to have provided occasion for a credo?! Materialism—even in its most vulgar form—is able to address the problems raised by the study of contemporary literature. [Letter breaks off here.]

50

BENJAMIN TO SCHOLEM

HÔTEL FLORIDOR
28 PLACE DENFERT-ROCHEREAU
PARIS XIV
MAY 6, 1934

This, my dear Gerhard, does not represent the first attempt to reply to your letter. But if the repeated endeavors point to a difficulty, that difficulty does not lie in the content of information you request, but in the form of your request. You dress it up as a—perhaps rhetorical—question: "Is it intended to be a Communist credo?"

Such questions, it seems to me, tend to absorb salt on their way across the ocean and then taste somewhat bitter to the person who has been questioned. I do not deny that such is my case. I cannot imagine what really new things the essay in question could have taught you about me. It leaves me utterly amazed that you seem to want to find a summa—or a credo, as you call it—precisely in this text.

We both know from experience the kind of circumspection necessitated by the meaningful correspondence we are wresting from a long-standing separation. This circumspection by no means precludes touching on difficult questions. But these can only be treated as very private ones. To the extent this has happened, the letters in question have definitely been filed—you can be sure of that—in my "inner registry." But I cannot promise this for your last question: it seems to me to be born more out of a controversy than out of our correspondence.

It should be apparent that we cannot maintain a correspondence in the manner of a controversy. And when items appear in the course of our exchange that suggest such a treatment, there is—it seems to me— no other course for its partners than to turn to the vivid image each carries in himself of the other. I believe that my image in you is not that of a man who easily and needlessly commits himself to a "credo." You

109

know that my writings have certainly always conformed to my convictions, but that I have only seldom made the attempt—and then only in conversation—to express the whole contradictory grounds from which those convictions arise in the individual manifestations they have taken.

And a survey of French literature is supposed to have offered me the rubric under which to do so!?—As far as I can remember, I was actually once given the opportunity to write something under that rubric. At least, it could have been considered as such, since it occurred in the context of a controversy. I found it in the form of a letter Max Rychner wrote to me several years ago. It wouldn't surprise me if I sent you a copy of my answer at the time.[1] If not, then I cannot make up for it now: that letter is among my papers in Berlin.

But what could even that letter tell you which would be new?! That, among all the possible forms and means of expression, a credo is the last thing my communism resorts to; that—even at the cost of its orthodoxy—my communism is absolutely nothing other than the expression of certain experiences I have undergone in my thinking and in my life; that it is a drastic, not infertile expression of the fact that the present intellectual industry finds it impossible to make room for my thinking, just as the present economic order finds it impossible to accommodate my life; that it represents the obvious, reasoned attempt on the part of a man who is completely or almost completely deprived of any means of production to proclaim his right to them, both in his thinking and in his life—that it is all this and much more, though in each case nothing but the lesser evil (see Kraus's letter to the female landowner who declared her opinion of Rosa Luxemburg)[2]—is it really necessary to say all this to you?

I must say I would naturally be dismayed if you found anything in these words even remotely resembling a retraction. The evil—compared to those that surround us—is of so much less that it should be affirmed in every practical, productive form, except for the unpractical, unproductive form of the credo.

And this practice—a scholarly one in the case of the essay you accuse—leaves the theory (the credo, if you like) a much greater freedom than the Marxists suspect. Alas, you seem to approve of their innocent ignorance in this case.

---

[1] Max Rychner (1897–1965), a Swiss literary critic with whom W.B. corresponded. See *Briefe*, pp. 522–24, for the letter to R. mentioned here. W.B. did send me a copy of the letter at the time. See my reply in the subsequent letter contained in that collection [pp. 525–29].

[2] Kraus's dazzling reply to the "Antwort an Rosa Luxemburg von einer Unsentimentalen" in *Die Fackel* 554 (November 1920), pp. 6–12.

You force me to state that the alternatives which are obviously the reason for your concern do not possess the merest glimpse of vitality in my eyes. These alternatives may be fashionable—I do not deny a party's right to declare them—but nothing can move me to accept them.

If the significance of Brecht's work—and it is to his work that you allude, but, as far as I know, without having ever passed judgment—can be characterized for me, it is rather this: it advances not *one* of the alternatives that do not matter to me. And the not insubstantial importance to me of Kafka's work resides not least in the fact that he doesn't take up *any* of the positions communism is right to be fighting.

So much for your question. And this is the right point for a transition to the ideas contained in your letter, for which I thank you very much. I need not say just how important a commission to write about Kafka would be to me. But if I had to treat explicitly his position within Judaism, I could not do so without pointers from other parties. I cannot encourage my ignorance to improvise in this case. Of course, word from Weltsch has not as yet been forthcoming.

I am sorry for both of us that your efforts with Schocken were futile, without finding this surprising. Nor was I surprised by your portrait of Reiss, about whom I knew nothing, although I do now, and—as I freely admit—it was precisely the image that I had awaited of him. I have heard nothing more from him on the subject since.

I would certainly be glad to work for the small series edited by Spitzer; it is just that no suitable idea has occurred to me as yet. On the other hand, I will spare us both from a recitation of the many attempts—some of which were certainly inferior—to create a basis for my existence here. They did not keep me from writing a longish essay, "The Author as Producer," which comments on current questions of literary politics. I don't yet know if it will appear in print.[3]

Green's *Visionnaire* was a great disappointment to me. At the moment I am busy with a *wretched* study of Flaubert's aesthetics, published by Klostermann in Frankfurt in a very pretentious form, and written by a certain Paul Binswanger.[4] I am by contrast enjoying Brecht's new political drama *Die Rundköpfe und die Spitzköpfe*,[5] which I received a few

---

[3] This essay was one of the most outspoken Marxist texts Benjamin ever wrote. It was a lecture he finished on April 27, 1934, and which was supposed to be held (but never was) at the Institute for the Study of Fascism, a communist-front organization. He later abandoned efforts to get the text printed at the time (*GS* 2:683–701, 1460f.). [In *Reflections*, pp. 220–38.]

[4] *GS* 3:423–25.

[5] Brecht's advance copy of the play for *Versuche* 8 (1933), only the proofs of which are extant, reads: "The play 'Die Spitzköpfe und die Rundköpfe oder Reich und Reich gesellt sich gern' is the 17th of the *Versuche*." The play was first published by Malik Verlag in

days ago in the final manuscript form. Incidentally, I am now getting quite a few books, since a number of the larger publishing houses have accorded me a sort of *service de presse.*

I must ask you to at least hint at the designs you associate with your suggestion that I look up Lev Shestov. What I have read of his, e.g., in *Kreatur*,[6] doesn't give me enough background to make such a step. I cannot find any concrete facts about him in my memory.

Might I add a postscript concerning Weltsch at this point? Besides the essay on Kafka, it would be most desirable by far if the *Rundschau* would entrust me with a regular book review section, preferably one that finds its expression in the remittance of review copies. And I say this less in the interest of my library than from the experience that such sections tend to become the smoothest part of editorial operations. Such a regular section need not appear frequently. I would be very pleased if you could put this suggestion to Weltsch. That also seems the only course to take in the long run, because the Jewish link would then at least be thematically established.

The whole question is not without a certain importance, since the discrepancies between contributing to journals published in Germany and contributing to emigré journals are becoming more and more insurmountable, even for the writer who is flexible. Even pseudonyms can offer no more than a brief subterfuge. I myself am trying to put off the decision for as long as possible, as is understandable in my position; but indications have been accumulating that this decision will have to be made in the foreseeable future.[7]

I am truly disheartened to learn from your letter of Escha's poor health. I hope very much that you will soon have better news to report, and I ask you in the meantime to convey my genuine wishes for a speedy recovery.

And fondest regards!

Yours, Walter

London in 1938. It is published in Brecht's *Gesammelte Werke*, vol. 2 (Frankfurt am Main: Suhrkamp Verlag, 1967).

[6] The quarterly edited by Buber, Viktor von Weizsäcker, and Joseph Wittig from 1926 to 1930, to which W.B. also contributed.

[7] W.B. did in fact succeed in placing contributions in the *Frankfurter Zeitung* until June 1935 under the pseudonym Detlef Holz.

BENJAMIN TO SCHOLEM

HÔTEL FLORIDOR
28 PLACE DENFERT-ROCHEREAU
PARIS XIV
MAY 15, 1934

Just a few rushed lines for today. And more, to inform you that Weltsch's anticipated invitation has arrived.[1] I expressed my great willingness to take on the Kafka assignment. But I also wrote him that I thought it would be both loyal and practical to advise him that my interpretation of Kafka diverges from Brod's. I did so because I thought it correct to establish clarity on this point, in order to avoid having the essay, which will require my full dedication in any case, rejected for reasons having to do with my viewpoint.

No answer has as yet been forthcoming; but I don't want to wait for it to tell you that I ask you to support me in this project as much as possible. That could take two forms. First, I don't know to what extent I'll be able to muster together Kafka's most important books here; as you know, not all of them can still be found in bookstores. If everything else fails, I could telegraph you the titles of the most important books I don't have—i.e., ask you to lend them to me if possible. (Unfortunately, this, the technical side of the matter, is complicated by the deadline.) Second, as I believe I intimated in my last letter, your own special views on Kafka —emanating as they do from Jewish insights—would be of the greatest importance for my undertaking, that is to say, virtually indispensable. Could you sketch them for me?

I have just—though I've surely written you this as well—finished an essay I regard as not unimportant. You will receive a copy as soon as I can dislodge one of the few available.[2] It is entitled "The Author as Producer."

That's all for today, along with the kindest regards and all the best wishes for Escha's health.

Yours, Walter

---

[1] The letter to Weltsch is published in *Briefe*, pp. 607–8.

[2] The essay was never sent, which is probably not as coincidental as might seem from these letters. Even when I asked him for a copy of it in Paris in the course of our great argument about his brand of Marxism, he replied quite openly: "I think I had better not let you read it" (see Scholem, *W.B.*, p. 201).

BENJAMIN TO SCHOLEM

HÔTEL FLORIDOR
28 PLACE DENFERT-ROCHEREAU
PARIS XIV
JUNE 2, 1934

Dear Gerhard,

I am sorry that your reply to my letter before the last still has not reached me, for it was an important one. The reason for these lines is certainly not to admonish you—you will find the right time yourself—but rather the fear that I may have embarrassed you somewhat about the Kafka matter in my last letter, which you must have had in hand for a week by now.

It would of course be of immense value for me to receive reflections on Kafka from you. But, on the other hand, let me tell you that my essay is virtually finished, more or less. I am indeed grateful for the opportunity you provided for me to write it. I did not harbor the intention of writing it for so many years in vain.[1] But what is to the subject matter's advantage is to the disadvantage of the occasion. The article promises to become quite long, such that I can hardly expect it to be published unabridged in the *Jüdische Rundschau*. But I do hope—not without some despair—to be able to prune it down to a version that would run to a third of its actual length.

Well, as I said, the text is not quite there yet, and I would not be bringing it up if it did not mean a great deal to me to make use of this now doubly precious opportunity to write to you. Doubly precious, because on the one hand I am completely preoccupied with the work in question, and am therefore without private life or private thoughts until it gets done, and second, because I just happen to have a secretary at my disposal.

I must exploit this opportunity all the more since it may be the last for some time. I am traveling to Brecht in Denmark at the middle of the month and will spend the summer there.

What my stay there will accomplish remains in doubt. At any rate, I have my books there; and living there is supposed to be especially cheap. Once I arrive, the problem of the Baader collected edition will again become acute, for under these circumstances I will have to part with it, should Jerusalem be willing to purchase it for a suitable price. I would be very grateful if you could effect something along these lines—in accord with your earlier suggestions.

---

[1] Hermann Schweppenhäuser published the voluminous notes W.B. had made for such a work in the critical apparatus to *GS* 2:1190–1270.

On the other hand, I am now in a position to release you from any obligation with regard to Kafka's *Trial*. Quite by accident, I found the book in a French bookshop at the original price, which I paid, no matter how remote in the foggy distance the days have become when to buy a book was a matter of course. But since Palestine hasn't exactly distinguished itself on the Kafka question, especially in the person of Kitty Marx, whose allegiance and resourcefulness I thought very highly of, I don't want to neglect to say that the person who could come up with a copy of *Betrachtung*, which my library still lacks, would achieve great, if late, honors.

I gather from Weltsch's last letter that Schocken is planning a complete Kafka edition.[2] No matter what his attitude to my work may be, I hope you can in all good conscience show him my Kafka essay one day in such a way that he feels inclined to send a complimentary copy of the collected edition to my address.

So much for now, and with the hope of receiving news from you here before my departure. Incidentally, mail will be forwarded to me, but please take into account that it is not impossible that letters from France to Denmark might travel through Germany. I will send you my Danish address as soon as I am over there.

Kindest regards and further good wishes for Escha's recovery,

Yours, Walter

53

SCHOLEM TO BENJAMIN

Dear Walter, JUNE 20, 1934

Your last three letters are lying in front of me, together with a letter to you, which has been superseded by your last letter and therefore urges me to write the new letter you want. I am very pleased that you have taken on the work on Kafka, but I see no opportunity in the weeks to come to express myself on this topic. You will no doubt best follow your line without the mystical prejudices that I alone am in a position to spread, and you can moreover rely on great resonance from within the *Rundschau*'s audience. Anyway, why shouldn't the *JR* publish the un-

---

[2] This edition appeared in six volumes from 1935 to 1937. (The first volume was actually already on the market at the end of 1934.)

abridged text of your essay, in installments? I definitely don't regard that as hopeless, especially given the personality of the editor-in-chief. That you already have *The Trial* both pleases and saddens me—I had hoped to acquire it for you from Ernst David's effects (as I had just informed you in my letter when your last letter arrived). On the other hand, I can only tell you at the outset that I cannot make any promises about a copy of *Betrachtung,* because such a rarity would first go to me, who has already made many attempts to obtain it.[1] I have only now located someone in Jerusalem who even owns the book, although it cannot be bought or schnorred. I can guarantee that you shall receive the entire Schocken edition, mainly because Weltsch will print your essay, at the very earliest, after the new edition (promised for the near future) has been published (since the tenth anniversary of Kafka's death was June 3, anyway). In that case, you can get it from the *JR* as a review copy. Anyway, you are sure to get it.

Regarding your Baader proposal, I truly regret that you never gave even a negative reply over the last few years, when I made concrete proposals to you on the library's behalf. I am unconditionally in favor of the library's acquiring your edition, of course, and I see the situation as follows: I *guarantee* you a price of *16 English pounds*; the library has *absolutely nothing* at the moment, but it is eminently conceivable, as I was able to ascertain in a conversation with [Hugo] Bergmann, that we would get the whole sum once we have the volumes here and can therefore *show them directly* to a tourist who happens along and ask him to write a check for them, in which case I think it *might* be possible to get up to 20 pounds. I am of the opinion that the books ought to be in the library, but since I cannot be 100% certain, I declare that if you send them and the library is unable to buy them, I would myself undertake to pay you £16. I say this primarily to induce you to make your decision at once and, if affirmative, to have the books sent here in several parcels right away. You would be reimbursed for the shipping costs; if I am not mistaken, a shipment of 16 or 17 volumes (16, I believe) shouldn't amount to more than £2. I am also of the opinion that, if you send the books very soon, it would be possible to secure their purchase price from a lady who is residing in Jerusalem for the time being and has helped us out several times in the past in similar cases. I would ask her for £18–20.[2] Please let me know your decision as soon as possible. You can have the books sent to the library or to me personally, as long as you inform me which course you decide upon.

---

[1] I succeeded in getting a copy of Kafka's *Betrachtung* [Leipzig: Rowohlt Verlag, 1913] for myself only after the war.

[2] The lady was Vera Bryce Salomons (1880–1969), a woman to whom Jerusalem's cultural institutions are greatly indebted for her services.

As for your letter of May 6, I find myself in a strange situation. Many facts of our correspondence must have escaped your memory, as you no longer remember what seemed to draw you to an explanation of your situation once in the past, even if only temporarily. You write that you were given the genuine rubric only once, in the form of a letter Rychner sent you several years back, and "It wouldn't surprise me if I sent you a copy of my answer at the time." Alas, dear Walter, the main point lies somewhat differently: it was not Herr Rychner who wrote a letter to you —that was just a short, though weighty question[3]—but myself, in reply to your letter to him which you did indeed send me and which I felt was principally directed toward me. And it is to this letter, which has so utterly vanished from your consciousness but at the time impressed you so differently, that I am still waiting for the reply, a reply you had declared you were unable to make.[4] We are debating with feigned positions, and I do not view this with pleasure. I have been waiting for years for an exposition on such implicit questions as I asked you back then and which you must have long ago forgotten. And when I go searching for an answer and very cautiously believe to have found it in a superbly written essay which I understood as a responsible statement, you are surprised, to take a verb that carries the least weight, and tell me that I have to go back to the letter that specifically elicited my fundamental criticism three and a half years ago if I really want to know what your position is. I didn't understand your attitude then at all, and I haven't become any wiser in the meantime. You felt very strongly then that an answer was absolutely necessary, yet that answer has been sorely missing so far. I would like to hope that the essay you promised me, "The Author as Producer," will help me a lot further along, since its title seems to smack of such an answer, but I haven't received it yet. Your postscript, in which you tell me that I have to take into account the possibility that this letter may not find you in Paris anymore,[5] prevents me from going into matters in detail right now and prompts me to send this letter to your present address as fast as I can.

What is a *service de presse* for large publishing houses? Can you remedy my ignorance?

If the idea of Shestov doesn't say anything concrete to you, then my earlier suggestion obviously loses its point. I thought that the man's

[3] He sent W.B. an article of his that was critical of a Marxist article written by Bernard von Brentano and entitled "Kapitalismus und schöne Literatur." He directed his question at W.B. in the form of a medieval Latin proverb: "Dic cur hic" ("Tell me why you stand here," that is, on the grounds of Marxism).

[4] It is apparent from W.B.'s letter to me of April 17, 1931, that this letter of mine had made a big impression on him. Cf. *Briefe*, pp. 525–29.

[5] The reference is to W.B.'s warning against a possible interception of the letters in Germany.

writings would be vividly in your mind, and that you had been impressed by them, but of course there is no sense in going to see him with the mere conception of an author who writes in the *Kreatur*. I think very highly of the man.

The semester has just ended and I have several months to pursue my own work. And I shall do just that with a vengeance. Escha's sciatica has improved over the last fortnight; she is back to working three hours a day but is still far from recovered. I will possibly, even probably, be writing several things in German this summer, so I will have something to offer you; in general, my writing is now done in Hebrew. These days I can celebrate a rare jubilee, on the appearance of the final part of an essay I published in a journal here which runs to the modest length of 15 pages: an analysis of the development of certain mystical terms. I plan to write on religious nihilism.[6] And, just to be on the safe side, I acquired a seat in a synagogue "for life"; judge from that how delicate the topic is![7]

Please, write from Scandinavia! Could you send me—at my expense, if need be—a copy of Brecht's *Saint Joan of the Stockyards*?

Kindest regards,

Yours, Gerhard

54

BENJAMIN TO SCHOLEM

C/O FRAU RAAHANGE
SKOVSBOSTRAND PER SVENDBORG
DENMARK
JULY 3, 1934

Dear Gerhard,

I cannot find an explanation for your silence, and only hope that the circumstances causing it will soon be remedied.

Moritz Spitzer sent me an invitation—still framed in general terms, for the present—to contribute to the Schocken Library, an offer that pleased me very much. I can't see where it will lead to for now, since "the sensitive Brod" is likely to look upon "another publication on K.

---

[6] I ended up writing this essay in the summer of 1936, in Hebrew. It was a longish piece designed to give insight into the Sabbatian messianic movement (1666–67) and its consequences for seventeenth- and eighteenth-century Judaism.

[7] I did indeed attend the Sabbath services at this synagogue during the two years I spent on this project, even if not exactly for the ironic reason given here.

prior to the appearance of his own biography" as a "territorial violation."[1]

I don't need to reiterate that I can hardly wait for your comments on my "Kafka."

Weltsch sent me a preliminary letter acknowledging receipt and has reserved to himself the right to print the whole or a part.

I am delighted to have regained possession here of part of my library; moreover, it includes the Baader. An offer for it by the Jerusalem library would be very welcome, as you know.

I am counting on receiving news from you soon (not to mention news about the Kafka manuscript) at the address given above.

With kind regards,

Yours, Walter

55

BENJAMIN TO SCHOLEM

Dear Gerhard,   [JULY 9, 1934]

I just received the lines you sent to Paris on June 20th. The first thing I gleaned from them is that my memory seems to have a vulnerable point. Indeed, the letter of inquiry you refer to seems to have slipped it altogether. That is regrettable, even though it can be explained. A memory that has to digest impressions imparted by unforeseeably changing living conditions will rarely be as reliable as one sustained by continuity. On the other hand, questions can be repeated. Whether that would be the right approach here is of course not for me to decide. For I can't guarantee you that I am in a position today to answer them in written form. And you will share my view that it would be unwise to lessen the prospects of an—though perhaps still distant—oral exchange of views through inadequate attempts at written explanation.

There are, besides the direct ones, numerous indirect avenues of approach for us to take. And thus—treading one of these paths—I don't shy away from repeating my request that you tell me something of your reflections on Kafka, despite your last refusal.[1] My request is all the

[1] Obviously quotes from Spitzer's letter.
[1] I had set forth such reflections in my letter of August 1, 1931, which he had with him

119

more justified since my own reflections on this subject are now before you. Even though I have articulated their principal features, they have further preoccupied me since my arrival in Denmark and, if I am not mistaken, will continue to do so for a while. You are the indirect cause of this work; I see no subject more perfectly suited to our correspondence. And it doesn't seem to me that you can refuse my request.[2]

Otherwise, I must get busy working on things that have little in common. Because one goal of my activities in Paris is to come out next winter with an article in the *Nouvelle Revue Française*, and since they suggested Bachofen as the theme to this end, I shall have to study Bachofen.[3] Other subjects are slated for the *Zeitschrift für Sozialforschung*, and it looks as if I won't be able to sidestep the study on Eduard Fuchs indefinitely, no matter how bitter I may find it.

I have part of my library here, as you know, and it is well housed with my neighbor. Still, it amounts, in total, to just under half of my books. But it isn't only my books that will make my work easier over the next few months; rather, the very fact that I have this neighbor has relieved me of my most immediate worries and I can once again catch my breath. Mme. Weigel,[4] to whom I must ask you to address my letters, is as friendly as can be imagined; her husband, unfortunately, entered the hospital shortly before my arrival and is still there. The two children, aged ten and three, are quite charming, and we have become fast friends.[5]

Two of the four parcels in which I am sending you the Baader are being sent with the same mail as this letter. The work stood in my library for 19 years; may it occupy a more secure berth in Israel, be it in the Jerusalem library or in yours. See what you can do and be assured of my gratitude in any case. What is so special about Shestov? I would like more precise information. Can you refer me to some of his books? Perhaps lend me some, should the need arise? I will make an effort to obtain a copy of the play you ask for as soon as my neighbor is home from the hospital. I am sure that it can be obtained, one way or another.

Your question about the *service de presse* brought on a dream in which mine was revoked; let me therefore hasten to provide you with the expla-

---

in Paris among his Kafka papers but which must have slipped his memory as well. It is printed in Scholem, *W.B.*, pp. 170–71. In 1928, when he began his "Notizen zu Kafka," he had already decided to dedicate his projected work "to Gerhard Scholem" (*GS* 2:1190).

[2] I replied with the then unpublished poem in letter 57, which I wrote in early 1933.

[3] The Bachofen essay, written in French, was rejected by the *NRF* and was first published many years after Benjamin's death (*GS* 2:219–33, as well as pp. 963–67 in the editorial apparatus).

[4] Helene Weigel, Bertolt Brecht's wife.

[5] Stefan and Barbara.

nation while I still enjoy its benefits. There are various kinds of *service de presse*: one whereby certain critics or editorial offices are sent every new publication—but that is not the case for me—and one whereby the publishing house agrees to make its new titles available to the respective tabloid or reviewer upon request: this is how it works for me.

So much for today. I must ask you to remain patient a little longer concerning "The Author as Producer"; I had too few copies made, so I don't at present have any at my disposal.

Please write as soon as possible. With kindest regards and all the best wishes for Escha's further recovery,

Yours, Walter

P.S. The first volume of the Baader, which I sent you care of the Hebrew University Library, includes the—of course extremely rare—invitation to subscribe to the series, which I came across by chance long after I acquired the Baader itself. It may be of some use to you if you have to show the copy to a third party.

56

BENJAMIN TO SCHOLEM

Dear Gerhard, [POSTMARK: JULY 11, 1934]

The first two parcels of the Baader went off yesterday, registered in your name but addressed to the library of the university; the other two will follow tomorrow.

Please notify me of their arrival immediately. I hope the Kafka manuscript has already been sent off to me. I need it all the more because I have undertaken a very extensive revision, so the one you possess has now been superseded in some respects.

Nonetheless, I must renew my request for your thorough and—should it be necessary—vigorous criticism.

Kind regards,

Yours, Walter

57

SCHOLEM TO BENJAMIN [1]

51 RAMBAN ST.
REHAVIA, JERUSALEM
JULY 9, 1934

Dear Walter,

I hope you received my lengthy letter, which I still sent to Paris, assuming that it would be forwarded to you. In the meantime, I was in Tel Aviv for a week, to spend a few weeks doing nothing after the semester's end, and upon my arrival I found your shipment with the Kafka article, along with your request for its immediate return.[2] I freely admit that this request was a great disappointment: on the one hand, I can't count on the [*Jüdische*] *Rundschau* printing the essay completely unabridged (unless it decides in favor of four installments), and, on the other hand, I don't know how I am supposed to comment on your findings if you demand its return, and, third, I am of the opinion that it definitely belongs in the archive kept here anyway and why do you begrudge me this copy?

Some months back, I gave a theological didactic poem on *The Trial* to Weltsch, who wanted to print it together with your essay. We will present a most pleasant contrast because, as utterly distanced as I feel from the somewhat harmless-idiotic quotations of the "theological" interpreters you mention,[3] I am still firmly convinced that a theological aspect of this world, in which God does not appear, is the most legitimate of such interpretations. Since one doesn't know when the *Rundschau* will be presenting us in brotherly unity, I don't hesitate to present you with this product, which I composed some time ago for Kitty Marx's theological instruction. It appears to me that we meet in some areas, despite the different directions from which we clearly approach the matter. Your

---

[1] [This letter is printed only in part in the German edition of this book. Scholem wrote: "It is especially regrettable that precisely the first sheet (or the first page) of this letter has been lost, or has at least not been found in the Benjamin archive of the East Berlin Academy of Arts. Written around July 10–12, it contained confirmation of the Kafka manuscript being received, as well as the first statement of my position on it. It crossed with his letter of July 9 (no. 55). In the letters that follow, both of us make reference to this letter and the accompanying poem (printed here). Is it possible that a renewed search might still bring the missing piece to light?" The complete letter presented here in translation was first published in the posthumous collection of Scholem's essays and miscellany on Benjamin, *Walter Benjamin und sein Engel*, pp. 193–95.—TRANS.]

[2] This request was made in Benjamin's handwriting on the copy.

[3] This had to do with a number of quotations from articles by Max Brod and Hans Joachim Schoeps, as well as their jointly composed afterword to the first edition of Kafka's posthumous *Beim Bau der Chinesischen Mauer* [Berlin: Gustav Kiepenheuer Verlag, 1931; not reprinted in *The Great Wall of China: Stories and Reflections*, trans. Willa and Edwin Muir (New York: Schocken Books, 1946, 1970); see also the typescript found among W.B.'s papers, "Franz Kafka: Beim Bau der Chinesischen Mauer," *GS* 2:676–83.—TRANS.].

portrayal of the preanimistic age as Kafka's seeming present—if I understand you correctly—is really quite piercing and magnificent. The nullity of such a present[4] seems to me to be very problematic, problematic in those final points that are also decisive here. I would like to say that 98% of it makes sense, but the final touch is missing, which you seem to have sensed, since you moved away from that level with your interpretation of shame (you definitely hit the mark there) and of the Law (which is where you get into difficulties!). The *existence* of secret law foils your interpretation: it should not exist in a premythical world of chimeric confusion, to say nothing of the very special way in which it even announces its existence. *There* you went much too far with your elimination of theology, throwing the baby out with the bathwater.

But that requires greater elaboration. I send you this in haste for now, and to express my most sincere gratitude.

And one question: Who is actually the source of all those stories? Does Ernst Bloch have them from you or you from him? The great rabbi with the profound dictum on the messianic kingdom who appears in Bloch[5] is none other than *I* myself; what a way to achieve fame!! It was one of my first ideas about the Kabbalah.

My kindest regards,

Yours, Gerhard

[ENCLOSED WITH LETTER 57 ON A SEPARATE SHEET]
With a Copy of Kafka's "Trial"

Are we totally separated from you?
Is there not a breath of your peace,
Lord, or your message
Intended for us in such a night?

Can the sound of your word
Have so faded in Zion's emptiness,
Or has it not even entered
This magic realm of appearance?

The great deceit of the world
Is now consummated.

[4] [This is where the letter printed in the German edition starts.—TRANS.]

[5] In Ernst Bloch's *Spuren*, the same sentence ascribed by W.B. to a "great rabbi" (*GS* 2:423) is quoted from a "truly kabbalistic rabbi." But in 1932 W.B. had already borrowed the sentence verbatim in the version originating from me, in his text "In der Sonne" (*GS* 4:419): "Everything will be as it is here—only slightly different." I learned from this what honors one can garner for oneself with an apocryphal sentence.

Give then, Lord, that he may wake
Who was struck through by your nothingness.

Only so does revelation
Shine in the time that rejected you.
Only your nothingness is the experience
It is entitled to have of you.

Thus alone teaching that breaks through semblance
Enters the memory:
The truest bequest
Of hidden judgment.

Our position has been measured
On Job's scales with great precision.
We are known through and through
As despairing as on the youngest day.

What we are is reflected
In endless instances.
Nobody knows the way completely
And each part of it makes us blind.

No one can benefit from redemption.
That star stands far too high.
And if you had arrived there too,
You would still stand in your way.

Abandoned to powers,
Exorcism is no longer binding.
No life can unfold
That doesn't sink into itself.

From the center of destruction
A ray breaks through at times,
But none shows the direction
The Law ordered us to take.

Since this sad knowledge
Stands before us, unassailable,
A veil has suddenly been torn,
Lord, before your majesty.

Your trial began on earth.
Does it end before your throne?
You cannot be defended,
As no illusion holds true here.

Who is the accused here?
The creature or yourself?
If anyone should ask you,
You would sink into silence.

Can such a question be raised?
Is the answer indefinite?
Oh, we must live all the same
Until your court examines us.

[Mit einem Exemplar von Kafkas "Prozess"

*Sind wir ganz von dir geschieden? / Ist uns, Gott, in solcher Nacht /
nicht ein Hauch von deinem Frieden, / deiner Botschaft zugedacht?
/ Kann dein Wort denn so verklungen / in der Leere Zions sein—/
oder gar nicht eingedrungen / in dies Zauberreich aus Schein? /
Schier vollendet bis zum Dache / ist der grosse Weltbetrug. / Gib
denn, Gott, dass der erwache, / den dein Nichts durchschlug. / So
allein strahlt Offenbarung / in die Zeit, die dich verwarf. / Nur
dein Nichts ist die Erfahrung, / die sie von dir haben darf. / So
allein tritt ins Gedächtnis / Lehre, die den Schein durchbricht: /
das gewisseste Vermächtnis / vom verborgenen Gericht. /
Haargenau auf Hiobs Waage / ward gemessen unser Stand, /
trostlos wie am jüngsten Tage / sind wir durch und durch erkannt. /
In unendlichen Instanzen / reflektiert sich, was wir sind. / Niemand
kennt den Weg im ganzen, / Jedes Stück schon macht uns blind. /
Keinem kann Erlösung frommen, / dieser Stern steht viel zu hoch, /
wärst du auch dort angekommen, / stündst du selbst im Weg dir
noch. / Preisgegeben an Gewalten, / die Beschwörung nicht mehr
zwingt, / kann kein Leben sich entfalten, / das nicht in sich selbst
versinkt. / Aus dem Zentrum der Vernichtung / bricht zu Zeiten
wohl ein Strahl, / aber keiner weist die Richtung, / die uns das
Gesetz befahl. / Seit dies trauervolle Wissen / unantastbar vor uns
steht, / ist ein Schleier jäh zerrissen, / Gott, vor deiner Majestät. /
Dein Prozess begann auf Erden; / endet er vor deinem Thron? / Du
kannst nicht verteidigt werden, / hier gilt keine Illusion. / Wer ist
hier der Angeklagte? / Du oder die Kreatur? / Wenn dich einer
drum befragte, / du versänkst in Schweigen nur. / Kann solche
Frage sich erheben? / Ist die Antwort unbestimmt? / Ach, wir
müssen dennoch leben, / bis uns dein Gericht vernimmt.]*

58

SCHOLEM TO BENJAMIN

Dear Walter,

My plan to write to you on your birthday and at least symbolically render you the tribute you deserve has not been realized. As you may have learned from the newspapers, the sudden death of C. N. Bialik intervened; his funeral took place on your birthday. The impact of the unexpected death of the most morally significant figure in Palestine and the Zionist movement has been enormous. His death also touched me personally very deeply. This man—the author of that treatise "Halacha und Aggada": you may recall my translation of it from our time together in Berne; it was a very significant piece of literature[1]—was one of the people with whom I had the most contact. His spiritual character threw a singular light upon our landscape, he was the most productive spokesman of this land—and that itself means a great deal, indeed very much, to those who know the atmosphere here, where there is no shortage of such people. He was a "teacher" precisely in the sense in which one imagines the great talmudists to have been, a Rabbi Akiba or Johanan. Upon my return from Tel Aviv I found your letter, which crossed in the mail with my letter dealing with Kafka. Meanwhile, you will already have seen that I followed your suggestion even before it reached me, and today I can only reinforce the position taken in those initial remarks. Kafka's world is the world of revelation, but of revelation seen of course from that perspective in which it is returned to its own nothingness. I cannot accept your disavowal of this aspect—if I should really regard it as such, that is, and not just as a misunderstanding brought about by your polemics against Schoepsen and Bröder.[2] The *nonfulfillability* of what has been revealed is the point where a *correctly* understood theology (as I, immersed in my Kabbalah, think, and whose expression you can find more or less responsibly formulated in that open letter to Schoeps you are familiar with) coincides most perfectly with that which offers the key to Kafka's work. Its problem is not, dear Walter, its *absence* in a preanimistic world, but the fact that it cannot *be fulfilled*. It is about this text

---

[1] The essay appeared in *Der Jude* 4 (1919): 125–30. W.B. made use of it in several of his works. [English translations appear under the titles *Law and Legend, or Halakah and Aggada*, trans. Julius L. Siegel (New York: Bloch, 1923), and *Halachah and Aggadah*, trans. Sir Leon Simon (London: Education Department of the Zionist Federation of Great Britain and Ireland, 1944).]

[2] Authors such as Schoeps and Brod.

that we will have to reach an understanding. Those pupils of whom you speak at the end are not so much those who have lost the Scripture— even though a world in which that can happen is already not very Bach-ofen-like either!—but rather those students who cannot decipher it. And it seems to me utterly compelling that a world in which things are so uncannily concrete and in which not a step can be fulfilled will present an *abject* and by no means idyllic sight (which you, for some incomprehensible reason, seem to regard as an objection against the "theological" interpretation, for you ask, astonished, since when a tribunal of a higher "order" has presented itself in such a way as that convened in the attic). On the other hand, you are of course largely right in your analysis of the characters who can only maintain themselves in this way. I am not about to contest that—there is something of the "hetaeric" class in it, and you brought it out in a really incredibly masterful way. I did not understand a few things—least of all what you quote from Kraft. But if you let me hold on to the manuscript, I hope still to enter into some areas in more detail, particularly regarding the "Jewish" aspect, which you seem to be searching for—with Haas—in every corner. And yet the main point raises itself so noticeably and bluntly—namely, in the terminology of the Law, which you stubbornly persist in viewing only from its most *profane* side—that one finds your silence about it quite puzzling. And for this you hardly needed a Haas! You had the *moral world of Halakhah* right before your eyes, complete with its abysses and its dialectics.[3] I am going to close for today, because this has to get in the mail. You will naturally receive word about Baader (we have already been notified of the first shipments) as soon as I can tell you something definite. I thank you most sincerely for everything and send you my regards, also those of Escha, who is unfortunately still ill.

Yours, Gerhard

---

[3] This refers to the contradictory interpretations given by the "religious man" in the cathedral of the parable "Before the Law" in Kafka's *Trial* itself [chapter 9]. (I was of the opinion that the religious man in the cathedral was a disguised halakhist, a rabbi, who knows how to transmit—if not the Law itself—at least the traditions circulating about the Law, in the form of a parable. He is not an official of the "tribunal" by accident, even if only with the rank of a prison chaplain, for that tribunal is somehow linked to the "Law," no matter how one interprets these concepts.)

59

BENJAMIN TO SCHOLEM

C/O HELENE WEIGEL
SKOVSBOSTRAND PER
SVENDBORG
JULY 20, 1934

Dear Gerhard,

Yesterday the long-awaited confirmation that you received my "Kafka" arrived. I prized it immensely, above all because of the enclosed poem. It has been years since I felt such discomfort at the limits imposed on us by our (solely) written communication. I'm sure you understand this sense of limitation and do not assume that I might be able to forgo the manifold experiments in formulation only conversation makes possible, and still say something decisive about the poem. Only the question of the "theological interpretation" is relatively simple. Not only do I unhesitatingly recognize the theological possibility as such in the poem, but also maintain that my essay has its own broad—though admittedly shrouded—theological side. I aimed my remarks against that unbearable posturing of the theological "professionals," who—you won't deny—have held sway over all Kafka interpretations to date and whose smuggest manifestations are yet to come.

To sketch my position with regard to your poem—whose language concedes nothing to that on the *Angelus Novus* which I rank so highly—in at least a little more detail, I only want to name the stanzas with which I unreservedly identify: 7 to 13. And several that precede those. The last stanza raises the question of how one has to imagine, in Kafka's sense, the Last Judgment's projection into world history. Does this projection turn the judge into the accused? And the proceedings into the punishment? Is it devoted to raising up the Law on high, or to burying it? Kafka, so I contend, had no answers to these questions. But the form in which they presented themselves to him—and which I tried to delimit through my comments on the roles of scenic and gestural elements in his books—contains indications of a state of the world in which such questions no longer have a place, because their answers, far from being instructive, make the questions superfluous. Kafka sought—and sometimes glimpsed as in a dream—the structure of this kind of answer that renders the question superfluous. At any rate, one cannot say that he found it. And that is why insight into his work is, among other things, bound up with the simple realization that he failed. "Nobody knows the way completely / And each part of it makes us blind." But when you write: "Only your nothingness is the experience, / It is entitled to have of you," I may relate my interpretive effort to precisely this passage with the following remarks: I endeavored to show how Kafka sought—on the nether side of that "nothingness," in its inside lining, so to speak—to feel his way toward redemption. This implies that any kind of victory over that nothingness, as understood by the theological exegetes around Brod, would have been an abomination for him.

I believe I wrote you that this essay promises to hold my attention for a while yet. And that is also the main reason for requesting that you return the manuscript. The one you have in hand has already been superseded at important points; for the essay, as I already wrote you, has continued to preoccupy me here. I am prepared, however, to promise you a manuscript of the final version for the archive.[1]

Since we will now, to my delight, be appearing together in the *Jüdische Rundschau*, this circumstance might afford you the opportunity to prevail upon Weltsch as to the form of the essay's printed version—an opportunity you are assured by virtue of the fact that you are the initiator of my essay. An examination of the definitive version—which I'll send you after you return the copy now in your possession—will convince you far more than any general considerations just how unsatisfactory it's abridged publication would be for me. The fact that the *Jüdische Rundschau* is published twice weekly is at least some sort of basis for the prospect of having the essay appear in installments. Please give some thought to whether you could accomplish something to this end with Weltsch.[2]

The question, as you can imagine, is also important for me as regards the fee.

I hope to receive word from you very soon that the Baader has arrived. On the one hand, I would be pleased to see it preserved for me in your library, at least *in my imagination,* but, on the other hand, economic considerations are at present so terribly relevant, that any higher figure which might result from a purchase through the library would be exceptionally important to me. A small measure of support provided by German friends, thanks to which I had a bit of leeway in recent months, has failed to come, apparently in the wake of the events in Germany.[3] Since

---

[1] I did indeed receive the new version (see letter 66). It is conceivable that I did not save it if the typescript didn't contain any handwritten emendations, once it had been published in *Schriften* [ed. Theodor W. Adorno (Frankfurt am Main: Suhrkamp, 1961). The English text appears as "Franz Kafka," in *Illuminations*, pp. 111–40)]. In any case, I am no longer able to find it among my papers.

[2] I intervened without success.

[3] An allusion to Hitler's purge of Ernst Röhm and other SA leaders, and its consequences. It may be possible to ascertain the identity of the "German friends" on the basis

I made use of the last of my funds to have my Paris books shipped here, so as not to lose hold of my library by virtue of its being spread throughout Europe, I am left without even a drop of reserves for the time being, which means I am dependent upon B.'s hospitality to a degree that might someday turn out to be precarious.

I believe I wrote you that I began working on an essay on Bachofen for the *Nouvelle Revue Française*. This means that for the first time I shall get to read him myself; up to now I have always relied on Bernoulli and Klages.[4]

Among Svendborg's superior amenities is a radio, which one now needs more than ever. Thus I was able to listen to Hitler's Reichstag speech, and because it was the very first time I had ever heard him, you can imagine the effect.

So much for today. The origin of the stories in "Kafka"[5] remains my secret—one you would only succeed in unraveling by being present in person, in which case I could promise you a whole series of even more exquisite ones. Convey my regards to Kitty Marx and point out that I am still carrying the arrow in my breast which she fixed there by not replying to my last letter.

Most sincerely,

Yours, Walter

60

SCHOLEM TO BENJAMIN

Dear Walter,   JULY 26, 1934

The Baader has arrived, complete and in good condition, and I have taken every step to induce the library to make the purchase, which will no doubt come about. Now I have to ask you to take care of a technical matter: the library requires a signed bill from you for the acquisition, to verify the entries in its books. I enclose a bill, which I ask you to sign

---

of the letters addressed to W.B. kept in East Berlin. My conjectures would include Fritz and Jula Radt.

[4] K. A. Bernoulli, *Johann Jakob Bachofen und das Natursymbol* (Basel: Benno Schwabe, 1924). See *GS* 3:43–45, and *Briefe*, 1:409–10 on W.B. and Klages.

[5] From Pushkin's *Anekdoten und Tischgespräche*, ed. Johannes von Günther, (Munich: Allgemeine Verlagsanstalt, 1924), p. 42.

and return right away. The money will be forwarded to you immediately upon receipt of this bill. Is your *Danish address* still valid? Would it be acceptable to transfer the funds by check, our preferred method? We are *not* able to send postal money orders to all countries from here, and such a procedure takes quite some time anyway. We calculated your mailing costs according to the stamps, but some stamps were missing and so we weighed the books to determine what it would cost to send them to D. from here, adding the fee for registered mail. If the actual amount was higher, then please amend the bill and retype it. The library can't pay more than £16 for the books themselves. I therefore hope that this matter has been settled to the mutual satisfaction of both parties, and it is with reverence and joy that I welcome such a valuable author to our university library.

You should have both of my letters on Kafka. I still plan to make some further observations. I am writing to you in haste because I received this important notification for you just as I am preparing to travel to Tel Aviv, where I want to attend—along with Agnon—the circumcision of Kitty Steinschneider's firstborn son, who made his appearance a week ago.

Best wishes,

Yours, Gerhard

61

BENJAMIN TO SCHOLEM

C/O HELENE WEIGEL
SKOVSBOSTRAND PER
SVENDBORG
JULY 26, 1934

Dear Gerhard,

Only very few lines for today.

I just received from Paris your essay against Breuer, which I read with great enjoyment.[1] When it comes to the manifold relationships this essay is aimed at, you are best able to gauge the measure of my igno-

---

[1] Isaac Breuer (1883–1946) was the main literary spokesman for radical Jewish Orthodoxy in Germany. My essay "Politik der Mystik," which the *Jüdische Rundschau* published (July 17, 1934) with a fairly impressive layout, was directed against his book *Der Neue Kusari: ein Weg zum Judentum* (1934). His book was the first piece of Jewish theological literature ever published in German to draw upon the Kabbalah as the center of the world of Jewish thought. My essay was also published separately, in a special reprint. [In English as "The Politics of Mysticism," in Scholem, *The Messianic Idea in Judaism: And Other Essays on Jewish Spirituality* (New York: Schocken Books, 1971), pp. 325–34.]

131

rance. Nevertheless, I have grasped—as I hope will be apparent to you
—the fundamental issue raised here. It seems to me, at least, that your
attack focuses on the idea of a theocracy and a history of salvation that
is practically immunized against profane history. And it isn't necessary
to emphasize just how much I agree with such an attack.

The copy that I read was on loan; please furnish me with one of my
own as soon as possible. At this point I also repeat my request for the
return of my "Kafka"; you will be sent the much-revised, definitive essay
immediately thereafter.

Unfortunately, I have nothing definite from Weltsch on this matter
yet.

The long delays in mail between Palestine and Denmark are very
regrettable. It is the only way I can explain to myself the fact that I don't
yet have the confirmation of your receiving the Baader, which was sent
off to you in four registered parcels.

And how important this is! Now that, in the wake of events, it seems
as if even the small amount of assistance from Germany I was able to
rely on will no longer be forthcoming.[2] Hence the relationship with my
host threatens to become very difficult sooner or later.

I am busy working on a Bachofen essay for the *Nouvelle Revue Française*. Naturally, I am also preoccupied with political events, which are
brought home to me by an excellent radio. Last night's transmission—
immediately following the assassination of Dollfuss—was a sensation
that could stand comparison with the broadcast of Hitler's July 17th
speech. I am sure that this source of information is just as accessible to
you and you shouldn't spurn its use on certain occasions, which should
hardly be lacking in the near future.[3]

Please notify me as soon as possible. With fondest regards,

Yours, Walter

[2] Cf. letter 39, note 3. This support must have come from Fritz and Jula Radt, who then
still lived in Berlin; it apparently continued until their emigration to Holland. This much is
obvious from letters by W.B. that were found by their son, Professor Stefan Radt, and
presented to me shortly before this book went to press.

[3] I did not have a radio at my disposal.

62

BENJAMIN TO SCHOLEM

Dear Gerhard,   [AUGUST 4, 1934]

Just a few lines for today, to thank you and to accompany the bill.

First of all, I still haven't had conclusive word from Weltsch about the "Kafka," despite two requests. Of course, his job is not without its worries, given the present circumstances. But he should have been able to reach his decision in a month and a half. It has less to do with the question of acceptance—which he agreed to—than with the arrangements of printing the essay completely or in part. It is, of course, very important to me that it appears unabridged.

I am writing you this because I think it possible that you communicate more or less regularly with him.[1] In this case, you would be doing me a favor by reminding him of the matter.

By the way, I have asked Weltsch—as I asked you—to return the manuscript to me so that I can bring it up to date. If I direct the identical request to you again today, then I do so in the hope that your manuscript is already on its way.

You may be interested to know that Dora is on the verge of setting herself up professionally in Italy.[2] Stefan is still in Germany for the time being, but, as far as I can tell, he will also be leaving for Italy before the year is out.

Summer here has its bright and its dark sides. The latter includes the weather, as well as all things associated with the usual delights of summer, such as promenades, bathing opportunities, hikes. My hosts[3] are even less attracted to these joys of nature than I, and the place where their farmhouse stands, pretty though it may be, cuts them—and me, as their neighbor—off almost completely from such pleasures. This is now slowly manifesting itself in my condition, which leaves something to be desired, not physically, but doubtless mentally. And this, even though my rapport and dealings with the B[recht]s have taken a pleasant form in every way.

Perhaps the form political conditions have taken has contributed to

---

[1] This assumption was incorrect. I met with Robert Weltsch whenever he was in Jerusalem, but I did not correspond with him, except about this matter.

[2] That fall she opened a boarding house, Villa Verde, where she often put up W.B., sometimes for months, and thereby was able to make his life considerably easier.

[3] Brecht and Helene Weigel. W.B. liked to go on long walks, as has also been portrayed by J. Selz. I went for many a long walk in his company.

my present sullenness, insofar as the very moderate optimism I thought it possible to entertain at times last week has given way to a less hopeful assessment of the situation at home.

As I said, you should regard this only as a note to accompany my thanks. I will write to you at greater length when you have written me in more detail. After I mail my second "Kafka" version, I will also address your more recent observations on the subject. I certainly don't have to tell you that I am impatiently awaiting their continuation. Sincere wishes for Escha's recovery and the fondest regards,

Yours, Walter

P.S. I request that the money be sent by check to the usual address, c/o Frau Raahange.

63

BENJAMIN TO SCHOLEM

Dear Gerhard, [AUGUST 11, 1934]

I am making use of the moment, in which I am putting what are probably the finishing touches on the "Kafka," to return explicitly to some of your objections and to append some questions concerning your position.

I say "explicitly," because the new version implicitly does just that in some respects. It has been revised considerably. As I said before, the manuscript in your possession has been superseded. I expect it any day. For technical reasons, I cannot possibly send you the revised one before I have the original in hand.

First off, several urgent requests: 1) if at all possible, give me access to Bialik's "Halakhah and Aggadah" as soon as possible; I need to read it. 2) Send me the letter to Schoeps you reminded me of, as background to our pending discussion.

Now the few major points:[1]

1) I wish tentatively to characterize the relationship of my essay to

---

[1] Notes to this "Kafka letter" to Scholem, drawn from W.B.'s posthumous papers, are printed in *GS* 3:1245–46. They correspond only in part with the letter that was actually sent, referring as well (as does the last sentence of the printed letter's sixth paragraph) to my commentary in the missing section of letter 57 [now included in this translation.— TRANS.].

your poem as follows: you take the "nothingness of revelation" as your point of departure (see 7 below), the salvific-historical perspective of the established proceedings of the trial. I take as my starting point the small, nonsensical hope, as well as the creatures for whom this hope is intended and yet who on the other hand are also the creatures in which this absurdity is mirrored.

2) If I characterize shame as Kafka's strongest reaction, this in no way contradicts the rest of my interpretation. On the contrary, the primal world, Kafka's secret present, is the historical-philosophical index that lifts this reaction out of the domain of the private. For the work of the Torah—if we abide by Kafka's account—has been thwarted.[2]

3) It is in this context that the problem of the Scripture [Schrift] poses itself. Whether the pupils have lost it or whether they are unable to decipher it comes down to the same thing, because, without the key that belongs to it, the Scripture is not Scripture, but life. Life as it is lived in the village at the foot of the hill on which the castle is built. It is in the attempt to metamorphize life into Scripture that I perceive the meaning of "reversal" [Umkehr], which so many of Kafka's parables endeavor to bring about—I take "The Next Village" and "The Bucket Rider" as examples. Sancho Panza's existence is exemplary because it actually consists in rereading one's own existence—however buffoonish and quixotic.

4) I emphasized from the very beginning that the pupils "who have lost the Scripture" do not belong to the hetaeric world, because I rank them as assistants to those creatures for whom, in Kafka's words, there is "an infinite amount of hope."[3]

5) That I do not deny the component of revelation in Kafka's work already follows from my appreciation—by declaring his work to be "distorted"—of its messianic aspect. Kafka's messianic category is the "reversal" or the "studying." You guess correctly that I do not want to shift the path taken by theological interpretation in itself—I practice it myself —but only the arrogant and frivolous form emanating from Prague. I withdrew the argument based on the judges' behavior as untenable (even before your proposals arrived).

6) I consider Kafka's constant insistence on the Law to be the point where his work comes to a standstill, which only means to say that it seems to me that the work cannot be moved in any interpretive direction

---

[2] In his notes, Benjamin adds a sentence not found in the letter: "And everything that Moses accomplished long ago would have to be reaccomplished in our world's age."

[3] [See Max Brod, "Der Dichter Franz Kafka," Neue Rundschau 11 (1921): 1213; Franz Kafka: A Biography, trans. G. Humphreys Roberts and Richard Winston, rev. ed. (New York: Schocken Books, 1963), p. 75.—Trans.]

whatsoever from there. I do not wish to go into explicit detail on this concept.[4]

7) I would like to ask that you elucidate your paraphrase: Kafka "represents the world of revelation seen from that perspective in which it is returned to its own nothingness."

So much for today. By now you will have in hand the bill I sent you. Best wishes for Escha's recovery, all the best to you.

Yours, Walter

P.S. Still no definitive answer from Weltsch!

Not a line from Spitzer in response to a long letter with my proposals!

64

SCHOLEM TO BENJAMIN

Dear Walter,   AUGUST 14, 1934

Your letter of the 4th arrived here yesterday. They are going to expedite payment (by check) as much as possible, and you can count on it being sent to you this week—straight from the library, by registered letter. Your brief note of July 26 and the newspaper clippings have arrived in good condition as well—I returned the Kafka manuscript[1] to you as requested, indeed ten days ago, and I also wrote to Robert Weltsch about the matter. I am almost tempted to suspect that he wants to wait and see if he can't print your essay as a contribution once Schocken has published the new Kafka edition.[2] I am very doubtful that he will be able to print it unabridged. In any case, I advised him to do so. You would then of course probably have to explain yourself more clearly in certain passages; your discussion is so terse, especially in the second chapter, but sometimes in the third as well, that in my opinion it almost invites misunderstanding or no understanding at all. In terms of execution, the first chapter is absolutely the best and really compelling, whereas later on there are sometimes too many quotes and too little interpretation. The

---

[4] This point is more fully formulated in the notes as well: "In case it [the emphasis Kafka keeps putting on "the Law"] were to have a function in Kafka's work in spite of everything—whether it does is something I want to leave open—an interpretation that takes images as its point of departure, as mine does, is sure to lead to it in the end."

[1] In the letter I mistakenly wrote "the Kraus manuscript."

[2] The essay did indeed appear as an announcement of the imminent publication of this edition.

piece on the "Nature Theater" is outstanding. But your allusions about the gestural are *utterly incomprehensible* for all those who aren't familiar with your work, particularly its more recondite parts. Take my word for it, so much abbreviation is maddening.

It would be worthwhile to consider expanding the essay to about twice its length, to formulate your arguments against other views somewhat more unequivocally and to arrange the quotations more clearly, and then offer the whole thing to Schocken as a special, small book. Of course, it must have a chapter on halakhic and talmudic reflection, which figures so prominently in "Before the Law." By the way, the references to Kraft are unfortunately utterly incomprehensible and don't contribute anything to the argument. They might, if you were to spell them out in more detail.

By the way, everyone who knew Kafka personally reports that his father was *in fact* a figure like the one in "The Judgment." He is said to have been especially contemptible and an unspeakable burden to his family. You might find this of interest.

Your repeated recommendation that I make use of radio to keep myself informed about German affairs cannot be expected to meet with a positive response. I employ this instrument for neither my political nor any other kind of edification, and I am willing to surmise that you will bury your optimistic opinion about radio together with those other hopes you recently wrote that you abandoned. I once heard ten minutes of a speech by Hitler on the radio, and since then I've had no further desire for such acoustic pleasures. Since, undistracted by any murders and such, I steadfastly uphold my pessimistic view of German matters and consider every other view to be completely illusory, you can well imagine that I am unable to share your zeal for gathering information of this order. What we learn of events with a week's delay here still more than amply covers all illegitimate claims of keeping up with the latest.

The fact that you have already read my essay on Breuer robs me of the surprise I had intended for you by sending you the offprint (which I herewith enclose). Even if I cannot expect that the world in which this discussion takes place will seem anything but obsolete to you, the rare spectacle of my appearance in German should not remain concealed from you. The essay caused a large scandal, as was expected and in some measure intended as well, and I must now pay the price of writing letters in reply. Incidentally, I am in no way responsible for the resplendent surfeit of titles, which were accorded me by Weltsch, apparently to improve street sales.[3]

I gather from the last clipping, which seemed familiar, that your "Ber-

---

[3] Street sales of the *Jüdische Rundschau*, which was then also read by many non-Jews, had not yet been prohibited, although it would be later.

liner Kindheit" keeps trickling into the *Frankfurter Zeitung* bit by bit. What ever happened to the French translation you were working on in Ibiza, together with a person unnamed? I never heard another word about it.

I read F. Borkenau, *Der Übergang vom feudalen zum bürgerlichen Weltbild*, a hefty Marxist tome on Pascal and Descartes.[4] Are you familiar with it? A warning to Marxists and those who wish to become such. This Institute for Social Research, which actually publishes this kind of thing, must really have leanings toward orthodoxly dressed intelligent prattle. More sensational by far is the sudden reappearance of *Die Fackel*[5] in 320 pages—what do you say to that? And to think I had all of the issues conclusively bound!! Werner Kraft appeared in Jerusalem at the same time as it did,[6] but I haven't seem him yet.

They just brought over your check! I enclose it.

Sincerest regards,

Yours, Gerhard

I haven't heard a thing from Dora for a year now. What is she up to in Italy? And where?

65

BENJAMIN TO SCHOLEM

Dear Gerhard,   SEPTEMBER 15, 1934

I must confess having actually intended to wait to write until I received confirmation that you received my last, numerically arranged observations on Kafka. But my thankful confirmation of the receipt of the check for the Baader forbids postponing these lines any longer. I also owe you thanks for the offprint of the Breuer critique and the copy of the letter to Schoeps. I refer explicitly to these exterior causes, since my inner constitution, which is very exposed at the moment, robs me of all other impetus to write. On the other hand, a lucky coincidence has succeeded in creating total solitude around me, since the B[recht]s are gone for a while. I am putting this to use as well as I can for the new piece—I

[4] See letter 11 above, and the following letter as well.
[5] That was the famous issue 890–905, "Warum die Fackel nicht erscheint."
[6] Kraft was an especially avid reader of *Die Fackel*.

138

already notified you of it, didn't I?—for the *Zeitschrift für Sozialfor-schung*: a retrospective recapitulation of the cultural politics of the *Neue Zeit*.[1] The theme has its manageable sides and its drawbacks. That it doesn't belong to my preferred themes is a trait it shares with the epoch of my life in which work on it is embedded. But if I tell you that Weltsch thought to offer me a fee of 60 reichsmarks for the fragmented—abridged by half—printed copy of the Kafka essay, you will understand that for the time being my intense preoccupation with purely literary subjects has clearly reached an end with the "Kafka."

That isn't to say that the "Kafka" itself has reached an end. On the contrary, I intend to nourish it further from a series of considerations I have continued to spin in the meantime—and a remarkable formulation in your letter to Schoeps promises to provide me with a greater insight in the deliberation. It goes: "Nothing ever . . . is, with reference to his-torical time, more in need of concretization than . . . the . . . "absolute concreteness" of the word of revelation. The absolutely concrete can never be fulfilled at all."[2] That surely states a truth which definitely applies to Kafka, and also thereby broaches a perspective that for the first time makes the historical aspect of his failure obvious. But it will be quite a while before these and other reflections take shape such that I can formulate them definitively. And you will empathize with this all the more because your repeated reading of my work, as well as my commen-tary in letters, must have made it clear to you that precisely this topic is ideally suited to become the crossroads of the different paths my thought has taken. By the way, in the course of marking that spot more precisely, I won't be able to refrain from making reference to Bialik's essay. Wouldn't it be possible for you to track down the relevant issue of *Der Jude* and lend it to me?

To dwell just a moment longer on external questions—I will hardly make any more headway today on internal ones—I had no other choice than to allow Weltsch—even given such a fee!—to go to press. I asked him, however, in the politest way possible, to revise the fee he had decided on. I hope that at least the collected edition will find its way to me when the time comes. Even as dismal as my library's fate remains—only a fraction of it is here in Svendborg—I still summon up the strength to make appeals now and again; I have, for example, just applied to Samuel Fischer, in order not to leave the attempt undone, to acquire the

---

[1] If I am not mistaken, Brecht had the whole series of the *Neue Zeit*, the ideological journal of the Social Democratic Party. The work itself never got beyond the draft stage, but it receives frequent mention in W.B.'s letters of this period.

[2] This sentence had already impressed W.B. when he first read my "Open Letter"; see letter 12.

new "popular edition" of Hofmannsthal's works.—Incidentally, I don't know if Dr. Spitzer is to be relied upon. He hasn't even replied to a detailed letter in which I presented him with detailed proposals—notwithstanding his announcement that they couldn't pay any royalties—for contributions to the Schocken *Almanach*!

Yes, the latest *Fackel* also found its way into my hands. But after such contact even the hands of a Galician would lose their loquacity—not to speak of my lips. A new Timon[3] has truly risen here, who mockingly distributes the yields of a lifetime among false friends!

In closing: How good of you to remember the French translation of the "Berliner Kindheit." Five sections are done; but I can't consider using them because I had a falling-out with my coworker for reasons that are quite picturesque but unsuited to epistolary portrayal—and which incidentally have nothing to do with the work in question.[4] But perhaps things will once again take a turn for the better, and some restful evening can present you with an account of the splendor and misery of that last summer on Ibiza.[5]

So much for today. In the hope that I will soon be receiving news and with kind regards, not forgetting my wishes for Escha's health: how is she doing?

Yours, Walter

66

SCHOLEM TO BENJAMIN

Dear Walter,   SEPTEMBER 20, 1934

Your last letter is dated August 11, and it must have crossed one of mine in the mail. At that time, both the Kafka manuscript you asked to have

[3] W.B. is referring to Shakespeare's *Timon of Athens*, one of Karl Kraus's favorite plays; see also W.B.'s letter to Kraft in *Briefe* 623.

[4] Jean Selz, whose version of the circumstances under which the relationship was broken off can be read in "Walter Benjamin in Ibiza." Their break took place in March 1934, and the explanation W.B. hints at here does not agree with Selz's story. But Selz's report about what was probably the only time on Ibiza that Benjamin was intoxicated (or suffering from alcohol poisoning?)—which he witnessed—bears every mark of authenticity (which cannot be said with the same conviction about many other details of his recollections, unless W.B. had consciously regaled him with lies).

[5] This sentence also reflects the background against which the text "Agesilaus Santander" should be interpreted.

returned and the check from the library for the Baader were on their way to you. But I haven't heard anything at all from you since then, and thus every day has seen me postponing a letter to you, because I expected your confirmation of receipt, and the weeks went by accordingly. Now I am finally getting ready to write you, one day after the Day of Atonement, which is only appropriate. In the interim, I have received two shipments of printed matter from your Detlef Holz, as well as the reworked version of your "Kafka," by way of a French address I didn't know, for all of which I am most grateful. I myself haven't heard from Weltsch for months, and I don't know what has been decided about your essay's publication. I also didn't receive a reply to my letter about the matter. (I am told by someone—who should know—that the *JR* finds itself in an extraordinarily sensitive situation politically vis-à-vis the regime and has to maneuver under the greatest difficulties, but I don't know whether this is the reason for Weltsch's disinclination to write.) The revision has kept me very busy; indeed, I wish it were available for public discussion by now [1] In recent weeks I also read Rang Junior's essay on Kafka,[2] which Kraft lent to me, and I found myself indescribably angry and indignant as I read. Such an interpretation doesn't merit the honor of being mentioned: such barren prattle interests me about as much as an investigation by a Jesuit on Lao-tze's relationship to the world of ecclesiastical dogma. As I read, I longed for the now-despised times when feuilletons were understandable, as they have been replaced by such pompous trivialities. Your interpretation will become the cornerstone of intelligent discussion, as far as such discussion is at all possible. I found myself enlightened and instructed by much of it, but I also feel more strongly than ever that your interpretation cannot essentially weaken the central Jewish nerve of the work. You don't manage without doing flagrant violence to the text; you are constantly obliged to interpret in defiance of Kafka's own testimony, not only in the matter of the Law I already wrote you about, but also in that of women, whose function you construe so masterfully, but from a totally one-sided Bachofean perspective, which runs counter to the most obvious evidence. And yet Kafka's women bear the signs of other things to which you pay too little attention. The castle or officialdom with which they have such a horribly undefinable but precise relationship is clearly not just your primal world, if it is that at all. If it were the primal world, then what need would there have been to make the women's relationship to it into a riddle? Everything would have been clear, whereas in reality everything is not clear and

---

[1] The Kafka essay first appeared three months later, on December 21, 1934.

[2] Bernhard Rang (the son of W.B.'s friend Florens Christian Rang), "Franz Kafka," in the journal *Die Schildgenossen* 12, nos. 2–3 (1934): 107–19.

their relationship to officialdom is very exciting, especially since officialdom itself even warns against them (for instance, through the mouth of
the chaplain). Rather, the castle or officialdom is something the "primal
world" must first be related to.

You ask what I understand by the "nothingness of revelation"? I
understand by it a state in which revelation appears to be without meaning, in which it still asserts itself, in which it has *validity* but *no significance*. A state in which the wealth of meaning is lost and what is in the
process of appearing (for revelation is such a process) still does not
disappear, even though it is reduced to the zero point of its own content,
so to speak. This is obviously a borderline case in the religious sense,
and whether it can really come to pass is a very dubious point. I certainly
cannot share your opinion that it doesn't matter whether the disciples
have lost the "Scripture" or whether they can't decipher them, and I
view this as one of the greatest mistakes you could have made. When I
speak of the nothingness of revelation, I do so precisely to characterize
the difference between these two positions.

What do you do in Denmark? I hope soon to receive more detailed
stories from your present life. About myself, I can say that I am working
a great deal. I've spent every day during these last three months diligently at my desk, working on the speculative interpretation of the Kabbalah in Safed. I met more than once with two European visitors you
know: Kraft and Ludwig Strauss.[3] Both are looking for a way to stay
here. Kraft didn't tell me very much about you; I only got the story of a
visit the two of you paid to a French writer and of your admirable mastery
of spoken French.[4] But otherwise my knowledge of your situation wasn't
much improved. Did I write to you that Kraft's son [Scha'ul] is more or
less the most interesting example of total deracination from the domain
of the German language and transplantation into Hebrew that I have
ever witnessed among the offspring of German-Jewish intellectuals?
I've never seen a child who has responded so harmoniously to the
radical expulsion of his German past. That presents a rare, fortunate
prospect.

Lectures begin again in a month's time. I have a group of young
students with whom I continued to work throughout the vacation—an
hour each day of reading from the Zohar—and who have remained most

[3] The poet Ludwig Strauss (1892–1953) had been in contact with W.B. as early as 1913–
14, when Strauss's first poems appeared, as W.B.'s letters from those years document. In
those years they also engaged in a (still-extant) correspondence about Zionism, of which
Strauss was an adherent. I myself had known Strauss (who later became Buber's son-
in-law) since 1917.

[4] Kraft described this visit to Charles Du Bos (1882–1939) in his memoirs *Spiegelung der
Jugend* (Frankfurt am Main: Suhrkamp, 1973), p. 80.

loyal to me these past two years.[5] I've devoted great effort to their education, and this has become truly gratifying.

I read a bulky Marxist tome on Descartes, Pascal, and Gassendi, which led to rather gloomy reflections.[6] I wanted to see for once how Pascal looks in the light of the class struggle.[7] Well, at any rate, I hope you have better colleagues. After I had finished the 600 pages, I found myself as ignorant as before, and now I am reading—as a penitent return to the reactionaries—Saint-Martin's obscurantist writings, which I have acquired in part. Originally I also wanted to read Thomas Mann's new mythologeme on our common ancestor Jacob,[8] but have resolved to wait until I am ill someday and can find the time and stamina to undertake it.

Have Dora and Stefan really emigrated to Italy? For good?

I am tempted to suspect that the silence of the editor at Schocken, which you complain about, is due to the refusal of the German exchange office to transfer royalties out of the country to Schocken authors living abroad. This is the beginning of a new phase.

Please write soon and accept the best wishes for the New Year,

Yours, Gerhard

67

BENJAMIN TO SCHOLEM

SKOVSBOSTRAND
PER SVENDBORG
OCTOBER 17, 1934

Dear Gerhard,

The "Kafka" is steadily progressing, and hence I am grateful to you for your recent observations. It remains to be seen whether I will ever be able to arch the bow so that the arrow zings into flight. But whereas my other works tended to find their termination rather quickly, at the point where I took leave of them, I won't be through with this one for a while. The image of the bow suggests why: I am confronted with two ends at once, the political and the mystical. By the way, this is not to say that I

---

[5] Fania Freud, who later became my wife, belonged to this group, as did Chaim Wirszubski (1915–1977), one of my most outstanding students, who would later become my friend and colleague.

[6] See the end of letter 64. Borkenau later made a radical break with Marxism.

[7] Lucien Goldmann (1913–1970) made the same attempt—with just as little success—thirty years later.

[8] *Die Geschichten Jaakobs* (Berlin: S. Fischer, 1933) [*Joseph and His Brothers*, vol. 1, trans. H. T. Lowe-Porter (New York: Alfred A. Knopf, 1934)].

have been concerned with the essay these past weeks. The version in your possession will remain valid for a while. I have limited myself to preparing some material for subsequent reflection.

I still haven't had any word from Weltsch; to write him doesn't seem very promising, given the present state of his enterprise.

I am probably correct in assuming that both of our last letters crossed in the mail. In any case, by now you must have long ago received my thanks for the check, interwoven in a lengthy report. But I don't really know how to comply with your request for biographical frescoes and full-length paintings. The overt side of existence has become so precarious for me that I won't touch on it unless necessary; and the pieces I write will help you now and then to visualize the less overt, though no less precarious, side. I won't conceal that at this very moment an exchange of views between us could be especially fruitful. I am readying myself inwardly—my outward circumstances depend on others and not on me—to return to the project of the "Paris Arcades"; you are presumably familiar with its vaguest form. Nonetheless, I am returning to it with significantly changed points of view. One of my next projects will be to work through the quite considerable material generated by my studies to date. Unfortunately, in a letter it is almost impossible to give you an idea either of my intentions or of the difficulties inherent in this project. Incidentally, it probably cannot be written anywhere but in Paris. But for the moment I am not able to afford living there.

The fact that the Institute for Social Research is to emigrate to America doesn't bode well. The upshot could easily be its dissolution, or at least a loosening of my relationship with its members. I don't want to spell out in detail what this means.—If you've read Borkenau's book, then you are better informed about the Institute's activities than I am. After your report, it is no longer conceivable that I shall narrow the orbit from which I have circled this fat tome.

I was away from here for a fortnight, in Copenhagen and a small town in the provinces, where I met a woman I know from Germany. Unfortunately, I spent the greater part of my absence confined to bed. At least I discovered the shop of a tattoo artist in Copenhagen and was able to expand my small collection of pictorial broadsides (which I started after being separated from the children's books) by a few marvelous original tattoo patterns from the master craftsman's own hand.[1]

---

[1] Benjamin's collection of children's books came into Dora's possession as part of the financial settlement following the divorce and is now in the possession of their son's widow. [What remains of this collection has been acquired by the Institute for the Study of Children's Books of the University of Frankfurt and catalogued in *Die Kinderbuchsammlung Walter Benjamins* (Frankfurt am Main: City and University Library, 1987).—TRANS.]

My neighbor is in London. I regret that I wasn't able to get the *Joan*[2] for you—even here copies are extremely scarce. Perhaps you can get it by way of Vienna—the cost is, after all, minimal. I also don't have it here; my collection of the *Versuche*, including the first issue, which contains my handwritten commentary, is still in Berlin. But a new edition of B.'s works is in the making at Malik Verlag. Furthermore, the *Three-penny Novel* should appear any day now and, if need be, you could have it from me on loan. But you will perhaps be even more interested to learn that a new volume in the Arsène Lupin series—you know the famous gentleman-*cambrioleur*—is to appear shortly in the form of a new book by Ernst Bloch.[3] *Heritage of Our Time*—I'm quite keen to see it; first, being curious in general, second, because I would like to learn what I, as a child of my time, am likely to inherit of my work from it. I hope to see Bloch in the near future.

I leave here three days from now. In fact, I will be going to stay with Dora, who has taken over an establishment in San Remo. Stefan is still in Germany, but he too is supposed to move down there next spring.

I am writing with clammy fingers in an ice-cold room and can't add much more. Should you see Kraft, please thank him for his letter and tell him that I will write him from Paris.

I return your wishes for the New Year belatedly but most warmly, and my reason for wishing you the best health imaginable is all the more cogent, since you plan—by your own admission—to read Mann's Jacob novel should you fall ill.

Yours, Walter

68

SCHOLEM TO BENJAMIN

Dear Walter, NOVEMBER 22, 1934

I received both of your last letters long ago, but I have been ill for quite some time, and now, just when I could have written and wanted to write, the new academic year has begun (4 weeks ago), and there is a lot going

---

[2] Brecht's *Saint Joan of the Stockyards*.

[3] This bitter remark continues a series of many similar complaints W.B. made about Bloch in his letters to me before 1933. These reservations placed a major burden on W.B.'s longstanding relationship with Bloch.

on here this time around. That is why I am only now able to reply and convey my thanks. Both your silence and your allusions enable me to construct an image of how difficult your external position becomes, the more conditions in Europe continue to develop along the line they have now taken. I don't see a way out. It is a horrendous vicious circle. It seems the only question people are asking these days is which country they should best be in when the war breaks out—which I don't believe is imminent, by the way. I had hoped for at least a brief note from you, with your new address in San Remo, but I don't want to put this off any longer, so I am sending this to you in Denmark, hoping that the mail reaches you via this roundabout route as well. At the same time, an essay[1] has been dispatched as printed matter to the same address; at last I can once again present you with something written in German, even if it belongs more to the provinces frequented by your friend Ernst Bloch, whose latest borrowings in the field of literature I believe myself entitled to hear about.

Will you stay in San Remo throughout the winter? I am not making preparations for another European trip, unfortunately. Who knows how long before I can contemplate such a journey again? I was able to look at everything I need for my work on my two long trips, and now instead of having to travel, I can have everything photographed instead. The only thing left is that I want to travel to Poland one of these days, to see Galicia, but that is still very much up in the air.[2] And before I can carry out a plan which I have my heart set on—to examine the manuscripts in New York—money has to be found again in America to spend on inviting people like me. Thus we are likely to remain without the chance to air our views face to face for quite some time, unless we are able to manage things the other way around and finance a trip that would bring you here. This is still a plausible consideration: I wonder if it could not be realized for, say, three to four weeks. Palestine itself would hardly cost you anything; a number of arrangements are conceivable, the question remains whether you can successfully track down an especially cheap passage, on a freighter or the like, from Genoa or Trieste or Marseilles. A round trip on the deck of an express liner would be even cheaper, from what I hear. I would like to discuss an itinerary with you, if you consider arranging a passage at all possible. Give the matter some further thought. Summer would be most advantageous.

Since, as I just read, the universities in Germany have admitted a grand total of *sixteen* Jews for their first semester, we outshone them

[1] "Der Begriff der Kawwana in der alten Kabbala," *Monatsschrift für Geschichte und Wissenschaft des Judentums* 78 (Breslau, 1934): 492–518.

[2] This trip unfortunately never materialized.

fantastically. A considerable influx has begun, although trends are still rather indefinite: many hundreds of new students are filling our few institutes and departments. On paper it is up to 1,000! (In reality, a large part of them don't come to us, but set out straight from the harbor happily to work.)[3] The subject of Jewish Philosophy, in its two branches, Rationalism and Kabbalah, is now at long last most auspiciously represented by the Professors Guttmann and Scholem, and it attracts accordingly. Whether Julius Guttmann (an outstanding authority and lecturer, in Hebrew as well) will stay here for good is still uncertain, but likely. We complement each other quite nicely, in that he represents the type of the liberal of 1880–1890 (only much more intelligent and principled than people then really were). The students thus have the interesting choice between two very different *pathoi*, for now that the "other side" is suitably represented, I display much less reserve in my historical-philosophical observations before young people than I used to when I didn't want to present a one-sided position. I have a small group of very committed students, who are coming along nicely. Your Baader recently performed its first services in my seminar. I most likely wrote you that I am reading Saint-Martin. A truly dialectical text, wearying and fantastic at the same time. Atrocious in part.

Kraft is relatively unhappy living in Jerusalem, and nobody knows what will become of him. He isn't very flexible, and the whole atmosphere here remains very foreign to him. I made an energetic attempt to interest Schocken in him as a secretary, but Schocken subjected him to a thoroughgoing examination and declared him entirely unsatisfactory, even though he considered K.'s essays on Kafka to be superb. That was the only major prospect I could come up with for him to date.

Please write soon. I am able to inform you not only of Escha's best wishes but that she finally seems to be completely rid of the sciatica. With kindest regards,

Yours, Gerhard

[3] Among the various ways of reaching the British Mandate of Palestine (before illegal immigration started, or rather was organized, on a larger scale) was confirmation by the University of Jerusalem (then the only one in the country) that one had been accepted as a student, which for many was relatively easy to obtain. The government then issued a student visa, which in very many cases was fictitious. The responsible department head (Eric Mills, one of the highest officials in the country), who sympathized with the plight of the Jews, turned a blind eye to this.

69

BENJAMIN TO SCHOLEM

VILLA VERDE, SAN REMO
DECEMBER 26, 1934

Dear Gerhard,

The letter you addressed to me in Denmark has at long last, two weeks ago, found its way to me here. Not so the German essay it announces, which must have gone astray. I hope very much that you can manage to send me another copy soon. Otherwise, I would have to conclude that a higher force is taking great pains to cut me off from the sources of mystical literature—and not merely the pure but the turbid. For example, Bloch's *Heritage of Our Time* has been out for weeks. But do you think I have so much as laid eyes on the book? I know only this much, that restlessness and bickering are about to break loose in the ranks of the faithful, insofar as I am both congratulated on the tribute shown me in the text and defended against the invective it directs at me—allegedly contained in the same passages. Even a letter from the author himself has already arrived. All that I lack is the material itself, which would allow me to make some sense of all this.

But you will permit yourself even less to hesitate in providing me with authentic documents when I confide that I have fallen into the headquarters of the genuine Magic Jews. For [Oskar] Goldberg has taken up residence here,[1] and he has delegated his disciple [Adolf] Caspary to the cafés, and the *Wirklichkeit der Hebräer*[2] to the local newspaper stand, while he himself—who knows?—probably spends his time conducting tests of his numerology in the casino. Needless to say, I haven't engaged in conversation with this flank. Less obvious, though unfortunately no less true, is the fact that no opportunities for me to communicate otherwise exist, nor are they foreseeable for me here.

The sheer loneliness in which I spend my days here, and whose effect is most hazardous in the long run, has recently been interrupted by Stefan's presence, if only for a few days. He will be returning to Berlin when school starts—at least those are the plans—in order to be registered at a school here after Easter. After a separation of almost two years, he left me with the best possible impression of his composure and confidence of judgment. He is now sixteen and a serious partner in conversations, which—I regret to say—tend mostly to be serious.

---

[1] See above, letter 29, note 5.

[2] Goldberg's magnum opus (1925). Adolf Caspary (born 1898) was one of G.'s foremost disciples (*Die Machinenutopie* [Berlin: David, 1927]).

The words with which your last letter touches on my situation cannot be called mistaken. The worst of it is that I am growing weary. And this is an immediate consequence less of my insecure existence than of the isolation in which its vicissitudes tend to place me. This isolation has rarely been more absolute than here, among bathers and tourists from whom I can scarcely expect anything rewarding but from whom—given the circumstances—I am forced day in and day out to reestablish my distance.

Not much would be required to make a trip to Palestine attractive to me; indeed, nothing would be more appropriate than if for once we could together inspect the foundations of our correspondence, which over the years has grown into a skyscraper. I would even be able to raise the fare for the passage, if the cost of the voyage there and back could be spread out over a sufficient period. When you have a chance, please write me in greater detail how you conceive the journey might be organized, whether I might be able to combine it with lectures, etc.

As you have surely seen, the first part of the "Kafka" has recently appeared, and what germinated for so very long has now at least borne reasonable fruit. This publication will induce me, sometime soon, to open my dossier containing suggestions others have made, as well as my own reflections, which—departing from my usual practice—I compiled especially for this essay.[3] My lengthy review essay on the theory of language—which I wrote as a novice, as you will probably notice sooner than I would like—is going to be published in the *Zeitschrift für Sozialforschung* in the foreseeable future. But I have been able to put the learning process resulting from this *coram publico* to good use, and in fact even very recently, through acquaintance with Karl Bühler's *Sprachtheorie.*[4]

To return to the Archives for Social Research, you have perhaps already heard from me or someone else that its administration has moved to America, and in fact just at a moment when *rebus sic stantibus* I set great store in a meeting with its heads. Prior to that, I can't even consider making use of the considerable material I worked through over the summer during my research on the *Neue Zeit.*[5]

Meanwhile, I am busy with intermediate projects: at the moment with a review of Brecht's *Threepenny Novel*, a book I urge you to read. En-

---

[3] The dossier containing W.B.'s own reflections has been preserved in Frankfurt and printed in the apparatus to *GS* 2. I don't know whether the "observations others have made" (excluding myself) have been preserved in East Berlin among the letters to W.B., but I consider this to be probable.

[4] See *GS* 3:454–55, 468–71.

[5] See the letters to Horkheimer printed in *Briefe*, pp. 621–22, 625–27.

closed you will find a little filler joke which recently appeared in the *Frankfurter Zeitung*.[6]

A great shame to hear that your effort on Kraft's behalf came to naught! I gather from his letters that life is not easy for him in Palestine. I never met his wife.—I wrote Spitzer not long ago, to notify him of the mailing of my Kafka manuscript, which he had requested. At the same time I was able to confirm receipt of the Schocken *Almanach*, in which —among sundry pieces worth reading—a short passage from the Mishne Torah[7] made an overwhelming impression on me.

Best wishes to you for your semester, a third of its course already run, and to Escha for her recovery.

Yours, Walter

70

SCHOLEM TO BENJAMIN

Dear Walter,   FEBRUARY 6, 1935

Your last letter, of December 26, has remained without a reply for a long time. In the meantime, there are many new things to relate, unfortunately not all of them good. First of all, Escha's eschiatica (as the illness would be more aptly named) has flared up again (which was one reason for the delay in writing this letter), and this is very unpleasant in many respects. She will be traveling to Tiberias in a few days, in the hope that three weeks of taking the waters will be more effective than it was last year. And, in connection with our last exchange of letters, we have also been mulling over your possible visit here. Before writing to you, I wanted to wait for certain decisions about my work that are of significance in this regard. I now want to lay the situation out for you as I see it. I will be withdrawn from the world from *July 1* until about November 1. During this time (the summer holidays), I want to write a book for Schocken, or at least make considerable headway on it. The time is ripe

---

[6] The reference is to the piece "Auf die Minute" (*GS* 4:761–63), published in the *Frankfurter Zeitung* of December 6, 1934.

[7] Moses Maimonides' magnum opus. It was the passage "Von der Lebensführung des Weisen" (printed in N. Glatzer's translation in the *Almanach des Schocken Verlags für das Jahre 5695* [1934–35], pp. 37–44). (Also published in volume 27 of the Schocken Library, *Rabbi Mosche ben Maimon, ein systematischer Querschnitt durch sein Werk*, 1935, pp. 87–92.)

for it, and it will demand all my concentration for several months: a kind of outline of the Kabbalah, somewhere between 500 and 1,000 pages in length, in which I want to present a concise exposition of the results of my last 15 years of study. I won't have collected the materials necessary to begin work before the holidays. There would clearly be no point in asking you to come here during that time; my mind would be on other things, and I wouldn't be able to have any kind of fruitful dialogue with you. Which leaves, in our opinion, either the time before or after. Before —that would mean from May 15 until July 1 or thereabouts. If you wanted to stay longer, without close contact with me, this could of course be arranged, but it is not a very advisable solution, since July is not a good month for guests here. Or you could come later, in the winter. Our friend Senator[1] would be very happy to have you stay with him then, assuming he has managed to liberate his apartment from his family by that time. If Escha's health allows, the two of us would be just as pleased to invite you to stay with us for several weeks. Senator's apartment (½ minute from ours) offers more seclusion and comforts. Anyway, we see no difficulty there, and we believe you wouldn't have any expenses for board and lodging if you were to stay 4 to 8 weeks. We are also of the opinion that something could be done in the way of a private lecture series in the winter—*not a chance* of that in summer!—which would bring in a few pounds of pocket money; but this could only be ascertained shortly beforehand. A public appearance in German is out of the question in Jerusalem, except maybe once as a special lecture. Perhaps something could be arranged privately. But it would definitely be better not to count on such a source of income in advance, since in this country things always turn out other than planned. I repeat: If you decide to come in the *spring*, then we would try to organize arrangements that would have you staying with us, the Bergmanns,[2] or Senator, in a way you would find comfortable. Let us say, then, that a stay of two months in Jerusalem without cost would be no problem to arrange, but we would of course not be able to finance excursions around the country, that is a matter of the right occasion arising, and prospects which may materialize later. It is *very* likely that a number of such opportunities without expense for you will arise in the natural course of events, but I don't want to make any

[1] Werner Senator (1896–1953), who was close to me in terms of shared convictions, was at the time a member of the Executive of the Jewish Agency, which was responsible for supervising the building of a Jewish entity in the country. He later became head of the administration of the Hebrew University.

[2] The philosopher Hugo Bergmann from Prague (1883–1974), then director of the Jewish National Library, became the university's first rector in the summer of 1935. Both Senator and Bergmann had more spacious accommodations than we did, and both relished the prospect of being able to have a man of W.B.'s stature as a guest in their home.

assurances. I need hardly tell you that, if you do indeed come, I would see what I could do to such an end. As far as the *visa* is concerned, I believe we can get a tourist visa from the government *without* having to pay the usual charge of 60 pounds in cash if we declare that you have been invited as our guest and for a lecture. In that case, we would need precise biographical details. May and June tend to be very nice and warm. So please give very serious thought to this proposal.

How do things stand with the Kafka essay, which you hint has prospects of being published by Schocken?

I have not read the *Threepenny Novel*. I have imbibed very little over the last six months that was not scholarly, and then only when it happened to be at hand. Brecht's popularity in Palestine is limited to an extraordinarily thin group, and similarly scarce are copies of his works. I rarely buy copies of such reading matter, since my Kabbalah collection presents me with more intriguing bibliographical tasks. I haven't heard anything about Bloch's new book at all, other than from you. Have you meanwhile obtained a copy and found your portrait in it?

I hope to hear from you and about your plans soon.

It would be very pleasant if we could see one another soon.

Sincerest regards,

Yours, Gerhard

Dear Walter,

It would be very nice if you could manage to come here. Of course, the voyage itself would probably be more interesting than agreeable, since you would surely have to make it on an emigrant ship populated by restless Jews. But once you are here, I can almost promise you rest and comfort. The real heat won't have arrived yet, nor the mosquitoes, and Jerusalem is a magnificent and beautiful affair. To this day, whenever I go for a walk, I feel as though I were on holiday.

I hope you agree soon to come, so that we can set about taking care of passport matters and other preparations early enough.

Best wishes,

Escha

To make things perfectly clear: I feel certain that I will be sufficiently healthy to have you stay with us. But you would also find living with our friends agreeable, and in some ways more attractive.

71

BENJAMIN TO SCHOLEM

VILLA VERDE, SAN REMO
FEBRUARY 22, 1935

Dear Gerhard,

I was delighted to hear from you at length. In view of Escha's relapse, I shall forgo the exordia and lamentations which in other circumstances would have befitted such a long hiatus in our correspondence, even if only in retaliation for instances on my part in the past. In their stead, I send my sincere wishes for Escha's rapid recovery and my gratitude for her postscript.

Now to the question of my putting in an appearance in Palestine. First of all, I want to thank both of you very much for the repeated and explicit invitation. And I hope that my deciding to come in winter, contrary to your expectations, will not be unwelcome. I do so for two reasons, one of which is conclusive. As I told you before, the Institute in Geneva—among whose rafters, as you know, my exceedingly battered mortal thread is becoming lost—is moving to America.[1] Since I must endeavor at all costs to maintain personal contact with its leadership, the probable European trip of one or two of its most influential people with whom I am in contact there—they are the directors or at least members of the administration[2]—represents a date I simply cannot ignore. I recently learned that this trip has been planned for May. It goes without saying that the arrangements may be postponed; but since I am dependent on them, I cannot arrange anything for myself during that period.

Add to this: The chance, vague as it may be, to intercede personally on behalf of my work—even to a modest extent—carries great weight with me, given the present span of history and the course of my life, which have both made the finite collection of my infinitely scattered production seem less predictable, not to mention less probable, than ever before. And even as important as a lecture series—supposing one could be arranged—would be to me for financial reasons, the paradox of it all is that considerations other than financial carry more weight, even in circumstances that make the latter especially compelling. And they also speak in favor of winter.

I still am not able to envision, by the way, how I will arrange my

---

[1] The allusion to Kafka's *Trial* is obvious; the comparison with the Institute for Social Research allows his feelings or his fears to surface a little more clearly than they did when speaking with other people.

[2] The reference is to Max Horkheimer and Friedrich Pollock.

summer, and whether I will remain here past Easter is especially uncertain.[3]—Stefan will probably have settled here before then. If possible, I will most likely travel to Brecht again in Denmark at the height of summer.

Engulfed in the seething haze of an almost permanent bout of depression, I finished off a few projects recently; above all, the French essay on Bachofen, which is now with the editorial board of the *Nouvelle Revue Française*,[4] followed by a longish review of the *Threepenny Novel*.[5] A longish review essay of literature on the theory of language published over the last four years should be on its way to you in printed form in the near future. By contrast, the French translation of "Hashish in Marseilles," which appeared in the Marseilles *Cahiers du Sud*[6] a short time ago, will have to figure as a desideratum in your archive for the time being.

It is with a most gloomy disposition that I see the moment fast approaching when, after a two-year span of adroit and ingenious stalling, I will no longer be able to avoid the detailed portrayal of Eduard Fuchs's studies and collections, which the Institute has urgently requested.[7] I would conceivably speak about the latter, if they were not inaccessible, or rather most likely destroyed; but to deal decently with the former is a hard nut for me to crack, as you will readily understand. I hope I don't have to take this nut between my teeth but can instead develop something of a makeshift nutcracker by addressing the task within the walls of the Bibliothèque Nationale.

At the moment, things have not progressed that far, and I have taken the arrival of the first volume of Kafka's collected works as a reason to reapply myself to my manuscript, and have begun by expanding and reorganizing the second part. The fourth chapter will be subjected to by far the most drastic changes; but they are also the most formidable ones, and I am not clear about them yet.[8]

I am even less so as regards Spitzer, whom I sent, at his own request,

[3] In any case, W.B. was still in San Remo and Nice on April 8, as a letter to Horkheimer attests.

[4] The *NRF* did not accept the essay.

[5] Just how carefully W.B. proceeded in terms of what he communicated to whom is revealed if we note that he mentioned the Bachofen essay in a letter to Horkheimer sent three days earlier but did not refer to the (highly laudatory) review of Brecht's *Threepenny Novel*, since H. did not number among Brecht's admirers. (Printed in *GS* 3:440–49) [*Reflections*, pp. 193–202].

[6] *Cahiers du Sud* 22 (1935), pp. 26–33 (not translated by W.B. himself). [English translation in *Reflections*, pp. 137–45.]

[7] See the aforementioned letter to Horkheimer.

[8] This remark should allow for a more precise dating of some of the longer notes printed in the editorial apparatus to the Kafka study (in *GS* 2).

the complete manuscript in the form you are familiar with, and who, without addressing the question of publication he himself had raised in the first place, sent it back with a few polite words, and yet at the same time solicited my advice concerning a publishing house. I can't make head or tail out of the matter.

It is fortunate that your relations with Schocken have taken on a much more concrete form. I assume it is already decided that you will write the book in Hebrew. At least I can expect you, if we see each other in the foreseeable future, to provide me with some oral information as to its character.

A gentle rain has been falling here for two days now, which is good for the flowers and the disposition as well—but less so, presumably, for Nice's carnival, whose acquaintance I shall thus be making in one of its less than flattering moments. I will be going there today, in order to report on an exhibition called "L'Enfance."[9]

So much for today. I dearly hope that the recent, several-months-long lull in your letters will remain an isolated episode in our correspondence, and one that will soon fall into happy oblivion.

Please let me know when you next write what personal information you need in order to settle the administrative details of my visit when the time comes.

With kindest regards and my repeated best wishes for Escha's recuperation,

Yours, Walter

72

SCHOLEM TO BENJAMIN

Dear Walter,   MARCH 29, 1935

Thank you very much for your last letter, from which I was able to grasp or glean some details of your plans, which I found most distressing. That you won't be coming here this summer is a fact that I, and with me Escha and other interested parties, must then accept. It seems particularly regrettable, since it appears by no means certain to me, to the extent I can judge your situation, that you will really be in a position to travel in

[9] "Gespräch über dem Corso" (GS 4:763–71).

winter, toward the end of the year. Too many barely predictable circumstances seem to influence (and in a decisive way, at that) such major decisions about travel, if only for coercive material reasons. The only person pleased with the news of your trip's postponement was Frau Steinschneider-Marx, who is going to America during the summer months and wanted very much to see you here. I hope we'll be clear about what will be happening once and for all by the latter part of summer. At that time, or by then, we will have been able to gather sufficient information about the requisite formalities and to clarify the prospects for lectures (even though I still think about these with the greatest skepticism). I hope at least that your perseverance will be rewarded by agreeable associations with, or commissions from, the gentlemen you mention from the Institute for Social Research. Of course, the news that you haven't even finished the essay on Fuchs yet, and have in fact developed severe inhibitions regarding it, is surely most unpleasant in this connection. In much earlier letters, you referred to the essay in a vastly more positive and optimistic way, so that I thought it long since finished. Since I am altogether unfamiliar from [with] the character of Eduard Fuch's work [1]—I only spent a few days looking through a book of his on caricatures of the Jew—I am unable to do anything more than vaguely imagine the dire straits you describe. Consequently, while you are grappling with such products of Marxist thought, if I understand you correctly—which affords you the chance to atone duly for your thoroughly theoretical sympathies for that kind of thought (as is only just)—I, who otherwise have decided to forgo such reading matter, have just read an anti-Marxist book (or pamphlet) by Berdyaev,[2] who combines very interesting expositions with peculiar mystical digressions on the nature of Russian materialism and its evolution. I learned a few quite interesting things from it.

Any day now, Schocken will bring out a book by Leo Strauss[3] (I devoted great energy to obtaining an appointment for Strauss in Jerusalem), marking the occasion of the Maimonides anniversary.[4] The book begins with an unfeigned and copiously argued (if completely ludicrous) affirmation of atheism as the most important Jewish watchword. Such admirable boldness for a book that will be read by everybody as having been written by a candidate for Jerusalem! It even outdoes the first 40

[1] I became the victim of an anacoluthon while writing this.

[2] Nikolai Berdyaev, *Wahrheit und Lüge des Kommunismus*, published by Vita Nova Verlag in Lucerne in 1934. W.B. must have already been in contact with Vita Nova Verlag, who published his *Deutsche Menschen* in 1936.

[3] Leo Strauss, *Philosophie and Gesetz* (Berlin: Schocken, 1935) [*Philosophy and Law*, trans. Fred Baumann (Philadelphia: Jewish Publication Society, 1987)].

[4] This refers to the 800th anniversary of Moses Maimonides' birth, which was widely celebrated in the Jewish scholarly world and beyond.

pages of your postdoctoral dissertation! I admire this ethical stance and regret the—obviously conscious and deliberately provoked—suicide of such a capable mind. As is to be expected here, only three people at the very most will make use of the freedom to vote for the appointment of an atheist to a teaching position that serves to endorse the philosophy of religion. I hope I will be able to furnish you with a copy of the book once it comes out. I have spent these last weeks working on a little book I hope you will soon be able to read: I have translated the Zohar's explanation of the first lines of Genesis into German, for Schocken.[5] This exceedingly difficult and strenuous labor occupied me completely for three weeks, but also gave me great pleasure. So now folks will at least have something decent to plunder; Ernst Bloch will bemoan not having had it sooner. I have to finish the little book during the holidays, by the end of April. If it turns out well, I will regard that as a good omen for my work later this year, for which I have grand designs.

Buber arrives in Jerusalem tomorrow, for several weeks. The Ge Sta Po has forbidden him to hold lectures in Prussia, by the way, as you may have read in the newspapers. A most mysterious affair, whose true motives remain utterly obscure to date. He will be staying nearby, at Bergmann's. At the beginning of this month my brother Werner came before the "People's Court," in a large trial with about 25 defendants, after he had been in detention for almost two years. After four days of sequestered proceedings, he was one of 4 to be acquitted, but he was promptly taken into preventive custody and there has been no trace of him since. He has undoubtedly been taken to some concentration camp or other.[6] We are all very upset. I feel even more sorry for my poor mother, who has already suffered through so very many and much too dramatic incidents in this case, than for my brother himself, whose behavior in those crucial days I will be unable to comprehend until the end of my days. Nobody knows yet whether he will be held ad infinitum as a special object of the Gestapo's hatred, as is Torgler,[7] for example, or if he can successfully be gotten out. We learned that the indictment fell apart through the testimony of a single respectable witness, an "Aryan" lawyer, after said charges had been fabricated on the basis of "testimony" given by former party members who had been blackmailed and in some cases beaten or bribed. Is your brother still in Germany?

[5] *Die Geheimnisse der Schöpfung: ein Kapitel aus dem Sohar* appeared in the Schocken Library.

[6] He was first held in the Torgau concentration camp, later taken to Dachau and then to Buchenwald, where he was murdered on July 17, 1940.

[7] The Communist Party Reichstag member who was acquitted in the Reichstag Fire trial.

I have already made a number of efforts on Kraft's behalf, but without the slightest success. He is having a hard time of it. I have been forced to realize that there is something about him that puts people off. He has difficulty winning people over. He still feels himself an utter stranger here.

What is Stefan going to do in Italy?

With fond regards. All the best,

Yours, Gerhard

73

BENJAMIN TO SCHOLEM

HÔTEL FLORIDOR
28 PLACE DENFERT-ROCHEREAU
PARIS XIV
MAY 20, 1935

Dear Gerhard,

It has been some time since you last heard from me. You will have guessed the reason. An exceedingly critical period set in after the move to Paris, underscored by external fiascos. Rejection of the "Bachofen" by the *NRF*, which passed it on to the *Mercure de France*, where I can see it languishing now; dissolution of my brief, and still all too long, literary relationship with Klaus Mann, for whom I had reviewed the *Threepenny Novel* and who returned my review, already typeset, when I refused his unmentionable fee.[1] And a few more things of that ilk, *novissima* in my career, long surpassed in my civil life.

Then, following a short breathing spell, a further circumstance arose that put a halt to my entire correspondence. The Institute in Geneva asked for a précis of the "Arcades," without any commitment on its part, I would even say, out of politeness. Now and then I had hinted here and there about it, never divulging very much. Since this coincided with the annual closing of the Bibliothèque Nationale, I was really alone with my studies on "Arcades" for the first time in many years. And since creative matters have a way of arising all the more unpredictably, the more important they are, so it happened that, with this précis, which I had promised without giving it much thought, the project entered a new phase, in which for the first time it bears more resemblance—even if from afar—to a book.[2]

---

[1] Klaus Mann had offered him 150 French francs.

[2] Compare the two letters to Adorno (no. 260) and Horkheimer (no. 261) in *Briefe*, pp. 260–67.

I don't know how many years my drafts, originally conceived for an essay for *Der Querschnitt* which was never written, date back. I wouldn't be surprised (should this Paris book ever come into being) if it turned out to be the classic nine years, which would exceed the time I spent arching the bow of preparations for the *Traverspiel* book. But that of course is the real question, since I am not the master of my working conditions. Prospects for really arousing the interest of the Institute in Geneva for this book are minimal. It [the book] allows no concessions to be made to any side, and if I know anything about the book at all, then it is that no school will rush to claim it as its own.

Otherwise, I periodically succumb to the temptations of visualizing analogies with the Baroque book in the book's inner construction, although its external construction decidedly diverges from that of the former. And I want to give you this much of a hint: Here as well the focus will be on the unfolding of a handed-down concept. Whereas in the former it was the concept of *Trauerspiel*, here it is likely to be the fetish character of commodities.[3] Whereas the Baroque book mobilized its own theory of knowledge, this will be the case for "Arcades" at least to the same extent, though I can foresee neither whether it will find a form of representation of its own, nor to what extent I may succeed in such a representation. The title "Paris Arcades" has finally been discarded and the draft is entitled "Paris, Capital of the Nineteenth Century."[4] Privately I call it "Paris, capitale du XIXe siècle," implying a further analogy: just as the Baroque book dealt with the seventeenth century from the perspective of Germany, this book will unravel the nineteenth century from France's perspective.

No matter how high an opinion I held of the studies I had made over the course of so many years, I now realize somewhat more clearly what I actually should have been doing, my opinion of them has diminished considerably. Innumerable questions are still unanswered. Admittedly, I am so completely at home in the relevant literature, and all the way down to its *bas fonds*, that I will gain a grasp on its answers sooner or later. In the midst of the incredible difficulties I am faced with, I sometimes enjoy dwelling on the following thought: how much of a dialectical synthesis of misery and exuberance lies in this research, which has been continually interrupted and repeatedly revived over the course of a decade, and which has been driven on into the remotest of regions. Should the book's dialectic prove to be just as sound, then it would find my approval.

[3] According to the famous chapter in the first part of Marx's *Capital*.
[4] Printed in *Schriften* 1:406–22 and later in *Reflections*, pp. 146–62.

The fact that the master plan now lies before me is, by the way, also probably an indirect result of my meeting with one of the Institute's directors, which took place immediately after my arrival in Paris. The result was that I could live one (!) month without the customary day-to-day problems. But the month has passed, and I do not at all know what the next one will bring. If I'm supposed to set to work on the Fuchs essay —which, to tell the truth, I have yet to begin—this would be doubly repugnant. On the other hand, it would be a stroke of luck, which I can in no sense rely upon, if the Institute really took a material interest in the Paris book.

What I wish for myself now would be to work in the library for a number of months and then be able to travel to Jerusalem after bringing my research to a more or less definitive conclusion in October or November. But even if there are numerous things that leave more of a mark on world events than my desires, we should still both keep the second of these wishes in mind. At the appropriate time I might be able to raise the money here for the trip, by means of a few tricks.

I eagerly await the books you announce: first and foremost, your little Zohar volume. I fear that it comes too late for Bloch, as will be the case with my book as well if it ever gets written—let alone published. Anyway, if Bloch's latest book should ever fall into your hands, you will easily be able to gain an impression of how successful his attempts at burglarizing my property have been. He should be surfacing in Jerusalem before long, accompanied by his new genie, Karola Piotrkowsky, as his wife.[5] Yes, it had almost slipped my mind: He will most likely be coming to Jerusalem with her; she is an architect and wants to build something there.

I am also very interested in Leo Strauss's book. What you tell me about him fits in with the pleasant image of him I have always made for myself.—Even if for the time being I am reading nothing but primary material, I recently happened upon a book whose author you had occasionally pointed out to me, the *Potestas Clavium* by Shestov.[6] I could not examine it very thoroughly but only determined that its polemic against Platonic idealism turns out to be more entertaining than in the usual stuff of this genre. I haven't read Berdyaev, whom you mention in your last letter.

Yes, Stefan will soon be attending school in San Remo. My brother, by contrast, is still in Germany, where his wife has a well-paid position with the Soviet trade mission in Berlin. He went abroad once after his

[5] The visit never took place.

[6] Shestov's book appeared in German in 1926 [English translation by Bernard Martin (Athens, Ohio: Ohio University Press, 1968)].

160

release from the concentration camp, but that was just for a holiday.[7] He has a son who is very handsome, judging from pictures I have seen. How very dreadful that your brother's predicament is so desperate. But whose field of vision is not crowded with such images!

Kraft wrote me an almost touching letter in which he offered his services to mobilize an influential Frenchman on my behalf.[8] Naturally I cannot avail myself of this, since setting this very problematic scheme into motion would require an effort that lies far beyond my present concerns. He seems to have traveled deep into the heart of the country and is sending me a nice report about it.

Write me when the occasion arises as to what details you need to make preparations for my coming. Kindest regards to you and Escha,

Yours, Walter

74

SCHOLEM TO BENJAMIN

Dear Walter,   JUNE 28, 1935

Your last letter, from the end of May, has been languishing here for some weeks, during which time I was as much preoccupied with completing the slender volume on the Zohar for Schocken as I was with a severe case of laryngitis, which I annoyingly came down with. Today marks the beginning of the last week of the semester, and in a few days I hope to apply myself to beginning my major study, the outline of the history of the Kabbalah, with whose composition in two languages I plan to spend the near future, "near future" meaning not only the vacation but presumably a substantially longer period. I am starting with the Hebrew text, which I want to publish first for moral reasons, but then have committed myself to writing the book anew in German, since translations from the Hebrew are not to be recommended. The two styles are altogether too unlike one another.

Developments concerning this book, as well as several other important factors, unfortunately make it rather doubtful whether I can still honor the invitation to you for the winter, as both of us, Escha and I, so very

---

[7] Georg Benjamin had visited Switzerland and the northern Italian lakes in the spring of 1934 (Hilde Benjamin's biography of G.B., p. 336).

[8] Probably Charles Du Bos.

much wanted. This has as much to do with family matters,[1] which do not lend themselves to detailed description, as with my possible absorption in work on the book until it is completed. It is therefore unlikely that we could have you stay with us for two months, as agreed upon. It is highly likely, on the other hand, that I will be traveling to Europe for several weeks next year, if only because of my mother's 70th birthday. Anyway, it's absolutely impossible at this moment for me to arrange my personal schedule for the winter in such a way that I could make firm commitments to you. On the other hand, I understand from your letter that you have really achieved something by staying where you are and that your work, like mine, is approaching a point of crystallization. I was most interested by what you wrote about the new fortunes of the "Arcades" study; I hope for you that the Institute shows interest in the project and absolves you of the Fuchs in return. Am I wrong in considering Paris as your summer residence? Or will you be going to Denmark again?

I cannot even venture a guess as to what the content of your new work will be; does it concern historical observations or theories about objects from ordinary spheres of life? Or a resumption of those surrealist trains of thought you wanted to link up with in this matter in the past, if I'm not mistaken? In my case, things are much easier to express; it has to do with a "textbook" that will give an extract of the last fifteen years of my work in which the element of proof will be totally eliminated. There'll be no lack of amazing and very amazing things, and the historical observer is guaranteed to get his money's worth. The whole thing is conceived of as the announcement of a stock-taking, if one which is also fairly voluminous.

I found Bloch's book in the library, to which it was donated (though by no means from the author!), but no longer found the time to study it closely. I would like to predict with relative certainty that his appearance in Palestine that you announce will never take place. I am convinced that he will not be able to count on any success whatsoever here, and I cannot imagine that of all people his latest wife is needed to build things here. But after all, I have already met with so many surprises here, as far as visitors are concerned, that I am inexhaustibly ready for anything —and besides, except on Friday evenings, I am not receiving any visitors for the present.

Kraft, who now shares a house with his lyrical colleague Ludwig Strauss, will have great difficulty in establishing a life for himself here. He doesn't seem to possess the divine gift of making friends, and I am often at a loss when I imagine what is going to happen when Hitler stops

---

[1] This was an allusion to my impending separation from my wife.

the payments he is still sending to Palestine for the moment.[2]

Shestov, whom you write about, is expected in Palestine; the workers' organization invited him to hold a series of lectures, which I will however be unable to profit from, since they will be given in Russian.[3] All of this is supposed to take place during the winter as well.

Kindest regards and wishes for you, from Escha as well,

Yours, Gerhard

75

BENJAMIN TO SCHOLEM

Dear Gerhard,   [PARIS, JULY 5, 1935]

Even though I know the time you intended to devote to your great work has arrived, I am rather troubled not to have received a single line from you—I don't even know for how long now.

If I had those sounds of reproach and lament at my command that once flowed from your lips whenever my letters were delayed for more than a fortnight, then today you would be receiving, instead of this post-card, a document worthy of a place as the final piece of my *Deutsche Menschen*.

As it is, I am satisfied with letting this rocket ascend into the evening sky of your silence. Let it brush your temples like fiery coals in the form of a question mark as it sinks down.

Cordially,

Yours, Walter

[2] Kraft was receiving a librarian's pension.

[3] In fact, Shestov's lectures were held in French, but much later, and I was asked to introduce them.

76

BENJAMIN TO SCHOLEM

7 VILLA ROBERT LINDET
PARIS XV
AUGUST 9, 1935

Dear Gerhard,

Our latest reports have indeed made their journeys across the Mediterranean very slowly. I hope these lines reestablish the old rhythm of our correspondence.

Your suspicion about my "summer residence" is correct. I am staying in Paris as long as I can somehow hold out. But I have no clear idea where I will go afterward, when this is no longer feasible. The winter months in the remote Danish corner where Brecht lives would probably be all the more difficult to bear, since Brecht himself usually makes his Russian and English trips at that time. On the other hand, how long I can stay here is entirely uncertain. I owe the present, really relatively pleasant weeks—pleasant so long as I utterly refrain from gazing into the future—to the fact that my sister has put her apartment at my disposal during her absence.[1]

I have several weeks of intensive work in the library behind me. They have greatly furthered the documentation for my book. But I now have to interrupt such efforts for a while—without having finished them. No god can save me now from the study of Fuchs. Yes, I have more reason than ever to demonstrate my willingness to comply with the Institute's suggestions. The cooperation forthcoming during the negotiations in May did not materialize without my having to disclose the prospect of my disappearing to Palestine for several months and relieving them of having to support me. An attractive perspective for them, as you can imagine, and I am now faced with the delicate task of having to dispel it. I have, as I said, every reason to demonstrate my compliance.

That I have better and more personal reasons to be very sorry to see our meeting postponed won't surprise you. And we dare not expect from a reunion in Europe—which could only be very brief anyway—what several weeks in Palestine would have given us. For my part, insight into your creative work and its circumstances; for you, insight into my work, whose character it is impossible to convey in a letter—even in conversation it would only be feasible if such insight were not limited to occa-

[1] W.B.'s sister had her own apartment in Paris, at least since spring 1935, where he often stayed in one of the rooms. According to Hilde Benjamin (*Georg Benjamin*, p. 232), in the summer of 1935 Dora traveled one last time to meet Georg and Hilde B. at the East Baltic resort of Misdroy. But in those years she was already seriously ill.

sional isolated ideas. It would thus be all the more rewarding for both of us, since I am getting going on this book with uncommon care, and the greater the isolation in which my work on it proceeds at this stage, the more willing and able I am to put all counsel originating in friendly dialogue to productive use. I believe that its conception, however personal in origin, addresses our generation's most decisive historical interests. No further word should be needed to suggest how very much I would like to familiarize you with it.

Things can essentially be summed up as follows: a précis for the Institute—I want to say for superficial, even the most superficial, use—which has been circulating for quite some time, has made me realize the precise point at which constructive work (which simultaneously entails deciding on the literary form and its potential success) will one day have to begin. That day has yet to arrive. Circumstances whose repulsiveness nonetheless implicates me as an accomplice are delaying it. Should I still live to see it, however, I would not grouse about very much anymore.

I don't want to leave the subject without telling you that both of the alternative conjectures you ascribe to it are correct. The work represents both the philosophical application of surrealism—and thereby its sublation [Aufhebung]—as well as the attempt to retain the image of history in the most inconspicuous corners of existence—the detritus of history, as it were.

I already informed you, if I remember correctly, of my sister's address, which for the moment is mine. Without knowing whether or not I will still be living here when Frau Marx-Steinschneider makes her return visit, I ask that you give it to her.[2] If I have moved, she can get my address from my sister or the concierge. I regret very much having missed seeing her. How can she possibly imagine I would have someone deny that I was here! The climate in Paris is most agreeable at the moment; the social atmosphere less so, stripped as I am of the few acquaintances I have. Even the emigrés gather their few centimes together and take a summer vacation. I am seeing Ernst Bloch—it took a great deal of effort to make my position on his latest book clear to him.[3] I am not discussing my own with him, and you will understand why if you have looked at the section on "Hieroglyphs of the Nineteenth Century" in his. [Siegfried] Kracauer is writing a book on Offenbach, and I

[2] She and her husband traveled through Paris in October 1935 on their way back from America.

[3] No reports or notes concerning this conversation have come to light up to now. Bloch's *Heritage of Our Time* caused W.B. more than a little agitation, as attested to by a number of letters. Over the years Bloch defended himself frequently against the charges and reservations leveled at his book. But he barely dealt with W.B.'s allegations, which he may well not even have known in this trenchant form.

have to keep my own reflections under wraps with him as well. All of which is not easy and could be more pleasant.

I am really looking forward to your little Zohar book. Isn't it supposed to appear, if my memory serves me correctly, this September in German?

So let me hear from you as soon as you can. And accept my best wishes for your great Hebrew endeavor. Greetings to you and Escha,

Yours, Walter

77

SCHOLEM TO BENJAMIN

Dear Walter, AUGUST 25, 1935

I am replying to your letter of August 9, which I only received on the 20th—never has mail taken so long as it has from France—and you shouldn't say that I'm a lazy correspondent. If these lines meet you in the midst of your work on Herr Fuchs, by which I gather you will be atoning for some of your sins, they will have their beneficial effect too: as is well known, one is quick to allow interruptions from that kind of work. If I read you correctly, there seems to be a prospect, or even more than that, of your anonymous patrons, the Institute, publishing your book on the 19th century, which would seem to be cause for rejoicing. So here we both sit, each engaged in a matter very important to himself, for I too have with no small effort begun to weigh every word I put to paper. I am availing myself of the language of our forefathers for the present, if only as a precaution against Ernst Bloch. Enough will be stolen later on, anyway. How I will fare in this endeavor, to present my historical knowledge in a single—if fairly thick—volume, cannot yet be foreseen; I am still jotting down this and that, so to speak. Unfortunately, you won't have to learn Hebrew to read it, since I will write it all over again in German afterward. By the way, à propos your suggestion regarding Bloch: I reread the paragraph you indicated and can only say how much I empathize with you. It doesn't speak well for the comfort of your situation that you have to tolerate this truly "touching" fellowship of thieves, and I really think it's too much of a good thing. I am warning you: Do not allow this man to travel here, or at least don't recommend that he visit me, for I would be capable of giving him a piece of my mind,

166

from which he would be able to infer that it too had been appropriated from you, following his notorious example. By the way, permit me to say that I have only rarely encountered a more prevaricative and bleak "communism" than in this tome. You've really paid a high price for the glory of his including you among the avant-garde, and I'm telling you: I would like to know who will think well of you as a result of such "fantastic, undignified praise" (to quote a familiar passage from your writings).[1]

Whether we can arrange our meeting here before next summer, which I would like just as much as you, mostly depends on how my work progresses. I can't commit myself yet; I need hardly mention that I am keeping it in mind and have taken your opinion in the matter very much to heart.

My small book is supposed to be published by Schocken on September 1; I gave them your present address, and a copy will be sent to you directly from the publisher. Did I actually ever send you a printed version of the Kafka poem? I am not clear about this.[2] If not, you can have one. It has also been a long time since I received anything in printed form from you. Are your doppelgängers Holz, etc., dead?[3]

The political turbulence generated by the Anglo-Italian crisis[4] has resounded down here as well: the eastern Mediterranean is a very likely theater of war, should hostilities break out. Italy is already casting about for confederates among the Arabs in case of a conflict with England, and money is apparently no object. Nevertheless, things are relatively calm here for the time being. Did you know (I didn't) that over the last three years the number of Jews here has exactly doubled? That tells you what is happening here! Immigration has assumed legendary proportions, 5,000 people arrive every month. Although the proportion of Jews from Germany, numerically speaking, is not all that great, it does attract inordinate attention. By the way, such immigration, for the moment, comes largely from groups that were already Zionist beforehand; the others are just talked about more, but only very gradually has the terror, which has now assumed savage forms, started bringing them here in growing numbers. For example, more or less all of my companions from the Zionist youth group are here, and what I find most striking (even though the contrary is so often heard) is just how very few among them have pursued paths that have taken them in entirely different directions.

---

[1] The quotation is taken from W.B.'s remark about Zacharias Werner's sonnet on *Elective Affinities* (GS 1:143).

[2] The poem appeared in the *Jüdische Rundschau* of March 22, 1935.

[3] Detlef Holz disappeared from the literature section of the *Frankfurter Zeitung* following the enactment of the Nuremburg Laws.

[4] In the context of Italy's designs on Abyssinia.

Some weeks back, I saw your cousin's wife, Hannah Stern,[5] who is now in Paris, preparing children for life in Palestine, but I did not get the impression that she could have been in close contact with you or else she presumably would have conveyed greetings from you, and so I refrained from inquiring about you. She was at one time a prize student of Heidegger's.[6] But this visit is only one among many: last Sabbath both the Gutkinds—he and she[7]—suddenly showed up at our doorstep; they are in Palestine for six weeks, on money they hastily paid the Cunard Line for further passages before leaving Germany. Have you lost all contact with them? That was my impression. They asked about you as if they hadn't heard anything from you in years. They are living in New York, where he keeps afloat by teaching philosophy courses, some of them at a Jewish, strictly Orthodox college, some at the quasi-communist New School for Social Research. Neither has changed a bit, he's as stupid as ever, but witty; she's an elegantly tamed, flat-chested chatterbox, so to speak. The old platitudes keep gushing right along: the world is heading for a cataclysm, Europe is falling apart, deteriorating. They have become somewhat more reserved on the subject of Russia, but America, America is trumps. People have a completely false impression of the Jews, of the goyim as well . . . it is "absolutely shocking"—well, you will be familiar with the terminology. I invited three guests, they all flew off the handle. It was melodramatic, and Escha makes herself scarce whenever she can. I am planning to bring him together with Werner Kraft, admittedly a diabolical act. They sailed straight from London to our part of the sea, and they are sailing straight back from Naples to New York at the beginning of September, and consequently are not going to Paris. By the way, he really looks superb, no two ways about it. Bergmann asked him with truly genuine seriousness about his manuscripts and forthcoming books; they replied with that affable candor so characteristic of children and confidence men.[8] They were our last visitors for the time being.

[5] Hannah Arendt, at the time the wife of Günter Stern, whose mother was a cousin of W.B.'s. I had made her acquaintance in Berlin in October 1932.

[6] For several years Hannah Arendt was a favorite student of Martin Heidegger's in Marburg, before (following some sort of crisis) she went to Heidelberg to study with Karl Jaspers.

[7] Erich and Lucie Gutkind.

[8] Gutkind had not published a book since 1911 (*Siderische Geburt* [excerpts translated as "Sidereal Births" in Eric Gutkind, *The Body of God: First Steps Toward an Anti-Theology*, ed. Lucie B. Gutkind and Henry Le Roy Finch (New York: Horizon Press, 1969), pp. 177–232]), but at the time he was writing *The Absolute Collective: A Philosophical Attempt to Overcome Our Broken State*, which was published in English translation [trans. Marjorie Gabain (London: C. W. Daniel, 1937)] . It amounted to a philosophical grounding of certain kabbalistic theses.

There's nothing else right now. Write like a well-bred addressee: soon, and at length. We send you our best wishes,

Yours, Gerhard

78

BENJAMIN TO SCHOLEM

23 RUE BÉNARD
PARIS XIV
OCTOBER 24, 1935

Dear Gerhard,

Despite the best of intentions, I have been unable to comply with the recommendation at the close of your August letter to let you hear from me soon. Things around me were too bleak and uncertain for me to dare deprive my work of my scarce hours of inner equilibrium. A new move took place during the same period, with everything that precedes and results from moving under such conditions. I finally found some consolation in the opportunity to have a greeting conveyed to you verbally through Kitty Steinschneider.

The immediate cause for writing to you today is to thank you for the Zohar chapter I just received. There can be no question of my reading the book—with the exception of your foreword—from beginning to end. But I did read enough to be able to proffer my highest praise for what you have accomplished. And I can do so without in the least being able to judge the—doubtless immense—technical craftsmanship this translation represents. For the translation is unmistakably informed by the eminent humanity expressed in your ambition to draw such a hermetic text so appropriately and astonishingly close to the unschooled intellect, which is thus able to rely on nothing other than its attentiveness. Translating this text was surely no easier than translating a flawless poem. But translators of poetry are not customarily endowed with the austerity which here both is the precondition of success and imparts the methodological imperative to combine the translation with commentary. In this respect I view your translation as exemplary beyond the pale of the material at hand.

You won't be surprised to learn that this is a matter still close to my heart, even if you probably didn't read the short paper in which it found its expression on Ibiza ("On the Mimetic Faculty") in quite that way. Whatever the case, the concept of nonsensuous similarity developed there finds manifold illustration in the way in which the author of the

Zohar conceives of the formation of sounds—and written signs to an even greater extent, most likely—as the deposits of cosmic connections. Yet he seems to be thinking of a correspondence that is not ascribed to any mimetic origin. This may well follow from his commitment to the doctrine of emanation, to which my theory of mimesis presents the strongest possible opposition.

I have already taken note of many passages I need to speak with you about. I would like to know more about your thoughts on the origin of the rather strange theory of the moon, pp. 80–81. Furthermore, it would be quite important to examine the doctrine of hell. I suspect I have spotted a misprint on page 90 in the parenthesis containing the exegesis of I Samuel 15:29.

In the preface, I found the remarks on Moses de Leon of particular interest. (Didn't Pflaum write his doctoral dissertation on him??)[1] And then the passage on the primitive and folkloric sides of Zohar demonology.

These sides have a blithe and playful counterpart in your disclosures about the Gutkinds. Yes—I had already given up on them years before leaving Germany. The sole cause was their characteristic folly or numbness in everything regarding simple human relations. They possess extraordinary kindness, and not a slight amount of charm (though I grant this only to Erich, to be sure); nonetheless, they combine this with a far too feeble ability to pick up on things, and their lack of sensitivity turns out to be unbearable in the long run. On the other hand, I approve of the fact that they have found a comfortable and droll existence in America. They always had their minds set on far vistas, and they were always resourceful in developing their contacts.

So as not to spoil you unduly with visitors, fate has decreed that Ernst Bloch's planned trip to Palestine not take place. Hence, the matter rests at the proclamation in your letter to me. What you suggest about Bloch's work doesn't deviate from my own opinion, as you know, and least of all from the one I have of his most recent book. On the other hand, you seem to acknowledge as well—if with a certain reluctance—that my interest in this affair has been satisfied to the extent that I have been spared having to conceal that opinion in its essentials. That has, as I wrote you, meanwhile taken place. And as true as it is that, given these circumstances, the relationship can never evolve to the complete satisfaction of both parties, I will nevertheless most definitely accept responsibility for preserving the association. I, whose weaknesses have surely

---

[1] Heinz Pflaum had written his doctoral dissertation (Tübingen, 1926) on Leone Ebreo (Judah Abarbanel) and his *Dialoghi di Amore.*

never included illusions or sentimentality, do so in view of my pure insight into the limitations of this relationship; and, on the other hand, the dispersion of my friends isolates every single one of them, including myself. Weighed against these problems, the way his book treats my writings cannot even become a topic of conversation. I'm only surprised that you discern praise in it, without taking notice of the sometimes drastic reservations.

You didn't send me the printed version of your Kafka poem, and I would like to have it. If nothing of mine [has] arrived for a long time, the causes are, first, that next to nothing has been published and, second, that the papers—e.g., the *Neue Zürcher Zeitung*—tend to provide only a single author's copy, on account of the current crisis.

Despite these circumstances, I have composed a small stack of novellas, just to double and triple my quota of work.[2] One of them should be no trouble to place, if I'm not entirely mistaken, and you will receive it from me then. From time to time I dream about the frustrated book projects the "Berliner Kindheit um 1900" and the collection of letters—and then I am surprised when I find the strength to embark on a new one. Of course, under such conditions that its fate is even more difficult to predict than the form my own future is likely to take. On the other hand, a book is, as it were, the shelter I step beneath when the weather gets too rough outside. Part of the inclemency is due to Fuchs. But as time passes I am gradually steeling myself against his words, to which I continue to expose myself, having taken a variety of precautions. Moreover, I am considering his books solely to the extent that they treat the nineteenth century. That way, he doesn't lead me too far away from my own work.

This work has recently been decisively advanced by several fundamental observations on aesthetics. Together with the historical outline I drafted approximately four months ago, they will form a kind of grid or systematic point of reference on which all further particulars will have to be inscribed. These reflections anchor the history of nineteenth-century art in the recognition of their situation as experienced by us in the present. I am keeping these reflections very secret, because they are incomparably better suited to theft than most of my ideas. Their provisional formulation is entitled "The Work of Art in the Age of Mechanical Reproduction."

I will be giving a lecture on *Elective Affinities* at the Institut des Etudes Germaniques in February.[3] I don't know how long my powers of resis-

---

[2] These novellas are printed as "Kleine Prosa" in *GS* 4:721–87.

[3] I don't know if this lecture was ever actually delivered.

tance will last in view of all the circumstances, since I am provided with only the bare necessities for *at most* two weeks a month. The most trifling purchase depends on a miracle taking place. Instead, several days ago I lost my fountain pen—which was an expensive gift, or rather an heirloom. And that was no miracle, rather the most natural consequence of profound ill humor and moreover an instructive confirmation of the saying that he who has nothing will be robbed of what he has.

It seems that today I will not find my way back to more cheerful observations, so this letter ends none too soon. Write soon, and accept my kindest regards for you and Escha,

Yours, Walter

79

SCHOLEM TO BENJAMIN

Dear Walter,   DECEMBER 18, 1935

This time around I am the one who is to blame: your letter from the end of October, which for me was extremely rich in substance, has been waiting for an answer all this time. I was immobilized by a sluggishness in my writing all the while, and I'm not very satisfied with myself in other respects either. I have been sitting here alone for some weeks, without housekeeping, since Escha had to leave Jerusalem for an extended period and is recuperating in Tiberias, where she hopes to shed her sciatica and her gall-bladder troubles. Right after she left, our Yemenite maid took ill, and I began leading a student's life, which is also not very conducive to working. At the same time, Escha was fired by the library, where her position had become both superfluous and unpleasant anyway, in the wake of changes in directorship following Bergmann's departure (he has gone on to become the first rector of the university and must now apply himself to university affairs). The simultaneous necessity of maintaining two households and the depletion of our accustomed income is fatal, and our plans for actually going ahead with your invitation to stay here have been most drastically affected by this, just as we were discussing (especially after we heard what Kitty Marx had to tell us about her meeting with you) what could still be accomplished in this regard this winter. For the time being, I am pretty much out of commission. Another factor has been a final attempt on my part (still in the works) to rescue

172

my unfortunate brother from the concentration camp by means of a special form of intervention; I still have no idea what the outcome will be (I must ask you not to mention this to anyone at all, no matter who), and this difficult matter tends to strain my nerves to their limit—the chances of success have now become quite slim. What little drive remained I put to the preparation of lectures, which have started once again. I have about 15 students, and this time they represent a remarkably mixed blend of all the tribes of Israel, before whom I allow myself to be examined about the connections between mysticism and eschatology.

You perhaps know that the situation at the top echelons of the university has undergone extraordinary changes. Magnes was deposed this summer, i.e., he has been excluded from all real activities and only retained as "president"—for decorative purposes, suspended above the waters. His previous extensive powers have been delegated to two people: Schocken as trustee, and the rector, who is elected (and happens to be Bergmann at the moment, as I mentioned above). This is supposed to initiate a more substantial transformation, but only time will tell whether these changes will bring it about. In the interim, it is almost certain that Buber, who has been banned from speaking publicly in Germany (probably because of his connections with the clerical opposition centered around the [Karl] Barth group), will be offered a chair in Jerusalem, the only question not yet quite clear being in what department. You may also have heard, although it doesn't seem to be common knowledge, that the Gestapo or somebody banned the Schocken edition of Kafka's works as revenge for a review by Klaus Mann in which he rubbed the regime's nose in the fact that these books had been published by a Jewish publishing house, whereas otherwise nobody else would have made it their business to worry about these books being read.[1] Schocken himself told me this. But he wants to print the remaining volumes for readers abroad, which is said to be possible as long as the work is not distributed inside Germany. And the last volume is just the one we have been waiting for so impatiently.[2]

I am enclosing a copy of my poem, as requested, for your collection. To whet your appetite, I hope soon to be able to send you a copy of a critique of Oskar Goldberg's *Maimonides*,[3] a showy kind of work written

---

[1] [Cf. Klaus Mann, "Dank für die Kafka-Ausgabe," *Die Sammlung* 2, no. 11 (1935): 664. —Trans.]

[2] This was volume 6 *(Tagebücher und Briefe)*, which, edited by Max Brod, would first appear in 1937, published in Prague by the house of Heinrich Mercy Sohn [as agents for Schocken Verlag—Trans.].

[3] Goldberg's *Maimonides—Kritik der Jüdischen Glaubenslehre* (Vienna, 1935), an un-

173

in the most unabashedly pimpish style, and one I don't want to remain silent about.

My small book on the Zohar seems to be quite a success and to have found many readers. I was very interested by your comments about it. I wish I were able to write my entire book on the Kabbalah in the terse style of my introduction, but I am still wrestling with it terribly. I would like to write an especially excellent book and have realized that I'm dependent on inspiration that seems to consist of forgetting all the material I've already worked up on my desk. This doesn't always work. I don't get much time to work on it now that the semester is on again. Instead, I spend my free hours filing away at an essay in Hebrew on the ideology of religious nihilism in Judaism, as a continuation of my early work on Cardozo. But this essay, which would be of great interest to you, can only be written in Hebrew anyway, at least if the author is to remain free from apologetic inhibitions.[4]

I met a somewhat grotesque-looking lady here, by the name of Dr. Franziska Herzfeld[5] . . . Anyway, she claims to be well acquainted with Bloch, you, and Kracauer, and so I talked with her about Bloch's writings, and her remarks weren't exactly stupid. Since you're interested in Schuler, let me point out that a lot of material on him is to be found in the late Theodor Lessing's newly published autobiography[6] (a dreadful book, by the way, even given its rather interesting contents). Should you lay your hands on the book at some point, read the relevant chapters.

Escha may remain in Tiberias the whole winter. The day after tomorrow, for Hanukkah, I will be going there for a few days.

Fondest regards,

Yours, Gerhard

---

usual pamphlet in which M. is accused of idolatry. I didn't write the critique in the end, because I didn't think the work was good enough to write about at the necessary length.

[4] This lengthy essay appeared in Hebrew in 1936. It appeared in English translation only in 1971, as "Redemption through Sin," in my book *The Messianic Idea in Judaism*, pp. 78–141.

[5] See also the following letter. I don't have a more detailed recollection of Frau Herzfeld, but I think I may have met her several times around 1921, during my student days in Munich, where she attracted attention because of her unusual coiffure. She studied literature and philosophy.

[6] Theodor Lessing (1872–1933), *Einmal und nie wieder* (Prague: Orbis Verlag, 1935). The author was murdered by the Nazis in 1933.

80

BENJAMIN TO SCHOLEM

23 RUE BÉNARD
PARIS XV

Dear Gerhard,

MARCH 29, 1936

Whichever of the gods may count the correspondence of earthlings among his duties, it seems as if the threads of ours have slipped from his hands to fall into the power of some demon of silence.

I freely admit, however, that his workings are by no means inscrutable to me, insofar as my own inner life serves as their stage. The manifold and disappointing vacillations of the date of our reunion are of great consequence. And they burden me down all the more when they raise the question in my mind of whether you are as infused with the significance, not to mention the timeliness, of this reunion as I am. The time that has passed since we first started looking forward to it represents a stream with an increasingly steep incline, against which our written communications find it ever more difficult to struggle.

I don't mean just the letters, but also communications like my latest offprint,[1] whose unacknowledged receipt might not have been a coincidence.

And if, in this context, I bear in mind the wish to bring my most recent work, which I can spare even less than ever (since it is more important), into the zone of our correspondence (and hence its latency periods as well), then I am not always able to refrain from feeling uneasy.

By the way, the work on this essay, which kept me completely occupied throughout January and February, is one reason for a streak of light in the tableau of my silence.

It will first—perhaps soon, perhaps only at the end of the year—appear in French: in fact, the *Zeitschrift für Sozialforschung*, which is bringing it out, prefers the translation to the original text. It is entitled "The Work of Art in the Age of Mechanical Reproduction." At present I see little chance of getting the original text published.

I am postponing further details of this work—or rather its text—until a later letter. For today, I just want to address an eager question to you about the substance of your quarrel with Goldberg's Maimonides book. This would allow me to gain a first impression of the book itself, and I hope I can count on getting it very soon.

I don't wish to hold forth again today on the external facts of my life

---

[1] "Probleme der Sprachsoziologie." [First published in the *Zeitschrift für Sozialforschung.*—TRANS.]

175

here. The major book has taken a back seat to the new work, which is not at all close to it in terms of material, but intimately related to it methodologically. Before I resume working on it, I have to write a short study on Nikolai Leskov to which I have committed myself. I have managed to relegate the Fuchs to the back burner once again.

By the way, I hope you've had occasion to read something by Leskov, who is a masterful storyteller.[2] Being acquainted with him is much more profitable than with, say, Fränze Herzfeld.

What results did your efforts on your brother's behalf have? Mine is still in Germany, unscathed for the time being.

I hope I will now be receiving news from you soon, and I send you my kindest regards,

Yours, Walter

81

SCHOLEM TO BENJAMIN

Dear Walter, APRIL 19, 1936

Your letter brought me great joy after such a long hiatus and such a turbulent interval, even though I can't turn a deaf ear to the difficulties you speak of in connection with our reunion. But I am only now able to write you in detail about the circumstances that, unknown to you, have weighed upon me so very much this past year. And it is to them that your trip has fallen victim, even though I couldn't tell you so before. You will understand my difficult position and excuse it, I hope, when I now inform you that a short time ago I was divorced.[1] Separating from Escha caused very great inward and external difficulties in my personal life. As a friend who has been through a similar experience, you don't need a description of just how great. Carrying through the decision to separate, which I finally made last summer, cost me close to 8 months and has of course brought about a most decisive change in the way I live. Because I filed the suit for divorce, I will be placed in a rather formidable financial situation should Escha not remarry, footing the bill for two households. The result was (and is) that I have had to carefully limit and rethink my

---

[2] I hadn't read anything of Leskov's, and only after the essay was published did I start to read the few volumes I managed to get hold of.

[1] See letter 74, note 1.

standard of living and my obligations, and here you have the reason why I could not, in my present situation, push forward with the arrangements for your trip, as we had conceived it. I would have had little to offer you during those trying months, and intellectually even less than in other respects. The divorce has meanwhile been finalized, but everything else is still relatively up in the air. Escha has remained in Tiberias for the time being. By the way, we dismissed the whole matter in as congenial a manner as possible. If Bergmann were to succeed in getting his divorce (which, however, is exceedingly problematic), then she would remarry.

These personal affairs have hindered me for nearly a year in my work and my plans, and only now can I hope to resume leading a regular and normal working life. So I am not able to provide you with the Goldberg critique just yet; my ability to work has been quite paralyzed. Another consequence of the events is that for financial reasons I can't even contemplate a European trip for the moment, but rather have to lead a subdued existence here. My mother came two weeks ago and will be staying for six weeks, so I won't be traveling to Europe for her seventieth birthday. Conditions don't yet permit us to envisage my mother staying here permanently.

An attempt to bring my brother Werner here, which I had pushed through to a relatively promising stage (certificate for Palestine, negotiations for his release being conducted by the British authorities), was thwarted at the last moment, when all concerned, especially the British and my poor brother himself, believed everything had been properly arranged. Goebbels needs to keep a couple of Jews on hand in order to demonstrate that he has stamped out bolshevism, and my brother is apparently among those selected to play the part.[2] I only learned the dismal news a week ago, and we have now lost hope entirely. On April 20 he will have been in custody for three whole years. There is no other course of action left to take. The brutes had already told my brother he would be released, and he had already been allowed to send a letter with the news to his wife. So now the reaction will be horrible, since that represented his last shred of hope. The affair has also taken a severe toll on my mother.

I regret not having anything more positive to report this time, but at least you are now fully informed about my situation. I will surely be able to write you soon with details about the future, specifically whether I will be moving out of the house, which has become far too expensive for me,

[2] At the time when the final decision had to be made, it came to light that a list existed of people who could be freed only with Goebbels's permission and that the Gestapo had known all the time that my brother was on this list. When my mother went to the Gestapo to hear about, or to receive, the final agreement, she was ridiculed contemptuously.

as comfortable as it would be for my work. In general I am not, for the time being, up to the routines of everyday life at all. But I assume that things can only get better.

I received your offprint on the sociology of language—this is the only mailing you can conceivably mean—and read it diligently, but without understanding everything. But I haven't been very intellectually receptive of late.

I wish you the best of luck on your new work, and I hope it will also lead you back to the completion of the other major project, which I expected you to be already editing in its final version.

I don't know Leskov, unfortunately, and have also never seen anything of his.

I hope we will regain our freedom to move and meet in the foreseeable future. I'm convinced that you are absolutely right in regarding the latter as imperative if we wish to know where we stand and how we really exist.

Kindest regards,

Yours, Gerhard

82

BENJAMIN TO SCHOLEM

23 RUE BÉNARD
PARIS XIV
MAY 3, 1936

Dear Gerhard,

With your last letter, our correspondence over this past year has sustained a sorry epilogue. It is an epilogue to which I can proffer nothing more than a mute listener who is able to follow it all too well—even where it moves only in intimations—to intrude with words of no consequence. Of the little that can be expressed, I hope that whatever loneliness you feel vis-à-vis the outside world will be short-lived and will bring about some inner fecundity.

Even if our correspondence these last months hasn't fared much better than you have, at least you can't deny me the testimonial that I have stood by it with patience. Not in vain, if it regains something of its original character as time passes. That's why we must both hope that the elemental spirits of our existence and our work, who are entitled to our dialogue, will not be kept waiting indefinitely on the threshold. On the other hand, one must not disregard the chance that they may be able to

178

converse, set free of the physical zones of our being owing to an imminent purge of geopolitical differences.

For the moment, I can only hope that at least the events in Palestine that come to my attention are exaggerated reports. But that leaves enough to be distressed about in many other respects. Knowing this, I would really like to obtain French citizenship, were it not bound up with costs that could lead to my new nationality being bestowed upon a skeleton.

I read the account of your brother's fate with horror. I don't know him,[1] but the mere fact of having to connect a name to that kind of existence is dreadful. My brother is still in Germany too, but at liberty. He doesn't suffer any direct privation, since my sister-in-law works at the Russian trade mission in Berlin.

As to my own work, it seems to be vastly surpassed by the thoughts you have for it—in every stage of its development. In any case, I take it that you mean the "Paris Arcades" when you refer to the "major project." Nothing has changed there: not a syllable of the actual text exists, even though the end of preparatory studies is now within sight. And for the moment the emphasis is not on the text so much as on the planning of the whole, which needs to be thought through very carefully and will certainly give rise to this or that experiment for some time to come. My last work, whose French version—"L'Oeuvre d'art à l'époque de sa reproduction mécanisée"—should be appearing in three weeks' time, has also evolved from this planning. It touches on the major project only superficially, but it indicates the vanishing point for some of its investigations. Of the aforementioned attempts at an overall plan, only one has thus far taken final shape. I will attempt a companion piece to it as soon as I return to this subject.

Unfortunately, I will scarcely be able to sidestep the work on Fuchs this summer; but meanwhile I managed to obtain certain liberties in connection with it.

I hope soon to hear more details of your big Kabbalah project for Schocken; not to speak of the Goldberg critique.

Is Leo Strauss in Palestine?[2] I would not be averse to addressing his works in the journal *Orient und Okzident*—for which I'm writing the Leskov piece. Perhaps you'll be seeing the author; if so, you can prevail upon him to send me the books.

I close for today with most cordial greetings,

Yours, Walter

[1] W.B. had met my brother once, at a Seder in the house of my friend Moses Marx in 1923, but he had forgotten about it.

[2] Leo Strauss was in England at that time, from where he traveled to the U.S. in 1938.

83

SCHOLEM TO BENJAMIN

Dear Walter, JUNE 6, 1936

The unrest of the last four weeks since receiving your last letter, for
which I am very grateful, didn't provide a good reason to write, and
unfortunately even less time. I don't know to what extent you can glean
reliable information about the unrest here from the Paris newspapers,
how much sensationalism is involved or, conversely, how coolly these
things are treated there.[1] Anyway, the situation here is grave and a test
for strong nerves. The Arabs have been waging genuine partisan warfare
over the last four weeks, with an intensity that keeps escalating and
exhibits an unexpected terror and barbarism. The general strike is forced
on Arab towns by means of internal terror against their own people, as is
for the most part its financing, but the fact that it is still so pervasive,
that the opposition can't get its way, demonstrates resolute discipline.
Since the Jews (instead of what would have only been natural, that is, to
answer with counterterror) have until now maintained an unexpectedly
disciplined poise—itself a moral achievement—they have also preserved
a very strong position in the political sphere *up to now*. If the Jews or
groups among them don't lose their nerve—an effect toward which many
of the extremely nerve-racking acts of terror and sabotage obviously aim
—it's hard to see how the Arabs can make even the slightest gains before
putting a stop to the terror. On the other hand, they apparently see no
escape from the adventure, which was undoubtedly begun in the expectation of being able to force the English government into suspending
Jewish immigration by these rather overly oriental methods. This has
proved to be a total miscalculation up to now, and the government has
remained uncompromising. We will certainly have to pay the price in the
end, of course, because once the present phase of terror is over, concessions will become more likely in the wake of successful "pacification."
Despite its much more savage massacres, the attack of 1929 was really a
small matter in its gravity and consequence compared to what we are
now experiencing. The fact that 400,000 Jews are not as easy to throw
around as 150,000 is well known to both sides, of course, and exerts a
moderating influence on the Jews this time: one feels stronger and is thus

[1] The reference is to the severe Arab unrest, which lasted from May to the end of
October 1936 and resulted in a general strike and insurrection by Arab guerrillas in Palestine.

able to endure more with patience. A state of siege has been in effect in Jerusalem for many weeks now, i.e., after 7 at night everybody is supposed to be at home. But it is in no way restful to have to listen night after night to incessant shooting going on in the mountains. Life does go on as usual on the surface, but in reality everything has changed. Almost every younger person, which above all includes students at the university, has been conscripted, as it were, even if privately, to defend against open raids which may occur at any time (and are often attempted). If this keeps up much longer, I will also be obliged to spend several hours at night surveying the landscape from a rooftop. I am telling you all of this in order to portray the bitter atmosphere we are breathing in at the moment.

My mother was here for six weeks. At least she is already so old that she apprehends what's going on only indistinctly, and things are better that way. As a result, she was fairly, or even wholly, content. She left during the very week when the situation became especially dangerous. She will turn seventy in the fall, but this sudden visit to me will substitute for my trip to Europe. I cannot work the way I would like to under these circumstances, which are of vital concern to us all. So today I won't be able to relate anything of my "inner life." In three weeks the vacation begins, and I hope the tension will have finally subsided by then—but that seems, to such a pessimist as I, to be most unlikely. I'm afraid we are still in for some very hard times.[2]—Did you receive the private edition of my book from Berlin (Schocken Verlag) in the mail? I had given them your name.

Leo Strauss doesn't live in Palestine, but rather has spent the last 2 years in England, in Cambridge. Which means I don't come into contact with him, I'm sorry to say. So much for this time. Please let me hear from you! I urgently advise you to acquire French naturalization.

Most cordially,

Yours, Gerhard

[2] This turned out to be the case. The next three months were filled with frequent Arab raids on villages and travel routes, resulting in extraordinary tension. This triggered heated discussions on the Jewish side as to whether the greatest possible restraint, limited to defense, was called for—this was the position taken by the responsible Jewish authorities —or whether the times dictated retaliatory blows, as a strong faction demanded.

84

BENJAMIN TO SCHOLEM

23 RUE BÉNARD
PARIS XIV
JUNE 25, 1936

Dear Gerhard,

I take it that this letter will be the last you receive from Paris for a while. I want to take a summer vacation in mid-July, for several months if possible. City life, which I have endured without a break for more than a year now, has considerably increased my need for a vacation. And even if I can't expect to escape the outward difficulties of my existence through a change of scenery, I won't let that hold me back. Nothing has been settled yet about which direction the trip will take! I waver between Denmark and the Baleares.

Your letter of June 6 goes into the political situation in Palestine for the first time. It has been of great concern to me, in my thoughts about you and, secretly, because of the mere fact itself. Of course, I lack the particulars to form my own opinion (which is not at all my strong point in concrete politics). Thus I am all the more vigilant in pursuing detailed and, if possible, firsthand reports. As far as I am able to do so, I have yet to run across anything that would serve to defuse your pessimism. I've been particularly impressed by the prospective impact of the negotiations currently taking place here on the Syrian question. Were Syria —as seems likely—to enter into a relationship with France comparable to the one between Iraq and England, that would hardly result in an easing of tensions in the Palestinian conflict. And it would be grave cause for concern if the Arab movement were really as popular in the Orient as some here contend. I fear that the psychological reactions of the Jews might prove scarcely less harmful than the physical actions of the Arabs. And if you, actually being there yourself, can't see a way out, then it's all the more impossible for me to do so.

I don't view the European situation—in terms of its latent structure— any more confidently than the Palestinian one. It seems to me to be moving quickly toward a state of affairs in which one would be virtually helpless, even with French citizenship in hand. By the way, I don't even have the material resources to acquire it. My German passport is valid until 1938 anyway, and if the problem still exists then, I would try, with foreign help, to do something toward that end.

Your letter crossed with the package containing my most recent essay in its French version. I don't know if it is accessible to you. If so, then I would be exceptionally interested in the impression it leaves you with, notwithstanding the reserved reception it is likely to receive. In the meantime, I have completed a new and not quite so lengthy manuscript, and I am especially sorry not to be able to let you read it at once, because you would find it much more agreeable, and not just from the linguistic point of view. It is called: "The Storyteller: Reflections on the Works of Nikolai Leskov."

Tomorrow I will finally meet Shestov.

I received the beautiful private edition of the Zohar chapter and thank you very much for it.

I am quite confident that the concerns my last letter touched on will regain their proper place in our correspondence, despite the ordeals we've both had to endure. And it is with this confidence that I want to close for today.

Most cordially,

Yours, Walter

85

SCHOLEM TO BENJAMIN

Dear Walter,   AUGUST 26, 1936

I found your card[1] on my return from a trip to Tel Aviv and am pulling myself together immediately to write you at last. Ever since your last letter arrived, I have been so lost in moodiness that I need a proper outside incentive in order to reply. The situation here, as you probably know, is most uncomfortable. It's true that the end of the almost anarchic situation in the country is said to be in sight in a matter of days, but "nobody knows anything for sure." We've been living under a state of siege in Jerusalem for three months, every evening you hear more or less incessant shooting, and from time to time one spends a few hours standing guard on a "strategic" rooftop at the edge of the quarter. In between, you wait patiently for the latest news. The terror is considerable, and it has required immense restraint on the part of the Jews not to resort to the very natural and all too practicable instrument of counterterror up to now. But I'm not certain whether it will remain this way. Several days

[1] This card has been lost; the single undated postcard (no. 87) from Ravenna, which might fit here, cannot be dated during this part of the summer (when he was with Brecht) by virtue of its content.

183

ago my colleague [Levi Billig], the assistant professor of Arabic Literature, was murdered while reading a book in his study, and you can imagine the uproar. You become accustomed to a certain measure of fatalism, since nobody knows whether or not a bomb will be thrown at him at the next corner; on the other hand, only seldom do these bombs ever explode or at least actually do some damage, so in the long run you become fairly unflappable. Ten minutes before I left Tel Aviv, a bomb was thrown from a train onto a railway crossing along the route we were to take, causing fatalities, and we arrived amid sheer pandemonium, but, in general, life in the cities is still ideal compared to the open country. There, pitched battles are being fought, partly between the army and groups of Arab partisans, and partly between those groups and the Jewish colonies, whom they attack incessantly. It will take a long time for peace to prevail once again. The British have adopted an irresolute and unclear policy; they are afraid of making a bitter enemy out of one of the two peoples and are hoping for a diplomatic miracle. The Jews are all the more incensed since their indignation, as I said before, is not vented in acts of violence, but they "keep quiet" for the soberest political reasons, which will carry weight at future political negotiations. We undoubtedly have a tumultuous six months ahead of us. On the other hand, immigration continues to be quite large despite Arab strikes and acts of terror, and in the final analysis, of course, everything will depend on this. The international situation exerts such abnormally strong pressure on Palestine that a genuine attempt to put a halt to immigration is hardly likely in the long run. Since everyone wants to get rid of the Jews, it is more difficult today than it was 7 years ago to shut the gates of Palestine to them. Yet a setback might also have its benefits, with reference to the moral side of our undertaking.—Speculation is widespread as to which country is behind the Arabic movement: Rome, Berlin, or Moscow—or all three. The whole business is most mysterious and, incidentally, rather spectacular as regards the role of the communists in the anti-Jewish agitation. Surefire philological analysis has determined that, irrespective of the language they appear in, the communist leaflets sent to my house were written by German Jews who have only recently entered the country. The Jewish camp accordingly is profoundly hostile to these groups, and the conflicts of conscience that people who know the names of such fellow citizens must then face are in no way minor. In short, it is unfortunate that every step has been taken to insure that life here does not become dull.

I myself am sitting here and working as effectively as I can. I have already produced a few essays, among them a very long one on mystical nihilism in the ghetto, which would be of interest to you except that it is written in Hebrew. I prepared a short abridgment of it in German for the

184

Schocken *Almanach*, which will somehow or other reach you upon its publication. At the moment I am doing some work on my history of the Kabbalah. I have so much in my head, but nevertheless things still go very slowly! But I'm happy just to have begun working again. My financial situation is such that I cannot even consider a major trip for the time being. My mother, as you seem to have heard,[2] fell ill when returning from her visit here and had to undergo an operation. But everything seems to have gone well and she is said to be on the way to a complete recovery. Her seventieth birthday is 3 months from now.

I found your essay very interesting.[3] This is the first time I have come upon something thought-provoking in a philosophical context about film and photography. But I am far too lacking in specialized knowledge to be able to pass judgment on your prognoses.

Has your Leskov essay appeared? I am, by the way, entirely uneducated and have no idea who he is. Perhaps I will be able to turn up some of his books here.

These days I spend my free hours reading memoirs, which I find much more entertaining than belles lettres, and in this way I am improving my education to some degree. I have a grand time reading four or five volumes of memoirs from the same circle: no poet lies as eloquently as do people with vested interests.

Will you be staying in Denmark very long?

With sincerest regards from

Your Gerhard

86

BENJAMIN TO SCHOLEM

23 RUE BÉNARD
PARIS XIV
OCTOBER 18, 1936

Dear Gerhard,

Your informative letter of August 26 lies before me. It reached me in Denmark, where I spent several weeks with Brecht before traveling down to Dora in San Remo.

The temporary lull that the summer brought in our correspondence

[2] There must have been a remark to this effect in the missing postcard, since there is no such reference in W.B.'s extant letters.

[3] The "Work of Art" essay, of which he had sent me an offprint. W.B. was not all that mistaken to sense reservations in my brief observations, as is borne out in the next letter. These reservations were brought up most emphatically in the course of verbal argument when we next saw each other.

seems to me of less consequence than some that preceded it, because public events, which affect and concern one or the other of us directly, and hence one or the other at least indirectly, are assuming ever more drastic forms. A report on Palestine which I received from a third party contributed some details to the picture I have of your existence there. And you have likewise now [and] then surely visualized in your own mind how things look in the political world that is more closely touching if not already engulfing me.

We cannot disregard the fact that the geographic separation we have endured for so long now, owing to the immensity and monstrosity of current events, weighs more heavily on our correspondence than otherwise would have been the case. I am of the opinion that for this reason we must seek to wrest all the more from our respective writings. Consequently, I am sorry you did not advise me of more specifics in the excerpts of your study on nihilism appearing in the Schocken *Almanach*, and I wonder if I should not have already received them by now. The *Almanach*, I imagine, must already be out.

I admit to you, along the same lines, that I have sadly taken to heart the fundamental impermeability with which my latest essay seems to confront your understanding (and I use the word not in its technical sense alone). If nothing in it pointed you back to the realm of ideas in which we both used to be at home, then I am going to assume, for the time being, that the reason was less that I have drawn a very novel map of one of its provinces but more that it was in French. Whether I will ever be able to make it available to you in German must remain as open a question as whether it would then find you in a more receptive mood.

In any case, you will get more out of a small book you will be receiving in the course of the next month. All of its contents, I suspect, will be known to you. It's the collection of those letters I had published with the anonymous prefaces in the *Frankfurter Zeitung* around 1930. Vita Nova Verlag in Lucerne is publishing it. I would have liked nothing better than to use the occasion of publication in book form to double the size of the collection, but the publisher was in a great rush, and it's virtually impossible for me to lay my hands here on the source material [I] would require.

Let me point out that the book's title, *Deutsche Menschen*, can be explained as flowing from my pen only due to the desire to camouflage the collection, from which some may be able to profit in Germany.[1] I am signing it with the pseudonym Detlef Holz.

---

[1] W.B. also gave this important explanation of the book's title (in place of the projected *Deutsche Briefe*) to Horkheimer (two months later); see *GS* 4:948.

Speaking of Germany, I want to inform you that just days ago[2] my brother was sentenced to 6 years' imprisonment. My sister saw him twice: he is said to have reacted with totally unforgettable courage and composure.

I don't know whether you sometimes receive issues of Maximilian Beck's *Philosophische Hefte*, which is published in Czechoslovakia.[3] The last one has an announcement at the end of its bibliographical section of both your publications on the Zohar. I am not able to judge the competence of Beck's observations about them (and, if I remember correctly, they were intended quite favorably). I consider myself a little better qualified to judge those he adds, in the same bibliographical section, to several quotations from Buber's writings. Here he seems to have hit the nail on the head. These quotations mark out the grounds of my long-standing, insurmountable mistrust of that man with a precision I could never bring myself to achieve in gathering the requisite material. It is a sad thing that Schocken's endeavors stand under the sign of that man, who has shown himself capable of seamlessly transposing the terminology of National Socialism into debates about Jewish questions.[4]

At this year's ten-day session at Pontigny, which dealt with the problem of the "Volonté du mal,"[5] Buber is said to have left quite an ambiguous impression.

I conclude by repeating the request to forward to me, without delay, that fraction of your publications accessible to me. I promise to do the same for the more accessible of my own.

I hope the cease-fire, which I assume has been reached in Palestine by now, will be conducive to your work. Fill me in about it soon. Let me also hear something about Agnon for once.

With kindest regards,

Yours, Walter

[2] On October 14, 1936. W.B. wrote "years" instead of "days."

[3] Maximilian Beck (1887–1950) was an acquaintance with whom I had often discussed philosophy and Jewish subjects in Munich. He was one of Wilhelm Pfänder's foremost disciples, and a sharp-witted man who didn't feel very comfortable with his Jewish-Bohemian birthright. He regularly sent me the *Philosophische Hefte*. The reviews of Buber and myself were printed in 5, nos. 1–2, (1936): 108–11, 112–15.

[4] I didn't share this judgment of Buber's terminology, and I wrote W.B. to that effect.

[5] Buber introduced the fourth discussion of the Pontigny Conference on August 29, 1936, on "La Volonté du mal" with a lecture which, in its revised form, has been included in his work *Good and Evil: Two Interpretations*, part 2 [trans. Michael Bullock (New York: Scribner's, 1953)].

87

BENJAMIN TO SCHOLEM

RAVENNA
Dear Gerhard,   [TOWARD THE END OF 1936]

These tidings and warm greetings on a day that has turned out to be glorious after all, one on which I've finally fulfilled a desire nursed for twenty years: I have now seen the Ravenna mosaics. The impression the mosaics made on me only barely surpasses that made by the sober, fortresslike churches, which have long been stripped of every intermittent ornament adorning their façades. Some have sunk somewhat into the ground; you have to walk down steps to get to them; this heightens the impression one has of turning back into the past.

Thank you very much for the essay on the connections between messianism and the Enlightenment.[1] It is nicely written; I read it with the utmost interest. I would be pleased to receive any sequel you might write.—And to have detailed news soon, which I request you send to my Paris address. Most sincerely,

Walter

88

SCHOLEM TO BENJAMIN

PENSION HELENA COHN
ABARBANEL RD. 28
REHAVIA, JERUSALEM
Dear Walter,   DECEMBER 29, 1936

I am beginning this letter, as you will observe from the address, in a new setting, which is the most succinct expression of some of the changes my life has undergone. I have left my former house, where Escha has now taken up residence. She herself has since been transformed into a Frau Bergmann. Moreover, in order to give other news its due right away, I should say that I was recently married again, to a young woman from the

---

[1] My essay "Zum Verständnis des Sabbatianismus: Zugleich ein Beitrag zur Geschichte der Aufklärung" in the *Almanach des Schocken Verlags für das Jahre 5697* (1936–37), pp. 30–42, was a very succinct German resumé of the theses in the long Hebrew essay mentioned above.

depths of the Sarmatian forests by the name of [Fania] Freud. Your first impression of her will have to wait until you meet her in person, which I don't despair about in the least. In any case, I find myself in the midst of extreme changes in my living arrangements, which we hope will be for the best. We don't have a place of our own for the time being, and are lodgers in a boarding house. It is very difficult for me to find something suitable, since my library has so swelled in size that it makes me virtually immobile. For the moment, the majority of the books are still housed in the old apartment. The next months will reveal how things are likely to develop. We are bound to come up with some place to live. You yourself are presumably a greater expert in this kind of diaspora existence than I and can easily imagine what ours is like.

And that is how I have passed the time since I last heard from you. I was delighted to get your card from Ravenna, from which I could at least glean that you still find some pleasure in the world—I only wish that it were far greater!

The book version of the letters, which you announced in October and which I am waiting for with bated breath, isn't out yet? Please keep me informed as to how this matter stands. I was extremely happy for you and us readers at the prospect of at last being able to hold the letters in my hand as a book, and I do hope that nothing has interfered with this.

The only news I've heard of your brother's sentence has come from you. Do you know any details of his trial? Six years is a terribly long time. My own brother is still incarcerated without any prospect of help or of an end. Ever since [Carl von] Ossietzky was awarded the Nobel Prize, they have redoubled the revenge they wreak on those political prisoners in preventive custody who have remained healthy: my mother writes me of the many new ordeals involved. But worst of all is the utter unpredictability of how long the imprisonment will last.

I did read Beck's critical reviews on Buber and myself (the author is an old acquaintance of Escha's and mine from our Munich days); he sent me the issues in question. I've forgotten what he wrote about Buber; it also didn't interest me particularly, since he has a long-standing aversion to all Zionists, which of course should not prevent his realizing the truth about some nonsense or other of Buber's. I must admit that, after 20 years of studying this Buber, I am still not able to give a categorical reply to the question of whether there is something of substance in what he writes or not. I don't have it as easy as you do, I see too much from both sides. I am of the opinion (and that is why I worked energetically to secure his appointment here) that this can only be *conclusively* determined once he is forced to speak Hebrew. I expect this will bring about an important crisis in Buber's life, and to plunge him into that would be

189

an act of piety. But I cannot in all honesty subscribe to what you write about his "National Socialist" terminology. I have nothing against him along those lines, and I don't think you are right.

Just 3 days ago a commemoration was held for Franz Rosenzweig's 50th birthday, at which we (four of us were speaking, I being the last and most tempestuous) all indulged in a critique of the great man and his thought.

I have published in Hebrew the expanded version of the article on the theory of kabbalistic nihilism, whose main theses you received in an abbreviated German version in the Schocken *Almanach*.—Shouldn't I send you this version as well? Perhaps the Holy Ghost will translate it for you? This work will bring me some notoriety as a Hebrew writer for the first time, for it is really good, and well suited to make an impression. Perhaps I will refashion it into an equivalent German after all; Schocken would like me to. But I have far too much planned this year as it is, including a slender volume in German on the history of the Kabbalah (a shortened version for the Schocken Library). May the Lord grant it a finished form!!

Most cordially,

Yours, Gerhard

Many regards to the much-read and much-discussed author, although we haven't yet been introduced.

Fania

89

BENJAMIN TO SCHOLEM

Dear Gerhard,   [POSTMARK: FEBRUARY 11, 1937]

Though I'm not a man who gives up easily, there are hours when I feel uncertain whether we shall ever see each other again. A cosmopolitan city like Paris has become a very frail entity, and if what I'm told about Palestine is true, then a wind is blowing there in which even Jerusalem could begin to sway to and fro like a reed.

(My opinion about England is that for some years now its policy has been solely determined by the certainty that the Commonwealth would cease to exist after the first forty-eight hours of a war.)

To return to our reunion, I visualize it now and then—just to be able to cling to its image—like that of the leaves of trees that are far apart and meet in a storm. Thus I will presumably have to be content, for the present, to return your wife's greetings with a wave from afar.—

Stefan's development has taken a disturbing turn.[1] His transplantation to Vienna (which Dora initiated a year ago without informing me, let alone asking me) has proven to be an error, as wasn't hard to predict, but on top of that it is particularly dangerous. It remains to be seen to what extent Stefan is the victim of disturbances that detrimentally influence his moral attitudes and to what extent his intellectual attitudes have been unfavorably affected as well. I regard the latter as satisfactory for the time being. Whereas his moral attitude is not. Whether or not he will take his final high-school exams is still uncertain.

It's a pity that neither San Remo nor Paris, each in its own way, can seriously be considered as a place for Stefan to stay. (San Remo would be very risky, and transplanting him to a totally foreign linguistic environment hardly less so.) We are therefore not yet clear about what steps have to be taken.

My thoughts are somber, as you will have noticed, whether they move about in nearby or remote regions. My work at present is not cut out to lighten them. It consists of finishing the essay on Fuchs, to which all others have to take a back seat.

By now you must have my book in hand. May you soon be able to find a fitting accommodation for the remainder of your library. I convey my best wishes to you and your wife for the new lodgings.

Yours, Walter

P.S. Send me the Hebrew text on nihilism and the Enlightenment!

90

SCHOLEM TO BENJAMIN

ABARBANEL RD. 28
MARCH 1, 1937

Dear Walter,

I received your book and thank you most sincerely. I read some parts of it for the first time, since I didn't get the first seven letters at the time

---

[1] Stefan had fallen in with gamblers.

they came out. I was as moved by the text as much as the commentary, and my only regret is that you were unable to bring out twice as much. Following this procession of letter writers in this way is a vivid experience. I wonder if the epigraph "Of Dignity without Pay, etc.," which has to be understood in an indirectly polemical way, might not offset the innocuous nom de plume and cause the book, despite all that, to be banned under Hitler? Besides, it might just occur to somebody to read your comments, which are unmistakably "corrupting." But you haven't heard of any difficulties up to now? I wish you the best of success and I intend to make propaganda for it among my acquaintances. My wife is very impressed by it.

Your last, brief letter was fraught with melancholy. I am much less skeptical than you are, for one thing because I don't believe in a world war before 1940, and for another because I hope our situation here will improve to the point that I can once again think of traveling (at the moment I simply lack the funds). Admittedly, I'm not entitled to take leave for a summer semester until two years from now (every seven years!), but I will duly keep my eyes on that date. If we should be in a position to invite you to visit us before then, as I wanted to in earlier days, you can rest assured that we will pursue it as vigorously as possible. Misfortune saw to it, as you can now recognize more easily in retrospect, that my personal affairs came to a head precisely at the time when we hoped to see you, and nothing could be done. We have just rented an apartment—it is at this very moment being renovated—which I hope to be able to inhabit in peace and quiet for a time. The next weeks (that is, the whole of this year's spring vacation) will be spent transporting and setting up my library. The boarding house we were living in is being broken up, and we have rented a floor in it, a minute away from our old rooms. I've spent the past several days emptying the bookshelves, in order to disassemble them, and I'm writing you this letter from the old apartment—Escha is with Bergmann in America, on university business, which allows me to make the move more leisurely. During the summer months I have to finish a book for Schocken, with which I hope to edify you.

The collection of your writings has already made its way with great care to the new residence. I hope you will be able to put your accursed Fuchs tearfully behind you and can then turn toward more intriguing questions of the intellectual world. I myself am going three days from now to a village in the Valley of Jezreel, where they are very rigorous Marxists and don't want to hear about anything else. I plan to poke fun at them dialectically and deliver a series of three lectures on the theme: The Kabbalah as a Revolutionary Factor in Jewish History. In the end we'll surely be at each other's throats.

I am having a copy of my Hebrew study on religious nihilism sent to you. I think you should learn from it—it is an interesting piece of work.

Accept my kindest regards and cheer up,

Yours, Gerhard

91

BENJAMIN TO SCHOLEM

23 RUE BÉNARD
PARIS XIV
APRIL 4, 1937

Dear Gerhard,

I was extremely gratified that you so thoroughly understood the character and intention of the volume of letters. Your unfulfilled wish was precisely the same as mine: to expand the book to twice its size. This wish is one I could no longer hope to realize in emigration; at best I might have been able to attempt it with the resources of the Swiss libraries or the British Museum—never in Paris. I also feel sorry for the sake of several commentaries: there is hardly one I would have preferred to write more than that on the incomparable letter written by Rahel on Gentz's death.[1]

I am pleased to hear that your life will soon have a definite shape again, and I congratulate you and your wife on the new apartment. I warmly return your wife's greetings. If this year passes without bringing the outbreak of war, then perhaps we can look into the very immediate future with a little more confidence, and I don't have to tell you that I would be happy to see our reunion bathed in such brighter colors—against either the backdrop of Jerusalem's battlements or that of the grayish blue façades of the boulevards.

Now dress me in your mind's eye in a herald's armor and imagine me at the bow of a four-master cutting through the Mediterranean surf as swiftly as an arrow, because that is the only fitting way to convey the grand news to you: the "Fuchs" is done. The finished text does not entirely have the character of penitence, as my laboring on it quite rightly seemed to you. On the contrary, its first quarter contains a number of important reflections on dialectical materialism, which are provisionally tailored to my book. My subsequent essays will be moving more directly toward that book from now on.

The "Fuchs" has been greeted with great acclaim. I see no reason to

---

[1] The reference is to Rahel Varnagen's letter of June 15, 1833, to Leopold Ranke, which was first printed in Varnhagen von Ense's collection *Rahel: Ein Buch des Andenkens für ihre Freunde*, part 3 (Berlin, 1834), pp. 576–78.

hide the fact that the tour de force it achieves is the substantial as well as major cause of this success. I hope you will be getting the printed article before the year is out. It always pleases me to hear of the care you bestow upon the collection of my writings. Troubled premonitions tell me that perhaps only our combined archives could present an exhaustive collection of them. For as conscientious as I am in administering my own, I most likely lost several pieces through the hasty departure from Berlin and the unsettled existence of the early years of emigration. To be sure, only a handful of my own works have been lost—as opposed to almost all of a relatively complete collection of comments published on them. Even you cannot provide replacements for those. With regard to more recent work, I am missing issue number 5 of the first volume of the *Wort* (Moscow), in which I have an essay on fascist theories of art. I am not giving up on my efforts to furnish you with one.—A small section of the *Elective Affinities* essay will be appearing in French translation any day now in the *Cahiers du Sud*.[2]

I am still waiting for the Hebrew text you promised.

The weather here is marvelous. "I wish someone would come along and take me away"—outside. But it will probably be summer before I get out of doors. The news I have about Stefan sounds better of late.

On that note, I'll close for today. Write very soon.

Most cordially,

Yours, Walter

P.S. I have recently been given *very* precise information about Karl Kraus's last weeks. It is worthy of that illustrious life, and it makes the end of Timon of Athens seem like an invention by Frieda Schanz,[3] compared to the Shakespearean spirit of the age that wrote Kraus's.

---

[2] "L'Angoisse mythique chez Goethe," *Cahiers du Sud* 24, no. 194 (1937), pp. 342–48. The journal's central figures, Jean Ballard (the editor) and Marcel Brion, were among Benjamin's few admirers in France.

[3] Frieda Schanz was W.B.'s favorite example of literary vacuity.

92

SCHOLEM TO BENJAMIN

ABARBANEL RD. 28
MAY 7, 1937

Dear Walter,

Your last letter pleased me all the more because I detected in it for the first time in quite a while a somewhat more optimistic tone and a sense of relief, and this touched me deeply. That alone augurs well, even if it has only been brought on by the fact that you have at last succeeded in dislodging the burden of the Fuchs essay, which weighed upon you for so very long, and it would be worth much more if your political prophecy were to turn out to be true. I myself am still betting on a fairly long continuation of present European conditions, and I put little stock in any change coming about soon, which means we can gradually make some preliminary plans with more optimism. Meanwhile, I had hoped to keep abreast of your latest activities via Kraft, who has returned from Paris (and for the first time has found a modest part-time position as secretary of a local French institution of a profane nature responsible for cultural propaganda).[1] But these expectations were not altogether fulfilled; either you or he did not display the desired communicative zeal.[2]

I now eagerly await the essay on Fuchs, all the more so since you do not seem so very dissatisfied with it any longer. When it arrives, I'll borrow the Fuchs volumes from my neighbor, a gynecologist, and study them agape. I tried in vain to obtain your essay in the Moscow *Wort*[3] by purchasing the whole issue. A pity you didn't draw my attention to its appearance right away, then I could have easily turned up a mint copy. I naturally knew nothing about it. I am now sending you the Hebrew essay on the doctrine of Sabbatianism, to rouse your spirits, and I believe there is something to it. I may do an extensive reworking of it into German for Schocken.

Your delphic allusions to accurate reports you received on Karl Kraus's last weeks have whetted my curiosity. Would it not be a worthwhile gesture to donate an hour to me sometime and breathe some word of it to Zion? I would be most grateful. So pull yourself together tomorrow evening. The World's Fair—whose impact on your biography, if only

---

[1] Kraft worked from 1937 to 1941 as secretary of Jerusalem's French Cultural Center, which was under the jurisdiction of the Lay Mission, a French government institution.

[2] The second time W.B. and Kraft saw each other again, in March 1937, ended with them having another falling-out. See the notes to W.B.'s essay on C. G. Jochmann in *GS* 2:1398–1403. Both remained silent about the affair to me.

[3] "André Gide und sein neuer Gegner" [Thierry Maulnier] (1936), *GS* 3:482–95.

because of the price increases it caused in Paris, you should explain to me—hasn't begun yet anyway, so you can dedicate your attention to me.

We here, who know nothing yet about Kraus, are preoccupied, as you will well understand, with the coarse hints about the solution of the Palestine problem that the Royal Commission has floated in the English press. The less people know for sure what is really behind the alleged plan for a division of Palestine into a Jewish state with dominion status and an Arab territory, whereby Jerusalemites would also become "irredenta"—that is, internationalized—the more commotion there is everywhere.[4] In humorous circles they are already joking that the university would remain here in order to represent the Jewish people *in partibus fidelium*. I myself have made a bet that it's all just invention, even though the matter looks rather serious. But it's not likely that anything will be known about the political proposals before the end of June. At any rate, the tension is great. There are procantonists, contracantonists, and "unsure cantonists"—I count myself among the latter for the time being.[5]

Our apartment is quite beautiful, and I would like to draw your attention to the fact that there is room to put you up. We will have to negotiate the problem of whether a plan can now be devised to take advantage of such space. During the summer months I have to write a book and would not be a proper host, but you should seriously consider whether you would like to be our guest during the winter months, say from December to January. That period (December 1 to February 1) includes about 4–5 weeks of especially beautiful weather, and thereafter rain. But we have central heating to offer. We'd see to it that you also have ample opportunity to read. You will appreciate that my personal circumstances now allow me to discount such unusual disruptions as those that intervened last time. My wife would be delighted to get to know you—she is off on a trip to Syria with classical philologists, which is why she is not able to announce this directly.

I hope to hear from you soon.

Kind regards,

Yours, Gerhard

---

[4] The Royal Commission, appointed in December 1936, concluded its report in June 1937 by proposing the separation of Palestine into an Arab and a Jewish state. The rumors circulated by the commission, and even more the "full" report published in July, created a tremendous stir.

[5] After reading the report—an extremely important document—and after many debates and long deliberation, I joined the "cantonists."

93

BENJAMIN TO SCHOLEM

VILLA VERDE, SAN REMO
JULY 2, 1937

Dear Gerhard,

I regret that I haven't satisfied the wish you voiced in your letter of May 7: I have not been prompt in sending you news, let alone been able to provide you with a report on Karl Kraus the day after your letter arrived.

The last few months in Paris have passed rather turbulently. The worsening of the Parisian economic climate, which you were quite right to suspect—and which is more a result of French financial policy than of the World's Fair—has forced me to take a series of wearying steps. And, in spite of them, I still haven't managed to secure the continuation of the modest improvement in my living conditions which the spring seemed to promise, even on the most minor scale. On the contrary, I am apprehensive when I contemplate the coming months.

You will understand that I mean this quite literally when I tell you that I have yet to set foot on the grounds of the World's Fair. I hope that before the year is out you will be seeing the rest of what kept me away from our correspondence. For now, I only want to report that the San Remo weeks are entirely reserved for the study of C. G. Jung. It is my desire to safeguard certain foundations of "Paris Arcades" methodologically by waging an onslaught on the doctrines of Jung, especially those concerning archaic images and the collective unconscious. Apart from its internal methodological importance, this would have a more openly political one as well. Perhaps you have heard that Jung recently leaped to the rescue of the Aryan soul with a therapy reserved for it alone. My study of his essay volumes dating from the beginning of this decade—some of the individual essays date back to the preceding one—teaches me that these auxiliary services to National Socialism have been in the works for some time. I intend to make use of this occasion to analyze the peculiar figure of medical nihilism in literature: Benn, Céline, Jung. It has not yet been settled, though, whether I will be able to land a commission for this work.

By now you will have received "The Storyteller"; the next text I can send you will presumably be the "Eduard Fuchs." Since I am understandably very concerned about the comprehensiveness of your archive of my writings, I would like to ask you to order the missing issue of the

Wort—volume 1936, no. 5 or 6—directly from the publisher, Jourgaz, Strastnoy Boulevard 11, Moscow.

We are expecting Stefan from Vienna. I won't be able to form a picture of his development over the last months until I've spoken with him. Unfortunately, the date of his final examinations seems to be postponed further and further into the future.

The prospect of a meeting between us in Palestine, which your letter opens up for me, is—how should I express this?—welcome and full of significance. I must confess that I can only fix my gaze upon it as if through a frosted windowpane. My autonomy vis-à-vis the Institute is not what it was two years ago. Even though there is no official tie between us, it would be most unwise on my part to move away from Europe for any substantial amount of time without obtaining New York's permission. If there is a prospect—and this is not out of the question—of having visitors from New York around wintertime, then I would not even attempt to ask for permission.

That is one side of the matter. The other side, though, is that my passport will expire a year from now. It is extremely doubtful that I will receive a new one. That speaks convincingly for postponing my trip to Palestine until this winter, since there may be special difficulties connected with obtaining a visa for Palestine on French temporary papers, which I would be able to get in any case. Meanwhile, I would be glad to hear from you how things look in the large and small world of Palestine. I understand the "large" world as being the English one, the small one *si licet* as that presided over by Buber. I've heard that he has meanwhile embarked on his way there.[1]

I acknowledge, with many thanks, receipt of the work on Sabbatianism. I would render even more thanks to Schocken if he decided in favor of a German edition of your work.

Are you writing anything on the Kabbalah at the moment?

In closing, I must request your permission to reserve the report on Karl Kraus's last months—for all you may say—for when we see each other. The reason is that I have it secondhand, so you would be getting it thirdhand. Were this to coincide with the switch from the oral to the written, all that remained would be something wholly distorted. It already represents no small risk to attempt to convey verbally some of what vividly caught my attention in the version I heard.

I will most likely be staying in San Remo for another four weeks. A speedy letter from you would have a chance not only of reaching me here but of being answered from here as well.

---

[1] Buber would first move to Jerusalem for good about a year later. He came for a visit in June of 1937.

Most cordial greetings, which I ask you to forward to your wife as well.

Yours, Walter

94

SCHOLEM TO BENJAMIN

28 ABARBANEL RD.
JULY 10, 1937

Dear Walter,

Your letter arrived the day before yesterday and you already see me here at work! I am trying to rouse your finer epistolary instincts by setting such a noble example, and I hope you will make good your ambition to still write from San Remo. In the meantime, there are various things to report! As you can imagine, excitement here and probably everywhere in the Jewish world is running high right now, ever since the long-awaited report of the Royal Commission appeared two days ago and the English government ceremoniously proclaimed it as the cornerstone of its policy, according to which Palestine is supposed to be partitioned again, as you will already know from the newspapers. The question of the Jewish state, with all of its implications, has consequently entered a historically decisive and dead-serious stage, 40 years after the 1st Zionist Congress and 20 years after the Balfour Declaration. People here are talking about nothing else, of course, and no one—including myself—is quite sure what to think for the time being. The report (a historical document of *spectacular* interest in virtually every respect, a weighty tome, by the way) gravely disappointed Jewish expectations (which they clearly made a general effort to meet as far as possible) on very delicate points on three or four issues, vital issues of honor of the highest order, so to speak. As for the damned serious decision to be made by the Zionist Congress in Zurich in four weeks' time, very much depends on whether or not the English government will give in on those issues. If it does, then the Jews are likely to vote in favor of the founding of a Jewish state—indeed, they would hardly have any other choice, as the alternative would be very much less favorable to them (continuation of the Mandate with a decrease in both immigration and the acquisition of land). Jerusalem is to remain an English mandate forever, "to protect the holy places," which would not be terrible in itself, were it not linked with the recommendation—a blunder, from the psychological standpoint alone—to rescind the Balfour Declaration and the recognition of Hebrew as the official lan-

199

guage in this territory. Even if we disregard the fact that the vast majority of Jerusalem's inhabitants are Jews, it is obvious that a solution that would abolish existing rights in the city that everyone regards as *the* metropolis of the Jewish people offends feelings greatly, and there are a few more such matters. But I believe that these things can be redressed more or less appropriately by means of negotiations, since the English are most anxious to get the Mandate off their hands if at all possible and to relinquish to the Jews the responsibility for their own future under the somewhat duplicitously lustrous title of the "Jewish state." Nobody can make any truly well founded predictions about the future—the internal and the external viability—of this new state: it could just as well be a great success as not, the calculations consist of nothing but two-edged factors. What is obvious is that historically it represents a watershed for the place of Jews in the world. Like many others, I am personally against partition as such, since I believe joint Arab-Jewish sovereignty in the whole of Palestine to be the more ideal solution, but this opportunity is one we will probably never be granted. The question of the day is only whether something better can be gained by rejecting the partition (they could hardly carry it out in practice without our acquiescence), and, unfortunately, this can scarcely be answered in the affirmative. The decision for or against the Jewish state, incidentally, runs like a rift through *all* camps here: of all the Jewish factions throughout the world, only the assimilated anti-Zionists are—understandably—unequivocally *opposed* to partition. Their fears about the recognition of a state of a Jewish people whose existence they have always denied are as vehement as they are understandable. On the other hand, the most remarkable groupings have formed *in favor* of accepting partition in principle. In short, things here are in turmoil once again. There won't be any real disturbances, since the English don't want this and they have made that unmistakably clear. Had they done so a year ago, we would have been spared a great deal. By the way, there's an old Jewish saying: Nothing is cooked as kosher as it's eaten—whose profundity you will easily grasp in this variant. So much for events in the world at large. Of Buber, whom you ask about, I can give you reassuring news: on the day after the partition plan was announced, he rented an apartment here, for the next few years. He's traveling back to Germany this week to organize his move (including a very dignified library!) and he inquires about you more or less as often as you ask about him. He has visibly aged. He has spent his time learning Hebrew, in which he has greatly outdistanced you, unfortunately. He will begin reading at the university this winter, and if you visit us, as I hope, you won't be spared from seeing him. I get along fine with him by relying heavily on my purest Berlin dialect and my customary frankness, and I have also already heard him say some sensible things. It is well known that Rosenzweig allowed the exquisite but not untrue variant of the saying about Buber to be printed in his (posthumous) letters, to wit, that he is an emperor *only* without clothes—it's there to read on p. 461! I have found this confirmed rather often. Otherwise, he is essentially inscrutable: enlightenment on this point is imparted verbally free of charge.

I hope you will take our invitation seriously and give it some thought. There is a new development, however, which assures us of an opportunity to meet in case you can't come this winter after all: in the next few weeks I will, in all likelihood, or almost certainly, receive an invitation (please keep this *strictly* confidential) to lecture as a guest professor at the Jewish Institute of Religion in New York. This would take place in the spring, which would give me the opportunity to spend half a year examining the Kabbalah manuscripts over there. I would be invited for only 2 months, but I could eventually stretch things out financially, by the utmost frugality, so that it would be possible for me to stay until I have seen everything (a tremendous task—about 1,500 manuscripts, all in New York and Cincinnati). If this works out, I would expect to leave here around February 15. It would be very nice if you were to come here before then; otherwise, I could pay you a short visit on one leg of the trip, and a longer one on the other. I would have to hold 6 lectures there, which I would naturally need to prepare beforehand this winter and have translated into English. This labor, with all the attendant bother, would burden our time together here somewhat; nevertheless, I believe that, if you can come, we will still have more time on the whole than would be possible in Europe. All you would have to do is to arrive a little earlier, as there would be no point in being here the last four weeks before the trip: too many things would be converging all at once. On the other hand, we would be delighted to have you as our guest in the period between November 15 and January 15. We can't guarantee the cost of the trip here or any trips around the country, but at least the stay in Jerusalem. So, by autumn I presume you will also have a clear idea of your plans, and my preparations will be settled by then as well, provided the business with the invitation is true.

Fania is traveling to Poland this week to see her father. I am staying here and have to work: a book in Hebrew about two handwritten Sabbatian manuscripts, and one in German on the Kabbalah, as the harbinger of a thick tome that has been ripening on a large scale all these years.

"The Storyteller" has arrived, and it made a great impression on me. I hope we will soon be supplying each other with even more! Now pull yourself together and write.

Kind regards,

Yours, Gerhard

I hope you will visit us this winter after all; it would be a great joy for Gerhard.

Greetings, Fania

95

BENJAMIN TO SCHOLEM

23 RUE BÉNARD
PARIS XIV
AUGUST 5, 1937

Dear Gerhard,

These lines, which are to express my gratitude for your letter of July 10, are being written from Paris, at six in the morning. From Paris, because I was summoned away from San Remo to cover the philosophers' congress taking place here; at six in the morning because this congress doesn't leave me with a minute of free time all day.

It would certainly be tempting to write you about the congress in a few words, but the prospect of talking to you about it in person is far more inviting. This brings me to the part of your letter that evokes above all my thanks to you and your wife. I would indeed be happy to come to you, happy to come to Palestine, under the conditions you specify and for the period you have in mind. And I would already be sending you my acceptance today if I were master of my own arrangements. *Rebus sic stantibus*, I will advise the Institute of my plans in the next few days. Difficulties—but the kind that would impel me to abandon the plan—should only arise if one of the directors intends to visit Europe this winter.

I hope to be able to accept your invitation in about a month.

Circumstances that would take too long to describe have entailed my following very closely the sessions of the special convention that the Viennese logistical school—Carnap,[1] Neurath, Reichenbach—has been holding. One feels free to say: *Molière n'a rien vu*. The *vis comica* of his debating doctors and philosophers pales in comparison with these "empirical philosophers." I haven't allowed this to deprive me of the chance

---

[1] In *Briefe*, p. 735, I read the name as "Bernay," which not only contradicts the way W.B. wrote his capital *B* but also distorts the name of Paul Bernays. The *C* at the beginning of the word is written in the customary form. Rudolf Carnap (1891–1954), Otto Neurath (1882–1945), and Hans Reichenbach (1891–1953) were the acknowledged central figures of the "Vienna Circle" of logical positivists.

to listen to the German idealist Arthur Liebert[2] at the main conference. He had hardly uttered his first few words when I found myself carried back twenty-five years into the past, into an atmosphere, to be sure, in which one could have already sensed all the decay of the present. Its products were sitting before me in the flesh in the form of the German delegation. Bäumler is impressive: his posture copies that of Hitler down to the last detail, and his bull neck perfectly complements the barrel of a revolver.—Unfortunately, I missed hearing old Tumarkin (from Berne) speak.[3]

I will be traveling back to San Remo in the middle of next week and will stay there for about a month. If you reply soon, as I very much hope, you can still direct the letter to the Villa Verde. I still don't have a very clear impression of Stefan's present condition; insofar as conclusions may already be drawn, he seems to have partly overcome the crisis in his development.

Under the aforementioned circumstances, I have no choice but to be brief. Allow me to congratulate you most sincerely on your anticipated— or by now received—invitation to New York. (Will you possibly be able to attempt something on your brother's behalf from there, with greater prospects of success?) What pleases me most about the invitation is that it promises us a chance to see each other in case I should not be able to come.

I was pleased to hear that the "Leskov" meant something to you.

A small fragment of my essay on *Elective Affinities* just appeared in French. Publication of the protracted essay on Fuchs seems to be imminent. I am about to embark on another project, which deals with Baudelaire. *En attendant,* in San Remo I have begun to delve into Jung's psychology—the devil's work through and through, which should be attacked with white magic.[4]

So much for today. Please write posthaste. Best of luck with the prolegomena to the Kabbalah book, which I am very pleased to learn will be accessible to me.

Most sincerely,

Yours, Walter

---

[2] Liebert (1878–1946) had long been the editor of the journal *Kant-Studien* until it was "gleichgeschaltet" [forced into line] by the Nazis.

[3] In the summer of 1918 we had both attended Anna Tumarkin's lectures in Berne. W.B. originally planned to write his doctorate under her.

[4] W.B. also expressed his views on C. J. Jung's psychology in letters to Horkheimer and Adorno (as early as 1934!), but as far as I know he did not leave a substantive critique behind in his papers.

96

SCHOLEM TO BENJAMIN

Dear Walter,

I am writing to you at once upon receipt of your letter of August 5. Two matters of importance have arisen that concern our plans for a meeting, which may cause them to be altered. First, I did get the invitation to New York (which is a great honor for me, of course), and I have to leave Jerusalem on February 1. But since I won't be able to work out the details of my New York lectures until December–January, I don't know whether we would be well advised to arrange a meeting here immediately prior to my trip or whether we wouldn't be better off timing it differently. Circumstances also force me to lecture more than I had expected. One of the following would be possible:

1) You come here now, but only for a month, let's say November 15 to December 15. That would be the best time I could conceivably have for you, even though it also falls during the semester. This only depends on the second difficulty that has arisen, namely, *when* my wife can return from Poland, for she is unfortunately not in good health. But if you are free then, that would be one course to take.

2) You don't come this winter, but I travel to Paris on the way to N.Y., and I could then stay there with you for about three days during February, and on the return trip (probably in *August* or September, if not earlier) we could meet, perhaps even with my wife, in France for two weeks—in Paris (where I would have some work to do) or in northern Italy, which is where I have to have my mother come, since Jews are not allowed to travel to France, as you well know. Thereafter, an extended visit by you to us in Jerusalem could be organized with *greater* ease for the winter *following* my trip—we would be sure of still having the apartment (the precondition for being able to accommodate you). I hope you see that we can now look forward to a meeting in 1938 with *certainty*, thanks to Stephen Wise's invitation,[1] and that I want to try to organize it in a way that turns out best for you, my wife, and myself.

Tell me, has Georg Lukács died? I heard something to that effect, but rumors were very vague.

---

[1] Stephen Wise (1874–1949), one of the best-known figures in U.S. Jewish life, was also the founder and president of the Jewish Institute of Religion, a Jewish college open to all religious tendencies.

Please don't be angry over these serious and well-intentioned proposals.

Kind regards,

Yours, Gerhard

P.S. Since my English isn't good enough, I have to write the lectures here *first* in German and *then* work them out in English together with someone else.[2] It is this duplication of labor that is so time-consuming.

97

BENJAMIN TO SCHOLEM

VILLA NICOLO
3 RUE NICOLO
PARIS

Dear Gerhard,   [POSTMARK: SEPTEMBER 6, 1937]

Your letter took and gave. I abide by the latter and am pleased with the definite prospect of our European reunion next year. The Palestinian one, however, has become altogether problematic. A trip to Palestine for only one month cannot even be considered, because of the costs involved. By next winter—as I wrote you already—I won't even possess a German passport. To complicate matters further, I had just succeeded in gaining the consent of the Institute in New York to give up my position here for a few months, having invoked all kinds of circumstances, when your letter of the 12th arrived. In particular, I am meanwhile denied the opportunity to solicit help there in the way that awaited me only five days ago upon my return. I wasn't let back into my apartment, which I had rented out during the trip. What that means in the context of the reigning climate toward foreigners, you can perhaps imagine better than I. I was flabbergasted. You will find my temporary address on the other side of this.

At the moment, a real breath of ice is blowing through the blue autumn haze, which the Promised Land will not be protecting me from this time around. And what the good Lord, who has so much to do for the resident

---

[2] I really wanted to write the lectures in Hebrew, but at the time I couldn't find anybody in Jerusalem with a command of both literary Hebrew and English who would be prepared to translate such a lengthy manuscript. I therefore arranged to work with George Lichtheim (1912–71), who had brilliant command of both German and English and who was in very close contact with us.

205

Jews (and so much against the Arabs), can undertake for me, remains to be seen.

So much for today. I won't close without adding my cordial wishes for your wife's recovery and for the successful outcome of your sojourn in America.

Bien à toi

Walter

98

SCHOLEM TO BENJAMIN

Dear Walter, [CA. NOVEMBER 10–12, 1937]

I am writing to you at the address given in your last letter of 9/6, and I hope you receive this, even if meanwhile you have your old apartment back, as I very much wish for you. Your account of the difficulties was well suited to excite the reader's imagination; I only hope nothing unpleasant happened to you. I am writing with two things in mind: First and foremost, I have to thank you very much for the copy of your esssay on Fuchs, which arrived here a few days ago. Reading it has kept me very busy, thinking along many different avenues. I would like to be able to talk to you about them as soon as possible. You have shown, in an unsurpassable manner, that the author or collector you discuss is not your equal. It can be read as a piece of diplomatic prose, but the success of the Marxist approach—whose problematic nature leads the reader of Walter Benjamin again and again to dark broodings, even against the author's will—is less visible to an unfortunate admirer like myself. I will permit myself to express the same sentiment in Paris. It is to the detriment of your work, I'm afraid, that you have to cast your fine insights before dialectical swine. The reader often muses that you would have been better off giving Fuchs a kick in the pants and dismissing him with considerable invective, rather than devoting 35 pages to him; your attitude has by no means been veiled to the point of unrecognizability. What strikes me strongly is this: Marxist insights always remain mired in methodology and never reach the realm of the factual (in the *ideological* domain—as goes without saying). Where the factual appears, it explodes the limits of the so-called method. Your feeling for art agrees only in the most dialectical fashion with the apparatus you serve up so admirably. I would feel better without it, and I am sadly convinced: you would as well. There is too damned much self-denial in this manner of writing, which I hope soon to be able to do more justice to in the flesh—when I have to tailor my American lectures to fools. There, I will have to learn that virtue *nolens volens*.

I am busy at the moment planning the trip. If I embark, providing the ship sails, February 16 from Cherbourg on the great *Queen Mary* (as I would like to do), then I would presumably arrive in Paris on the afternoon of the 15th and be able to spend half a day with you. But things could well turn out differently. Unfortunately, there are no ships sailing from here to Europe that would let me spend two or three days in Paris. I cannot travel on the ships of the Messageries Maritimes because they are dreadfully bad and filthy—at least those in my price range. I will therefore sail directly from Trieste or Genoa. I hope this will allow me enough sleep to be able to follow you alertly in the wintry Paris air. For technical reasons, it's unlikely that I could sail a whole week earlier. I would be grateful to you in any case if you would inform me what a stay in Paris will cost per day at that time of year, without any luxuries, but the room has to be clean. I have no idea what prices in Paris are like anymore, and if I am forced to stay there for 5 or 6 days after all, before sailing to N.Y., I have to form an idea of how much I will need. I was thinking of meeting my wife in Paris in the summer, on the way back, and then spending more time with you.

I have to set aside my German book in the middle of working on it, in order to concern myself with America; I have yet to put a single line down on paper for my lectures, and everything has to be finished by January 1. There you have my activity for the next six weeks in a nutshell.

I hope to hear from you soon and how you are doing. My wife returned three weeks ago, in better health, but still not entirely her old self.

Accept my fondest regards,

Yours, Gerhard

99

Benjamin to Scholem

C/O DORA BENJAMIN
7 VILLA ROBERT LINDET
PARIS XV

Dear Gerhard,   [NOVEMBER 20, 1937]

This time I'm avoiding letting even the slightest term elapse before replying to your last letter. It contained the announcement of your coming and the critique of the "Fuchs." Both are joined in my mind, just as they are in yours. It is really urgent that we speak with one another soon, indeed it can hardly be delayed. Not that the reservations you have about the "Fuchs" surprise me in the least. But the subject of the work—precisely because it seems so threadbare—offers an opportunity to debate the merits of the method it lets shine through, an opportunity that may not present itself so advantageously soon again. It is well suited to gain us access to the realms in which our debates were originally at home.

Under these circumstances, the dates you have in mind for your stay in Europe are a great disappointment, following the many frustrated schemes for my appearance in Palestine. Does it really surprise you that half a day seems to me less than nothing, after so many years and given the present status of both public events and our private affairs? Half a day is of a dimension that could very easily turn out to be negative, even if the blame for it is not to be sought with one or the other of us. My reservations about this proposal carry all the more weight since no guarantee exists that the summer meeting, if you want to set it for Paris, can take place. I don't yet know where I will be during the summer; I will probably spend a number of weeks with Dora in San Remo. Also under consideration is a trip to Denmark, from where I would like to transfer a part of the fraction of my library back to Paris.

This leads me to the brief remarks I wish to devote to the present state of my private life. I did not recover my former lodgings, and I have struggled along for the last two months with wretched ones that were put at my disposal for free. They are situated at ground level on one of the main thoroughfares outside Paris, where countless trucks roar from morning till night. My ability to work has suffered considerably under these circumstances. I haven't got beyond doing the background reading for the "Charles Baudelaire" I am preparing.

As of January 15th, I will be renting my own place. It has only one room.[1] And yet furnishing it presents me with an unresolved problem. In

---

[1] The room was quite spacious, however, as I was able to ascertain during my visit.

208

the interim, I ask that you quickly send what I hope will be more welcome news to me at my sister's address [above]. If you have 65 or 70 francs a day at your disposal, you can make do in Paris rather comfortably.

Sincerely,

Yours, Walter

100

SCHOLEM TO BENJAMIN

Dear Walter,   NOVEMBER 29, 1937

I have just received your short letter and hasten to reply by return mail. I am not unconstrained as far as my outward voyage is concerned, at least not to the extent I will be thereafter, in the summer. On the one hand, I have to stay here until a certain date; on the other, I have to be in Cherbourg on February 16 (if I sail on the *Queen Mary*). So I am confined to the few ships sailing from here during that stretch of time. The upshot of this is that I would have to be in Paris either for six days or for half a day, and it is not clear whether I could in practice take advantage of the first choice at all. I would of course exceedingly welcome it if we could find a way to allow me to stay in Paris for three days, but world history is unfortunately not about to deliver it up to me. As soon as I know the precise arrangements for my trip, I will pass them on to you, but this matter is a tough nut to crack. I would have to find a ship that sails from here on February 4 or 5; that would be ideal—but there is as yet no such sailing listed.

As for the summer, you need not worry too much. I assumed you would be in Paris. I myself don't know whether I will be returning from America in July, or not until September 1, and I will find out only shortly beforehand: it simply depends on my finances. I will stay as long as the money I get there lasts. I can't supplement it out of my own pocket. I must admit that *Denmark* would be very bad news for me. If you were to be on the Riviera, or somewhere in Italy, however, instead of in Paris, then that wouldn't necessarily present an obstacle. I am quite inclined to take a short holiday for myself anyway, if possible. That would then be merely a matter of mutual agreement. And I must meet my mother in Italy anyway—she wasn't granted a visa for France—unless I am supposed to go to Switzerland for a few days. We cannot settle all that yet, but I am absolutely counting on seeing you in a leisurely atmosphere. I want to travel back from Rome-Naples—that means I can be at any place on the Paris-Rome axis, providing the timing is favorable.

My work at the moment consists of formulating my New York lectures, which I have to deliver in English. That is a very unfamiliar task and costs a lot of time. The art of composing short sentences is not something that attracted my attention in the past. I will have to make up for it.

I hope that a small Hebrew book of mine, which is now being printed, will be in your hands a month from now.[1]

I hope you will find your way back to a larger format of writing paper once you have found the peace to work in your new apartment, if not sooner.[2] That would be an auspicious sign.

With this wish I remain, with the kindest regards,

Yours, Gerhard

101

BENJAMIN TO SCHOLEM

10 RUE DOMBASLE, PARIS XV
AT PRESENT: VILLA VERDE, SAN REMO
DECEMBER 31, 1937

Dear Gerhard,

I took note of your card of December 14 with great joy;[1] I also thank you for your lines of the 29th of the previous month. Our imminent reunion makes it seem bearable that so far I haven't returned to a more generous format of letter paper. You will find me, I hope, halfway installed in my new, tiny apartment.

I came down to San Remo just a few days ago and will be staying until about the middle of the month. Stefan is here. We have had to abandon our hope that he would take his final high-school examinations. He is helping out in the boarding house for now. Unfortunately, I am far from being able to say that I am reassured about his future development.

The book with the Hebrew text you announced hasn't arrived yet.

My Paris address is 10 rue Dombasle, Paris XV.

So much for today. I say see you soon with all sincerity. Let me know

---

[1] The book dealt with the dreams and inspirations of Mordechai Ashkenasi, a follower of Sabbatai Zvi from the last years of the seventeenth century.

[2] The format was 13 cm. by 5 cm.

[1] This card has not yet been found among the Berlin papers.

in good time if I can make any arrangements for your arrival. Please be sure to send me a short message in any case.

Yours, Walter

102

SCHOLEM TO BENJAMIN

ABARBANEL RD. 28
JERUSALEM
[CA. JANUARY 20, 1938]

Dear Walter,

This is my last written message. I thank you very much for your most recent lines and ask you, in the event any mail comes for me at your address, to please hold it for me. I sent this address to my mother as my last in Europe.

I will probably have to stay in Zurich for a day, because of a meeting that may become necessary. I would then be in Zurich on the 9th/10th and arrive in Paris either on the evening of the *10th* or on the *11th*. I cannot specify that beforehand, and I will cable you from Z. I hope you can meet me at the station.

Should I *not* have to travel via Z., then I will be coming directly from Venice and will be in Paris on the afternoon/evening of the 9th. In that case, I will inform you of the exact details from here. In any case, you have to be prepared for my arrival from the 9th onward. I would like to have a room that is not overly small in a well-kept and, above all, heated hotel, and I ask you to reserve one for me in advance, if possible. The location is not important, I would just like to have a direct connection nearby to the city center. I take it that you know about all that better than I do. I have some work to do at the library, and, weather permitting, I would like to do some roaming around the center of the city. I have to continue my journey on the morning of February 16.

So here's to a healthy reunion in Paris. Until then, kind regards,

Yours, Gerhard

103

BENJAMIN TO SCHOLEM

10 RUE DOMBASLE
PARIS XV

Dear Gerhard,
JANUARY 23, 1938

I hope this card still reaches you.

Your last card[1] reached me with some delay, since I only returned from San Remo the day before yesterday. My address is 10 rue Dombasle, Paris XV. Have your mail sent there c/o Dr. W. Benjamin, and inform me by telegram of the train you will be arriving on. As soon as I receive your telegram, I will procure a hotel room for you in the immediate vicinity. The connections to the Biliothèque Nationale are the best imaginable from there. Thank you very much for your "Kabbala-Forschung."[2] I will read it today.

In anticipation of our approaching reunion, the kindest regards

Yours, Walter

104

SCHOLEM TO BENJAMIN

JERUSALEM

Dear Walter,
JANUARY 25, 1938

This only to keep you informed. My mother just now sent me word that she will be coming to Zurich for a day or two, and thus I have to meet her there. She is not allowed to travel to Paris. From Zurich I'll cable you the exact time of my arrival in Paris. I will probably be arriving there on Feb. 11. But it could also turn out to be the 10th, and in the end it is always uncertain up to the last minute whether or not they will really permit her to travel and whether she will actually be there when I arrive.

As far as the room is concerned: Would it be possible to stay not too

---

[1] The reference is to another postcard that has not yet been found. W.B. only received this card once he was back in Paris, whereas he confirmed receipt of the other card while still in San Remo. Both cards apparently contained new details about travel dates and other practical matters.

[2] The reference is to an essay of mine that appeared in a publication of the Hebrew University in many languages and gave an account of my field of research.

far from the station where the train to Cherbourg leaves from? I don't want to have to navigate the city loaded down with luggage.

So, I'll be seeing you.

I will go to the main post office in *Zurich* on the morning of the 9th. If you want to send me a message beforehand, then please write to: Poste restante, Main Post Office, Zurich.

Kind regards,

Yours, Gerhard

105

BENJAMIN TO SCHOLEM

10 RUE DOMBASLE
PARIS XV
FEBRUARY 6, 1938

Dear Gerhard,

I hope that you have a pleasant journey behind you and, more, that the days in Zurich may pass without being overly taxing on your nerves.

Cable me as soon as you can.

If you have no objections, I will put you up at my sister's, where you will be better off than in an affordable hotel. She is away for the time being. Unfortunately, she is not in a position to offer you the hospitality as my friend. (She had rented the room out until just a few days ago.) But if 25 francs for a spacious, quiet room with bath, a five-minute walk from my flat, is not too much for you, then this arrangement would clearly be the most convenient one.[1]

In the hope of an auspicious reunion, kindly,

Yours, Walter

---

[1] W.B.'s sister had returned when I arrived, but she was quite ill, so I ended up moving into a hotel very near his place after all.

106

SCHOLEM TO BENJAMIN [1]

MY ADDRESS IS:
C/O LIBRARY OF THE JEWISH THEOLOGICAL SEMINARY
BROADWAY AND 122D STREET, NEW YORK CITY
MARCH 25, 1938

Dear Walter,

The flood of New York life has kept me completely submerged all this time, and only now are you seeing me come up for air. I have completed my lectures (with enormous success), and I am now spending all of my time studying the manuscripts. That is likely to drag on for a while, intermingled with the attempt to see and to understand something of America. I am learning quite a lot here, and I am using every opportunity to explore this strange world a bit.

The following is important: I have already set the date of my return voyage and hope I may still be able to reach you in Europe. I am leaving here on July 23 and will be in France August 1. I want to send for my wife to come there. I then want to spend several weeks, partly in Paris, partly in Switzerland, and partly in Italy (the region around Merano), and return to Jerusalem from Rome at the end of September. That is my itinerary. The question is whether we could meet you in Paris between, let's say, *August 1st and 15th.* This would fit in well with my plans. It would be ideal if you could arrange things that way. Afterward, I must proceed to the mountains for a month, and I don't believe it would be possible for me to travel to Denmark. In Italy, by comparison, a meeting could well be arranged. I intend to meet with Schocken there (providing that he is in Europe); something with you and him might also be arranged. In addition, I want to make a trip to Berne.

All of this for your information and for you to bear in mind when making your own plans for the summer.

Wiesengrund wasn't aboard the ship, and he hasn't been in touch with me either. However, I did meet with Tillich [2] and his wife, who are resolutely determined to bring me together with Horkheimer and Wiesengrund, with whom, they said, they are very close, which placed me in a somewhat embarrassing position. Our conversation turned to you. The T.'s were profuse in their praise of you (as was I, most conscientiously), and the result was that a somewhat different picture of Hork-

---

[1] [Their reunion is described in detail by Scholem in *W.B.*, pp. 205–214.—TRANS.]

[2] Paul Tillich (1886–1965), the well-known Protestant theologian who, as professor of Philosophy in Frankfurt, had awarded Wiesengrund-Adorno his postdoctoral degree [*Habilitation*].

heimer's relation to you emerged than the one you had postulated in your various esoterically couched warnings. I put on a bit of an act in order to get T. to talk. He said that H. holds you in the *highest* regard, *but that he is entirely clear that, where you're concerned*, one is dealing with a *mystic*—now this is precisely what you had not intended to suggest to him, if I understood you correctly. It was not I, but Tillich, who used the expression. In a word, he said something like this: People are neither so simple-minded that they can't make you out, nor so obtuse that they are put off by it. They are going to make every possible effort on your behalf and were also thinking of bringing you over here. So it now seems to me, judging from the way T. portrays the Institute's relationship to you, that your diplomacy may well be barging through open doors. Which means I would be severely handicapped in the event of a meeting with those people. They seem to have long been aware of much of what you consider secret and don't wish to have brought up, and *nonetheless* are still placing their hopes on you. I hadn't wanted to see these people, really, but on the other hand it could appear very strange if I were to visibly avoid a meeting after speaking with Tillich, especially since T. seems to have ardently campaigned for such a meeting. So that's how matters stand at the moment, and my embarrassment is not slight.

I leave here next week for two weeks in Cincinnati and Cleveland. Thereafter, I will be staying here, for the most part.

The Gutkinds, whom I've been with twice thus far, sent their most cordial greetings. He has just published a pious Jewish *Siderische Geburt*, in English, which causes me to shake my esoteric head.[3] He is quite popular as a speaker here, and he fends for himself fairly well, virtually unchanged.

The events in Vienna[4] have had a huge impact here as well, but more of an abstract one—it's just too far away, and nobody has any real notion of what it might be like.

Let me hear from you, especially concerning your summer plans!

All the best,

Yours, Gerhard

[3] The reference is to *The Absolute Collective: A Philosophical Attempt to Overcome Our Broken State*. *Siderische Geburt* [see letter 78, note 8] was Gutkind's first and only book until 1937, written before he turned to Judaism.

[4] The persecution of the Jews following the annexation of Austria.

107

BENJAMIN TO SCHOLEM

10 RUE DOMBASLE
PARIS XV
APRIL 14, 1938

Dear Gerhard,

Your first news from America took a considerable time in coming.

It includes much that pleases me.

In the first place, word of the success of your lectures. That must mean that your stay over there is less problematic, at least as far as the language is concerned, than you had initially assumed.

In your ensuing communications, I also hope to profit from this by having you unfurl "cultural and travel images" from the diverse regions and social strata. [*Amerikanische*] *Reisebilder* by Theodor Dielitz was one of my favorite books as a youth, and it was set over there as well.

I further expect that you will initiate me into the secret of Jewish star-birth; courteously return the greetings of the united wizard pair [the Gutkinds].

Mercy really did send me Brod's Kafka biography at my request, and with it the volume beginning with "Description of a Struggle." So it seems that now the 6-volume edition lacks only the *Tagebücher und Briefe*. Has it already appeared? If so, where? Please reply without delay.

I speak of Kafka at this point, however, because the biography, in its interweaving of Kafkaesque ignorance and Brodesque sagacity, seems to reveal a district of the spiritual world where white magic and spurious witchcraft interplay in the most edifying manner. I haven't yet been able to read it much, but I at once appropriated for myself the Kafkaesque formulation of the categorical imperative: "Act in such a way that the angels have something to do." I only read it intermittently, my attention and my time are now almost undividedly devoted to the "Baudelaire." Not a word of it has yet been written, but I have been schematizing the whole thing for a week now. The organization is, as goes without saying, decisive. I want to show how Baudelaire is embedded in the nineteenth century, and the vision of this must be seen as fresh as that of a stone that has been lodged in the soil of a forest for decades, and whose imprint —after we have laboriously rolled it away from its place—lies before us with pristine distinctness.

Your portrayal of the conversation with the two Tillichs aroused my profound interest, but caused me much less surprise than you thought it would. The point here is precisely that things whose place is at present in shadow *de part et d'autre* might be cast in a false light when subjected to artificial lighting. I say "at present" because the current epoch, which makes so many things impossible, most certainly does not preclude this: that the right light should fall on precisely those things in the course of the historical rotation of the sun. I want to take this even further and say that our works can, for their part, be measuring instruments, which, if they function well, measure the tiniest segments of that unimaginably slow rotation.[1]

For these reasons I look forward with some confidence to your encounter with Horkheimer and Wiesengrund, which may have already taken place, if not repeated itself, by the time you receive these lines. My sense of confidence grew through my encounter, just days ago, with the Institute's codirector, which turned out to be as genial as it was brief.

I don't yet have a clear view of how my summer will be arranged. As far as I can tell, everything would be very simple if you still have the second half of August free for Paris. I'm not sure if I can be back from Denmark for the first half.—We will certainly return to this point later.

Don't make me wait nearly as long for news this time as last time. Write to me about the "paths and the encounters" that were yours. Convey my kind regards to my New York friends when you get the chance and, whatever happens, don't forget to give them to Moses Marx.

All the best,

Yours, Walter

108

SCHOLEM TO BENJAMIN

HOTEL PARIS, NEW YORK
MAY 6, 1938

Dear Walter,

Thank you very much for your letter. My plans have meanwhile been clarified to the extent that I know the following: 1) I arrive in Paris on July 31, and 2) I *cannot* travel to Germany unless a miracle occurs while

---

[1] Few passages (if any) in W.B.'s letters to me possess such an unmistakably esoteric, if not almost conspiratorial, tone as this paragraph on his position with regard to the Institute for Social Research. I dare not decide whether the reference to the role of "our works" means the work he did in the orbit of the Institute, or instead works by people like him and me. At the time I associated it, given the strange context in which it appears here (and following our conversations in Paris), with both of us, but I am no longer so sure about this.

I'm still in Paris. That's doubly unhappy where you're concerned, since I might not only have been able to do something for your books, but it would also have made it easier to meet during the second half of August. Now that is very uncertain: I doubt if I can remain in Paris that long. If my wife comes to Paris, I can't stay there much longer than 2 weeks, since I want to travel with her to Switzerland or northern Italy for a month. Should she be unable to come—her father died suddenly and she has immigration complications with her young sister, whom we want to bring to Palestine—then all my travel plans would of course be deferred. In that case, I would travel to Switzerland directly, if you are not in Paris, but I can't say with any certainty whether I would be able to come back in order to meet you in Paris at the end of August. That would then be the only arrangement possible.

Is your sister back again? If not, how about my renting her room? Is it suitable for 2, or only if I am in Paris alone? Otherwise, I would be grateful if you could recommend a clean hotel approximately in the neighborhood where I stayed in February, which was situated rather conveniently.

On September 25 I leave from Trieste or Brindisi for Haifa, and I may spend some time beforehand in Rome, especially if my wife comes.

So those are my travel plans. I would like very much to meet you in Paris if there is any way at all to arrange it. We could spend a few peaceful days and do something for our education at the same time.

I want to remind you of our conversation on Kafka, and also that you wanted to write me a letter about the Brod biography that could be shown around. Don't shelve this for too long; it's possible that I will be meeting Schocken in Europe and could make use of it. If you can, write three to four pages that outline a kind of program and don't sound too innocuous.

The volume of diaries has already come out—indeed, a year ago—and it will certainly be of great importance to you, since most of it had not been published before.

To report from here: After all my odysseys throughout the continent, I arrived back here in April and will remain until my departure. My mailing address remains the Library of the Jewish Theological Seminary, since I will only stay in this hotel, which is too expensive for me, until I find something better, i.e., cheaper. In Cincinnati, we spoke a great deal about you during the Seder, since 15 years ago you were sitting together with us at Moses Marx's. Marx hasn't changed a bit, and I got along with him famously.

In the meantime, I saw Wiesengrund on three occasions and Horkheimer once, at Wiesengrund's insistence, just a few days ago. H. seemed to be bored stiff by me (but he put on a good show), which I

218

couldn't say about Wiesengrund, with whom I was able to establish a very sympathetic relationship. I like him immensely, and we found quite a lot to say to one another. I intend to cultivate relations with him and his wife quite vigorously. Talking with him is pleasant and engaging, and I find it possible to reach agreement on many things. You shouldn't be surprised by the fact that we spend a great deal of time mulling over your situation.[1] In short, I found myself pleasantly disappointed by this couple.

My work here is as strenuous as it is agreeable. After all, I'm only doing what I like to do anyway. When I come back from the manuscripts at 6, I am pretty much dead. And here there's a tradition of eating the evening meal very early, so invitations are always made for an unexpectedly early hour. I'm trying to gain a general impression of New York Jewry (two million in one city!), and that brings me together with diverse people. There are at least two or three individuals among them of whom I can say that the trip here would have been worthwhile because of them alone, and that is saying a lot.[2] There is also no shortage of intellectual hyenas, to use one of Wiesengrund's expressions.

I rode with acquaintances in their car back here from Cincinnati across the Virginia mountains, a wonderful tour for the most part. Trying to see something of the country without a car is a project doomed to failure, so I am dependent on the few car owners I have access to.

I seldom have time to read, outside of my research, and when I do, I read English in order to work on my own.

I see the Gutkinds every now and then. They are as gracious as ever, especially he, and I must give them great credit for that. They seem to feel very much at home here.

Write me soon about your plans and think of me as well when making your arrangements.

Kindest regards,

Yours, Gerhard

c/o Library . . . Broadway and 122d Street, N. Y. City.

---

[1] Wiesengrund-Adorno's detailed report on our first meeting in a letter to W.B. is still extant. Adorno printed a substantial part of it in an essay on me in the *Neue Zürcher Zeitung* (December 2, 1967).

[2] I was thinking of three prominent minds among my colleagues in Judaic studies: Shalom Spiegel (born 1899), Henry Slonimsky (1884–1973), and Louis Ginzberg (1871–1954).

109

BENJAMIN TO SCHOLEM

[I]

10 RUE DOMBASLE
PARIS XV
JUNE 12, 1938

Dear Gerhard,

At your request, I'm writing you at length what I think of Brod's *Kafka*. After that, you will find some of my own reflections on Kafka.

You should know from the outset that this letter will be reserved entirely for this subject, which is of profound concern to us both. For news of me, you'll have to be patient for a day or two.

Brod's book is characterized by the fundamental contradiction that obtains between the author's thesis, on the one hand, and the attitude he adopts, on the other. The latter serves rather to discredit the former, not to speak of the other reservations that must be made about it. The thesis states that Kafka found himself on the path to saintliness (p. 49).[1] But the attitude taken by the biographer is one of supreme bonhomie. Its lack of detachment is its most salient feature.

The *very fact* that *this* attitude could avail itself of *this* opinion of the subject robs the book of its authority from the outset. *How* this has been done is illustrated, for instance, by the turn of phrase that introduces "our Franz" to the reader via a photograph (p. 127).[2] Intimacy with the saintly has its own special appellation in the history of religion: Pietism. Brod's attitude as a biographer amounts to a pietistic stance of ostentatious intimacy—in other words, the most irreverent attitude imaginable.

This slovenliness in the work's economy is underscored by habits the author may have acquired in the course of his professional activities. At any rate, it is virtually impossible to overlook the traces of his journalistic hackwork, down to the very formulation of his thesis: "The category of saintliness . . . is truly the only correct category in which Kafka's life and work can be considered" (p. 49). Is it necessary to state that saintliness is an order reserved for life, and that artistic creation does not belong to it under any circumstances? And does it need to be pointed out that the epithet of saintliness is nothing more than a novelist's empty phrase when used outside a traditionally established religious framework?

[1] [Page references are to Max Brod, *Franz Kafka: A Biography*, trans. G. Humphreys Roberts and Richard Winston, rev. ed. (New York: Schocken, 1963), although this translation has not always been followed.—TRANS.]

[2] [In the original *Franz Kafka: Eine Biographie* (Prague: Heinrich Mercy Sohn, 1937). —TRANS.]

Brod lacks the merest sense of that pragmatic circumspection which should be required of a first biography of Kafka. "We knew nothing of deluxe hotels and were nevertheless happy as larks" (p. 103). On account of the author's striking lack of tact, of a feeling for thresholds and distances, feuilletonistic clichés have seeped into a text that should have been obliged to exhibit a certain dignity, given its very subject. This is not so much the reason for, as evidence of, the extent to which Brod has been denied any authentic vision of Kafka's life. This inability to do justice to his subject becomes especially scandalous where Brod discusses the famous instructions in Kafka's will (p. 198), in which the latter charges Brod with the task of destroying his papers. There if anywhere would have been the ideal place to broach fundamental aspects of Kafka's existence. (He was obviously unwilling to bear responsibility to posterity for a work whose greatness he was well aware of.)

The question has often been considered since Kafka's death; one might have done well to let the matter rest for once. That would have meant some soul-searching on the part of the biographer, of course. Kafka presumably had to entrust his posthumous papers to someone who would be unwilling to carry out his last wishes. And neither the testator nor his biographer would be harmed by looking at things in this way. But that would require the ability to gauge the tensions that permeated Kafka's life.

That Brod lacks this ability is demonstrated by the passages in which he sets out to comment on Kafka's work or style. He doesn't get beyond dilettantish rudiments. The singularity of Kafka's being and his writing is certainly not merely an "apparent one," as Brod would have it, any more than you come near to Kafka's depictions with the insight that they "are nothing but true" (p. 52). Such digressions on Kafka's work are of a kind that render Brod's interpretation of Kafka's Weltanschauung problematic from the very start. When Brod says of Kafka that he more or less followed Buber's line (p. 198), this amounts to looking for a butterfly in the net over which it casts its fluttering shadow. The "as it were realistic-Jewish interpretation" of *The Castle* suppresses the repulsive and horrible features with which Kafka furnishes the upper world in favor of an edifying interpretation which the Zionist ought to be the first to view with suspicion.

Occasionally, such smugness, so out of keeping with its subject, divulges itself even to a reader who is not all that punctilious. It remained up to Brod to illustrate the intricate difficulties of symbol and allegory, which he considers important for the interpretation of Kafka's work, by the example of the "tin soldier," which constitutes a valid symbol because it not only "expresses much . . . that extends into infinity," but also touches us "through the story of his fate as a tin soldier, in all its detail" (p. 194). One might like to know how the Star of David would look in the light of such a theory of symbols.

Brod's awareness of the deficiency of his own Kafka interpretation sensitizes him to the interpretations of others. It makes one uneasy to see the way he brushes aside the surrealists' by no means foolish interest in Kafka as well as Werner Kraft's in some measure significant interpretations of the short prose pieces. Beyond that, he is clearly making an effort to belittle any future writing on Kafka. "Thus one could go on and on explaining (and some will indeed do so), but necessarily without coming to an end" (p. 53). The emphasis on the words in parentheses is obvious. That "Kafka's many private, accidental failings and sufferings" contribute more to the understanding of his work than do "theological constructions" (p. 174) is unwelcome coming from a man who is resolute enough to base his own presentation of Kafka upon the concept of saintliness. The same dismissive gesture is used against everything that Brod found disturbing in his acquaintanceship with Kafka—psychoanalysis as well as dialectic theology. It allows him to contrast Kafka's style with Balzac's "fraudulent exactness" (p. 52)—and all he has in mind here are those transparent rodomontades that cannot possibly be separated from Balzac's work and its greatness.

None of this originates in Kafka's intentions. Brod all too often misses the assurance, the equanimity so peculiar to Kafka. There is no man alive—as Joseph de Maistre said—who cannot be won over with a moderate opinion. Brod's book does not win one over. It oversteps moderation both in the way in which he pays homage to Kafka and in the familiarity with which he treats him. Both presumably have their prelude in the novel for which his friendship with Kafka served as the subject.[3] The inclusion of passages from that novel by no means represents the least of this biography's improprieties. By his own admission, the author is surprised that outsiders could believe that the novel contained an affront to the piety due the deceased. "This was misunderstood just as everything else is. . . . People failed to remember that Plato, who in a similar, albeit much more comprehensive way, wrested his friend and teacher Socrates away from Death, all his life seeing him as a companion who continued to live, work, and think by his side, and making him the protagonist of almost every dialogue he wrote after Socrates' death" (p. 64).

There is little chance that Brod's *Kafka* will someday rank among the great standard biographies of men of letters, in a class with Schwab's

---

[3] Max Brod's novel *Zauberreich der Liebe* (Berlin: P. Zsolnay, 1928) [*The Kingdom of Love*, trans. Eric Sutton (London: M. Secker, 1930)].

Hölderlin or Bächtold's *Keller*. It is all the more memorable as the document of a friendship that is not among the smallest mysteries of Kafka's life.

You will see from the preceding, dear Gerhard, why an analysis of Brod's biography—even if only in a polemical way—seems to me unsuitable as a vehicle to offer a glimpse of my own image of Kafka. It remains to be seen, of course, whether the following notes will succeed in sketching that image. In any case, they will introduce you to a new aspect, one that is more or less independent of my earlier reflections.

Kafka's work is an ellipse with foci that lie far apart and are determined on the one hand by mystical experience (which is above all the experience of tradition)[4] and on the other by the experience of the modern citydweller. When I speak of the experience of the citydweller, I subsume a variety of things under this notion. On the one hand, I speak of the modern citizen, who knows he is at the mercy of vast bureaucratic machinery, whose functioning is steered by authorities who remain nebulous even to the executive organs themselves, let alone the people they deal with. (It is well known that this encompasses one level of meaning in the novels, especially in *The Trial*.) On the other hand, by modern citydwellers I am speaking of the contemporary of today's physicist. If you read the following passage from Eddington's *Nature of the Physical World*, you can virtually hear Kafka speak.

"I am standing on the threshold about to enter a room. It is a complicated business. In the first place I must shove against an atmosphere pressing with a force of fourteen pounds on every square inch of my body. I must make sure of landing on a plank travelling at twenty miles a second around the sun—a fraction of a second too early or too late, the plank would be miles away. I must do this while hanging from a round planet heading outward into space, and with a wind of ether blowing at no one knows how many miles a second through every interstice of my body. The plank has no solidity of substance. To step on it is like stepping on a swarm of flies. Shall I not slip through? No, if I make the venture one of the flies hits me and gives a boost up again; I fall again and am knocked upward by another fly; and so on. I may hope that the net result will be that I remain about steady; but if unfortunately I should slip through the floor or be boosted too violently up to the ceiling, the occurrence would be, not a violation of the laws of Nature, but a rare coincidence. . . .

"Verily, it is easier for a camel to pass through the eye of a needle

[4] W.B. appropriated this identification from the technical term "Kabbalah," whose literal meaning is "tradition," as he knew.

223

than for a scientific man to pass through a door. And whether the door be barn door or church door it might be wiser that he should consent to be an ordinary man and walk in rather than wait till all the difficulties involved in a really scientific ingress are resolved."

In all of literature I know of no printed passage that exhibits the Kafkaesque *gestus* to the same extent. One could effortlessly match almost every passage of this physical aporia with sentences from Kafka's prose, and much speaks in favor of the fact that the "most unintelligible ones" would be among them. If I were to say, as I just did, that there was a tremendous tension between those of Kafka's experiences that correspond to present-day physics and his mystical ones, this would only amount to a half-truth. What is actually and in a very precise sense *folly* in Kafka is that this, the most recent of experiential worlds, was conveyed to him precisely by the mystical tradition. This, of course, could not have happened without devastating occurrences (which I am about to discuss) within this tradition. The long and the short of it is that clearly an appeal had to be made to nothing less than the forces of this tradition if an individual (by the name of Franz Kafka) was to be confronted with *that* reality of ours which is projected theoretically, for example, in modern physics, and practically in the technology of warfare. What I mean to say is that this reality can scarcely still be experienced by an *individual*, and that Kafka's world, frequently so serene and so dense with angels, is the exact complement of his epoch, an epoch that is preparing itself to annihilate the inhabitants of this planet on a massive scale. The experience that corresponds to that of Kafka as a private individual will probably first become accessible to the masses at such time as they are about to be annihilated.

Kafka lives in a *complementary* world. (In this he is precisely on the same level as Klee, whose work in painting is just as essentially *solitary* as Kafka's work is in literature.) Kafka was aware of the complement without being aware of what surrounded him. If one says that he perceived what was to come without perceiving what exists in the present, one should add that he perceived it essentially as an *individual* affected by it. His gestures of terror are given scope by the marvelous *field for play* which the catastrophe will not entail. But his experience was based solely on the tradition to which Kafka surrendered; there was no farsightedness or "prophetic vision." Kafka eavesdropped on tradition, and he who listens hard does not see.

The main reason why this eavesdropping demands such effort is that only the most indistinct sounds reach the listener. There is no doctrine that one could learn and no knowledge that one could preserve. The things one wishes to catch as they rush by are not meant for anyone's ears. This implies a state of affairs that negatively characterizes Kafka's works with great precision. (Here a negative characterization probably is altogether more fruitful than a positive one.) Kafka's work represents tradition falling ill. Wisdom has sometimes been defined as the epic side of truth.[5] Such a definition marks wisdom off as a property of tradition; it is truth in its aggadic consistency.

It is this consistency of truth that has been lost. Kafka was far from being the first to face this situation. Many had accommodated themselves to it, clinging to truth or whatever they happened to regard as such, and, with a more or less heavy heart, had renounced transmissibility. Kafka's real genius was that he tried something entirely new: he sacrificed truth for the sake of clinging to transmissibility, to its aggadic element. Kafka's writings are by their nature parables. But that is their misery and their beauty, that they had to become *more* than parables. They do not modestly lie at the feet of doctrine, as aggadah lies at the feet of halakhah. When they have crouched down, they unexpectedly raise a mighty paw against it.

This is why, in the case of Kafka, we can no longer speak of wisdom. Only the products of its decay remain. There are two: One is the rumor about the true things (a sort of theology passed on by whispers dealing with matters discredited and obsolete); the other product of this diathesis is folly—which, to be sure, has utterly squandered the substance of wisdom but preserves its attractiveness and assurance, which rumor invariably lacks. Folly lies at the heart of Kafka's favorites—from Don Quixote via the assistants to the animals. (Being an animal presumably meant to him only to have renounced human form and human wisdom owing to a kind of shame—as shame may keep a gentleman who finds himself in a disreputable tavern from wiping his glass clean.) This much Kafka was absolutely sure of: First, that someone must be a fool if he is to help; second, that only a fool's help is real help. The only uncertain thing is: Can such help still do a human being any good? It is more likely to help the angels (compare the passage, p. 171, about the angels who get something to do),[6] who could do without help. Thus, as Kafka puts it, there is an infinite amount of hope, but not for us. This statement really contains Kafka's hope; it is the source of his radiant serenity.

I leave you this image, somewhat dangerously foreshortened in perspective, with all the more ease as you may clarify it by means of the views I have developed from different aspects in my Kafka essay in the *Jüdische Rundschau*. What prejudices me most against that study today

---

[5] This definition is to be found in W.B.'s essay "The Storyteller" [*Illuminations*, p. 87].
[6] This passage was already quoted in W.B.'s letter of April 14, 1938 (letter 107 above).

is its apologetic character. To do justice to the figure of Kafka in its purity and its peculiar beauty, one must never lose sight of one thing: it is the figure of a failure.[7] The circumstances of this failure are manifold. One is tempted to say: Once he was certain of eventual failure, everything worked out for him en route as in a dream. There is nothing more memorable than the fervor with which Kafka emphasized his failure. His friendship with Brod is to me above all else a question mark which he chose to ink in the margin of his life.

That seems to bring us back to where we started from, and I place the kindest regards to you at its center.

Yours, Walter

110
BENJAMIN TO SCHOLEM
[II]

10 RUE DOMBASLE
PARIS XV
JUNE 12, 1938

Dear Gerhard,

I thought it wise to relieve the enclosed letter of personal matters, so as to keep it presentable.

This is not to say that it isn't meant for you most personally in the first place, as a token of my gratitude for your suggestion. Otherwise, I can't judge whether you will consider it useful to give it to Schocken to read *tcl quel*. All the same, I do believe I went as deeply into the Kafka complex here as I possibly can at the moment. In the days that follow, everything else will have to take a back seat to my Baudelaire study.

I was pleased to see that some things go smoothly as soon as my back is turned. How many complaints have I heard *de part et d'autre* about you and Wiesengrund! And now it all turns out to have been much ado about nothing. Nobody is more pleased about that than I am.

I will be writing to Wiesengrund in the next few days and will mention the Kafka letter. You may tell him about it, of course; but I must ask you to mention the publication prospects which may ensue from it only with the utmost caution, and as if this represents your own opinion, *unknown* to me. But whether or not you should refrain *entirely* from mentioning that aspect is a judgment you must make yourself, depending on your understanding of the situation. The matter must be well thought out,

---

[7] This aspect emerges as early as W.B.'s letters to me during the summer of 1934; see, for example, letter 65 above.

since the letter's semiofficial nature is sure not to escape Wiesengrund's attention. If need be, you could always tell him that you had induced me to write the letter for your archive of my esoteric writings. I am afraid this explanation may come very close to the truth.

In any case, that document entitles me to a prompt and very detailed report on your peregrinations through New York's Jewry. I must ask you to refrain from being overly laconic when composing this report, especially since the chances of seeing each other, after your last letter of May 6 and my own arrangements, remain uncertain.

Contrary to expectations, I will only be able to start my trip on June 21, and the earliest I could possibly return from Denmark would then be August 6. If your wife does come to Paris, then you would presumably have no objections to showing her around the city, minus my person, for that first week. But if she doesn't come?

I'd like to know exactly what your thoughts are on this.

It is very likely you will be able to have suitable and moderately priced lodgings—an apartment with bath, entirely satisfactory for two—in the immediate vicinity, at my sister's. It might be best for you to clarify everything further with her directly, in case I make the trip to Denmark: Dora Benjamin, 7 Villa Robert-Lindet, Paris XVᵉ.

I was especially delighted to read what you wrote me about Moses Marx. I frown upon the absence of greetings from the Gutkinds.

Most sincerely,

Yours, Walter

P.S. Don't forget to let me know your impressions of the Institute, and any new developments there. My address from now on: c/o Brecht, Skovsbostrand per Svendborg.

111

SCHOLEM TO BENJAMIN

Dear Walter,   JUNE 27, 1938

I was overjoyed to receive your two-part letter, and I hope to be able to ruminate some more on your observations on Kafka, which I found magnificent. If I should be seeing Schocken somewhere this summer, I will be sure to carry the letter in the secret pocket of my metaphysical vest.

The main purpose of these lines, though, is not to write you a long letter, but instead to appeal to you to organize things in such a way that you can still meet us! My wife will be arriving in Paris 2 days before I will; I arrive July 31, as you know, and if you really leave Denmark on August 6, you should be in Paris by the 9th at the latest. We would then have a few days together this time as well, and that would please me a great deal. Since my wife's trip is definite, you can make your arrangements accordingly. It would be very good if you could write more specific details to me (or via my wife), so that I have them on July 31: address the letter to Mme. Fania Scholem, Hôtel Littré, 9 rue Littré, which will allow her to welcome me with the letter. We will have to leave Paris by August 15 at the latest—I don't yet know our destination. But I hope there won't be any obstacle to our getting together during that time.

I will be paying my first call on the Institute in the next few days, and I think it might be better if I convey my impressions to you in conversation. I saw the Wiesengrunds a couple of times, but otherwise I have not spoken privately with anyone from the sect. They await your "Baudelaire" here with great excitement.

I am sorry not to be able to use your library in Paris—otherwise, I might have been able to do more for my education during your absence.

I now have to make extremely careful use of my time here, since the end of my stay is approaching. There is still much left to accomplish. I have moved into the Seminary and thus can also work here at night now. If all goes well, I will have my first chance to relax on the ocean voyage, which will take eight days this time. It departs from here on July 23. I have no complaints about the fecundity of the local treasure trove; many important papers are coming to light at the end of my stay.

On August 7, we could celebrate Agnon's fiftieth birthday, if you were here.

All the rest in person! I hope you come back from Denmark as well rested as you would like and that you are enjoying working. By the way, the Gutkinds do indeed send you many greetings. They struck their tents for the summer last week, as everyone here does. You wouldn't believe just *how* unchanged they are; it's almost amazing. He tends to lead the life of a bat: he nests in the dark corners of the ruins of great problems, and he has become a kabbalistic imperialist, if one is to believe those who attend his lectures.

On Kafka, preferably in person—otherwise at greater length another time.

Accept all my kind wishes in the meantime, and, should this arrive on time, best wishes for your birthday.

Yours, Gerhard

P.S. Providing you receive this note before July 10, you might still be able to reach me in N.Y. with news.

112

SCHOLEM TO BENJAMIN

NEW YORK
Dear Walter,   JUNE 14, 1938

My last letter to you went unanswered, unfortunately, which means I am no longer as free in my arrangements as I would have liked. I will be arriving in Paris on July 31 and hope to meet my wife there on August 2. I will probably be with her in Paris until August 15 (at the maximum, certainly no longer) and then head east, first to Switzerland, and I may have to go on to Budapest, for research purposes. I have to get in all of our European stopovers that follow Paris and manage a little vacation as well between 8/15 and 9/15, since I have to be in Rome on the latter date, from where, after a week's stay, we will return to Palestine. I must *nolens volens* leave it to fate to decide for better or worse if we will have the pleasure of seeing you in Paris. Unfortunately, I cannot place much hope at all in the prospect of going back to Paris yet again at the end of August.

I may decide to stay at the Hôtel Littré, on Wiesengrund's recommendation; he says you also know it and can recommend it.[1]

I have been working very hard here under extreme pressure all these weeks, just to get through my material, which turns out to be very valuable. I should accomplish this in the next 5 weeks—providing the heat waves don't get too severe. Up to now it has been quite bearable, even much better than I had feared.

Can you get me Hannah Arendt's address? I would like to go see her, together with Fania, if she is in Paris.

I can't travel to Berlin—I have no visa.

I sent you an offprint of an English essay (from one of my lectures) and I hope you received it.[2]

I have almost no time to read other things, since by evening I am

---

[1] This recommendation was altogether mysterious. The hotel turned out to be a meeting place for the Action Française, and we were continually met with strange looks.

[2] It was an excerpt from my first lecture in New York: "Philosophy and Jewish Mysticism," *Review of Religion* 2 (1938): 385–402.

incapable of reading another line. Which means I have to make do with company.

Please let me hear from you soon. Kindest regards,

Yours, Gerhard

113

BENJAMIN TO SCHOLEM

C/O BRECHT
SKOVSBOSTRAND PER
SVENDBORG
JULY 8, 1938

Dear Gerhard,

My spring presentiment turned out to be true after all, and it won't prove possible for our fall meeting to take place, much to my dismay, and no doubt to yours as well. The reason, against which all else is powerless, is my work. My stay here is tantamount to monastic confinement; and if it were no more than that, the long trip would be legitimate. But I need this seclusion; I really cannot risk letting a protracted interruption, let alone a change of milieu, to occur before the work has, for all intents and purposes, been finished. Add to this that the local working conditions are superior to those in Paris, and not just because of the seclusion. I have a large garden at my disposal, in peace and quiet, and my desk in front of a window with a clear view of the Sound. The small ships that sail past therefore represent my only distraction, apart from the daily chess interlude with Brecht.

Since I am staying at a Svendborg police officer's, in the house next to Brecht's, there presumably won't be any obstacles to an extension of my stay beyond mid-August. If I could at least keep the deadline desired in New York without sacrificing our meeting! But I am afraid that I will have to exceed it after all.

You could do me a good turn in this connection by informing Wiesengrund of this when the occasion presents itself. I will certainly write him myself as well; but first I am waiting for his reply to a detailed letter I sent him from Paris. So you would potentially be doing me a favor if you could slip in a few words to this effect.

Among the reasons that make me sad about the failure of our plans—besides my wish to meet your wife—is my wish to speak with you about the "Baudelaire." I had placed high hopes in such a discussion. It can be summed up as follows: The subject matter necessarily puts into motion the entire mass of thoughts and studies I have launched myself into over the last years. In this sense, I can say that a very precise model of the "Arcades" project would be furnished if the "Baudelaire" were to succeed. Another question is what guarantees there might be for this success. In my opinion, prudence is still best, and that is why I devote a long chain of reflections (which take the *Elective Affinities* essay as their model) to its composition.

Many thanks for your birthday wishes. Your letter did indeed take a remarkably short time—arriving on July 6. I can't say the same about the English offprint you mention. It might still be among my mail in Paris.

I am very pleased to hear that your spoils turned out to be so abundant. Permit me to hope that, once you have the hunting season behind you, you will tell me at some length about the many things that must once again—for who knows how long—be entrusted to our correspondence. I have in mind especially my Kafka letter and your impending visit to the Institute.

Hannah Arendt's address is Hôtel des principautés étrangères, 6 rue Servandoni.

With kindest regards,

Yours, Walter

114

BENJAMIN TO SCHOLEM

C/O BRECHT
SKOVSBOSTRAND PER
SVENDBORG
SEPTEMBER 30, 1938

Dear Gerhard,

I find it amazing that you have let no word be heard from you. Your silence has been an object of my concern for some time now. But I could find neither time nor strength to inquire about you before finishing my long essay "Baudelaire and the Paris of the Second Empire" yesterday, after more than three months of terribly concentrated labor. It represents the second part of a voluminous book on Baudelaire. The combination of this most intensive of labors and the political events[1] forced me to reach down into the very bottom of my resources.

[1] The Czechoslovakian crisis and the Berchtesgaden discussions between Hitler and Chamberlain.

It turns out that I made the right decision in not going back to Paris. I would have never been capable of carrying out this tour de force over there.

I was in Copenhagen for 10 days, in order to dictate the manuscript. I got back the day before yesterday.

I hope to be in Paris from October 17 onward.

My unusually detailed letter on Brod and Kafka, with which I obliged your urgent request while having to interrupt other work, allowed and still allows me to expect a reply other than a cursory remark, no matter how laudatory.

I would also have found it quite desirable to have heard more details of your last days in America.

Please think about all this and write without further delay.[2]

Most sincerely,

Yours, Walter

115

SCHOLEM TO BENJAMIN

JERUSALEM
NOVEMBER 6–8, 1938

So that nothing goes wrong, I am having this letter sent by registered mail. So much goes wrong in the mail these days.

Dear Walter,

You are perfectly right to be furious (as shown by your grim and resolute expression in the photograph, which I am most "obliged" to you for— notice how I've been assimilated by the Swiss again?) that you haven't heard anything from me for so long. It was on account of neither malicious intent nor particular astuteness but rather an incredible sense of lassitude which has virtually kept me from picking up a pen for close to three months. In America I worked very hard, so intensely that I let myself sink into a comfortable, or lazy, state of lethargy on our way back, and conversations formed the sole intelligent complement to this torpor. And I was not granted the privilege of having them with you, which is

---

[2] The photograph of W.B. taken in Svendborg, which has been frequently published, was enclosed in this letter.

deplorable a thousand times over. Thus, while I wanted to write to you at length the entire time we were traveling through Europe, I kept putting it off, just like everything else. And when I got back here on September 30, amid the most magnificent global catastrophe, to make matters even worse and to top off your righteous anger, something went wrong with my eyes. I had to undergo an operation and wasn't allowed to write at all —and precisely when my now-genuine affliction, as it were, appeared, so did your wrathful likeness, along with the thundering prefatory address. Well, I did do my fair share of penance. I hope that my eyes, my most precious possession, will be completely healed soon, and I am making use of the first moment of my renewed freedom to write in order to pay you the proper homage and especially to congratulate you on finishing your Baudelaire essay, which regrettably cost me[!] the opportunity to spend time with you. I am looking forward to it very much, and I take it we will get to read it very soon. They told me in N. York that they were expecting your essay for the journal's fall issue, and since you did indeed finish it, it can't take so very long before it is printed.

I arrived in Paris on August 1 and spent two weeks there with my wife, who was inconsolable about your absence after she had prepared herself, as it were, to see you at long last. We spent a couple of very pleasant hours there with Hannah Arendt and Blücher,[1] who made an exceptionally fine impression on me. After that, we went to Switzerland. In Berne I trod old paths once again, after 20 years—we arrived, opened the *Bund*, and read that on that very day our respected teacher and master, Herbertz,[2] young and indefatigable as ever, had happened to turn 60. I came close to paying him a visit, but he still lives in Thun. I heard from several sources that his behavior has been conspicuously decent and respectable, and that he hasn't gone over to the Nazis. After that, we went to Muri, which hasn't changed in the slightest. Only the people seem to have become even more supine than before. We went on to the Oberland (Simmenthal, Bad Weissenburg) and to Montreux, where politics took over our vacation and there was to be no more peace. In the middle of the catastrophe, we recklessly traveled on to Rome, guided by the sad certainty that nothing would happen in the end and that the saber rattling only camouflaged the retreat in the face of Hitler. That was on

[1] Heinrich Blücher, at that time Hannah Arendt's constant companion and later her husband, who was a great expert in military matters. Hence we spoke not only about Benjamin, philosophy, and the fate of the Jews, but also about military prognoses in Europe and Palestine, which Blücher (who, or so I heard at the time, had at one time worked in the military administration of the Communist Party of Germany) had a lot to say about. In the meantime, Blücher had become a very decided opponent of the Comintern and its policies.

[2] Richard Herbertz (1878–1959), from whom Benjamin received his doctorate, summa cum laude, in 1919.

September 17. We were right, unfortunately, which means of course we will all (including we "Orientals" here in this nook) have to pay for it. In Rome we stayed with my cousin Loni,[3] who took us entirely by surprise when she suddenly tapped me on the shoulder at the Bärenzwinger in Berne; she too was wandering along the winding paths of her youth. Everybody we met was in the midst of leaving, for Paris, overseas, or without destination. The Italians themselves were still quite numbed by their own "nordification,"[4] but they are proving to be fast learners. It was wonderful to see Rome once again, though I suppose it will be the last time for quite a while. We left there on September 25 with the somewhat spine-chilling feeling that the steamer was under orders to turn around on the high seas in the event of something happening after all, and to bring us back to Italy. We couldn't take another ship, they were all vastly overbooked. And so I made my way back again.

It's a great shame that I wasn't able to present you with my views about America in person. It's virtually impossible to write about it. It's a most attractive country, where life is easy only if you have sufficient means at your disposal, in which it is not unlike other countries—and yet it is a little more than one would expect after such a characterization. The air is still freer over there, and the great discussion you have to enter into wherever you go deals with how long you think this will last, whether Roosevelt's presidency is finished or not, and the like. I found it a lot better there than here with us, of course, but I was a guest, which I should not forget, and it's not just in America that guests are treated in a far superior manner to immigrants or those about to become so. The intellectual atmosphere is better than we in Europe are accustomed to presume. There is widespread openness to and interest in matters Americans aren't supposed to be interested in. The detachedness people have regarding what is happening to them is still very much unstrained, which is great insofar as their own affairs are concerned, but drives you mad where European or global affairs are concerned. On the whole, not a soul is interested in what is happening outside his corner of the globe, and indeed it is impossible to forget over there that you are dealing, not with one country among others, but with a whole continent. The security they feel in their awareness that they are still essentially protected from airborne attack by the two oceans and the present state of technology influences their behavior in the extreme. I would be very happy to spend

[3] Leonie Ortenstein (1896–1944), whom I wrote about in *From Berlin to Jerusalem*, pp. 109–12. W.B. knew her from our days in Berne.

[4] In Rome, the following derisive line was making the rounds among the Italians: "Eramo sudici [which means *Sudler*—"a slovenly person," "a southerner"!], ora siamo nordici!" [I used to be a southerner; nowadays I'm nordic!]

234

a whole year there sometime,[5] but I imagine it would be unbearable in the long run. But then again, that is only the case for us Jews. Because what you are makes a whole world of difference there too, to be sure, and for Jews at least the country is by no means one of unlimited opportunities, not even in the purely geographical sense. On the whole, you can only move about there in a certain living space (which is still undoubtedly large and important); insuperable barriers separate you from the rest. But the fascist–anti-Semitic calamity is still merely a relatively distant trembling of the Earth—but one that has already been sensed by all those I spoke with. Uncertainty is great. But it seems to me at least that the historical and social preconditions for fundamental change are lacking there too, for the moment. In France, where the problem of fascism is likely to become acute in the very near future, the possible repercussions of European fascism on America hang very much in the balance. Your admirers there, I was given to understand, are hoping to bring you to America before the dawning of such a new era in French history. America would be a very far cry from your way of life, but, on the other hand, there is probably no atmosphere in the world that is not preserved in some corners in a city like New York. It cannot be compared with the Parisian atmosphere, of course. The problem is not whether there would be more or fewer people there with whom one could have lively conversations—I am inclined to believe that you will find more such people in a place like New York than in Paris in the imminent future. It is rather a truly different atmosphere that wafts around you, and you will find it especially difficult to bear.

As to the people from the Institute, I only really got to know Wiesengrund, whom I saw a lot of. With Horkheimer, I didn't get further than the politest contact, which must have had its cause in mutual antipathy. It proved impossible to conduct even a single sensible conversation in his presence without having his infinitely and vividly bored expression make the words die in your (or rather my) mouth. In the meantime, I have read some of his essays, which are not uninteresting but which didn't shake me in my conviction that he is not a pleasant fellow. So I preferred to keep a respectful distance, whereas I found it possible to engage in conversations on a human level with Wiesengrund and his wife. Wiesengrund maintains that Horkheimer is an incessant admirer of your genius. That did become obvious to me after reading some of his writings, but the personal impression I have of the man reinforces my opinion that, perhaps precisely *because* he feels he has to admire you, such a man can of necessity have only an inscrutable relationship to you,

[5] This actually happened eighteen years later (1956–1957).

heavily burdened by a sense of embitterment. You are free to view all this as nonsense if you like.[6] I wouldn't be surprised in the least if he turned out to be a scoundrel someday. In view of the circumstances, I did not express this strong feeling to Wiesengrund. I thought it right not to say anything that could have tempered W.'s enthusiasm to obtain, someday soon and the sooner the better, as decent a living for you as possible, by way of said H. The people at the Institute have every reason, in my estimation, to mount you in gold (be it only in secret). I gained the impression (in the course of fleeting but innocuous contact) that people such as [Herbert] Marcuse or [Leo] Löwenthal were conscious of this as well.[7] You may trust me without amazement when I tell you that I did my bit to promote a salutory respect for you in those circles. Those people are all *highly* intelligent and all slightly unreliable. The question is only whether that pays tribute to their intelligence or to their social standing. By the way, I also found all of the Institute's members whom I got to know to be diligent and very outspoken anti-Stalinists, great and small, and I didn't hear a single good thing said about Brecht. (Which reminds me of the request that you make me a present of a handwritten copy of the sonnet on Beatrice that you read aloud to me in Paris.)

Since I didn't get to speak with Schocken in Switzerland (and thus in peace and quiet) as I had hoped—world history abruptly intervened—I have not yet conveyed your letter on Brod and Kafka to its diplomatic destination. But otherwise you needn't complain about my reception of it. It seems to me that the way of looking at things you've taken is exceptionally worthwhile and promising. But I would like to understand what you take to be Kafka's fundamental failure, which you virtually embed at the heart of your new reflections. You really seem to understand this failure as something unexpected or bewildering, whereas the simple truth [is] that the failure was the object of endeavors that, if they were to succeed, would be bound to fail. Surely that can't have been what you meant. Did he express what he wanted to say? Of course. The antinomy of the aggadic you mention is not specific to the Kafkaesque Aggada alone; rather it is grounded in the nature of the aggadic itself. Does this opus really represent "tradition falling ill" in your sense? I would say such an enfeebling is rooted in the nature of the mystical tradition itself: it is only natural that the *capacity* of tradition to be transmitted remains as its sole living feature when it decays, when it is

[6] My impression of Horkheimer's relationship to W.B. was later confirmed by two people familiar with the conditions of the Institute, entirely independent of each other.

[7] Marcuse (1898–1979) and Löwenthal (born 1900) were among the most important members of the Institute. I knew Löwenthal from Frankfurt in 1923.

on the crest of a wave.[8] I believe I have already written you something along the same line in connection with discussions on Kafka. I don't know how many years it must be since I made notes, in the context of my studies, on questions such as the mere possibility of transmissibility, and I would like very much to hunt them out again. It seems to me to emerge in the context of questions about the "essence" of the righteous, the type of the "saint" evident in a decaying Jewish mysticism.—That wisdom is a property of tradition is entirely true, of course: it has the essential unconstructability of all the possessions that inhere in tradition. It is *wisdom* that, when it reflects, comments rather than perceives. If you were to succeed in representing the borderline case of wisdom, which Kafka indeed does represent, as the crisis of the sheer transmissibility of truth, you would have achieved something absolutely magnificent. This commentator does indeed have Holy Scriptures, but he has lost them. Thus the question is: What can he comment upon? I take it that you would be able to answer these questions within the perspectives you expounded. But why "failure"—since he *really* did comment, it only on the nothingness of truth or whatever might emerge there? So much for Kafka—and much to my surprise, I discovered a faithful disciple of his in your friend Brecht, in the final chapter of *Threepenny Novel*, which I read in Switzerland.

As to Brod: You almost deserved the garland for polemical achievement there. It is so well said and true that I have nothing to add. I didn't give you any reason to expect anything else; it's just that your carefully chosen words in this case go so much better to the heart of the hogwash.

I want to send this letter off at last. In closing, I still have to tell you that now I shall have to bring my mother over here, since the turn of events is forcing her to emigrate as well. That could even be [by] this winter. This has made us rather inflexible in our arrangements. I view it as possible, though, that she might then travel on to Australia, where both of my elder brothers took up residence several months ago.

There is nothing much to relate about Palestine. Life is very difficult here, and not the way I expected to find it. But it seems that nothing much will be changing, judging from the most recent political course the English are taking now that partition has fallen through. That was a rare opportunity, which is now gone.

My lectures begin next week, but I haven't done a single thing for them yet, since mere thinking means little as long as I am not allowed to

[8] This is an obvious slip of mine: I wrote "crest of the wave" instead of "trough of the wave," which fits the sense of the sentence.

write. But now this is well on its way too, as you can see from the *figura* at hand.

Give Hannah Arendt our regards when you see her. We have certainly not given up hope of seeing you here as our guest, and if we had a moment's respite from all the ill tidings, then we could perhaps finally be allowed to make such arrangements. We often talk about that around here.

Accept our constant, kindest wishes in the meantime and write about your work. I am preparing my English lectures for publication. My wife, who was really looking forward to making your acquaintance, sends her best wishes too.

Yours, Gerhard

Did you find the English essay (offprint) I sent to you in Paris in May? Reply requested.

116

SCHOLEM TO BENJAMIN

ABARBANEL RD. 28
Dear Walter,   JANUARY 25, 1939

What bringeth his Lordship's fury? One hears nothing whatsoever from you, as if you had to revenge yourself for all my epistolary sins "measure for measure"! In the meantime—as my astonished and troubled eyes keep noticing—the most varied works of the by-now famous author of the "Berliner Kindheit" continue to appear, and I, wretched custodian of the treasures of this author's spiritual life, am left out in the cold. Yes, my dear Walter, so I then went out and bought myself an issue of *Mass and Wert*,[1] something I will surely never do again, but I now consider it to be a rite of atonement. In the meantime, you surely must have received and digested my latest, lengthy letter, and hence the following words of Holy Scripture now apply to you: "Arise, my friend, be swift as the gazelle on the mountain rocks."[2]

I sit and work, but unfortunately not on what I should be working on, namely, getting my English lectures ready for publication. I still hope

---

[1] It was the first or third issue of the second volume of *Mass und Wert*, in which W.B. had reviewed two important publications on early Romanticism (*GS* 3:538–41, 557–60).

[2] A reference to the Song of Songs (2:17).

they will appear in the course of this year. I still dream of unpublished manuscripts. Politzer,[3] the last editor of Kafka's writings, sits three houses away from me, and I am studying your various declarations on the occasion of this project. My pleasure increases the more I do so.

I should also appreciate, by the way, your sending me Wiesengrund's private address—I would just like to give him a sign of life from here. He had just moved when I left.

Meanwhile we, just like everyone else, have to struggle with the consequences of the German pogrom.[4] I wanted to bring my mother here, even got a permit for her, but she broke down under all the excitement and strain, and won't be able to travel to Palestine, even if she were to get well again. That creates many difficult situations for us, which are still far from clear. Very soon she will be all by herself in Berlin. In the meantime, relatively large groups of German and Austrian Jews keep arriving here, for though the number of immigrants officially permitted is rather modest, a sizable "illegal" immigration has ensued under the open eyes of the authorities. To be sure, the people arrive in a pitiful state. In brief, things are rather hectic here, and on top of that we are waiting for the London negotiations on our political future, which are certain to come to nothing, and what should come afterward.[5] It is astounding that one feels only marginally affected by all the tension, even though the results of it drastically influence and concern our daily life.

Schocken Verlag was shut down by the authorities on January 1. My books have a very good chance of becoming rarities. (In Berne, where I followed our tracks, I asked about your dissertation. Although it has been sold out at Francke's bookstore for 4 years, it can still be had at the janitor's from the cellars of the university, which may be of interest to you, since you had assumed that everything had been destroyed by fire.)[6]

Is your "Baudelaire" already at the printers? Good for you that you were able to bring it off!

If you run into Hannah Arendt-Stern, please greet her warmly for us, and accept our kindest regards yourself,

Yours, Gerhard

---

[3] Heinz Politzer (1910–1978), who had collaborated on several volumes of the first collected edition of Kafka's works before coming to Palestine, where he spent the war years. He used to visit me often.

[4] The *Kristallnacht* of November 9, 1938, and the mass arrests that followed.

[5] The British government's White Paper, which, after the failure of the London conference, was first published in May 1939, proved to be the beginning of that government's attempt to liquidate its own Zionist policy.

[6] See W.B.'s letter to me of March 5, 1924 (*Briefe*, p. 341).

117

BENJAMIN TO SCHOLEM

Dear Gerhard,

10 RUE DOMBASLE
PARIS XV
FEBRUARY 4, 1939

To free my ability to communicate, I had to declare a sort of state of emergency over our correspondence, as you may have inferred from the unusual script.[1] That I have done so is due to your letter of January 25, for which I thank you very much.

If my silence had been transparent to you, your looks would have penetrated *in medias res*. A period of severe depression accompanied the onset of winter, and all I can say about the depression is *je ne l'ai pas volé*. A number of things coincided. First of all, I was confronted by the fact that my room is practically useless for working in winter. In summer, I have the option of opening the windows and countering the racket the elevator makes with the din of Paris street noises; not so on cold winter days.

This state of affairs coincided most auspiciously with an estrangement from my work's present *sujet*: as I presumably wrote you, in light of editorial demands made by the *Zeitschrift für Sozialforschung*, I finished a part—the second part—of my book on Baudelaire sooner than anticipated. This second part is presented to the reader in three relatively distinct essays. I'd been hoping to see one or the other of them printed in the *Zeitschrift*'s latest issue, which just came out. But what came in its stead, at the beginning of November, was an extensively argued letter, from Wiesengrund no less, not necessarily rejecting the work itself but refusing to send it to press.[2]

It is of course impossible for me to introduce you to the details of this problem, which you will surely find of interest, before being able to make the manuscript available to you. I intend to do just that, if you could make do with an uncorrected manuscript, which doesn't always conform to the latest version. In any case, I promise myself to put your point of view, which may well be analogous to Wiesengrund's in essential parts, to good use when I continue the work. And I will *have* to start on that continuation at once.

---

[1] The letter had been typewritten.

[2] Wiesengrund's letter is published in our edition of W.B.'s letters (pp. 782–92). He accused W.B. of a much too crude and "nonspeculative" application of Marxism. [English translation by Harry Zohn in *Aesthetics and Politics* (London: New Left Books, 1977), pp. 110–33.—TRANS.]

It isn't easy for me. The isolation in which I live and especially work here creates an abnormal dependence on the reception my work encounters. Dependence doesn't mean sensitivity. The reservations that can be made in the case of the manuscript are reasonable in part and should trouble me all the less, since the key positions of the "Baudelaire" could not and should not emerge in this second part. But this is where I run up against the limits of communication by letter, and now it is my turn to regret that we did not speak with each other in August. Please inform your wife of this regret—modified as befits the subject—as far as my meeting her is concerned.

If I haven't sent you any of my scarce publications in the recent past, the reason is that only seldom do editorial boards these days feel obliged to provide the author with more than a single author's offprint. You have no cause to assume negligence on my part in these matters, since it has been my intention all along to keep your archives of my writings complete. That has become all the more urgent now, since the only fairly substantial collection, apart from yours, is in the hands of a third party and must be considered lost by now. It is among the effects a friend of mine[3] had to leave behind in Barcelona. (As a curiosum, let me tell you that just recently an extremely cursory bibliography of my writings appeared in a small English report by the Institute, alongside bibliographies of its other collaborators.) The latest issue of the *Zeitschrift* 7:3 contains an essay of mine on Julien Benda in the review section; I am sure you will like it.[4] But what am I to do? I don't have a duplicate copy.

To show you that I do everything within my power, from now on I will on occasion be sending you typewritten manuscripts to be incorporated into the archive. Whereas I must ask you to return quickly the Baudelaire manuscript I promised you, you may consider the accompanying reviews of Hönigswald and Sternberger[5] as dedicated to you. You should get your hands on Sternberger's book *Panorama: Ansichten vom 19. Jahrhundert* at some point, which you surely already know of as an attempt at plagiarism.[6] You will find the Beatrice sonnet enclosed as well.[7]

---

[3] The reference is to Alfred Cohn, to whom W.B. used to send his writings.

[4] *GS* 3:550–52.

[5] They were first printed in *GS* 3:564–69, 572–79.

[6] Dolf Sternberger made the following remarks about this review and Benjamin's accusations in the new edition of his book *Panorama oder Ansichten vom 19. Jahrhundert* (Frankfurt am Main: Suhrkamp, 1974) [*Panorama of the Nineteenth Century*, trans. Joachim Neugroschel (New York: Urizen Books, 1977)]: "The judgment W.B. made in Parisian exile at the time, in a manuscript which has only recently come to light, was a painful one for me. I owe him much, not least the sharpening of my eye for the foreign and dead aspects of historical details, as well as a feeling for proceeding configuratively, but I of course did not yet know any of his own relevant works. His essay begins sympathetically, ending in a harsh and angry tone. He too recognized the original critical motivation and characterized

I take note of the changes in the world of publishing with interest. Rowohlt showed up in my room at about the same time as your news about Schocken being closed down. He had to turn his back on Germany rather hurriedly. He can do no wrong in my book, not because of this, but because he made Hessel's life easier in Berlin for a long time (Hessel himself made it here three months ago)[8] and kept Jewish employees on his payroll as long as he could. I never took him seriously politically. He is going to Brazil, mainly to resettle his family, as I see it, and after that to look around in Europe again. He has his old publishing company halfway intact in Paris at the moment, should the occasion arise.[9] Polgar and Speyer turned up here a short time ago.

Dora passed through Paris 6 weeks ago. I have the impression that the liquidation of her enterprise in San Remo is going well. Meanwhile, she has opened up a boarding house in London, together with an English partner.[10] The chances of Stefan's naturalization appear to be good.[11] It is to be hoped that he will take his final high-school exams in London.

I would like to hear from you about how things are in your part of the world. Aren't the shootings in Jerusalem supposed to have died down somewhat? But above all: Is everything all right with your eyes by now? —Hearing that you are still weighing the possibility of having me as a visitor pleased me very much. I'm only afraid that the list of wild and tame peoples whom one has to seek permission from is getting longer by the day.

Your report on America was really marvelous. I was convinced by what you say about country and people (I have taken to relating this part now and then for the edification of a select audience); the passages devoted to the Institute hardly introduced thoughts that hadn't been my

---

it with precision, but he failed to see the 'concept' that would succeed in bringing the remote together, namely, social analysis. He wanted to achieve such an analysis in his own great work on the Paris arcades; my book, related in subject matter, could not possibly satisfy him. I could not then and cannot now confer on class concepts and economic categories the capacity to intercept or illuminate historical conceptions. Benjamin himself believed in it at the time, but could not act accordingly: even in his work, definitions are surpassed by images."

[7] See Scholem, *W.B.*, pp. 208–9.

[8] Franz Hessel, one of W.B.'s few close friends, only left Germany following *Kristallnacht*, when the atmosphere became imminently dangerous for Jewish writers.

[9] Implying that in W.B.'s opinion Rowohlt Verlag's most important authors were Jews (such as Alfred Polgar and Wilhelm Speyer, even though the latter had been baptized).

[10] Dora ran a number of such houses in the London neighborhood of Notting Hill until her death in 1964.

[11] These prospects were frustrated by the outbreak of the war. Instead, Stefan was deported to Australia in 1941 as an "enemy alien," and the treatment he was subjected to on the ship, where he was under the authority of German Nazis, severely traumatized him. (He later became an antiquarian bookseller in London and died in 1972.)

own for some time. I have all the more reason to thank you for the manner in which you behaved there on the basis of such an accurate assessment of my interests.

There is a doctor living here who treats Shestov's widow. The poor woman sits beneath the volumes of her husband's works, their pages still uncut. What will we leave behind someday, other than our own writings with their uncut pages? To make her interior look a bit more amiable, she hauls away a few of these writings now and then, and in this way I am slowly building up a collection of Shestov's writings. I decided on impulse that I would read *Athens and Jerusalem*[12] someday. If you imagine a good fairy who suddenly gets the urge to transform the filthiest cul-de-sac in the most desolate corner of a large city's outskirts into an inaccessible mountain valley, in which the sides of the mountain flanks plummet as steeply perpendicular as the façades of the block of tenements had before, then you have the image in which Shestov's philosophy appears to me. It is, I believe, rather admirable but useless. One can only take off one's hat to the commentator in him, and I think his style is superb. I hope I'll have occasion to write a review of the book.[13]

The route from Shestov to Kafka is not a long one for anyone who might have decided to disregard the essential. More and more, the essential feature in Kafka seems to me to be humor. He himself was not a humorist, of course. Rather, he was a man whose fate it was to keep stumbling upon people who made humor their profession: clowns. *Amerika* in particular is one large clown act. And concerning the friendship with Brod, I think I am on the track of the truth when I say: Kafka as Laurel felt the onerous obligation to seek out his Hardy—and that was Brod. However that may be, I think the key to Kafka's work is likely to fall into the hands of the person who *is able to extract the comic aspects from Jewish theology*. Has there been such a man? Or would you be man enough to be that man?

Hannah Stern returns your greetings most warmly.

All the best to you and yours,

Yours, Walter

P.S. What is the meaning of your reference to Kafka in connection with the ending of *Threepenny Novel*?

[12] *Athens and Jerusalem* was Shestov's last work.
[13] This review was never written.

118

BENJAMIN TO SCHOLEM

10 RUE DOMBASLE
PARIS XV
FEBRUARY 20, 1939

Dear Gerhard,

I suggested to Hannah Arendt that she make the manuscript of her book on Rahel Varnhagen available to you.[1] It should be sent off to you in the next few days.

The book made a great impression on me. It swims with powerful strokes against the current of edifying and apologetic Judaic studies. You know best of all that everything one could read about "the Jews in German literature" up to now has allowed itself to be swept along on precisely this current.[2]

I will begin to rework the section "The Flâneur"[3] in the next few days. When that is done, the problem of printing this chapter will be raised once again. For me, among all literary procedures, rewriting is the one I like least. I have greater things in mind, so overcoming that resistance might in this case prove worthwhile.

Entre temps I have returned once again to reflect on Kafka. I am also leafing through older papers and asked myself why you haven't yet sent my criticism of Brod's book to Schocken. Or has this taken place in the meantime?

I hope to hear from you in great detail forthwith.

Most sincerely,

Yours, Walter

[1] I kept this manuscript and later was able to send it back to Hannah Arendt when she thought all other copies lost. The book first appeared in 1956 (in English) [*Rahel Varnhagen: The Life of a Jewish Woman*, trans. Richard and Clara Winston, rev. ed. (New York: Harcourt Brace, 1974)]; the German original in 1959.

[2] W.B. had bitter memories of the article he had written for volume 5 of the German *Encyclopaedia Judaica* (1930) being completely rewritten by the editors and "purged of everything essential." See the remark he wrote on his copy of the offprint (*GS* 2:1521).

[3] *GS* 1:537–69. [English translation by Harry Zohn in W.B., *Charles Baudelaire: A Lyric Poet in the Era of High Capitalism* (London: New Left Books, 1973), pp. 35–66.—TRANS.]

119

Scholem to Benjamin

ABARBANEL RD. 28
JERUSALEM
MARCH 2, 1939

Dear Walter,

Your latest *billet* announcing Hannah Arendt's manuscript arrived just as I was sitting and puzzling over your Baudelaire MS, armed with an astonishing dearth of knowledge (the extent of which only became clear to me as I continued along). I am not very fast when it comes to reading manuscripts, and I hope Arendt's affords me some of the relief denied me by yours. If I am to summarize my impressions with some hesitation, then I must say that I liked the third part of your work[1] best, because I find in it a genuine harmony of text and commentary, a real interlocking which I found only at isolated points in the second part. It is also less naïve in its methodology, if you will permit me to set this ignorant person's "judgment" to paper, than the second part, where I find a dubious simplification in the way you relate the world of poems to its social context. If that is the common grounds for a critique you ascribe a priori to myself and Wiesengrund in your letter, you would be right. In addition to this, you surely provide far too little explanation here of your characterization of B. as a *flâneur* for readers unfamiliar with B.'s writings; you presuppose it rather than develop it (apart from the analysis of "A une passante"), and instead you emphasize entirely different, much more contrasting interconnections in literature. The introduction of the theory of the detective novel to characterize Baudelaire seems to me *here* to be bold and inconclusive. As much as I understand that the theory is likely to occupy a central position in a work called "Paris Arcades," you do very little to link it for the reader with your analysis of B.'s appearance or of his oeuvre, except by the thinnest of threads. I would suggest that the confrontation with Hugo, which takes up so much space here, is out of place, precisely in an analysis of the *flâneur*. But I was extremely impressed by many passages in which you put poems in their context. I simply don't know B.'s writings well enough to be able to judge whether your emphasis on certain features of the oeuvre does indeed have the significance you would like to claim for it (especially in the first chapter). You can presuppose only minimal knowledge on my part. At any rate, I find real interpretation in the third part. You would have done well to develop the allegorical element much more elaborately. The pages in

---

[1] The three chapters of the complete work were called: "The Bohème," "The Flâneur," and "Modernism."

question are composed altogether esoterically in my opinion (unless that was precisely what you wanted to achieve with this subject in *this* context, which I believe you capable of).

I am not returning the manuscript just yet, but keeping it around for further study; you can have it back anytime you need it, of course.

I haven't seen Hönigswald's book[2] yet, and the other one even less, and there is even less hope of that happening. Hönigswald has a number of admirers[3] in my circles; I would have to let them discuss things orally with you.

My dear sir—no *empty* promises please! You write: "You will find the Beatrice sonnet enclosed as well"—but it was nowhere to be found. Please redress this omission *immediately*, for my edification—you may be assured of my gratitude.

I have not received volume 7, issue 3 of the *Zeitschrift* [*für Sozialforschung*]—but all *previous* issues.

Your Kafka letter: I haven't been indolent in the least. On the contrary, I have done everything I could (within the bounds of advisable tactical considerations) to bring the conversation around to this subject. Without success—the man[4] hasn't read Brod himself, as became obvious, to my irritation, nor does he intend to, and he showed an emphatic lack of interest at the news of Brod's being torn to shreds. Right now he is lying in a hospital in Utrecht, suffering from a detached retina, waiting to be operated on. I therefore have to wait for a later opportunity to broach the matter from another side. Would you be opposed to my reading the letter to Kraft? RSVP.

I'm not familiar with Shestov's *Athens and Jerusalem*. He gave a lecture with that title when he was here, but unfortunately read from the manuscript so badly that it was quite impossible to understand anything of consequence, even for wholly favorably predisposed listeners such as myself (who had introduced him to the audience). The event was a terrible fiasco! But you are right, at any rate, when you call his style magnificent. It certainly is in his essay "Memento mori" on Husserl![5]

My eyes are unfortunately no closer to being well than are the political circumstances, which, ever since the brunt of the unrest shifted to Italy, will not and cannot [be] stabilized in the Mediterranean region without a severe crisis in Italo-Franco-English relations. On the contrary: Nothing

[2] *Philosophie und Sprache* (Basel: Haus zum Falken Verlag, 1937).

[3] Two of my colleagues knew Hönigswald (a baptized Jew) quite well from Breslau, where he taught. They thought highly of his penetrating intellect as well as his philosophical writings.

[4] The man was Salman Schocken.

[5] Shestov's "Memento Mori" was a chapter of his book *Potestas Clavium* (1926), which W.B. was familiar with.

good is happening and the London negotiations[6] have reached such a critical stage that a Jewish revolt against the proposed "solutions" could break out here any day. There's "trouble brewing" these days. The British are of course trying out Munich's "Czech recipe" on us, as was to be expected, and that is not going to be without its problems. Feelings are running very high, since the Jews believe (and rightly so, to some extent) that they have been sold out, and the willingness to answer with terror is extraordinarily high. That would be very stupid, of course, since our situation is very different from that of the Arabs, and terrorist activities from Jewish quarters can be countered much more easily. But the mood is now such that the possibility must be taken into account. If one is willing to take the risk, or rather the certainty, of ruining *everything*, then one can of course change the situation, but then nothing will be left of us either. I am as good as certain that it will *not* come to this and that we still retain the chance of seeing you here. We are definitely giving this thought; it appears to be a question of money on both sides, and nothing else. (You should inform me as to how things stand as far as your papers are concerned: can you travel on them?) I presumably wrote to you that my mother is not coming. She leaves Berlin on March 12, to travel to Australia via London. I hope I will be able to see her when she passes through Port Said.[7] The main problem now is how she can be supported and how much I will have to send to Australia, where my brothers have not even been able to find a means of existence as yet. I am not yet clear on all these things, otherwise we would already be starting to negotiate with you!

We (my wife and I) think that the end of *Threepenny Novel* is a materialistic imitation of the chapter "In the Cathedral" from *The Trial*. Doesn't this suggest itself quite naturally?

I have to close. As concerns "works," I wrote an article on Jewish mysticism for the Paris Yiddish encyclopedia and this would certainly be of interest to you, if only I had a copy of it. It would show you precisely the line my historical studies are taking, how I see them and am pursuing them at the moment. But I only have a copy of the German original. Perhaps Schocken will print it as a private edition in German—I'll try to get him to do so. Everything in a nutshell: a mere 45 pages! How I would like to have debated it with you.[8]

---

[6] A round-table conference at which Jews and Arabs would negotiate directly, under the aegis of the British, had been transformed into a separate, double conference by the Arab refusal to sit at the same table with the Zionists. The separate negotiations of the British with both the Arabs and Jews ended in failure.

[7] This meeting did indeed take place; see letter 121.

[8] An English translation first appeared in 1946 in the collection *The Jewish People, Past*

Write again soon, send the sonnet and your works, and fare as well as can be imagined. Greetings to all to whom they are due. Most sincerely,

Yours, Gerhard

120

BENJAMIN TO SCHOLEM

10 RUE DOMBASLE
PARIS XV

Dear Gerhard,

MARCH 14, 1939

While you still have a sundry cargo of ideas from my last letter lying at anchor waiting to be unloaded, this new barge is setting out to sea freighted far beyond the load line with much heavier cargo—my heavy heart.

Horkheimer informs me that the Institute is facing enormous difficulties. Without stating a definite date, he is preparing me for the end of the financial stipend that has been my sole subsistence since 1934.[1] Your eyes didn't deceive you, nor did your humble servant think for a moment that they had. All the same, I didn't foresee a catastrophe. As their letter indicates, these people had not been living on interest, as one would assume in the case of a foundation, but on the capital. The major portion of this is said to be still in existence but frozen, and the rest is supposed to be about to dry up.

If you can get anywhere with Schocken, it should be done without delay. The documentation you need to bring up the Kafka plan is in your hands. I would, of course, have to accept any other assignment he may be able to offer me within the range of my competence.

There is no time to lose. What kept me plugging along in earlier years was the hope of someday getting a position at the Institute under halfway dignified conditions. What I mean by halfway dignified is my minimal subsistence of 2,400 francs.[2] To sink below this level again would be hard

---

and Present (New York: Central Yiddish Culture Organization) 1:308–47. I also attempted to specify the social context of Jewish mysticism and its effects.

[1] This date does not accord with the desperate letters from the year 1934 and the news of the Institute's intervention, still partial in 1935 and more steady thereafter. As all available documents show, in those years W.B.'s material existence relied on three factors: the Institute and the long visits to Dora in San Remo and to Brecht in Denmark, where he could live entirely, or at least largely, without expenses.

[2] This sum was the equivalent of 285 Swiss francs in "hard currency," as I was able to establish, a sum that would allow a bachelor to lead a modest bourgeois existence in those days. It would have been supplemented by fees (not very high, to be sure) for his literary contributions to journals and newspapers.

248

for me to bear *à la longue*. For this, the charms exerted on me by this world are too weak to make it worthwhile, and the rewards of posterity too uncertain.

The crucial thing now is to survive the interim. The people at the Institute are almost sure to be handing out some money. It would be desirable still to be around for that occasion.

Do not give these things more publicity than may be necessary to help me, should an opportunity present itself. If I can manage to show Horkheimer and Pollock that they are not the only ones who are attentive to my plight, there is a chance they might try to do more for me.

So much for today. Don't keep me waiting for an answer, provisional though it may be.

Most sincerely,

Yours, Walter

P.S. I had just signed my name to this when your letter of March 2 arrived. In the meager inventory of opportunities open to me, I had regarded Schocken as one of the more considerable ones. Perhaps you know of something to replace it. I was pleased to see that, without knowing my present prospects, you have kept my visit to Palestine in mind. The way things are shaping up now, the question of whether or not it will be possible to assure me of sustenance in Palestine for a number of months has become important. (I don't imagine that this can be financed from your own funds.) The fact is that, of all the places in the world where Jews are systematically endangered, France is at the moment the most threatening for me, because here I am *completely* isolated economically.

I will go into you observations on the *Baudelaire* in a later letter. At first reading, most of them seem to me to be well worth thinking about.

Let me know how your eyes are doing and what exactly is the nature of the problem.

121

SCHOLEM TO BENJAMIN

Dear Walter,   MARCH 20, 1939

Your letter of March 14 arrived just now, and, as you can well imagine, I was quite stunned by it, for very obvious reasons. I am not even talking with Schocken about your dilemma; he is at present recovering from an eye operation in Holland and is only expected back after Passover, that is, one month from now. The dreadful thing, of course, is that your catastrophe at the Institute coincides with another one here for those most prepared to be supportive: the events of recent months, and now the blow struck these last days by the sudden collapse of Czech Jewry,[1] are forcing almost everyone here to go to the most unimaginable lengths to help their families. Rich people have been ruined within 24 hours, and their families here are suddenly forced to shoulder obligations they had never imagined. I am in exactly the same situation concerning my mother, whom I could obviously have pulled through this time a little more easily in my house in Jerusalem than now. It seems I will have to help finance her life in Australia (since my brothers apparently are still without any means of their own) from my salary (I don't have any independent means). Needless to say, I would like to help you with every possible means at my disposal, and I keep mulling over impractical ideas as to how this could still be done, in case of emergency. Political developments have reached the point where it now appears extremely doubtful whether we could even get you a tourist visa if we wanted to—*even that* has become problematic!! Not to mention the whole material side of financing your stay. 2,400 francs a month amount to £15 in local currency —a *large* sum by our standards. I dare not give an optimistic prognosis as to whether you could get some sort of commission from Schocken which would guarantee you such an income (or even a fraction thereof). On the other hand, it unfortunately seems that nobody can truly be confident that you will be *allowed* to remain in Paris undisturbed very much longer! There is such a sinister side to everything now that the imagination balks at keeping up with the reality (of tomorrow and the day after). Who knows where you even *can* go at all, just looking from the outside. Following the failure of the London conference, the question of immigration has now reached an extremely critical stage for Palestine. All these things appear in a very bleak light. I can only start finding out whether it would be possible to finance a few months' stay for you once the colossal wave of agitation about Prague's fate has subsided among the families most closely affected. You will always get something to eat at our place, as long as we have something ourselves, but the question about further developments must remain unanswered at this moment if we don't want to elicit certain refusals from the outset.

Couldn't you determine, at least in principle, whether it is even *possible* a priori for you to obtain a tourist visa for Palestine?

[1] The invasion of the Germans caused thousands to flee helter-skelter immediately.

I can't tell you anything more today, even though I would dearly like to convey something of promise. My wife is in Galilee, and I can't talk things over with her. I'll be traveling to Port Said at the beginning of next week, to see my mother for three hours once again when her ship puts into harbor there: this is likely to be our last meeting by human reckoning. I'll be writing much more soon. I will certainly make use of any opportunity I might somehow, somewhere, come across for you. I am asking myself whether you shouldn't try to get into the U.S.A. while you still can, and whether that wouldn't be better for you than everything else.

All the best,

Yours, Gerhard

122

BENJAMIN TO SCHOLEM

10 RUE DOMBASLE
PARIS XV
APRIL 8, 1939

Dear Gerhard,

Your letter was as sparingly imbued with verdant hope as the streets of Paris are suffused with the green of this cold spring. This made the wintry prospects between the lines of your letter all the more pronounced. Never an enemy of clarity, I am least of all so now, when the years have led me to believe I know exactly what I can or cannot make my peace with. The significance my mentioning a specific sum in my letter of March 14 had—and no other—was that I wanted this second side of the alternative to be represented.

The same conditions that threaten my European situation will in all likelihood make emigration to the U.S.A. impossible. Such a move is only possible on the basis of an invitation, and an invitation could only come about at the instigation of the Institute. You are surely aware that the quota is already filled for the next four or five years. I don't think it very likely that the Institute, even if it had the power to do so, would want to arrange my invitation at this time. For there is no reason to assume that such an invitation would solve the problem of my livelihood, and the Institute, I suspect, would find the immediate linkage of these problems especially irritating.

I haven't heard anything further from the Institute since I sent you my last report, but you may find it useful to learn that it brought out a 30-

251

page informational brochure in English about half a year ago, in which I am rather prominently represented by a cursory bibliography of my writings.

Here in Paris I met with a helpful party in the guise of Hannah Arendt. It remains to be seen whether her efforts will lead to anything. At the moment, I am still getting my stipend—but all guarantees are gone.

The documents I travel on are the French identification papers for *réfugiés provenants d'Allemagne* [refugees of German origin], and these go hand in hand with the French residence permit. They are recognized by England, and that is a sufficient administrative basis for a visa to Palestine. Some time ago—rather a long time, to be sure, and who knows what effect the events in Europe may have had for her—Kitty Marx-Steinschneider showed herself in the course of our conversations in Paris to be willing to facilitate my stay in Palestine. I myself am clearly not in a position to appeal to her, since I did not receive a reply from her to an involved letter, unclouded by personal concerns, which I sent her last summer.

In order to be as thorough as possible on my part: Should a stay in Palestine be economically feasible, then I would be able to finance the trip from here.

It was not welcome news to hear that you have reason to complain about your eyes these days. Do you have a doctor there in whom you have complete confidence? I know that this is especially important where eye troubles are concerned.

You can surely understand that I have difficulty applying myself to projects oriented toward the Institute at the moment. If you add to this the fact that making revisions is less attractive than new endeavors, anyway, you will understand that reformulating the *flâneur* chapter is making rather sluggish headway. It will, I hope, prove to be advantageous, if the planned book shows incisive changes. As a consequence, the character of the *flâneur* in Baudelaire's person may well achieve the plasticity you are probably correct in finding deficient in the present text. To this end, the problem of the "type" will be developed in a philosophically precarious sense. And, at last, the great poem "Les Sept vieillards," which has never been the subject of an interpretation, will be given a surprising yet, as I hope, convincing explanation.

Indeed, your objections do coincide with those of Wiesengrund where you suspected they would. I am not far from admitting that I wanted to provoke them. The overall conception of the *Baudelaire*—which now only exists as a draft, of course—shows the philosophical bow being bent to the greatest extent possible. I was sorely tempted to confront it with a

252

modest, even homegrown method of philological explication, which I give in to now and then in the second part. In this connection, I want to tell you that your suspicion was correct that the passage on allegory has been kept hermetic intentionally.

I could only drop my request that you return the manuscript to me immediately if you were to compensate me with the German or French manuscript of your treatise on Jewish mysticism. You can well imagine how much I desire to study that text. Enclosed is the Brecht sonnet, as a token of appeasement. (The next-to-last word in the second line deviates from the first version I recited to you by heart, as you will remember.)[1]

I would very much like to know what kind of impression *Rahel Varnhagen* made upon you. I am less urgently interested in hearing whether you have ever come across the novel *Der Sohn des verlornen Sohnes*, by Soma Morgenstern, which Erich Reiss published in 1935. If so, let me know what you think about the book. Its author, Heinrich Simon's son-in-law, used to cross my path in Frankfurt some years ago.[2] I have now run into him again here: he left Vienna just in time. The book is the first volume of a trilogy, of which the second volume is already in manuscript form.

Best wishes to you and your wife,

Yours, Walter

On Dante's Poems to Beatrice

Even today, above the dusty vault
In which she lies, whom he could never have
Although he dogged her footsteps like a slave
Her name's enough to bring us to a halt.

For he ensured that we should not forget her
Writing such splendid verse to her as made
Us listen to the compliments he paid
Convinced that no one ever put it better.

---

[1] The word in question was not "have" (*haben*), but "screw" (*vögeln*).

[2] [*The Son of the Lost Son*, trans. Joseph Leftwich and Peter Gross (New York: Rinehart, 1946); also published as *The Testament of the Lost Son*, trans. Jacob Sloan and Maurice Samuel (Philadelphia: Jewish Publication Society, 1950).] Dr. Soma Morgenstern (1896–1976) came from East Galicia. His wife was the niece and not the daughter of Heinrich Simon, co-owner of the *Frankfurter Zeitung*. M. was a close friend of Joseph Roth but had much stronger ties to Judaism than Roth or any other writer he associated with in the years prior to Hitler. At that time, I wasn't yet familiar with his books. During the last years of his life, he wrote me a series of protracted letters from New York about his relationships with W.B., Kracauer, and Adorno.

253

Dear me, what an abuse he started then
By praising in a manner so arresting
What he had only looked at without testing!

Since he made poems out of glimpses, men
Have seen what looks nice in its street attire
And stays bone-dry, as something to desire.

[Translated by John Willett]

[*Sonett über die Gedichte des Dante auf die Beatrice*

*Noch immer über der verstaubten Gruft / In der sie liegt, die er
nicht haben durfte / So oft er auch um ihre Wege schlurfte /
Erschüttert doch ihr Name uns die Luft. /*

*Denn er befahl uns, ihrer zu gedenken / Indem er auf sie solche
Verse schrieb / Dass uns führwahr nichts andres übrig blieb / Als
seinem schönen Lob Gehör zu schenken. /*

*Ach, welche Unsitt bracht er da in Schwang / Als er mit so
gewaltigem Lobe lobte / Was er nur angesehen, nicht erprobte! /*

*Seit dieser schon beim blossen Anblick sang / Gilt, was hübsch
aussieht und die Strasse quert / Und was nie nass wird, als
begehrenswert.]*

123

Scholem to Benjamin

ABARBANEL RD. 28
JUNE 30, 1939

My dear Walter,

You must have given me up for lost long ago, carried off into the Arabian
deserts and perished of thirst, or otherwise wounded and rendered mute
by one of the all too frequent bombs. Not even the dazzling shipment of
your commentary on Brecht's Lao-tze poem,[1] which possessed all the
requisite qualities for loosening the tongue of someone like me, could
entice me to do so. If you haven't lost your faith in the fact of my

---

[1] *GS* 2:568–72 [English translation by Anna Bostock in W.B., *Understanding Brecht*
(London: New Left Books, 1977), pp. 70–74.—Trans.]

existence after all this, you will have assumed, and rightly so in this case, that something more powerful than all my desires and obligations must have prevented me from writing. And that something is actually nothing physical (I don't even know whether I should say "thank God" or "unfortunately"), nor is it health related. Rather, it is unmitigated despondency and paralysis, which have gripped me for months in the face of the state of things here. It is indeed impossible *not* to reflect on our situation, and by "our" I am not merely referring to us Palestinians. The horrifying catastrophe that Jewry has gone through these last six months, and whose dimensions nobody is really able to grasp, this utter hopelessness in a situation in which hopes are invented only to mock us (like the shameful "project" of sending the Jews off to "colonize" British Guiana) —all these things descend on you sooner or later and brush away any brightness of spirit. And I would so much rather have written you about the prospects we might be able to find for you here, or about your staying here for several months, which has preoccupied us for longer than I can tell you. But I can't bring myself to invite you to us when murder and manslaughter are inevitable, if not tomorrow, then definitely the day after, with all the attendant effects on our "bourgeois comforts" (even if one is determined to make do with only the most elementary things), since inviting you would presuppose a minimum of calm, to say the least. My prolonged silence testifies to *nothing* other than the very critical and depressing lack thereof. You know me well enough to realize that I don't easily succumb to depression, but these last few months have managed to bring about such a miracle. To me, the debasement of Palestine to the arena of a civil war is ultimately more than one lost opportunity among many. After all the experiences of the last six years, I am unable to discover any grounds for the hope that all our troubles will be resolved through revolution. The workers' movement as a revolutionary political factor is deader than a dead dog, there is no point in upholding any illusions on this point. And the future of Judaism is totally cloaked in darkness: it cannot pretend to be invisible—inactive and asleep—as others may (perhaps) try to do, because it will no longer have the bodily basis of an existence which is still at the disposal of the vanquished socialists. We aren't able to make alliances any longer, since there is no one left who might be interested in doing so. We must not give up on this generation, and since nothing could replace Palestine in its function for Judaism but empty phrases evocative of nothing, how should I conceive of the years to come? In this darkness I only know how to be silent. The chance of salvaging a viable Palestinian settlement over the course of the next world war is being endangered just as much by us as by the Arabs and the English. Abominable things occur from among our ranks

255

as well, and I shudder when I try to consider what the sole consequence must be. We are living in terror; the capitulation of the English in the face of this terror leads the fools among us to believe that terror is the only weapon with which we, too, can achieve something, notwithstanding our special conditions. But such fools are too prevalent to be acknowledged as such. So that is the reason why the things that are happening are happening. I never believed the English could do much to us, as long as we ourselves did not abandon the civilized foundations on which our cause here rests. But we are well on our way to doing precisely that. Here you have all I am able to advance to explain my uncommunicative silence. I am ashamed to speak about what preoccupies me and equally ashamed to act as if it doesn't exist in all its menacing reality. Hence I remain mute. Your position, which I think I understand very well, is endangered, and I have nothing intelligent that might throw some light on it. Indeed, it could very well be that we can no longer even achieve the *technical* preconditions for your visit here under present circumstances, i.e., that they won't even let you in anymore, even if everything else were as smooth as I wished, and as it absolutely is not, I regret to say. We are still looking for somebody who would (to put it simply) at least be willing to give up a room for the duration of your stay. Kitty is so overburdened that we can't expect any help from her. If we managed to overcome the formidable practical difficulties, the question would remain whether you could be here in November/December, that is, whether the political situation—both here *and* there—might permit you to come. As far as climate is concerned, the period from November 1 to January 15 is superb. Thereafter, it gets very unpleasant.

As to my work: I have only been capable of gathering material, my mind wasn't receptive to anything else. I now want to begin preparing the text of my English book, which means expanding it to about twice its previous length. Schocken is willing to print up to 25 sheets. The vacation began this week, and this sums up my main ambition for it in terms of work.[2] I also have to write a few shorter pieces and to prepare my lecture on Sabbatai Zvi, which I want to attempt at last after such prolonged study.[3] For years an image of the fruits of all my efforts has been growing in me, so I can begin its formulation with a reasonably clear conscience.

I am not familiar with Soma Morgenstern's book, nor have I ever heard anything about it. On the other hand I was *very* pleased with

---

[2] My book *Major Trends in Jewish Mysticism* was written between the summer of 1939 and the summer of 1940. Published after Benjamin's death, it was dedicated to his memory.

[3] Sabbatai Zvi, the leader of the most important messianic movement in Judaism after Bar Kokhba's revolt under Hadrian, especially from 1665 to 1666.

Hannah Arendt's book on Rahel, even though I presumably read it with a different emphasis than the one with which she wrote it. It's a superb analysis of what took place then, and shows that a relationship built on fraud, such as the German Jews' relationship to "Germanness," could not end without misfortune. By fraud I mean the assumption that everything always had to come from one side, and that the other side was only ever allowed to deny itself (in the most precise sense) and to be receptive. Pity, I don't see how the book will ever find a publisher.

Many thanks for sending me the two Brecht pieces, which are literally being brought into my room at this very moment. I already received the one four weeks ago, and I am all the more pleased to have it again as I feared it misplaced. I think the poem is simply splendid, and I avidly studied your commentary, as well as making both available to a broader public by reading them aloud in company. As to the other essay on Brecht's theater,[4] I must raise the question of the social significance of a theater that is not allowed to be staged in the foreseeable future. And since you emphasize precisely this function, as opposed to so-called abstract "artistic" functions, I wonder what function is fulfilled by a theater that is tied to emigration from the start, and then made impossible by it. The "relaxed audience," which checks the events of this theater against its social experience, is a great idea, but just an idea, which doesn't correspond to anything in society. Such an audience doesn't exist, either in Russia or in America, and if it exists in Utopia, then the concept of a theater oriented toward such an audience (which I could imagine, following your instructions) is itself lifted into the realm of the utopian, something it evidently wants to reject.

Could you at least send me a list of your publications in the journals *Das Wort* and *Mass und Wert*, so that I can try to obtain the issues here that weren't accessible to me up to now? I was able to turn up the "Berliner Kindheit," by the way; it has already found its rightful place.

I have to close. Will you be going to Denmark again? I would really urge you to take steps toward getting a tourist visa to Palestine, just so you are equipped for the journey here, since I don't know how long such procedures might drag on. And in case we are able to give you positive news, it would be good not to be faced with administrative difficulties.

My fondest regards, then, and please don't think poorly of my inability to write.

Yours, Gerhard

---

[4] *GS* 2:532–39. ["What Is Epic Theater?" (second version) in *Illuminations*, pp. 149–56. —Trans.]

124

SCHOLEM TO BENJAMIN [1]

[French original]
Mon cher Walter,

ABARBANEL RD. 28
SEPTEMBER 11, 1939

Here I am, tormenting the French language! We were told that it would be acceptable to write in either English or French, and since I know you don't speak English, I am certain you (or the censors on both sides of the Mediterranean) will forgive me the relatively un-French phrases you are sure to find everywhere in these lines and those that will follow.

I don't know at all what you are doing, whether you are in Paris or with your friends, as you were last year, and the main goal of this letter is to beg you to send us some news. I don't know whether you received my last letter (of considerable length), which I sent registered several months ago. We did not receive a reply, and I hope it didn't get lost in the course of these last feverish days. You will still find us in the same circumstances, even though we don't know what is going to happen to our work and to the university in general. It all depends on the course of events, and I am not enough of a prophet to predict all the possible complications in our situation. We hope that the responsible authorities will find ways to allow Jews to take part in the war as Jews and in their capacity as Jews. After all, we are the ones against whom war has been waged all these years, and it would be a good thing if we did our part to bring about the downfall of Hitlerism. Many of my young friends are preparing themselves for all eventualities, and who knows, maybe our turn will come as well. Meanwhile, I proceed with my work, or at least try to. I have no radio, thank God, but that is not enough these days when you are not allowed isolation to write your book or shape your thoughts.

And you? I can't imagine that you are able to do much research. Is the library open? Or perhaps you have joined the ranks of the political writers?

I can see I shall have to read some French novels—Anatole France still occupies pride of place in my library—to be worthy of corresponding in French with you.

Kitty was here and she wants to know everything you've been doing. I informed her that she incurred Your Highness's displeasure.

---

[1] [Letters 124 and 125 were written in French to avoid postal censorship.—TRANS.]

That's enough for the first time! Let me have news from you as soon as possible, and accept the most cordial greetings from my wife and from your old comrade in arms,

Gérard

125

BENJAMIN TO SCHOLEM

[*French original*]

Cher Gérard,

10 RUE DOMBASLE
PARIS XV
NOVEMBER 25, 1939

I haven't left Paris this summer, even though I was invited to Sweden. I wanted to finish my "Baudelaire" above all—or rather that fraction of the book which could be presented as an essay. I was obliged, after war was declared, to go to an internment camp, like all German refugees. I found your letter of September 11 upon my return. My sister had told me that you were worried about me, but I was unable to write to you, since the mail that leaves the camps was limited to 8 letters per person per month. My release was among the first to be decided.[1] This means I left quite a few friends behind there, and you can easily imagine how sad that makes me. I had the good fortune of being released at precisely the time when the weather began to turn cold there. I have lost weight but feel good. Paris has donned an unfamiliar appearance. All is dark in the evening, cars drive slowly, people stay home. Nobody here doubts that Hitler is doomed. The important thing is not to make his end coincide with that of too many human beings.

I am told that the tension between Jews and Arabs has diminished in Palestine. Is it true? It would be a piece of good news amid so much sadness. Let me have news from you as often as you can. I don't think I will be leaving Paris for the moment.

My "Baudelaire" turned out to be quite a success in New York. I've already received the proofs, but haven't touched them yet and don't think

---

[1] When the war broke out, W.B. was interned, along with thousands of refugees, first in a stadium in Paris and then in a *"camp des travailleurs volontaires"* [camp for voluntary workers] at Clos St. Joseph in Nevers. He was not released until mid-November, one of the first to be freed on the basis of a decision made by the interministerial committee for the review of particular cases. People with the highest prestige in French cultural life interceded vigorously on his behalf, and Adrienne Monnier, Hermann Kesten, and Sylvia Beach were untiring in their efforts, as reported in *Briefe*, pp. 827–35. Hans Sahl and Max Aron have described how W.B. lived through this time like a stoic sage.

the task is urgent. The last news I had from my brother is two months old and could be worse. Do you know of your brother's fate?

Many greetings to your wife. Sincerely yours,

Walter

126

SCHOLEM TO BENJAMIN

ABARBANEL RD. 28
REHAVIA, JERUSALEM
DECEMBER 15, 1939

Dear Walter,

I think you would be wise to make the perusal of what I hope will be your endlessly long answer easier by writing as legibly as possible. Your card of November 25, which arrived here today to my great joy (as you can well imagine), took three weeks, despite its brevity and the fact that it was composed in French! In the meantime, since I had heard absolutely nothing from you, I have been asking heaven and earth for news of your whereabouts, and in the end inquired at the Paris office of the American Joint Distribution Committee. We can wonder if any of those asked will ever reply. At any rate, your card brought the first piece of news I've had for the entire time. I want to welcome you warmly to your regained serenity and hope we will succeed in safeguarding what we hold in common throughout this war, as we have managed to do for nearly 25 years, even given the vast distance separating us. Just as much has changed, in an astonishing way, as has remained the same, which is even more astonishing. Now, as then, we are trying to carry on our scholarly work, even though our most vital and decisive interests are affected and shaken by this war (this is different from the last time). I see from your postcard that you have accomplished more in this respect than I have, even though my working conditions are much more favorable. Your analysis of Baudelaire is already probably in galley form, while I am still sitting undecided in front of the manuscript of my American lectures, which Schocken wants to publish. I hope we will succeed in making the long time that lies before us in this war (or wars—the plural form is better) fruitful in terms of the things that concern us. For the time being, I find myself quite literally "far from the front line" (who knows for how long), and life here proceeds now as it ever did. We all admittedly have great material worries, but who doesn't? Anyway, with the new academic year, commencing the beginning of November, the university is back in business, as if everything were peaceful. Many local students, who used to go abroad and can't get away now, have taken the place of our foreign students. The many fictitious students from Poland are *nolens volens* given meals by the university, and since there is no work, they are also studying. In addition to all these—and to our amazement—students keep arriving, either from a few of the countries that "remain free," or because they managed to get their papers cleared in time. And so we hold our lectures as if everything were normal. I am now for the first time lecturing to historians on the history of the Sabbatian movement, to an audience that fantastically—to my mind—numbers 60 to 70 listeners (but there are no lecture fees here, we are progressive!), while no less than ten wizards have gathered for my aristocratic seminars on the book of Bahir. But—*pourvu que cela dure,* as Napoleon's mother is supposed to have said. Schocken has gone to America to replenish our finances, and we await news of what is to come of our salaries. In the meantime, however, one can work, if one is able to. I am full of good intentions for the coming months and I am just waiting for the all-decisive élan. My studies look very promising, since I have the opportunity of setting up a Scholem "school" of research. I'll tell you more about it another time. *Utinam,* oh if only my propaganda about your qualities and significance had met with as much success as my propaganda on my own behalf! I have dutifully done all I could: just before he left, Schocken, who bought the manuscript of *The Last Days of Mankind,* set up a little evening on Karl Kraus and invited Kraft and me as speakers. I didn't come up with any mustard of my own, but read large parts of your essay in the most emphatic voice. Everybody was deeply impressed by you, except the only man your admirer really wanted to impress. The demons are engaged in a direct defensive action against you!

I could answer in the affirmative your question as to whether the tension between Jews and Arabs has lessened, but I don't trust this peace. There are too many things involved that seem unreal. There is as much desire for a peaceful and quiet existence with the Jews among large parts of the Arab population as there is among the Jews, and that wish has expressed itself in concrete terms. On the other hand, that was also the case in the past, but nevertheless what happened could happen and did happen regardless. Nazi propaganda has much more of an effect among the Arabs than is generally admitted, and that is a bitter pill to swallow.[2] Of course, things are by and large quiet here at the moment, but the road to a pacification of hearts is a still long one.

[2] The former Mufti of Jerusalem, the leader of the forces in the country pressing for a violent confrontation with Jewish immigration and settlement, openly came out on Hitler's side and went to Germany.

261

I've had no news at all about my brother so far, not even indirectly. I'm afraid his situation remains unchanged.[3] It has become very difficult to communicate with Paris from here nowadays and to say what one really thinks, so you can imagine how things are in his case. Please write as soon as possible. Fondest regards from both of us!

Yours, Gerhard

I will have the bookseller send you a Hebrew essay of mine, in which I devour an author in a major critique.[4] For your collection. And convey my regards to Hannah Arendt!

Yours, Gerhard

127

BENJAMIN TO SCHOLEM

Dear Gerhard,   JANUARY 11, 1940

I had your letter of December 15 in hand by the end of the month. I hope this one will not require too much time for its trip either.

I was pleased and reassured to hear that you are going about your craft in as unperturbed a manner as the circumstances allow. I particularly hope you won't put off work on your New York lectures any longer. Every line we succeed in publishing today—no matter how uncertain the future to which we entrust it—is a victory wrenched from the powers of darkness. Anyway, it would be all too sad if you were to become negligent of your publications in English precisely when the undersigned is seriously getting down to learning that language. I am negotiating on private lessons at the moment. I intend to take them together with Hannah Stern and her friend.

You want us to "safeguard what we hold in common." As far as I can see, in that respect things are even better taken care of now than they were twenty-five years ago. I am not thinking of us when I say this, but of the arrangements made by the *Zeitgeist*, which has set up markers in the desert landscape of the present that cannot be overlooked by old Bedouins like us. Even though it is a sad thing that we cannot converse

---

[3] In the meantime, my brother Werner had been transferred from Dachau to Buchenwald, where he was murdered by an SS man in July 1940.

[4] The reference is to the account of a "whitewash" by the renowned Rabbi Jonathan Eibenschütz in Prague and Hamburg in the eighteenth century. He was suspected of belonging to the sect of Sabbatai Zvi.

with one another, I still have the feeling that the circumstances in no way deprive me of such heated debates as we used to indulge in now and then. There is no longer any need for those today. And it may well be fitting to have a small ocean between us when the moment comes to fall into each other's arms *spiritualiter*.

The isolation that is my natural condition has increased owing to the present circumstances. The Jews seem not even to be holding on to the little intelligence they have left, after all they have been through. The number of those who are able to find their bearings in this world is diminishing more and more. Under these circumstances, I rather enjoyed two short meetings with Dora.[1] She struck me as more quiet and serene than she had been for a long time. The news she gave me about Stefan was not exactly favorable, but not alarming either. By the way, she spoke of signs indicating Italian anti-Semitism will be taken out of circulation in the foreseeable future.

The description you gave me of the lecture at Schocken's soirée is truly gripping. I didn't keep it from Hannah Stern, who returns your greetings most cordially. Your report makes me thirst for revenge, since I am rather slow to see the work of demons in people's shabby behavior. But if I want to slake that thirst, I will have to wait for the first things Schocken himself publishes. Hannah Stern was of the mitigating opinion that Schocken thinks more of Brod alone, in the depths of his soul, than of you and me put together. *Rebus sic stantibus*, I wish you, and—with the requisite distance—your colleague too, every success in his American expedition.

I am very pleased to hear of the influence you have as a teacher, as you can imagine. Tell me as soon as possible what the Scholem school is all about.

The double issue of the Institute's journal inaugurating the 1939 volume has just come out. You will find two long essays of mine in it. I'll send you offprints of both, of course, as soon as I can lay my hands on them.[2] Even so, I would dearly advise you to buy the issue or get hold of it some other way. I have a double personal stake in it: first, it will place your propaganda for me on a wider platform, and for another, I want to hear your opinion of the essay "The Jews and Europe."

Some time ago, you asked about my contributions to *Mass und Wert*. Here's the index (to the extent that you don't own the issues, I am

---

[1] During her last stay in Paris, Dora still tried to prevail on W.B. to come with her immediately to London, but he refused. It was a fateful decision, which Dora told me about in April 1946, when I first saw her again.

[2] Those were the last of his works I was to receive from him: the essay on Jochmann and "On Some Motifs in Baudelaire" (*GS* 2:572–85 and 4:605–53). [The latter appears in *Illuminations*, pp. 155–200.—TRANS.]

unfortunately unable to get them for you, since the author's copy is all I have in hand. If you are unable to decide in favor of purchasing the ones you are missing—an attitude I certainly could not approve of—then, if worse comes to worst, I could place a typewritten copy at your disposal).

1:5 May–June 1939 ("Über die *Zeitschrift für Sozialforschung*")

1:6 July–August 1938 ("Berliner Kindheit um 1900")

2:1 September–October 1938 ("Krisenjahre der Frühromantik")

2:3 January–February 1939 ("Béguin: *L'Âme romantique et le rêve*")

2:6 July–August 1939 ("What Is Epic Theater?")

That should be enough for today. Please accept my most sincere greetings, which are also addressed to your wife.

Yours, Walter

128
SCHOLEM TO BENJAMIN [1]

[. . .]   [FEBRUARY 1940]

You want to know my opinion of Horkheimer's essay "The Jews and Europe." After repeated readings of the pages in question, I don't find it difficult to formulate in a readily understandable manner: this is an entirely useless product in which, astonishingly enough, *nothing* beneficial and new is to be discovered.

The author has neither any conception of the Jewish problem nor any interest in it. It's obvious that at root no such problem exists for him. Thus, it is only out of propriety that he deigns to express himself on the subject, as a kind of afterthought. The comparison with Marx's essay "On the Jewish Question," of which exactly the same thing is true, readily suggests itself. More than that: I am in all modesty of the opinion that the author wanted to rewrite this essay (which evidently impresses him as profound) *mutatis mutandis*: to address the situation that exists 100 years after Marx (years that have not exactly shown the wisdom of

---

[1] The original text of this letter seems to have been lost. It was written in February 1940 and included, besides my remarks on Horkheimer's essay, which I kept a copy of because it seemed important for further discussion, an inquiry concerning Werner Kraft's complaint about W.B.'s conduct in the Jochmann affair. Kraft had sent his complaint to Horkheimer. I described Kraft's arguments to W.B. and asked him for his view of the matter or for clarification of some kind. W.B. was very much preoccupied with the matter at the time. His reply never reached me. Concerning the Jochmann affair, see *GS* 2:1398–1403.

that—repulsive—essay in the best light, no matter how fashionable it may sometimes have been to quote from it).

The man explains nothing at all—except a cliché that one has been able to read for years in every provincial Jewish newspaper aimed at the man in the street, namely, that in the totalitarian state the Jews have been deprived of the old economic foundations of their existence. That is true and not new. But on the subject itself, the author has nothing whatsoever to say. He neither addresses a single sentence to the topic he announces—"The Jews and Europe." (He almost tries to show it has nothing to do with Europe because fascism is lurking everywhere.) But to my mind this is a *real* problem—the expulsion of Jews from Europe—whose meaning and significance he does not see and presumably is incapable of seeing. Nor does he ask *on behalf of the Jews*: What will *they* be like when they are deprived of this soil, after terrible demoralization and plans for their annihilation (he does not even care about this, for the Jews interest him not *as Jews*, but only from the standpoint of the fate of the economic category they represent for him—as "agents of circulation," p. 131). Nor does he ask *on behalf of Europe*: What would a Europe actually look like after the elimination of the Jews? Though there would be all sorts of things worth asking here. It is in keeping with this spirit that he has no *answer* of any kind to give to the Jews on whose behalf he does not even *ask*—except for the facile final phrase with the horrible allegorization of monotheism, which obviously has nothing to say to the *unallegorizable* Jew and *his* concerns within mankind. How this man would poke fun at others who employed such concepts as "answers"!! (In the foreign-language summaries, the whole, somewhat ludicrous helplessness of this final recommendation becomes even more apparent!) . . . The man makes it easy for himself, in an underhanded way. "*Politically* speaking, pogroms are aimed more at the spectators—to see whether someone will make a move," etc. Well, with such wisdom dialectics is prostituted, and all I can say is that anyone who has *such* an idea of the *meaning* of pogroms has nothing to say of worth on the subject. The *style* of Horkheimer's writings has always made me uncomfortable because of a certain brash insolence in its instrumentation, and in this essay that insolence has unfortunately found its way home in the most exact sense of the word. *This* Jew is the last person who is able to provide us with an unsentimental analysis (but one that hits the heart of the matter itself and not its most decayed emblems) of "The Jews and Europe," the genuine question that concerns *us*, you and me, equally and decisively. As an exhortation addressed to the Jews in the Second World War, the essay leaves one "as disconsolate as the speech of ghosts," to quote Benjamin.

ON THE END OF THE
CORRESPONDENCE

For those not familiar with my book *Walter Benjamin: The Story of a Friendship*, I include two passages from its closing pages. They can be read as a sequel to my last letter.

This was probably the last direct communication between Benjamin and me. I awaited his response with great suspense, and to this day I have no idea what it was like. Only in 1941 and 1942 did I learn from letters from Adorno and Hannah Arendt how Benjamin fared in those months before and after his flight from Paris. After all I have told here it is evident that Walter repeatedly reckoned with the possibility of his suicide and prepared for it. He was convinced that another world war would mean a gas war and bring with it the end of all civilization. Thus what finally happened after he crossed the Spanish border was not a surprising irrational act but something he had prepared inwardly. Despite all the astonishing patience he displayed in the years after 1933, combined with a high degree of tenacity, he was not tough enough for the events of 1940. As late as September, he mentioned his intention of committing suicide to Hannah Arendt on several occasions. The only authentic information about the events connected with his death is found in a detailed report written on October 11, 1940, by Frau Gurland, who crossed the border together with him, to Arkadi Gurland, a member of

Horkheimer's Institute.[1] I received a copy of this letter from Adorno in 1941.

I learned about Benjamin's death, on September 26 or 27, on November 8 in a brief letter—dated October 21, 1940—from Hannah Arendt, who was then still in the south of France. When she arrived at Port Bou months later, she sought Benjamin's grave in vain. "It was not to be found; his name was not written anywhere." Yet Frau Gurland had, according to her report, bought a grave for him in September for five years. Hannah Arendt described the place: "The cemetery faces a small bay directly overlooking the Mediterranean; it is carved in stone in terraces; the coffins are also pushed into such stone walls. It is by far one of the most fantastic and most beautiful spots I have seen in my life."

Many years later, in one of the two cemeteries (the one Hannah Arendt had seen), a grave with Benjamin's name scrawled on a special wooden enclosure was being shown to visitors.[2] The photographs in my possession clearly indicate that this grave, which is completely isolated and utterly separate from the actual burial places, is an invention of the cemetery attendants who, in consideration of the number of inquiries, wanted to assure themselves of a tip. Visitors who were there have told me that they had the same impression. Certainly the spot is beautiful, but the grave is apocryphal.

[1] Cf. Scholem, *W.B.*, pp. 224–26. Frau Gurland's letter of October 11, 1940, is printed in my book in its entirety.

[2] According to an essay by Helmut Niemeyer in the weekly *Die Zeit* of September 28, 1979, this alleged grave has not been shown "for quite some time."

INDEX OF NAMES

Caro, Siegfried (Hüne), 24
Caspary, Adolf, 148
Céline, Ferdinand, 197
Chamberlain, Neville, *231*
Cohen, Hermann, xii, xiii
Cohn, Alfred, *xxxiv*, xvi
Cohn, Jula. *See* Radt-Cohn, Jula
Coventry, Camilla, *107*

Daladier, Edouard, xxxvi
Dannhauser, Werner, *x, 70*
Dauthendey, Max, *47*
David, Ernst, 67, 71, 116
David, Lotte, 67, 71
Demetz, Peter, *xi, 19*
Descartes, René, 138, 143
Diebold, Werner, *27*
Dielitz, Theodor, 216
Döblin, Alfred, *12*
Dollfuss, Engelbert, 132
Du Bos, Charles, 142, *161*

Eagleton, Terry, *xix*
Eddington, Arthur Stanley, 223–224
Eibenschütz, Jonathan, *262*
Einstein, Albert, *25*
Eisler, Robert, 82
Ense, Varnhagen von, *193*
Exleben, *10*

Febvre, Lucien, *76*
Feuchtwanger, Ludwig, *18*
Finch, Henry Le Roy, *168*
Fischer, Samuel, *96, 100*, 103, 139
Fittko, Lisa, xxxvii
Flaubert, Gustave, 111
Förster, Georg, vii, xxvi
France, Anatole, 258
Freud, Sigmund, xix
Freud, Tom, 24, 25
Friedländer, Salomo, xi, xv
Fuchs, Eduard, *59*, 90, 94, 120, 154, 156, 160, 162, 164, 166, 171, 179,
191, 192, 193, 195, 197, 203, 206, 208
Fuld, Werner, *101*

Gabain, Marjorie, *168*
Gassendi, Pierre, 143
Gauguin, Paul, 58
Gentz, Friedrich von, 193
George, Stefan, 58–59, 62, 67, 70, 74
Gide, André, xxv, xxvii, xxxiv, *195*
Ginzberg, Louis, *219*
Glatzer, Nahum, 101, 104, *150*
Goebbels, Joseph, 177
Goering, Hermann, 45
Goethe, Johann Wolfgang von, viii, xvi, xxi, xxvii, 10, 15, 95, *194*
Goldberg, Oskar, 67, 148, 173, 174, 177, 179
Goldfriedrich, Johann, *100–101*
Goldmann, Lucien, *143*
Goldschmidt-Rothschild, Miriam, 68, 83
Gottheil, Walter, 20
Gracián, Baltasar, 11
Graetz, Heinrich, xiv
Grand Mufti of Jerusalem (Hajj Amin al-Husseini), *261*
Green, Julien, 104, 111
Grimm, Hermann, *35*
Grimme, Hubert, 35
Groethuysen, Bernhard, 40, 45
Gross, Peter, *253*
Gundolf, Friedrich, 11
Günther, Johannes von, *130*
Gurland, Arkadi, 267
Gurland (Frau), 267, 268
Gutkind, Erich, 49, 58, 90, 92, 168, 170, 215, 216, 219, 227, 228
Gutkind, Lucie B., *49, 90, 93*, 168, 170, 215, 216, 219, 227, 228
Guttmann, Julius, *32*, 75, 79, 147

Haas, Willy, 23, 38, 83, 86, 95, *96*, 100, 127
Halle, Toni, 57

271

Wertheimer, Max, 43
Wieland, Christoph Martin, 69, 71
Wiesengrund-Adorno, Theodor. *See*
  Adorno, Theodor
Wilder, Thornton, 11
Wilkins, Eithne, *41*
Willett, John, 254
Winston, Clara, *244*
Winston, Richard, *135, 220, 244*
Wirszubski, Chaim, *143*
Wise, Stephen, 204
Witte, Bernd, *xvi, xvii, xx, xxiii*

Wittig, Joseph, *112*
Wohlfarth, Irving, xxviii
Wolin, Richard, *xx*
Wyneken, Gustav, x, xi, xviii

Zohn, Harry, *xi, xiv, xxi, 3, 240,
  244*
Zola, Emile, xxvii
Zung, Leopold, xiv
Zweig, Arnold, *66*